Voices of the
Vietnam POWs

VOICES OF THE VIETNAM POWs

★ ★ ★ ★ ★

Witnesses to Their Fight

CRAIG HOWES

New York   Oxford
OXFORD UNIVERSITY PRESS
1993

Oxford University Press

Oxford   New York   Toronto
Delhi   Bombay   Calcutta   Madras   Karachi
Kuala Lumpur   Singapore   Hong Kong   Tokyo
Nairobi   Dar es Salaam   Cape Town
Melbourne   Auckland   Madrid

and associated companies in
Berlin   Ibadan

Library of Congress Cataloging-in-Publication Data
Howes, Craig, 1955-
Voices of the Vietnam POWs: witnesses to their fight / Craig Howes.
p.   cm.   Includes bibliographical references and index.
ISBN 0-19-507630-3 — ISBN 0-19-508680-5 (pbk.)
1. Vietnamese Conflict, 1961-1975—Prisoners and prisons, North
ietnamese. 2. Vietnamese Conflict, 1961-1975—Personal narratives,
American. 3. Prisoners of war—United States—Biography.
4. Prisoners of war—Vietnam—Biography. I. Title.
DS559.4.R68   1993
973.92'08697—dc20
[B]   92-41091

2 4 6 8 9 7 5 3 1

Printed in the United States of America
on acid-free paper

Acknowledgments

Consciously or otherwise, many individuals and institutions have helped to make this book possible. During the researching, the writing, and the revising, I have depended greatly on the kindness of strangers. The memoirs, histories, and critical works I discuss here range from bestsellers to privately published tracts. Most proved to be somewhere in the University of Hawaii at Manoa's Hamilton Library or in the Hawaii State Library system; the rest arrived promptly, thanks to the efforts of the University's Interlibrary Loan staff. The University of Toronto, Beloit College, and the University of Wisconsin at Madison also allowed me access to their databases and collections; I am especially indebted to the Wisconsin State Historical Library. When the time came for publication, Bill Hamilton from the University of Hawaii Press provided invaluable advice about book proposals and presses. At Oxford, Elizabeth Maguire, Susan Chang, and Susan Hannan have been friendly, patient, and professional. I also appreciate the work of the copy editor, Randi Laisi, and an anonymous outside reader.

A number of interested, sympathetic, or captive audiences have offered helpful comments along the way. The Center for Biographical Research's Brown Bag Biography Series, the Hawaii Committee for the Humanities' sponsored Conference on Just and Unjust Wars, and those students and colleagues enrolled in my honors and graduate courses on research methods and critical writing all read or listened to earlier versions of what appears here. I would also like to thank the UH Interdisciplinary Theory Group, and the members of the Manoa Garden Weekly Seminar for their encouragement.

By writing this book, I have happily run up many debts to teachers, colleagues, friends, and family. Though with very different projects in mind, Hans Aarsleff first showed me how to conduct research, U. C. Knoepflmacher convinced me to be hard on myself, and Alvin B. Kernan set a standard for teaching and writing which I have tried to keep before me. Through research reductions and other institutional support, the University of Hawaii at Manoa Department of English has for the past twelve years helped me complete this and other projects.

By reading early drafts, John Rieder, Valerie Wayne, and Alan MacGregor have all made this book better, and so have Mark Heberle and Jay Kastely, whose expertise in Vietnam and the literature of war has been invaluable. Cristina Bacchilega, Happy Chapman, Joe Chadwick, Steve Curry, Paul and Sandra Davies, Arnold Edelstein, Nyla Fujii, Barbara Gearen, Brien Hallett, Lanning Lee, Linda Middleton, Joan Peters, Loretta Petrie, George Simson, Sheldon Tyau, and Rob Wilson have all given me the benefit of their friendship, intelligence, and encouragement. Robert B. Martin gave me some crucial advice at a very early stage, and a happy reunion in Chicago with Tom and Margaret Peden led me to the story of Lance Sijan. I would also like to thank David and Annie Collins for their love and support, and Bill and Merle Howes, for more than I can hope to say.

This book is for Seth, who bravely and cheerfully put up with years of one parent flying off to Vietnam while the other parent wrote about it, and for Sara Collins, my remarkable wife, who brought Jeremiah Denton's *When Hell Was in Session* home one day and started everything.

Contents

Voices of the
Vietnam POWs

America's Vietnam POWs

On January 22, 1973, five days before the signing of the Paris peace accords, former President Lyndon Baines Johnson died. A month-long period of public mourning was declared for the president whom many Americans still identified with the Vietnam War's frustrations and deaths. Flags flew at half-mast. The Paris accords outlined procedures for repatriating those prisoners of war held by all sides. Roughly 600 were Americans, and over 400 of them had become POWs while Johnson was president. When the first Americans left Hanoi on February 12, President Richard Nixon ordered the Stars and Stripes back up the poles, with Mrs. Johnson's approval, saying "that for the American flag to be flying high on the day the first American prisoners return to America would be the finest possible tribute both to her husband's memory and to the heroism of the prisoners' families—as well as to the missing, the men who gave their lives and all who helped to win the peace with honor in Vietnam."[1] How Johnson would have responded to this tribute is debatable, but once home, the POWs did set to work on an agenda similar to Nixon's: to end the nation's feelings of failure and guilt over Vietnam by bearing witness to the powers of patriotism and duty.

The tools the POWs employed in accomplishing this task—their speeches, interviews, essays, memoirs, and histories—are the subject of this book. Before dealing with these narratives, though, some information about who these POWs were helps to explain why some told their stories and some didn't. Many insisted they were different from captives who had returned from previous wars, and the curious demographics of the Vietnam POWs certainly support this claim. What they believed set them apart most, however, was a performance in captivity superior not only to that of POWs in previous wars, but also to America's own performance during the Vietnam War. Hardly victims, many of America's Vietnam POWs arrived home determined to run Old Glory back up the flagpole personally.

Who were these POWs?[2] The answer depends on who's counting. American servicemen were captured and released before the Tonkin Gulf Resolution of August 1964, and Robert Garwood, the last living POW to return, came home to court-martial proceedings in March 1979.[3] In the intervening years, several hundred Americans, a few foreign nationals, and tens of thousands of Vietnamese became prisoners. A fairly consistent POW profile has however emerged from the various narratives. Though the Vietnamese numbers dwarfed all others, for instance, these captives are barely mentioned. The Americans called themselves the 4th *Allied* P.O.W. Wing because of a few Thais and Vietnamese who deserved "a place within the wing," but the Southeast Asian POWs remain shadowy or invisible.[4] POWs who returned home *during* the war are also second-class citizens. One tally lists 129 "captured or overrun" POWs who then "escaped from, evaded, or were released by their captors."[5] Ninety-five of these were paroled, and though some have commented on their captivity, they have largely remained silent. The parolees' spotty reputations with the POWs left behind had something to do with the quiet. Since antiwar statements were virtually mandatory at release, the parolees' integrity was an issue: the Hanoi POWs considered 11 of the 12 parolees released from there derelict in duty, and serious threats to camp morale.

More puzzling is the lack of attention paid to the 31 servicemen and 3 civilians who "escaped from or evaded" captivity. Though some men were missing for less than a month, and many for only a day or two, Navy aviator Dieter Dengler's book about his 1966 *Escape from Laos* is a remarkable story, and *Five Years to Freedom* (1971), James N. Rowe's memoir of his jungle captivity, is one of the great POW narratives from any war. The best explanation for this neglect is probably a simple accident of history. Though estimates of how many Western POWs survived run from 629 (U.S. military personnel only) to 766, the attention directed at those POWs repatriated in February and March of 1973 during the mass releases known as Operation Homecoming focused American attention tightly and permanently upon these individuals.[6] The totals vary by one or two in some accounts; however, it's generally accepted that 591 Americans left Vietnam at this time. Six foreign nationals—2 Canadians, 2 West Germans, and 2 Filipinos—left with them. Of the Americans, 26 were civilians—pilots, State Department officials, Voice of America personnel, agricultural specialists—and some civilians died in captivity—one census lists 7 Americans, 3 West Germans, 2 South Koreans, and a Filipino. Five hundred and sixty-five military POWs returned during Operation Homecoming, a population psychologist Edna J. Hunter calls "very small indeed when compared with the numbers held captive in Korea (7,140) or during World War II (130,201)."[7] The Vietnam POWs were also remarkably homogeneous. After learning that only 16 were black, for instance, the Black Congressional Caucus, acutely aware that "black soldiers have been disproportionately represented on the ground combat front lines," vowed to investigate.[8] What outraged the caucus was how the POW population reflected the way that race, rank, and career opportunity meshed within the military. Career aviators dominated the POW population. Over half—324—were Air Force personnel, and 315 of these were commissioned officers. *All* 138 Navy POWs were aviators and commissioned officers. Ten of the 26 Marines were also commissioned officers shot down and held in the North—4 more officers, a warrant officer, and 11 enlisted Marines made up the other 16. Only the 77 Army POWs even remotely reflected the proportions of their service branch: 19 commissioned officers, 10 warrant officers, and 48 enlisted men. "Top heavy" thus seems only a barely adequate description of the Operation Homecoming POWs. Only 79 weren't commissioned officers, and only 16 were privates. Most astounding of all, not a single Operation Homecoming POW had been drafted.[9]

When and where these POWs were imprisoned reinforced the patterns cast by rank and service branch. All the Army and 16 of the Marine POWs were captured during operations in South Vietnam and held in jungle camps; all 138 Navy POWs, all but 9 of the Air Force's 324 POWs, and the remaining 10 Marines "spent their entire captivity in North Vietnam."[10] As for the order and frequency of these POWs' introduction into captivity, imagining the shape of a brandy snifter is perhaps the best way to proceed.

Though two captures did take place in 1964, the number of POWs taken in 1965 was quite large—the snifter's mouth—then steadily swelled through 1966, 1967, and into 1968, when the POW population reached 400. Thanks to Johnson's bombing halts in March and October, however, at its broadest point the snifter abruptly stopped swelling. A thin stem, never widening beyond 15 POWs a year, reached down through the years 1969, 1970, and 1971; when the bombing resumed in 1972, this stem splayed out into a broad base of well over 100. (Only one American was captured in 1973 before the February releases.)

Rank, service branch, time, and location of capture defined the significance of this pattern. The first Operation Homecoming POW, Army Captain Floyd J. Thompson, was captured on March 26, 1964, and held for years by ground troops in the South.[11] Thompson was thus the first jungle POW; four months later, Navy Lieutenant Everett Alvarez bailed out during the first American air attacks on North Vietnamese targets and became the first Hanoi POW.[12] Since U.S. ground troops weren't fully committed until March 1965, and since their first large engagement wasn't until October's Ia Drang valley conflict, the 63 Operation Homecoming POWs taken in 1965 were all aviators, and except for Ernest Brace, a civilian pilot captured in Laos, they all followed Alvarez to Hanoi.[13] 1966 was more of the same. Only civilian Douglas Ramsey and an enlisted Marine were held in the jungle; the other 85 POWs were officer aviators who went straight to Hanoi. More POWs were captured in 1967 than in any other year—95 Air Force, 50 Navy, 5 Marine, and 10 Army, for a total of 160 POWs. By January 1, 1968, then, 294 of the Operation Homecoming POWs were already in Hanoi, and 18 more—2 civilians, 5 Marines, and 11 Army POWs—were scattered across Laos and the jungles of the South.

One hundred and six more POWs were captured in 1968, but the Tet Offensive and the bombing halts dramatically changed who was captured. For instance, 18 of the 26 civilian POWs released in 1973 were captured between January 31 and February 5, 1968, during Tet. The 34 Army and 11 Marine POWs made 1968 these branches' biggest year. On the other hand, Air Force and Navy captures dropped to a combined total of 43, making 1968 the smallest year for aviators since 1964. Johnson's March restrictions on air strikes and his October halt to all bombing in the North caused these changes. Sixteen Air Force fliers were captured in January and February, but only 12 more became POWs in the next ten months, and only one after August. As for the 15 Navy POWs, they were all in prison before October. The record pace of 88 POWs before July, due largely to Tet and early heavy bombing, thus trailed off sharply, as only 18 more Americans became prisoners in the next six months. The next three years each produced only a handful of captures—14 in 1969, 12 in 1970, and 15 in 1971—and because virtually all of these POWs were held in the South or in Laos, the population of roughly 320 Hanoi prisoners remained essentially static. As a result, these men not only spent "three years longer than any of the more recent shootdowns of 1971, 1972, and 1973," but as Edna J. Hunter notes, also *"spent more time in captivity than any other Americans in history."*[14] Nixon's 1972 bombing renewal ended the POW drought. Although only 5 Air Force fliers were captured in 1972's first three months, 10 Americans became POWs in April alone. May's northern air strikes really set things in motion. During the next six months, 65 POWs arrived in Hanoi, and 6 others were taken elsewhere. Then came Christmas 1972. Forty-four aviators were captured in December alone—a monthly total second only to the 59 POWs taken during Tet. By the end of the Christmas bombings, then, 130 POWs had been captured during 1972. This however was the final flurry: the only 1973 Operation Homecoming POW, Navy flier Phillip A. Kientzler, was appropriately enough captured on January 27, the day the accords were signed in Paris.

Two other variables should also be mentioned when discussing the POW population: the mortality rate and the MIA controversy. Calculating POW fatalities is difficult. Their own rough welcome led senior POWs to guess that injuries from bailing out, or from beatings inflicted by the Vietnamese, might have finished off half of all shootdowns.[15] Adding these unrecorded deaths into fatality totals poses obvious problems; if anything, though, figuring out ground-force POW casualties is even harder. Should, for instance, someone killed within hours of his capture be counted as a POW? Faced with such problems, POW manifests usually list only civilian or military men whom surviving POWs saw die or disappear. Even so, the numbers still vary wildly. Although the North Vietnamese listed 55 deaths, Stephen Rowan found that "the POWs believe the number may be considerably greater." *We Came Home*, a collection of POW first-person accounts, recorded 54 military deaths. In 1976, Benjamin Schemmer claimed that "at least 72 Americans died at the hands of their captors," and this number has continued to climb steadily over the intervening years.[16] However much this total might fluctuate, one thing remains certain: casualties were more frequent outside the Hanoi prison system. During the eight and one-half years that the "Hanoi Hilton" and its surrounding camps held Americans, only a handful of POWs died. Those who returned considered two of these deaths out-and-out murder, blamed another three on equal doses of brutality and neglect, and credited three more to appalling medical care for traumatic injuries or abuse.[17] For men so injured and ill-treated, though, the Hanoi POWs had a remarkably low fatality rate. The jungle prisoners weren't so lucky. In 1968 and 1969, one small camp lost more POWs to malnutrition and disease than Hanoi lost during the entire war.[18] Though many memoirs and histories downplay this fact, a Hanoi prisoner was far less likely to die than a jungle POW.

The MIA controversy has also distorted POW counts. From their earliest days, organizations seeking the release of the POWs also demanded a full accounting for those missing in action. When North Vietnam announced in 1973 who would be released during Operation Homecoming, hundreds of families were therefore devastated. Virtually no one whose captivity wasn't already confirmed was on the Hanoi list, and only ten of the several hundred men who disappeared in the vicinity of Laos were headed for home. The question of how many POWs might still be held captive has of course received a great deal of attention over the years, with some returning POWs changing their own minds about the answer. The frequent moves, tiny populations, and sudden disappearances of prisoners made it impossible for the jungle POWs to reach any conclusions about the possibility that men remained behind. They simply couldn't know. A justifiable pride in their communications network, and the senior officers' wish to return home with all present and accounted for, made the returning Hanoi POWs confident they had resolved the status of every person anyone had encountered during captivity. Rod Colvin could report as late as 1987 that "returned prisoners who had been in The System believe that anyone in it either died or came home."

These same POWs, however, had doubts about the accounting *outside* the system, and since "their methods for keeping track of other men" were "not flawless," these uncertainties later changed minds. "When I first came home I was among those who felt very certain that every prisoner the Vietnamese held had been released," POW Gerald Coffee recalled, "But over the years, the volume of circumstantial evidence indicates that men probably are still being held."[19] This conclusion has in fact become orthodoxy; "Remember the MIAs" is a Vietnam POW rallying cry. Over the last ten years, congressional hearings, fact-finding missions, privately funded paramilitary expeditions, shelves of books, and scores of media investigations have also tried to discover how many of the roughly 2,500 missing Americans spent time as, or still perhaps remain POWs. By definition, however, with one significant exception, MIAs do not figure in the POWs' memoirs, histories, or interviews—and that exception, a POW named Robert Garwood who returned home in 1979, I will be discussing at length.[20] I therefore join many surviving POWs in granting that some MIAs were probably POWs in Vietnam—perhaps living now, but more likely dead. Their histories, however, can be no more part of this book than they have been part of the returning POWs' accounts. Like the men themselves, their stories remain MIA.

Who then were the Vietnam POWs? Since the majority were career officers and aviators, the typical POW who emerges from the narratives was a high-ranking, long-term captive held in Hanoi—and the space and relative importance granted to this figure can often suggest he was the *only* Vietnam POW. Many Hanoi POW memoirs pass silently over the jungle POWs and later shootdowns, and Jay Jensen wasn't even silent: after claiming that almost 90 percent of the POWs were in solitary for periods ranging from three months to four years, he then acknowledged that "of course, here—and throughout my narrative—I am speaking about the prisoners of my group, those captured in the first three or four years of the war, not about those captured in the last few months of the war."[21] Later writers followed this example. In an "overview" of the POWs in 1970, Benjamin Schemmer describes "356 Americans" who "bailed out in the prime of their lives," even though the Army, Marine, and civilian POWs put the actual population well over 400. According to Schemmer, the "average" prisoner was "only about thirty-two years old"— actually an advanced age for combat personnel—and "a captain in the Air Force or a Navy lieutenant, married and the father of two young children."[22] The "typical" POW was thus anything but—a fact the Hanoi prisoners took great pride in. Though intending "no discredit at all to our great enlisted men," 1965 shootdown Ralph Gaither, for instance, modestly claimed that "never before in the history of mankind had such an unusual group of prisoners been gathered." Hanoi was the Harvard of POW camps: "Almost to a man, we were career-minded. Almost to a man, the IQ level was 135 or more. Almost to a man, the education level was bachelor degree or better." And almost to a man, they also put America's previous POWs to shame. POW Howard Dunn declared that the "young, immature, impressionable" Korean War prisoner had nothing in common with the "career-oriented" Vietnam War POW, whose "high-risk, specialized training" and "near-college degree level of education" were "vastly superior to any group of prisoners in any previous conflict in which the United States had engaged." James Stockdale saw the Vietnam POW as "a professional warrior, a professional fighter pilot" who proved that "chivalry is not altogether dead in that world." When POW Harry Jenkins described a "U.S. naval aviator" as "a man who has no equal, a competitor, a man who is convinced he is better than all other men," he was therefore sketching a self-portrait that many men claimed as their own.[23]

Even these air knights were, however, anxious about returning home, for as Howard Rutledge wrote, "We had no idea of what our reception would be."[24] Their first fear was being branded traitors. Between 1965 and 1969, the Hanoi POWs had been tortured into producing incriminating statements, and most of the men still felt guilty. As a result, "the POW, his mind sometimes clouded by captor recriminations and maltreatment, frequently weighed the possibility that he would return to the United States in total disgrace."[25] This intense fear appears frequently in POW memoirs. "I'm broken," cried Jim Mulligan after being tortured, "I'm a traitor. I've disgraced my family, my country and myself." This anguish—"You feel as if you're in company with Benedict Arnold," Bob Shumaker recalled—led even hard-line POWs to prepare for exile: "They agreed that they certainly could not return to the United States, where they would be in disgrace. It was decided that Reynolds would go to Canada while McKnight checked out Australia and South Africa."[26] A second, and contradictory anxiety also plagued the POWs. Since America had apparently turned against the war, the POWs worried they would be greeted with hate or contempt for doing their duty. Though he "felt some anger at those who had opposed the war," Howard Rutledge felt he "had been fighting to defend their right to oppose it." Nevertheless, he was worried: "But how would they feel about me now? Would we be booed in the streets? Would our families be humiliated, our children scorned?"[27] Unsure whether they would be greeted as traitors or war criminals, the POWs responded by holding tight to their motto, "Return with Honor." According to Operation Homecoming organizer Roger Shields, they "were concerned about whether they had really come out with honor," and once home, "they wanted to know if they had achieved it."[28]

Their answer came quickly, as the POWs stepped out into "a well-planned homecoming with all the hoopla of a hero's welcome." This greeting was heart-felt, deliberate, and politically motivated. In January 1973, Defense Secretary Melvin R. Laird changed the name for the ongoing preparations for the POWs' return from Operation Egress Recap to Operation Homecoming, a switch that caught perfectly the government's wish "not to repeat the mistakes and atmosphere of the prisoner repatriation that followed the Korean war." Instead of interrogations and suspicion, the POWs would be treated with "dignity, respect, and understanding." All initial questioning would be about POWs still imprisoned or missing; all medical tests would be aimed at getting the POWs back to their families as quickly as possible.[29] This program meshed perfectly with the POWs' own highly visible agenda. Since the men left Hanoi in their order of capture, the highest-ranking and most tortured POWs arrived home first. Almost to a man, their first words were as pious as Jeremiah Denton's when he stepped off the first plane: "We are honored to have had the opportunity to serve our country under difficult circumstances. We are profoundly grateful to our commander in chief and to our nation for this day. God bless America."[30] Gratitude, piety, and patriotism were the watchwords. "I want to tell you something, folks," Robinson Risner said to the crowds at Travis Air Force Base, "to us, this is truly the land of milk and honey, the land of the free and the home of the brave." Leo Thorsness declared he would "like to see every flag double in size and talk about apple pie and motherhood for the rest of my life," and the *New York Times* was certainly correct when it observed that most of the returnees would agree.[31]

So similar were the POWs' public remarks that many people began to wonder who was directing the chorus. *Izvestia* predictably announced that the Pentagon had brainwashed the POWs, who in turn were now brainwashing Americans about the war, but some American publications were uneasy as well.[32] On February 20, the *New York Times*' James P. Sterba reported that "careful military planning" of the POWs' appearances "has set the stage for a restoration of unchallenged patriotism and of the status of the military man to his honored place." This planning had barred American news reporters from Saigon or Hanoi during the releases, preserved silence on topics that might "tarnish the prisoners' image," and allowed the media access to the POWs only under the most controlled conditions. Though a strong whiff of reportorial sour grapes pervades these charges, a February 24 *Times* editorial took the stage managing seriously enough to worry that "history" will "remember the occasion largely as a succession of military hand salutes, stiffly prepared statements, medical bulletins and canned handouts concerning the joys of steak and ice cream." And because the POWs could not be blamed, the *Times* concluded that the villain must be "the Government" which "would prefer not to let people speak for themselves without first straining and homogenizing their words in a public relations blender."[33]

The POWs resented such remarks. "We were offended that anyone would think we would be used in any form of organized programming or orchestration," remarked senior Navy POW Jim Stockdale, "At no time have I ever been given words to say." Jeremiah Denton went after Robert Maynard, the *Washington Post* ombudsman, for making similar charges. If Maynard "meant, entirely meant, what he said...I'm sorry for him and pray he will come off it." The most ringing defense of the POWs' integrity, however, appeared on April 1 in the *New York Times*. After describing the strength necessary to survive the hellish cellblock the POWs called Alcatraz, Stockdale finished his short essay with three indignant and emphatic sentences: "We return to a fast-paced America as neither a monolith of common opinion nor a cheap commercial commodity. The men of Alcatraz return home as individuals. To treat us as anything less is an injustice none of us deserve."[34]

Denying that someone else wrote the returning POWs' words does not, however, rule out the possibility that the POWs orchestrated them on their own. Senior ranking officer (SRO) John Flynn suggested that "probably" the reason the POWs' statements "sounded so stereotyped" was that before leaving Hanoi, "as a matter of guidance" he had told them "he was going to say that 'I have been privileged to serve my country under difficult circumstances.'"[35] This explanation was however far too modest, and a touch disingenuous: the POWs had in fact been rehearsing their release from at least the moment when they entered the large compounds in Hanoi they called Camp Unity. Partially as a way to pass the time, the POWs "formed several toastmasters clubs and practiced public speaking." As the *Los Angeles Times* later reported, club members rehearsed "patriotic homecoming speeches" and staged "news conferences, with some prisoners playing the parts of reporters and asking barbed questions while others rehearsed the roles they are actually playing now." When coupled with the senior POWs' orders "not to discuss treatment until all the prisoners were out, and never to speak publicly of misconduct on the part of fellow prisoners," these activities, which some POWs called "reverse brainwashing," shaped their homecoming speeches far more than any government plan ever could have.[36] The execution could at times be rough: "When one man deplaned here, his wife rushed toward him—but he warned her off with a stern whisper: 'I have to salute the flag, don't bother me.'" Nevertheless, the early POWs had undeniably planned their return in a way that was all the more effective for being heartfelt, and as events unfolded, it became clear that their performance fit almost perfectly with America's own "public display of pride and relief."[37]

Neither a traitor nor a war criminal, the POW found himself "perhaps the *only* hero of the Vietnam conflict," and his "warm and tumultuous welcome," POW Robert Naughton later observed, created "a unanimity among Americans which had been lacking during the long years of the Vietnam conflict." Jungle POW Donald Rander agreed. "We're giving the American people what they want and badly need—heroes," he said in mid-1973: "I feel it's our responsibility, our duty to help them where possible shed the idea this war was a waste, useless, as unpopular as it may have been."[38] Though figures like California's Governor Ronald Reagan thanked the returning men for precisely this service—"You gave America back its soul, God bless a country that can produce men like you"—this ongoing POW agenda disturbed a variety of people.[39] To begin with, it thoroughly demolished some cherished stereotypes. Just before the first POWs returned, James Reston solemnly warned, "The prisoners come back different men, usually helpless or rebellious." Since "many of them have literally been 'killing time,' which means killing their fears, blotting out the present, romanticizing the past and dreaming of a family and an America that are changed beyond their imagining," coming home "to the same but different and older wives, different children, a different country, with different memories and different values" will be "an agony." As a result, Reston thoughtfully suggested that as symbols "of the tragedy of the Vietnam war and the conscience of America," these POWs deserved a full pension to support them as they struggled through the decades ahead.[40]

Given predictions like these, for some Americans the men who bounded off those first planes home were shocking, and even a moral affront. Disabled GI Joe Rekasis, for example, bitterly contrasted the typical Vietnam vet's welcome home to that now given to "the POW, the flier, the officer...the guy who flew at 10,000 feet, punched the buttons, and wore clean socks."[41] Other people worried that Operation Homecoming was encouraging America to forget its defeat and guilt. The American Psychological Association warned that the POWs "have been assigned the role of heroes in a war that has no heroes, the central role in an elaborate drama staged to provide justification for the President's policy, to create the illusion of victory and to arouse a sense of patriotic fervor."[42] Robert Jay Lifton felt the same way, observing that "this may be the first war in history" in which POWs became the heroes "around which civilian populations can cleanse themselves of guilt and reassert immortalizing principles." The POWs were apparently committed to restoring an image "of simple, old-fashioned American military virtue, as though nothing had happened in Vietnam, and as though the understandable emotion around these men can wipe away 10 years of an ugly, unjust war." For Lifton, this was dangerous. Instead of reaping the war's "one potential benefit: political and ethical illumination arising from hard appraisals of what we did and why we did it," Americans were letting "administration officials and returning prisoners not only reassert the official mythology of peace with honor, but also attack war opponents and proposals of amnesty, lest there be any suggestion that resisters and protesters were right and official America wrong."[43]

Nowhere was this conflict over interpretation more fierce than over the POWs' championing of Richard Nixon. Immediately after landing in the Philippines, SRO Robinson Risner phoned Nixon "to convey to you, Mr. President, that it would be the greatest personal honor and pleasure to shake your hand and tell you personally how proud we are to have you as our President."[44] Already wounded by Watergate, and committed to a "peace with honor" which increasingly looked like a "retreat with nothing," Nixon couldn't have been more pleased. Before the POWs' return he had ruled out being present at their arrival, declaring, "This is a time that we should not grandstand it; we should not exploit it."[45] As he came under heavier attack in the following weeks, however, Nixon often turned to his POW supporters. So transparent was this strategy that in a March column Art Buchwald claimed the president was "running out of POWs," leading Nixon staffers to worry that "by April there will be no POWs to display and Americans will start looking at the peace again and wondering what we really got out of it." According to Buchwald's anonymous "government official," the mass release had been a mistake. Prisoners should have been rationed instead, with "only two or three of them to be exposed to the media every week. In that way we could have kept the POW issue alive for three years." Buchwald ended this fantasia by hinting that Nixon would bomb Hanoi again simply to create more POWs, but before that, Buchwald's "source" drew some frighteningly accurate conclusions:

> The truth of the matter is the President needs the POWs now more than they need him. By rationing them to the public over a long period of time, Mr. Nixon could keep the amnesty issue alive, he could appeal to the patriotism of the American people, and he

could use the POWs to attack all the people who don't agree with them. They are a natural administration resource and it's a pity we use them up so fast.[46]

On May 24, at perhaps "the largest and most spectacular White House gala in history," Nixon proved Buchwald a prophet. Calling the hundreds of assembled POWs "the most distinguished group I have ever addressed," Nixon declared that America must "quit making national heroes out of those who steal secrets and publish them in the newspapers." In response, the POWs "stood and applauded and cheered for a full minute." After summarizing his administration's first term, Nixon then ended his speech by calling on the POWs to help him carry his policies forward. Another standing ovation brought the gala to a close.[47]

As the months passed and the presidency collapsed, most POWs stood with their commander in chief. At the height of the tapes controversy in December 1973, for instance, an impassioned Orson Swindle denounced "the apathetic and squeamish elements of our society," Nixon's "political adversaries and large elements of the news media" in a letter to the *Washington Post* which many POWs could have signed:

> I said it upon hearing of his election in 1968; upon learning of the Cambodian operation and the Son Tay raid in 1970; upon learning of the resumption of bombing and the mining of North Vietnam in 1972; upon hearing of his reelection in 1972 and witnessing the B-52 raids over Hanoi that followed; upon my return to freedom on March 4, 1973; and upon shaking his hand on May 24, 1973. To those panic-stricken Americans of so little faith and courage, I say it again today. Thank God for Richard M. Nixon...my President, my commander-in-chief and my fellow American.[48]

This partisanship was not confined to supporting Nixon. In May 1973 the Air Force told Leo Thorsness "to stop making politically tinged statements" against George McGovern; in November, Thorsness announced his plans to run for the House or Senate in 1974. In early April, James Kasler announced that "all pilots who flew over North Vietnam's Red River Valley have formed the Red River Valley Association" to pursue joint political goals and provide support for a strong military.[49] And over the next fifteen years, many POWs became elected and appointed state and federal officials.

All this political activity was one of many signs that as the glow wore off their welcome, many POWs were feeling frustrated and angry. A few were saddened by how little certain things had changed: one POW from Augusta, Georgia, revealed on the *Today Show* "that a parade had been scheduled for his homecoming until it was found out he was black."[50] Nor had all of the POWs leapt joyfully off the planes. In May, a medical examiner for March Air Force Base announced that "only six of the 51 POWs" he had seen "were in good health and that some of the men might require psychiatric care for the rest of their lives." (Shortly afterwards, he also revealed that his superiors had told him to say his earlier remarks "were 'taken out of context.'")[51] Domestic problems were common. The Pentagon announced that "thirty-nine of the 420 married American prisoners of war returned from Vietnam have either gotten or are getting divorces"; researcher Edna J. Hunter later reported that 30 percent of the Army, Navy, and Marine POWs went through "marital dissolution within the first year after return"; and ten years after Operation Homecoming, *U.S. News and World Report* reported that "at least 90 have divorced."[52] Though this same 1983 article described the POWs' robust mental health as "a far cry from what the experts feared," events in mid-1973 made such fears understandable. After remarking that many POWs were having "a lot of difficulty in moving back into their families," Pentagon health chief Richard Wilber announced in early June 1973 "that all

returned Vietnam War prisoners would be counseled and watched for five years to avoid
the high violent death rates among former American P.O.W.'s after World War II and the
Korean War."[53]

The next four weeks seemed to confirm Wilber's apprehensions. On June 3, Edward
A. Brudno, a Hanoi POW captured in October 1965, committed suicide. According to his
mother-in-law, Brudno "had been despondent ever since returning from North Vietnam,"
and his suicide note, written in French, "said roughly, There is no reason for my existence...my life is valueless."[54] This death created precisely the impression the POWs
wanted to avoid—that captivity had robbed them of the ability to fight back against
personal problems—and another suicide on June 27 began raising fears of an epidemic.
No one could have been less like Brudno than Marine Sergeant Abel Larry Kavanaugh.
Captured during a 1968 ground patrol, Kavanaugh was one of the eight men known as the
Peace Committee, a group POW Colonel Theodore Guy had formally charged with "disrespect to an officer, disobedience of a lawful order to stop collaborating with the enemy,
communicating with the enemy, conspiracy to undermine the morale of fellow prisoners
and attempting to undermine fellow prisoners' morale." When the government refused to
prosecute, Guy filed his charges as a private citizen. The day after Kavanaugh shot himself,
however, his wife Linda, "pregnant with their second child," declared Guy, the Pentagon,
and America itself responsible: "The North Vietnamese kept him alive for five years and
then his own country killed him." The response was immediate. Within a week, the Army
and Navy, citing the POWs' "long hardship" and "a Defense Department policy against
prosecuting any prisoners of war for propaganda statements made while in prison" as
"mitigating circumstances," dismissed Guy's charges.[55] Many POWs were outraged, but
the service branches held fast. No POW would face a court-martial for his conduct in
captivity until 1979, when the ghostly Robert Garwood emerged from Vietnam.

For all the media attention, though, Brudno's and Kavanaugh's suicides proved highly
atypical of the Vietnam POWs. *U.S. News and World Report* concluded in 1983 that "no
more than 30 have been treated for psychological or mental problems" since their release,
and although "two suicides, a few cases of alcoholism, and three deaths, from a malig-
nancy, a plane accident and a heart attack" had occurred, almost half of the POWs were
still in the military, and three-quarters had returned at some point to college.[56] The feared
tailspin by scores of POWs into despair and death simply didn't happen. Some hard-line
POWs were actually disgusted by this success. They had wanted a day of judgment, a
moment when the POW heroes would be sharply and publicly distinguished from the
prison traitors, and from those men who had passively waited for release. Behind their
warm welcome, the POWs also sensed an unwillingness to hear about their captivity. Their
debriefers seemed most interested in POWs still missing, and the push to reunite the men
with their families had led to some very brief interviews. About a year after coming home,
the POWs were asked to fill out "a classified 'survey of returned prisoners of war,'" and
about half did.[57] But all the misconduct charges had already been dismissed, and the
hard-line POWs were finding their demands for justice no more welcome than any other
public call for a hard look at the Vietnam War.

Dissatisfaction with this state of affairs was only one of several reasons for that
incredible outpouring of POW interviews, group histories, and memoirs which has never
really stopped. A sense of civic duty played its part as well. Edna J. Hunter concluded that
the POW "felt obligated to tell about his experience to anyone who might request a personal
appearance—Boy Scouts, church, civic groups, etc.," and by offering his book "to the
American people in appreciation for their evident concern for the POWs while we were

away and in deep gratitude for the warm and wonderful welcome they gave us on our return," POW Larry Chesley confirms Hunter's conclusion.[58] Some prominent Americans also requested these stories. At the White House gala, for instance, the POWs' commander in chief had asked them to help in raising "the national spirit, the faith that we need to meet our responsibilities in the world," by speaking to their most important audience: "The young people of America need to hear the truth. They will believe you. They will believe you because you have suffered so much for this country and have proved that you will do anything that you can to do what is best for America, not just for yourselves."[59] The POWs' altruism and duty, however, went hand in hand with a coordinated plan for managing how their stories would emerge. At the highly orchestrated "news conferences and public reenactments of their ordeals" held in late March 1973, forty prominent returnees explained that they had "defended U.S. war policy" in Hanoi "because they were part of it, and could not concede that their suffering was in a wasted cause." After weathering such captivity, these POWs understandably had no intention of conceding to their fellow Americans either. As POW James E. Hiteshew explained, "So we came out and in our minds we had done what we intended to do, we had accomplished it and wanted to tell everybody else that job has been accomplished."[60] The earliest POW publications made the same point. In *Prisoner of War: Six Years in Hanoi*, a vivid collection of drawings showing how the POWs suffered in Hanoi, POW John McGrath noted that while "a few Americans listened to the stories of torture and maltreatment," the majority turned away: "The stories were unpleasant, and most people wanted to forget." In addition to his own sketches, McGrath also promised that more contributions to "our own record of what really went on inside the walls of the Hanoi prisons" would soon appear.[61]

McGrath's reference to "our own record" points to a joint history which had in fact taken shape well before release. Even before all the POWs were home, one source was promising "a spine-tingling testament to a very old type of patriotism when all the POWs are free to talk without fear of hurting any of their comrades."[62] Seymour Hersh wrote about something much more deliberate when he reported in March 1973 that "some of the senior American pilots agreed—while still prisoners of war in Hanoi—to set up a corporation to manage their income from publishing, speech-making and other public appearances upon their return." Men with "their feet on the ground while in prison," these longtime POWs, "knew while in captivity that their return and safety was—as one officer put it—'a big issue back here in the States.'" Anticipating "demands for books, speeches and endorsements," some senior POWs decided to follow the Mercury astronauts' lead, and to pool their resources.[63] Of course, no such agreement appears in the POWs' own narratives, and Hersh did not reveal his sources. But the toastmaster clubs, the designation of certain POWs as camp historians and memory banks, and the steady flow of memoirs and historics make it impossible to believe that the senior POWs did not discuss their futures as historians and commentators in detail.

Who were the POWs? The most visible men were proud, patriotic, and largely white career military officers who had shared in captivity the desire and the time necessary to get their story straight. The group history, or official story, they came home with answered the prayers not only of their president, but that large audience of people who felt enraged and humiliated by America's failure in Southeast Asia. Even more welcome to this audience was the POWs' charge that the United States had drifted away from its values and duties. Captivity had not shaken the POWs' faith in America's cultural superiority to the rest of the world; rather, it had shown them just how dangerous the nattering nabobs of negativism and the liberal purveyors of doom and gloom could be. By proclaiming this truth in their narratives, the POWs thus often served as advance men for one of their earliest public champions, Governor Ronald Reagan. Though too injured to profit from the heartland revival that would eventually carry Reagan to Washington, when President Richard Nixon ordered the flags lowered for Lyndon Johnson back up the mast, he was certainly helping to prepare the way for "morning in America," a sunrise with no date, but one that glowed more brightly on the horizon on February 12, 1973—Lincoln's Birthday, and the day the first Vietnam POWs left Hanoi for home.

★ ★ ★ | ★ ★ ★

THE CODE, THE RULES, AND THE BODY

The prisoner . . . is doubly unfree, since he is not set loose from his former allegiance, or so he is told, by his captivity. If he is forced to face his captors, bound or at gunpoint, he must also look over his shoulder to the authorities of his own state. He is required continually to balance the obligations he knows he once had, and may still have, as a citizen and soldier, against the more immediate threats and coercions of his captors—and perhaps also against his new obligations to the society of prisoners. What should he do?

MICHAEL WALZER, "Prisoners of War:
Does the Fight Continue After the Battle?"[1]

★ 1 ★

The Fighting Man's Code

Our experience with Communist captors has shown that they consider the prisoner of war camp an extension of the battlefield. The Code of Conduct similarly enjoins the American serviceman to continue the fight after the battle.

HOWARD DUNN, POW, Dec. 1965–Feb. 1973[1]

The vast majority of POWs were guilty of violating the Code of Conduct. The ones who refused to give the North Vietnamese anything but name, rank, and serial number didn't come home.

FRANK ANTON, POW, Jan. 1968–Mar. 1973[2]

The Code of Conduct was one thing I remembered as an unchanging guide. Even when the issues were totally confused, it provided the standard of conduct that should be maintained, and if I could comply with it, I would be right. The only problem now was to stay alive while following it.

JAMES "NICK" ROWE, POW, Oct. 1963–Dec. 1968[3]

The "Code of Conduct for Members of the Armed Forces of the United States" was the POWs' single most important document. Issued in 1955 in response to the supposedly disgraceful behavior of the Korean War POWs, Executive Order 10631 briefly and clearly listed the POW's duties to his country and his fellow prisoners. If followed, the Code would keep him from violating the Uniform Code of Military Justice, from letting his morale slip, or from falling victim to the harsh conditions. The Vietnam War was the Code's first test, and most POWs declared it the key to their survival. Exactly what the document meant, however, proved difficult at times to determine. Faced with this quandary, the highest-ranking POWs developed guidelines for applying the Code to their Hanoi surroundings. If the Code thus served as the Ten Commandments and Declaration of Independence combined, then the elaborate system of regulations and procedures can be thought of as the POWs' constitution. Just as importantly, though, the Code of Conduct also provided the foundation for two central articles of POW faith: that by following the Code, the POWs had triumphed over the North Vietnamese; and that by drifting away from the Code, the American government and military had abandoned their duty, fallen into moral paralysis, and eventually settled for a shameful, negotiated retreat.

Captives of Korea, Captives of Vietnam

Widespread beliefs needn't be true to shape a nation's history, and certainly the accepted but dubious wisdom about America's Korean War POWs profoundly influenced military policy, and eventually the way many Vietnam POWs viewed their own captivity. *The*

ontains the essence of received opinion: in Korea, skilled Com-
brainwashed American soldiers into renouncing their country,
's, programmed to rise up on command as saboteurs, assassins,
This fifth-column paranoia, however, proved less damaging
he conclusions drawn about the men themselves. The most
Kinkead, whose sweeping charges appeared first in a 1957
later in his book, *In Every War But One*. He began by calling
ptional War," since never before had "a wholesale breakdown of morale
ale collaboration with the captors" occurred among American POWs.[4] Failure
er than ill-treatment was thus Kinkead's subject. The 38 percent mortality rate, for
example, "was not due primarily to Communist maltreatment," but to "the ignorance and
callousness of the prisoners themselves"—or as one of his sources, a "Major Anderson,"
put it, "a regrettable lack of the old Yankee ingenuity" resulting from "some new failure
in the childhood and adolescence training of our young men—a new softness."[5]

Though sometimes "psychic shock" was a factor, this softness was more often simple
cowardice. One "notorious collaborator," who "gave information to the Communists after
no more than thirty-five minutes of not very intense questioning," excused himself by
claiming, "They said they had ways of making me talk, so I talked."[6] Kinkead's most
striking claim, however, was that a POW's rank and service branch were good indicators
of his success or failure. Besides the POWs from Great Britain, Turkey, and elsewhere,
"31 Navy, 196 Marine, 235 Air Force, and 3,973 Army personnel" were held captive in
Korea. According to Kinkead, everyone performed better than the American Army enlisted
men, and for very specific reasons. The Turks' "astonishing record"—they didn't lose a
man—resulted from "the strict discipline they maintained from the time of their capture
till their release."[7] America's Marines "resisted indoctrination" because of their "leadership, discipline, and rigorous training"; the Air Force POWs had a higher "social and
educational level": "More than two-thirds of its members were officers, compared with 5
per cent for the Army. Over half had some college training as against 5 per cent again for
the Army."[8] Kinkead's indictment of the GIs was detailed and emphatic. Those who died
usually did so because they failed in their duty to their country and to each other. Those
who fell victim to brainwashing and betrayed America did so because they were young
and badly educated: "The indoctrination process, unfortunately, was greatly helped by the
ignorance of the captive GI's, whose formal education on the average had ended with the
ninth grade of school. Not only did the prisoners not know much about the history of
Communism, they didn't know much about that of the United States either."[9] They also
lacked a proper respect for military hierarchy. One of Kinkead's many career Army officer
sources blamed the enlisted men's failure on the 1945 Doolittle Board, which by supposedly narrowing "the distance between the commissioned and the noncommissioned ranks,
all with the laudable purpose of making the enlisted man happier with his lot," had
destroyed self-discipline and respect for authority, leaving the typical Korean War POW
a young grunt too stupid to resist his captors, too spoiled to take orders, and too weak to
survive.[10]

Kinkead and his sources had their critics. Albert D. Biderman's *March to Calumny*
(1963), a heavily documented attack on the hopeless GI myth, honed in on Kinkead's
officer-biased call for "a less permissive, more punitive, more rank-conscious Army." Such
"strident evangelism," Biderman warned, had its vindictive side as well: "Kinkead and his
Army informants have made prisoners of war, American society, and, indirectly, persons
with views I share, the villains of their piece." Furthermore, Kinkead's "piece" downplayed

an ugly and opposite truth: that "the major faults stemmed from the lack of innovation to meet new conditions and from the elements of traditionalism and the ritualism in the Armed Forces that are also reflected in the thinking of those who misread the Korean POW story." As Biderman's indignation suggests, however, despite its factual slips and hidden agendas, this misreading profoundly affected military and public opinion, and virtually all commentators agree that the Code of Conduct was a direct consequence. Though Biderman saw the Code as "an attempt to reconcile the incontrovertible value position of 'no aid to the enemy' with the many complexities of the prisoner's actual situation," other writers found it far less flexible.[11] Historian A. J. Barker states that "serious offences" and huge POW mortality rates in Korea led to the Code, which he sums up as "no surrender; no parole; no information; discipline and loyalty"—"principles which could be adopted by anybody who faces the possibility of becoming a POW." Philip R. Holt emphasizes the propaganda side. The Code was "an attempt to stymie any future efforts at thought reform," which the Department of Defense called "a new Communist aim: 'to make the prisoners serve the cause of international communism.'" And in 1978, Harold L. Hitchens simply stated that even though later research has called it into question, "the interpretation of the experience of American PWs in Korea which prevailed in the United States in 1955" greatly influenced "the decision to promulgate a Code."[12]

There is ample evidence that the Vietnam POWs took the hard-line interpretation into captivity with them. According to Vietnam POW Howard Dunn, the Korean War had shocked "the conscience of the American public" because the enemy had successfully "attempted maximum exploitation of the prisoners of war in its custody in furthering its war effort." POW Robert Naughton called it "unfortunate" that books like Biderman's had received less attention, but he too states that the hard-line interpretation "combined with the conclusions reached in the *Secretary of Defense Advisory Committee POW Report* prompted the issuance of the Executive Order Code of Conduct," an explicit statement of "the expected standard of conduct for POW's" which was implicitly "a *de facto* condemnation of Korean POW's." The Vietnam POWs' duty was therefore clear. Hold tight to traditional American values, maintain a command hierarchy, and follow the Code, which Kinkead had called the "most important of all the steps the Army took as a consequence of the discoveries of its prisoner-of-war study."[13]

It should therefore hardly be surprising that the returning Vietnam POWs loudly proclaimed that by following the Code they had rewritten the Korean War POWs' story in almost every detail. "We were unique prisoners who acted differently from those of Korea or World War II," declared POW Charlie Plumb, and by describing these "graduates of the U.S. Military Academy, the Naval Academy, and the Air Force Academy" as "the bright, clean-cut, cream of American youth," POW George Day made very clear what they generally credited for their success. The media picked up this message quickly. The first POWs left Hanoi on February 12, 1973; by the 17th, the *Los Angeles Times* was reporting "that virtually all of the men captured in Vietnam were professional officers, highly trained and dedicated," and that their performance stood "in sharp contrast to that of many returnees from North Korean POW camps 20 years ago."[14] The military's institutional response to Korea also received high POW praise. On February 18, Ray Merritt told the *New York Times* that the Code had been the key to their success—"If we follow that we have a way to live"—and the *Times* concluded that the POWs' good health arose from "their ability to maintain military discipline and a firm chain of command." Even before this, however, the *Los Angeles Times* had reported that "the new code and the survival training are given much credit by Pentagon observers for the way American POWs have come through Vietnam."[15] How the longtime POWs interpreted and then applied the Code to their situation is therefore one of the most significant stories to emerge from the cells of Hanoi.

The Articles, and the Debate

The Secretary of Defense's Advisory Committee on Prisoners of War first met in May 1955. Its five military members were retired generals or admirals. The five civilians were assistant secretaries from the service branches, or from the Department of Defense. This committee released a report; it also formed a subcommittee, chaired by General S. L. A. Marshall, to write a Code of Conduct. Marshall actually drafted the document: "Most of the language is mine, and I was the penman."[16] After appearing as Executive Order 10631 on August 17, 1955, the Code has been reissued frequently in Department of Defense pamphlets and in service General Orders. It has been revised twice: in November 1967 and in November 1977, after a committee studying the Code's usefulness in Vietnam recommended changing two words in Article V.

The Code's six short articles fit easily on a single page, and read like the sections of the Boy Scout pledge. As with similar documents, though, the Code's spareness led to some intricate and impassioned debates in Vietnam over what certain articles actually meant. These disputes and their resolution are perhaps the best introduction to the ethical, historical, and legal challenges the POW community faced as it struggled to follow the Code.

Article I

I am an American fighting man. I serve the forces which guard my country and our way of life. I am prepared to give my life in their defense.

Article I tells a soldier who he is, but this identity becomes complicated when he becomes a POW. The military's own opinion about a POW's combat status and expendability is clear. As Naval General Order (March 1957) explains, "an American fighting man" must oppose the enemy "whether in active participation in combat, or as a prisoner of war."[17] The title of the Defense Department's Advisory Committee report, *POW: The Fight Continues After the Battle*, makes the same point, and so does the title of Scott Blakey's biography of Vietnam POW Richard Stratton—*Prisoner at War*. As virtually all famous POW stories, films like *The Great Escape*, and even kitsch like *Hogan's Heroes*, suggest, in captivity this fighting takes the form of resisting. POW Ralph Gaither recalls that "holding out was the name of the game" in Hanoi: "Hold out as long as possible, every time. Make the enemy work for everything they get. Don't give 'em anything." Jeremiah Denton's reading of Article I was even more concise: "They had us, but they weren't going to enjoy it."[18]

These commonplaces gloss over what Michael Walzer, in his 1970 essay "Prisoners of War: Does the Fight Continue After the Battle?", argues is a real problem. If the Code of Conduct, and Article I especially, insists captivity is only "the termination of one sort of combat and its replacement by another sort, where the fighting is relatively circum-scribed and its conditions radically unequal," then surrender would "involve no commit-ment to cease (and not to resume) fighting," and the North Vietnamese would have no "positive incentive" to take prisoners, nor any reason to abide by the Geneva conventions, since its guidelines for POWs assume that hostilities have ended. According to Walzer, resisting is not a POW's right under Geneva, but a decision with possible consequences:

"The fight does not continue after the battle, not for the men who have been captured, unless they choose together to fight on and accept the risks that choice involves."[19]

Few Hanoi POWs would deny that the Code led them to see captivity as "a 'total war' to be fought within as well as without the bounds of the prison camp"; in fact, one of the major sources of conflict between the captives was their ongoing debate over which men were truly behaving as American fighting men.[20] Article I's relation to self-sacrifice was also hotly contested. "I am prepared to give my life" would seem to be utterly unambiguous, for as Philip Holt remarks, "A military man's contract with his government tacitly admits that his role must be played to the death if national interest requires."[21] For the POWs, however, the difficulty lay in deciding *when* to give their lives, and in some cases, in deciding what to do when *prevented* from dying. Those far from the scene have always found it easy to demand the ultimate sacrifice. Nathan Hale's famous regret that he had but one life to give for his country has made Americans impatient with those who don't make the same gift. When, for instance, Francis Gary Powers embarrassed his country by surviving his U-2 shootdown over Russia, many Americans asked, "Why didn't Powers use the poison needle he had on hand? Or the pistol he had with him?"[22] And in 1968, the returning crew of the *Pueblo* also learned that many of the folks back home considered suicidal resistance a fighting man's duty.

In Vietnam, time and place of captivity strongly influenced how a prisoner understood his duties under Article I. For POWs held in jungle camps, where the conditions often made death a certainty if the captives stopped struggling to survive, the issue seemed beside the point. Because of this constant threat, Army mortarman Ike McMillan found the Code "really hard to abide by once you're under pressure": "What's more important? Your life or the possibility of a court-martial when you get back? I never had the feeling I would rather die than disclose information." Jungle POW Donald Rander reached the same conclusion. Since surviving was his "prime objective as a prisoner," a hard-line reading of Article I would have been "unrealistic": "I don't think the object of the code is to get a soldier hurt or killed when through his ingenuity he can stay alive."[23] Self-sacrifice was a far more pressing issue in the Hanoi camps. A heroic suicide attempt figures prominently in the citation for Jim Stockdale's Medal of Honor, and so many POWs have claimed that they would have happily died rather than make statements under torture that Stephen Rowan entitled his collection of POW interviews *They Wouldn't Let Us Die*.[24] The North Vietnamese consciously exploited this duty to die by frustrating it. As one interrogator told Jay Jensen, "We know you are prepared to die for your country. But are you prepared to live for your country—to live under the conditions we will impose?" He then laughed and said, "No, you cannot live under those conditions. You will talk."[25] For many Hanoi POWs, then, Article I's demand for the ultimate sacrifice at times turned survival itself into their heaviest cross.

Article II

I will never surrender of my own free will. If in command I will never surrender my men while they still have the means to resist.

Article II proved to be the least significant part of the Code in Vietnam. The General Order notes explain that those who can no longer inflict casualties must evade, and that officers must never surrender their command, but since most of the POWs were aviators, their ability to inflict casualties ended when they bailed out, and "seven out of every ten men who lived to tell what happened suffered injuries so severe when they ejected that they were incapable of even *trying* to escape or evade capture after they hit the ground."[26] As for the uninjured men, their billowing parachutes virtually ensured a welcoming committee. Those taken in ground actions seldom had the chance to follow Article II either. Almost always overrun, their officers were usually dead, and only two or three men survived to be taken away. Article II was thus largely beside the point in Vietnam. Capture came instantly, and had to be dealt with.

Article III

If I am captured I will continue to resist by all means available. I will make every effort to escape and aid others to escape. I will accept neither parole nor special favors from the enemy.

Article III follows from Article I: if a POW remains a fighting man, he should resist. But how much? Michael Walzer argues that by demanding diehard resistance, Article III denies an American POW his right to the Geneva convention's mandated "benevolent quarantine" and provokes some men to actions which endanger "all those prisoners who do not choose to be heroes."[27] The hard-line Vietnam POWs would laugh at Walzer's reference to "benevolent quarantine," but they do frequently mention that harassing the guards or attempting escapes could lead to severe punishment for resisters and bystanders alike. According to commentator Harold Hitchens, for this reason the Code's injunctions "to attempt escape and resist the enemy activity were, to a great extent, disregarded, or at least interpreted in a far more shaded fashion than permitted by a literal reading of the words of the Code."[28] Camp conditions usually determined the shading. In the jungle, self-preservation could provoke or restrain escape attempts. Dieter Dengler shot his way out of Laos and James "Nick" Rowe fled after five years of captivity because death was clearly almost upon them, but in the jungle compound I'll be calling the Kushner camp, all thoughts of escape evaporated after the first attempt. "We tried to escape today," a terrified Joe Zawtocki told the other POWs, "We weren't successful. Weatherman was killed. Denny was shot in the leg." Small wonder, then, that these POWs "began to speak about holding out till the war ended."[29]

Article III was far more contentious in Hanoi. Even some of the toughest officers carefully separated their duty to resist from their duty to escape. "We were locked in cells, inside of cell blocks, inside a series of jagged-glass and hot-wire walls, in a massive prison with inner and outer walls, with twenty-four-hour guard surveillance, in the heart of the capital city," explained hard-liner Howard Rutledge, and "even if a prisoner survived an escape he would have no friends and no place to hide in downtown Hanoi"—"a town," as civilian POW Ernie Brace described it, "of three-and-a-half million people" who "all had black hair and brown eyes and were about five feet, four inches tall."[30] The punishments both failed escapers and the other POWs suffered through only stiffened the resistance to future attempts. Though the fire-breathing John Dramesi accused his fellow POWs of putting up as many barriers against escape as his captors, POW Charlie Plumb offers his account of what followed Dramesi's May 1969 failed escape as proof that such attempts were foolhardy. Dramesi himself was savagely tortured; his escape companion Ed Atterberry was beaten to death. Several other POWs were lashed hundreds of times with those rubber straps the POWs called "fan belts," and the systematic torture that soon followed destroyed the POWs' communication system and left twenty more POWs badly beaten up. After this nightmare, Plumb claimed that the men "didn't think much about escape—not that it would be impossible but that the aftermath for the remaining prisoners would be too horrible."[31] Though POWs like Dramesi might be respected and helped at times, they therefore also felt the hostility of those waiting "for the miracle of freedom to happen from the outside."[32]

And a miracle it would have to be, since Article III ruled out any possibility for parole agreements—"promises," as the General Order explains, "given the captor by a prisoner of war upon his faith and honor, to fulfill stated conditions, such as not to bear arms or not to escape, in consideration of special privileges, usually release from captivity or a lessened restraint." As an "American fighting man," the POW could not accept such conditions, and especially because his Vietnamese captors liked to turn parolees over to American antiwar groups, a "degrading and inhumane" form of political theater that Walton K. Richardson was urging the government to denounce as early as 1970.[33] Here too, rank and prison location tended to influence how a POW viewed parole. The Hanoi prisoners generally saw parole offers as a "fink release program." As with escape attempts, the major concern was how parole affected those left behind. Howard Dunn, for instance, found the actions of three officers who accepted parole in 1972 "contrary to the Code of Conduct, and potentially harmful to the welfare, discipline, and morale of the remaining prisoners."[34] But parole was also unattractive among the high-ranking Hanoi POWs because of the potential career damage. No excuse could justify a career officer's early release. The jungle POWs saw things differently. Since their captivity often looked like certain death, many men felt justified in grabbing at any chance for release. When enlisted POW Ike McMillan first encountered career officer policy after arriving in Hanoi, he thus knew instantly that he was in a different world: "Colonel Guy told us not to accept probation. I said to myself, 'Man, you're crazy. If these people call me and tell me I can go home—I'm going home.'"[35]

Article III was therefore a sore spot. Though the Hanoi POWs often finessed the duty to escape, they came down hard on early release, and justifed both actions by insisting that individual desires, and perhaps even duties, must give way to the greater cause of sustaining the POW community's health. This position alienated many jungle POWs and a fair number of diehard resisters; it also helps to explain why many senior men placed so much emphasis upon Article IV, the Code's statement on hierarchy and command.

Article IV

If I become a prisoner of war, I will keep faith with my fellow prisoners. I will give no information or take part in any action which might be harmful to my comrades. If I am senior, I will take command. If not I will obey the lawful orders of those appointed over me and will back them up in every way.

Article IV sums up the career officer version of the Korean War. According to Kinkead's hard-line "Colonel Brown," inferior American GIs and the military's betrayal of its own commanding officers led to POW failures in Korea. "'Look at the juvenile delinquents, the confirmed adult-haters, the slum kids who know nothing but the dog-eat-dog rule,' Brown exclaimed, 'How can you deal with them without discipline?'" Brown believed that "the way to correct this is not to give them a false impression of comfort, tell them about the movie hour, and the time they will have off—or giving them a company commander with the cooperative, democratic, let's-take-a-vote, and the please-come-along-now-fellows, and I-hope-you-will-like-me-fellows approach." Instead, company officers must command, sergeants must feel different from privates, and the grunts need commanders and rules, not big brothers and the chance to express their opinion. Unfortunately, though, by trying to iron out inequities "alleged to have existed at that time between the officers and the enlisted men," the infamous 1945 Doolittle Board had gutted this command hierarchy—and the result was treason, failure, and death.[36]

This version of Korean War captivity has been questioned on historical and ethical grounds. Biderman notes that many enlisted men kept resisting even after their officers were removed, and a group of diehard enlisted men known as the "reactionary platoon" had "agreed there would be no such thing as a leader. Before we would do anything, it would go before a vote and the majority would rule. The squad they called reactionary was run on democratic lines."[37] As for the ethics of Brown's conclusion, Michael Walzer points out a chilling similarity between the absolute hierarchy argument and the North Korean and Chinese strategy for controlling their own soldiers held as POWs in South Korea. To prevent widespread defections, the Communists sent political officers out to get captured. Once in the camps, through threats, murders, and camp riots like the Koje mutiny, these officers turned these POW compounds into nightmares—for their captors and for many of the prisoners. By suggesting that the Code encourages "action on the scale of the Koje mutiny," Walzer was thus expressing his fear that the military wanted to deny POWs the right to make decisions about their own behavior in captivity—a right the Geneva convention guaranteed.[38]

Though some may dispute its wisdom or legality, Article IV indisputably reminds the American fighting man that the command chain goes into captivity with him. "Without discipline, camp organization, resistance, and even survival may be impossible," the General Order notes explain, and since "strong leadership is essential to discipline," all "officers and noncommissioned officers of the United States will continue to carry out their responsibilities and exercise their authority subsequent to capture."[39] The Hanoi POWs strongly believed they had followed this article, and survived because of it. Edna J. Hunter concluded that these POWs had attacked their "lonely, monotonous and incredibly boring" existence "with two powerful, covert weapons: a POW military organization based upon seniority or rank, and a communication code to pass messages between walls." Interviewer Stephen Rowan learned that the same weapons prevented defections. Since "most military men would be totally lost without authority figures," keeping in touch with the chain kept the POWs from admiring their captors—a mistake Rowan suggests the jungle POWs sometimes made. The POWs themselves have credited Article IV for their success. According to Eugene "Red" McDaniel, "It wasn't until we organized our rooms according to rank and imposed discipline in the food that we were to avoid serious breakdowns." The highest-ranking Navy POW, Jim Stockdale, was even more emphatic. Since "survival and success in a combat situation" requires "a strictly disciplined military organization—if you will, a military dictatorship," the POWs "could not afford to live in a democracy." Following Article IV, they "built a successful military organization" instead: "a society of intense loyalty—loyalty of men to another; of rigid military authoritarianism that would have warmed the cockles of the heart of Frederick the Great; of status—with such unlikely items as years in solitary, number of times tortured, and months in irons as status symbols." This society eventually called itself the 4th Allied P.O.W. Wing—Vietnam was the fourth modern war involving American POWs—and many of its personnel returned home with strong opinions about the relative merits of military and civilian government. "We talk about the rights of individuals, but I think we've gone overboard," remarked Marine James Dibernardo, "People need authority. Maybe even dictatorial authority if we are to last as a civilization in the throes of a permissive society."[40] Comments like these suggest how totally many Vietnam POWs had inverted the Doolittle Board's recommendations. Instead of diluting military discipline, America itself needed a bracing dose of the authoritarianism that had saved the POWs in Hanoi—and by stressing the senior ranking POW's authority over all camp activities, including escape attempts, the 1977 Defense Review Committee supported the POWs' opinion.

This emphasis on command led to some startling conclusions. According to hard-liner George Coker, for instance, whether a senior officer "did a good job or a poor job made little difference, as long as he established a command structure." Even if he was "doing something stupid" or "holding hands with the enemy," this officer's word should remain law, since "as long as everyone worked together and did exactly the same thing, even when that thing was wrong it seemed to work out okay."[41] In practice, though, the Vietnam command chain was neither as universal or as absolute as many POWs suggest. One group of prisoners survived without any hierarchy at all. "The civilian portion of the camp was not run on a military basis, but rather according to democratic vote system," reported Chuck Willis, a Voice of America employee captured during Tet, "If something had to be done, Mr. Manhard asked for a vote and then represented the prisoners with the decision to the camp commander."[42] Nor did the military POWs find "obeying the lawful orders of those appointed over me" always easy. Simply establishing seniority could be a problem. A man captured in 1965 could for instance be suddenly outranked in 1970 by a new, younger POW who knew nothing about the camps, and whose promotions had come after captivity had frozen the older man in rank. Though Howard Dunn declared that "when the enemy starts making the room assignments, there must be only one service: the Armed Forces of the United States," differing service branches also caused difficulties. Naval officer Jeremiah Denton had to convince Air Force officer Larry Guarino in mid-1965 that they were not two one-man squadrons, and the same controversy resurfaced years later, when enlisted Army POWs from the jungle confronted Hanoi's Navy and Air Force officers.[43] Seniority thus had to be negotiated as well as recognized, and the POWs developed formulas that took length of time in rank, shootdown date, and promotion rumors from home all into account.

The distance between the POW command chain and Washington complicated matters further. Commanders in Hanoi "had excessive responsibility but none of the tools of authority—reduction of salary, suspension of liberty, court-martial." As a result, "SROs wielded gentle sticks of diplomacy" as often as they pulled rank. "They knew we were not 'boots' who asked 'How high?' at the command to jump," explained Charlie Plumb, "We were all trained leaders who acted independently. For the first few years, the SRO's authority was limited to advice rather than orders."[44] Compounding this problem were those officers who refused or were denied command. George Coker admitted "there were some real leadership problems" which blind obedience couldn't solve. While the good leaders "seemed to emerge and help guide others along the right path," it was also true that some ranking officers "just drifted into the background." These drifters did not escape criticism. On perhaps his worst night in captivity, Jim Stockdale worried about what his resistance might mean for other POWs: "Another purge, more deaths. My fault again. I don't have a hint about what happened at Alcatraz after I left. How many of them died in the ropes trying to protect me? Why is it I who cause all the trouble?" And yet, despite this self-doubt, his contempt for those who avoided command remained fierce: "Maybe it's better just to sit on your ass and keep quiet. Lie low in your cell like Colonel Kingpin over there in the Desert Inn and let Americans—misfits, psychos, and all—fend for themselves."[45]

Ironically enough, the existence of Colonel Kingpins led some senior POWs to violate the letter of Article IV consciously. When placed in isolation, or tortured into a state of mental and physical trauma—what the POWs called "rolling"—an SRO "could pass the lead to his successor without fear of criticism from the POW community." In early 1970, Jim Stockdale did this, but Jeremiah Denton's directions to Jim Mulligan indicated that the next exchange would not be as automatic: "'I'll pass the lead back to Stockdale just as soon as he gets his situation under control,' Jerry said. 'In the meantime, if the Vee get to me, Harry Jenkins is next in line, then you, then Howie Rutledge, and then back to Bill Lawrence,' he instructed, passing over a few officers who were senior to those just mentioned but who had never assumed the mantle of leadership in the camps when things were going rough."[46] Nor were those wearing the mantle beyond attack. The antiwar enlisted POWs known as the Peace Committee denounced the command structure as a bludgeon that stupid, reactionary, racist, or insane officers used to extort obedience. The senior POWs "have been subjected to the military mentality for a long time," POW Bob Chenoweth told the *New York Times*, "and if there's such a thing as brainwashing, the military does the best job."[47] For "prisoners holding varying views," the Code thus could appear to be an instrument of harassment—or as one of the Peace Committee's lawyers put it, "The reaction these P.O.W.'s received from Colonel Guy was the same as antiwar Senators received back here from people like Agnew."[48] An ugly fact therefore lurked behind Article IV as the key to POW survival. Disputes over rank, authority, and obedience were frequent, widespread, bitter, and at times divisive.

Article V

When questioned, should I become a prisoner of war, I am bound to give only name, rank, service number, and date of birth. I will evade answering further questions to the best of my ability. I will make no oral or written statements disloyal to my country and its allies or harmful to their cause.

This was the version in force during the Vietnam War. In 1977, the Defense Review Committee changed "bound" to "required" and dropped the "only" entirely—the only revisions made to the Code, and a hint that Article V's attempt "to spell out restrictions on the information a PW could provide while in the captor's control" must have "created the most difficulty."[49] Public opinion had something to do with this, since sticking to the Big Four of name, rank, service number, and date of birth is a POW's best-known duty. Jim Stockdale, however, regretted this emphasis, claiming that only outsiders "who have not served as prisoners of war but who write on such matters" see Article V as the Code's "heart." According to Stockdale, longtime POWs realized that Article V "is just a piece of good advice: to utter as little as possible except for the four items required under international law, at least until one is sufficiently certain of his ground to be able to use his words as weapons against his captors."[50] But as many narratives, including Stockdale's own, reveal, only after periods of self-hatred and despair for failing their country did most POWs arrive at this understanding of Article V.

Once more, Korea was partially to blame. Since the Geneva convention already "bound" legitimate POWs to supply their captors with the Big Four, the very existence of Article V suggests that the Korean War POWs had provided too much. According to Kinkead, besides the outright traitors, "three out of four" Korea prisoners took "the path of least resistance":

> They complied outwardly with the less extreme demands made by the Communists. The petitions they signed and broadcasts they made were relatively harmless. They cooperated in indoctrination and interrogation sessions in a passive sort of way, although there was a tendency to refuse to do anything obviously traitorous. Among the prisoners themselves, this outward compliance was known as "playing it cool."[51]

The other service branches and many Army officers agreed that most of those "playing it cool" were Army enlisted men. Perhaps for this reason, while post-Korea Air Force training began advising aviators to "comply willingly with enemy demands rather than to submit themselves to unspeakable tortures and mind-destroying 'brainwashing,'" the Army pushed a hard-line attitude of "absolutely rigid and open defiance of the captor . . . as exemplified by the rule 'give name, rank, serial number, and nothing more.'"[52] A few students of Korea proposed even more ingenious countermoves. In an essay called "We Can Baffle the Brainwashers," Admiral Daniel V. Gallery argued that POWs should be *publicly* authorized to say whatever their captors wanted them to. Since even a "true" confession would be ignored, the captors would have no reason for leaning on their captives, and the POWs would no longer feel like traitors for passing beyond the Big Four.[53] Article V took a middle route between Gallery's Cretan liar approach and the Army's Spartan demand for almost dead silence. S. L. A. Marshall himself later wrote that a POW "bound" to the Big Four is not "therefore prohibited from talking with his captors, so long as he does not disclose vital information," but subcommittee politics in 1955 led to "an intentional ambiguity" in Article V "to which I objected at the time the code was written."[54] This article had therefore posed difficulties even before the first American was captured in Southeast Asia.

In Vietnam, jungle camp conditions tended to overrule Article V. When jungle POW Frank Anton refused to describe his military duties, for instance, his interrogator pulled a .45: "'If you do not answer the question,' he said, 'I will shoot you. You may think about it.'" Anton then "answered everything he asked"; in the jungle, it was just too easy to disappear forever.[55] In Hanoi, personal differences, past training, and Article V itself always threatened to split the camp. To Howard Dunn, the article's second sentence, *I will evade answering further questions to the best of my ability,* acknowledged "the realities of interrogation and the individual's susceptibility to sustained coercion." But the last sentence, *I will make no oral or written statements disloyal to my country and its allies or harmful to their cause,* drove many POWs back into their hard-line training, which "led to a misperception of individual capabilities and to a very damaging sense of self-betrayal once contradicted by actuality." Most POWs ended up on one side or the other of these "contradicting absolutes." According to Charlie Plumb, "those who were disciplinarians by nature and interpreted the Code strictly" were known as the "Tough Guys," and "those who were liberal and rendered the Code loosely" became "The Softies."[56]

Over time, individuals also discovered they were blends of tough guy and softie. Convinced "that a pack of lies would not matter," Ensign Ralph Gaither for instance started off by supplying an autobiography which became legendary among the POWs:

> My father, I said, was a Big Foot Indian who belonged to the Foot-Washing Baptist Church of America. My grandfather was Chief Crockagator who lived in the Happy Hunting Grounds and hunted alligators and mudfish for a living. My wingman, I continued, was Dave Brubeck; my briefing officer was Walter Winchell. They knew what my ship was and where I was born, so I admitted that, and then added that my family worked for B. S. Railroad in Birmingham; that they always had and still do live there.[57]

Gaither ultimately became so committed to evasion techniques like this one that once home he became a Survival School instructor. By "trying not to give any more information" than Article V mentions, Gaither felt that some POWs had signed their own death warrants: "My buddies had died because they made mistakes. In captivity it is easy to die—tougher to live." At the time, though, Gaither felt profoundly guilty about his Chief Crockagator story. The tough guy reading of Article V still gnawed at him: "I felt that I had let my buddies down, and my country too."[58] Starting out as an Article V hard-liner did not however guarantee better results. Richard Stratton became perhaps Hanoi's best-known softie only after torture destroyed his hard-line resistance: "Picture the desire to die, to commit suicide! Yes! Had I the means then, even though I do not believe in it, I perhaps would have done it. After they broke me, I felt I had betrayed my country and my fellow men and my officer corps." Jim Stockdale also struggled with both possible readings of Article V. While staring at some "childlike pidgin-English propaganda" he's been ordered to copy and sign, Stockdale battled his urge "to delay commitment to the ropes, to 'play it smart,' to 'use my cleverness.'" Only by posing a rhetorical question, "Isn't credibility of defiance what it's all about in the long run around here?" did he free himself to conclude that evading "to the best of my ability" meant undergoing torture.[59]

Although very few POWs dared to claim they had followed Article V to the Spartan letter, most men were very familiar with the position of senior officers like Stockdale, who believed that resisting interrogation to the point of physical pain was an American fighting man's only honorable course of action. Article V's deliberate ambiguity thus drew the battlelines for a struggle that was still raging when the POWs arrived home.

Article VI

I will never forget that I am an American fighting man, responsible for my actions, and dedicated to the principles which made my country free. I will trust in God and in the United States of America.

"No argument there"—Jeremiah Denton felt Article VI was self-evident.[60] And yet, some men cited this article when justifying actions other POWs found traitorous. The General Order notes indicated that "responsible" refers to military law—"The provisions of the Uniform Code of Military Justice, whenever appropriate, continue to apply to members of the Armed Forces while prisoners of war"—and Korea's aftermath certainly suggested that the Vietnam POWs would be held responsible for their actions.[61] On their three-week boat trip home, the Korean War POWs went through "questionnaires, examinations, interviews, tests, and other details of processing." The average POW file looked like "an unabridged dictionary," and a few were over two feet thick. As one general remarked, "No group of men in Army history has ever been so closely studied as these repatriates were," and recording UCMJ violations was the interrogators' principal task. Negative service ratings and courts-martial followed, thus proving that the Army held its men "responsible for their actions as prisoners of war just as they are responsible for their actions in all other military and civilian situations."[62] Because of the Korean War POWs' experience, and because of Article VI, the Vietnam POWs therefore assumed that their actions *would* be examined, and that Code violations *would* be prosecuted under the UCMJ.

Michael Walzer guessed quite accurately how this awareness would affect the POWs. Though the "prison or prison camp is the scene of a new society" existing "precariously in the shadow of the detaining powers," POWs nevertheless "feel the pull of their previous commitments, not least because these are likely to be their future commitments as well."[63] But while Walzer saw this pull as dangerous, many Vietnam POWs felt that the certainty of judgment helped them maintain morale. In the war's early days, released POWs did return to a day of reckoning. While held by the Vietcong, Army Sergeant George Smith for instance denounced the war and praised the peace movement. His welcome after his 1965 parole included a reading of "Article 31—the military version of the rights against self-incrimination under the Fifth Amendment. A real friendly homecoming." During six months of debriefing in Okinawa, Smith also learned "that he was suspected of violating Article 104 of the Uniform Code of Military Justice—aiding the enemy"—a charge carrying the death penalty. Eventually, Smith received "something less than an honorable discharge, something more than a dishonorable discharge," and only because a court-martial would be too embarrassing politically.[64]

Though actions like these strengthened the Vietnam POWs' belief that the Code was a legal document, this opinion had never actually been unanimous, and as the war dragged on, government officials increasingly separated the Code from the UCMJ. By 1973, Roger Shields, the organizer of Operation Homecoming, could say that while the Code "gives a man the guidelines he needs to survive," it "is not a legal code, and you do not prosecute under it." Believing that the Code contains inspirational messages rather than legal obligations had become commonplace, and in 1977, the Department of Defense Review Committee concluded that the Code's principal value was "moral and spiritual." Though the POW must try to meet its standards, falling short was not sufficient cause for invoking the UCMJ.[65] For POWs like Jim Stockdale, "to be told that the Code did not have the force of law" was a "shocking discovery." When the government and military then refused to prosecute *any* POW under the UMCJ, many POWs felt cheated and betrayed. Even more serious, however, were the consequences of this decision for future POWs. Howard Dunn warned that "the role of the prisoner of war—whether senior or junior—will be more difficult if we do not insure now that the words 'responsible for my actions' in Article VI enjoy a firm basis of support." Jim Stockdale believed that "our POW military organizations would have been much less effective" without firm belief in Article VI's authority, and since the "Code of Conduct was the star that guided us," he and several other POWs had made "recommendations for its modification, particularly in the area of a prisoner's legal status."[66]

If anything though, deciding what "American" meant in Article VI was even more difficult than defining "responsible." For POWs like Larry Chesley, the link forged in the last sentence between God and the United States simply reflected the fact that "God and America is the great latter-day combination for freedom and happiness—if the American people will but do the right and put their trust in God."[67] When however a POW claimed that "American" neither guaranteed Divine Favor, nor referred to the U.S. government or its foreign policy, Article VI suddenly looked very different. By calling the Code "worthless as a guide to individual survival, primarily because it is based on the premise that the state is paramount to the individual," George Smith's editor was implicitly arguing for any American's right to dissent without fear of reprisal. Peace Committee POW John Young made this point explicitly—"Whether a soldier or not, I was an American first, and I decided it was my duty to speak out." So did Eugene Wilber, one of the two Hanoi POWs Jim Stockdale tried to press charges against: "Because I'm a military officer doesn't reduce my citizenship rights a bit; in fact it just *emphasizes* them. Being in prison probably made me hyper-critical about anything I was told to do. But, I *do* believe the First Amendment— the right to free speech—applies wherever I am in the world."[68] A POW charged with violating the Code thus cites Article VI as support for doing so—one more of anticipated and unanticipated ambiguities which in captivity led to a remarkable array of institutions and regulations designed to interpret and enforce those six pithy articles composing "the star that guided us."

Interpreting and Instituting—Reading the Code

According to Howard Dunn, disagreements over the Code "created greater schisms among the prisoners during the Vietnam conflict than their captors ever could have hoped to achieve." The document's "simplicity" was the trouble, since "a six-paragraph code can no more anticipate the myriad problems of combat and day-to-day prisoner of war life than can the memorization of 'SMEAC' and similar abbreviations completely prepare an individual Marine officer to write an operations plan for an amphibious operation."[69] Uncertainties were inevitable, as Jay Jensen's niggling questions about Article II's ban on "special favors" also suggest:

> Is special food (a little better or different food) a special favor, especially when you are sick? If the guards bring around something different like extra cigarettes, a banana, orange, grapefruit, cookie, or candy and just give it to you or drop it in your cell and leave, do you take it? Do you eat it? Or would that be a special favor, since you don't know if the other POWs in the camp got any?[70]

Appeals to a higher authority were futile as well. "No longer could we pick up a telephone and call the Pentagon for advice," Charlie Plumb notes: the buck stopped in Hanoi. The Hanoi POWs responded to these challenges by composing their own rules. Though they accepted the Code as "the basic law," because it "did not provide for day to day existence," they "wrote the laws we had to live by."[71]

Since telling junior officers "Do the best you can and decide for yourself how to resist" or even "'Obey the Code of Conduct' would have been the biggest cover-your-ass maneuver of all," these rules could not be vague. Instead, "fair and easily understood law" had to translate the Code's absolutes into individual circumstances. "The Code," Jim Stockdale explains, "as good as it is, is like a constitution—arguments can go on endlessly about how it should be applied to specific situations. I had to spell out our Hanoi-specific applications, to select out certain of Cat's [the Camp Commander's] key programs that we would likely be able, by corporate effort, to defeat." The senior officers of course not only wrote but enforced these laws, and the junior officers could not recall their commanders, making Stockdale's constitutional analogy somewhat strained. The Code, however, was a military Code, and its insistence on the POW's duty to lead and be led was familiar and welcomed. "Authority was not something that had to be imposed from the top," Stockdale insisted, "to be led, to obey fair and universal orders within the capability of all, was a right that this community of Americans demanded."[72] The history of Hanoi POW policy had three crucial stages. Stage one was the shortest, simplest, and probably the most controversial. In late 1965, the senior officers responded to widespread torture by ordering all POWs to "bounce back." As Jeremiah Denton bluntly put it, this policy mandated that "we should resist until they broke us and, when we recovered, make them break us again." Bouncing back not only shored up the POWs' resistance, but the Code itself. Since it "provided no further guidance once the prisoner was broken," by "bouncing back," the POW proved that the impossibility of following the Code to the letter had not made him question its relevance.[73]

The second stage of camp policy was a set of "standardized orders" issued in the spring of 1967. Known by the acronym BACK US, and written by Jim Stockdale, these orders "were absolutely prohibitory"—"that is, you were required to take torture, forcing the Vietnamese to impose significant pain on you before acceding to these specific demands." By identifying what was worth being tortured for, BACK US prevented senseless suffering. For instance, the B stood for bow—"Don't bow in public." Since prison officials demanded that the POWs bow to any North Vietnamese they met, refusing to bow would have led to several beatings a day, and a battered and weak community. Stockdale thus prohibited bowing only when photographers, reporters, or foreign officials were present.

The North Vietnamese could hardly beat their captives in front of outsiders, and even more importantly, no pictures or firsthand accounts of repentant and submissive American POWs could appear from "objective" sources.

A stood for air: the POW must stay off the air—"no broadcasts, no recordings"—until he is tortured. Though this rule echoed the "no write, no tape" order Jeremiah Denton had been issuing since 1965, it arose primarily from Jim Stockdale's observation that when everyone refused to read on the camp radio, the Camp Authority would give up for awhile. Bitter experience necessitated the C rule—"Admit no crimes." Stockdale felt that Article V to the contrary, "It would be the height of ignorance to order sententiously 'Make no confessions'"; after all, "the toughest of the tough were forced to make them from time to time." POWs should however avoid using the word "crime" in extorted statements, since this practice not only drained "a lot of the emotional steam" out of any confession, but also weakened North Vietnamese claims that since these admitted "air pirates" and "criminals" had violated international law, they did not qualify for Geneva Convention treatment. K stood for "kiss"—"Don't kiss them good-bye." POWs should neither "kiss up to the Communists," nor participate in staged farewells or other activities upon release which might suggest they had come to like their captors. As for US, these two letters stood for America, for the POWs, and for a simple but demanding rule: "Unity over Self." No POW could benefit himself at another POW's expense. As Stockdale explained it, "our highest value had to be placed on the support of the man next door. To ignore him was to betray him. The bottom line was placing prisoner unity over selfish interests."[74]

Stockdale wrote BACK US for a small and scattered society of POWs who lived with torture. When most of the POWs crowded into the Hanoi Hilton in 1970, the senior men responded with new regulations. Called the Plums, like BACK US they required the men "to support the Code of Conduct by doing and saying nothing harmful to the U.S. interests, to actively resist propaganda efforts of the Vietnamese, and to work together in order to go home with honor."[75] The detail, however, had radically increased. Plum 1 for instance expanded on "Don't kiss them good-bye" by outlining proper release procedures. Sick and injured POWs would leave first, then the enlisted men, and then the officers; nor would anyone describe their treatment until everyone was out of Hanoi. Other Plums established a hierarchy of resistance postures, rising from Res Con No. 6—"our military bearing with the enemy—to offer consideration to them, but with disdain"—to Res Con No. 1—"a hunger strike." Some other Plums could be ten paragraphs long, and "very specific, with times and dates and particular conduct in a variety of situations." Unit security added a further level of complexity: "Plums dealing with the communication system itself were highly classified, and unscrambling these codes was tedious business." So Byzantine did these rules become that POWs called memory banks "memorized every plum to keep the regs consistent," but even at their most elaborate, like the Code, the Plums could lead even loyalists like Charlie Plumb to worry about shaky ground: "Were the plums really binding by military law? How would a man withstand court martial proceedings if he disobeyed? Were the squadron commanders exerting more control than they rightfully possessed? None of us knew for certain."[76] Less orthodox POWs like Eugene Wilber went farther, denouncing many POW rules as the whims of high-ranking diehards: "Strict authoritarianism, which goes on in the military, we just can't buy. 'Forward march right over the wall' sounds great in text books. But, when it comes time to applying these things in real life, you have to listen to what you're told and try to apply it to the legal and moral situation you're in."[77]

For most Hanoi POWs, however, their growth as a community paralleled the growth of their laws. As Jay Jensen explains, "To begin with, you are on your own completely. You are in solitary. You make your own decisions. Then you get another cellmate, and he is higher rank, so he now interprets the code. Later if you get communication with other adjoining rooms and get a system set up you can get specific instructions from the building SRO (senior ranking officer) or the camp SRO. And that's what we did."[78] Following the Code certainly led to some complicated regulations, but it also gave many POWs their reasons for sticking together. Unity was thus not only a triumph over self, but a way of tying your personal fortunes to those of the entire POW community. For men worried about the Code's legal status and their eventual return home, the S in US could stand for safety as well.

The Code in Practice

Unity did not, however, mean assumed equality in ability, or in freedom of action. This too was a legacy from Korea, for one of Kinkead's striking revelations was how willingly many officers condemned their own troops. Presumably one possible explanation for the enlisted Korean War POWs' "failure" would be the incompetence of their officers, but this was seldom suggested; in fact, the career officers' faith in their own superior intelligence, education, and self-discipline actually widened the gap between enlisted and commissioned POWs. One example suggests how great this distance could be. Captured on August 25, 1950, General William F. Dean was the highest-ranking American held in Korea when an enemy general asked the most embarrassing question Dean had ever been asked: "Do your officers and men know why they are fighting?" Before capture, Dean had agreed with an American officer who asked him this question that "we're fighting for liberty" was "as good an answer as any." Confronting the enemy general, however, made Dean realize that he "just hadn't gotten around to any such explanations," and though he "lied like a trooper" in reply, Dean also "made a personal resolution never to let that explanation detail slide again, no matter how tough the situation or how little time I had." As a POW, Dean also granted himself a remarkable degree of latitude. He talked comfortably to interrogators, visitors, and reporters, and even his "friend" Wilfred Burchett, the leftist journalist whom the Vietnam POWs would call "Well-fed Bullshit." To pass the time, Dean helped translate a biography of Kim Il Sung into English, and at occasional drinking parties, Dean joined his captors in toasts he suspected had to do with the destruction of North Korea's enemies. Though the Code did not yet exist, Dean certainly seemed to be violating the spirit of Article 5. His punishment however was the Congressional Medal of Honor, and the moral is obvious: the higher the rank, the greater a POW's freedom when dealing with his captors.[79]

Some of the most influential Vietnam POWs followed the same path. Before his capture, Jim Stockdale learned in his Stanford political science classes that a POW's success in Korea had largely depended on his willingness to act out stereotypes. The best enlisted prisoner was "the redneck Marine sergeant from Tennessee." Though his eighth-grade education limited his grasp of international affairs, "He was a straight guy, red, white, and blue, and everything else was B.S.!" Officer POWs triumphed for the opposite reason. Well-educated, thoughtful, and patriotic, these "sophisticates" knew America's history and its problems well, but believed their country was "on the right track." Though they usually chose not to, these men could easily master their ill-educated captors in debates: there was no need to yell B.S. As "high school graduates who had enough sense to pick up the innuendo, and yet not enough education to accommodate it properly," Korea's POW failures lay between these poles. The most vulnerable POWs were thus enlisted man who mistakenly believed they had the brains of an officer—men just smart enough to think up stupid things to do.[80]

Though Stockdale admitted these categories were "possibly oversimplistic," they certainly influenced how the Code was read in Vietnam. POW Howard Dunn for instance denounced "Pre-Vietnam Navy and Marine SERE training" for telling officers that lying convincingly to interrogators was "a form of weakness," while at the same time declaring that such lying was "not suited to the training of the masses, for it generally requires the concoction of credible answers to particular questions." "Premeditation," "constant vigilance," and "common sense," the skills of a successful POW liar, were in Dunn's opinion beyond the enlisted man's reach.[81] Similar attitudes accounted for glaring differences in service branch training. While the Air Force assumed the potential POW was "an officer of the Strategic Air Command, carefully selected and highly trained in sophisticated tactics and missions," the Army assumed the "bulk of its troops liable to capture are enlisted men, often with little education and training." As a result, the Air Force set "a policy that could fully utilize the intelligence, dedication, and resourcefulness expected of its combat crews," but the Army "argued for a 'simple policy that every soldier could understand,'" since "training troops for fallback positions under severe interrogation would weaken their will to resist and lead to other dangers."[82] The Navy and Marines generally followed the Army's path: before Vietnam, then, most training stressed the Spartan Code—and the lower the rank, the harder the line.

When enlisted Vietnam POWs talk about the Code, this lack of training becomes obvious. "I can't answer that," jungle POW David Harker said when asked for his parents' address. But his captor asked "Why not?" and Harker realized, "That's a good question. I don't know why." He then tried "to recall the exact wording of the Code of Conduct," which he had memorized during basic training, but the words seemed ambiguous—and especially with a bayonet at his neck. A "lonely, exhausted, empty" Harker thus chose to survive, and he talked about his family for the next hour. Navy enlisted man Douglas Hegdahl found his equally vague memories about as helpful: "He volunteered his name, rank, serial number, and date of birth. That much he did remember about the Code of Conduct that he'd read on a bulletin board in boot camp. He did not answer the next question, because the code said he did not have to; he remembered that too." Two unanswered questions, however, proved to be his captors' limit. "A rifle butt slammed into the back of his head, nearly knocking him senseless," and Hegdahl went immediately into his act as the world's stupidest sailor—an ill-trained, virtually illiterate child with nothing to reveal. Other enlisted POWs made similar adjustments without playing the clown. Jungle POW Donald Rander "conceived the idea of counter-subversion": "In the interrogations I'd use the names of people I knew in sports, for example. Then I'd organize these stories in my mind, go over them again and again. I realized I was telling them fiction so in case I was interrogated later I could remember them exactly." Ignoring the Spartan emphasis on the Big Four also let Rander turn his own life into a weapon: "I also told them a lot of truth about my background. Things I knew were contradictory to what their government was telling them about the U.S. After 3 years of this I believe I was successful in causing two or three to wonder just what was the truth."[83]

Hegdahl's and Rander's successes were all the more impressive because they contradicted many senior POWs' belief that enlisted men could not manipulate their captors so expertly. In fact, many enlisted POWs came to believe that the officers' "by the book" approach would have amounted to suicide in the jungle. When Army doctor Floyd Kushner, a captain but no military leader, arrived at his camp, the "pale, drawn, hollow-eyed" prisoners regarded his rank with "unmistakable hostility." "We don't go by the Code of Conduct here," one man told him, "I know you're an officer, but you will learn." As Kushner soon learned when he questioned two Puerto Rican POWs, these sick, ill-fed men were utterly indifferent to their duty:

> "What's going on here? Have you been brainwashed? Do you feel as Roberts does about the war?"
> Ortiz did not speak English. Agusto, who did, answered for both of them: "I know only three things: I am an American. I am a Catholic. And I want to go home. And that's all I'm going to tell you."[84]

Since these POWs often blamed their commanding officers' ambition or stupidity for getting them captured, when any officer POW "felt he had to do his duty" by shaping up the troops, to prisoners like John Young it seemed like "he was trying to earn medals at our expense." Peace Committee member Young even turned the tables by arguing that it was the *officers* who often proved to be inflexible, and even brainwashed: "Colonel Guy was a flier who had never seen the war on the ground as we had, a career officer who went by the book whereas we were young enlisted men who still hadn't been influenced that much by the military and were still able to think for ourselves."[85] Poor training thus left the enlisted men with two ugly alternatives: stay hard-line and die; or survive by waffling the Code, and confirm the career military's belief in a GI's weakness, even though the officers themselves felt entitled to adopt the second alternative. John Young is admittedly a dubious source; nevertheless, the *New York Times* also found in Guy's formal charges against the Peace Committee some of that long-standing antagonism between grunts and career officers which polarized the military both inside and outside the POW camps.[86]

Even the senior Hanoi POWs found gaps in their precaptivity training. Though nothing could have fully prepared someone for seven years of imprisonment, many returning POWs would have agreed with Howard Dunn's complaint that "our evasion training prior to and during the conflict in Vietnam dwelt more on history and fraternity-hazing techniques." POWs who praised their training also manage to suggest it was something of a joke. Jay Jensen for instance played hide-and-seek in the Philippines with natives who got rice for catching someone—"quite a game," Jensen fondly recalled.[87] The interrogation training was contaminated by a lingering fondness for the Spartan Code. S. L. A. Marshall, the Code's author, deeply regretted this macho mistake. By downplaying anything but a hard-line reading of the Code, "the Services, with the exception of the Air Force, did not try to make it work." As early as 1968, the "disparity between expected stress and the realities of the captive situation" in Vietnam had Philip Holt guessing that Spartan training "may prove to have been a great disservice to these prisoners," and when POWs like Jim Stockdale did come home, they confirmed Holt's fears. For Stockdale at least, the Spartan approach to torture "generated one big false impression": that "it all happened in the first month or two, and that 'if you hang tough through them, the jailers will put you aside as a waste of their time and leave you alone.' "[88] In Vietnam, the captors also hung tough, and many POWs became "sophisticates" simply in self-defense.

Though unhappy about falling short of the Spartan Code's demands, as educated and experienced military officers, these POWs were confident that they could easily outwit their captors. Some of the most senior POWs were sparring with their interrogators almost from day one. Since Jeremiah Denton had learned in Survival School that POWs with

"advanced schooling in international relations" should "feel free to defend their government's policy," during his first interrogation "he launched upon a vigorous defense of the
American effort in Vietnam." Robinson Risner, camp SRO during 1965 and 1966, did
the same thing. When an official asked, "What do you like about the United States?"
Risner "would go on and on for hours, giving him the red, white and blue version of
what I liked about America." As for senior Navy POW Jim Stockdale, he actually
debated politics and philosophy with the architect of Hanoi's worldwide media campaign, "master Communist propagandist" Nguyen Khac Vien.[89] In each case, however,
the justification for this jousting rested upon the POW's intellect and rank. The senior
officers saw themselves as the brains of the POW community, and later commentators on
the Code have seconded this opinion. Colonel Charles E. Marean bluntly stated "that a
major or lieutenant colonel should be given greater latitude (than lower ranking personnel)
to interpret the Code according to the situation he might find himself in," and Harold
Hitchens criticized the Defense Review Committee's failure to " 'bite the bullet' and
recognize, clearly and explicitly, the realities." Granting senior officers more freedom
might "from a narrow political or military standpoint" be "undesirable or difficult to set
forth publicly before the American people," and might thus require being "phrased in more
moderate, 'democratic' terms." Nevertheless, since "service members who are officers,
and particularly those of higher rank, are more important to the enemy than enlisted men,"
officer training "should be more intensive and should formally allow more latitude than
for lower ranking personnel."[90] Both senior POWs and commentators thus agreed that
rank granted greater responsibility and freedom. The POW sophisticate could duck, return
fire, or even retreat; the redneck Marine could not.

On the Outs: America's Revision of the Code

While the Vietnam POWs were adapting the Code to their situation, however, the authorities back home were altering their reading as well, with results often at cross-purposes.
As the POWs struggled to maintain a military community, for instance, legal and military
commentators were recommending that POWs should not be prosecuted for violating the
Code. John E. Wehrum, Jr., argued that given the widespread domestic protests, "To expect
a soldier to conform to a higher standard than his country would be not only unrealistic,
but also unreasonable." L. James Binder, editor in chief of *Army* magazine, agreed, asking
"how can the Government fairly condemn men for antiwar statements, which were in most
instances much milder than those being made daily by many citizens, up to and including
many members of Congress and other elected officials?"[91] Many Vietnam POWs blamed
this kind of reasoning for the government's retreat from its own duties. The Department
of Defense training instructions clearly informed POWs that "just as you have a responsibility to your country under the Code of Conduct, the United States Government has a
matching responsibility—always to stand behind every American fighting man." A POW
will thus "not be forgotten," and the government "will use every practical means to
establish contact with and support our prisoners of war, and to gain their release."[92]
Unfortunately, government officials proved dangerously ignorant about these responsibilities. When Jim Stockdale's wife Sybil heard Secretary of State Dean Rusk remark in 1967
that the captured pilots were hostages rather than prisoners, she was terrified. Since the
North Vietnamese were justifying their violations of the Geneva convention by claiming
the captured Americans were war criminals rather than POWs, by denying the POW label

himself, Rusk was helping the enemy, and giving rebel POWs an excuse for ignoring the Code.[93]

These gaffes could, however, be corrected fairly easily. The government's eagerness to get the POWs back proved more difficult. As early as 1966 the United States "hoped to start a chain reaction of informal unnegotiated releases," and some captured Vietnamese were actually returned on the chance that the North Vietnamese might return the favor.[94] Sybil Stockdale also worried about the official response to those POWs released to antiwar groups: "For a military man to accept parole and come home early was forbidden by the Code of Conduct. Yet our government encouraged and condoned this sort of release. What kind of honorable situation existed when our own government disobeyed the code it had sworn our servicemen to uphold?" Jim later shared Sybil's disgust. During the Iran crisis, almost eight years after his release, he still rankled at what he called False Assumption No. 3: "Any release is a good release: if they'll agree to return 5 out of 52 next week, encourage it." For Stockdale, Unity always came before Self, and "what our politicians and countrymen in general need to understand is the true and total perniciousness of early releases as seen from within that band of brothers behind barbed wire." Parole sets a "time bomb of depressive remorse" ticking in the parolee, and leaves a "trail of lifelong grudges and broken unity" behind him. But when Stockdale tried to prosecute those POWs who had failed in their duties, "I couldn't find anybody in Washington who understood the problem."[95]

How did the government drift so far from its own military's code? Once again, the most public cause came from Korea. On January 23, 1968, the U.S.S. *Pueblo*, a surveillance ship, was captured in international waters off North Korea. A flood of confessions, prepared statements, and photos flowed out of North Korea until December 23, 1968, when the POWs were released and over 100 "debriefers" and "technicians" began interviewing the crew. Convened on January 20, 1969, the Court of Inquiry eventually recommended that Commander Lloyd Bucher and research officer Lieutenant Stephen Harris "be brought to trial by general courts-martial"; that the executive officer receive a letter of reprimand; and that an admiral and a captain who had helped to plan the *Pueblo's* mission be disciplined as well. These recommendations withered as they passed up the command chain, until Navy Secretary John H. Chafee announced there would be no disciplinary action. What also withered, however, was any commitment to the Code. The Court had started out Spartan, asking all witnesses why they had violated the Code. The findings however sidestepped everything that occurred after capture, and praised Bucher's leadership in captivity, lending support to his belief that the Code, not his crew, had failed. With its beatings, mock executions, displays of mutilated Koreans, and death threats against his men, Bucher's own captivity paralleled that of the senior Hanoi POWs. Shame and despair tormented Bucher as well. Shortly after signing his first extorted confession, he attempted suicide. Bucher, however, reached some radically different conclusions: "The Code of Conduct was unenforceable and impractical and unrealistic in a case such as ours when an entire ship's company with some documents falls into the hands of a ruthless enemy who does not shrink from applying torture methods to extract what they want." Since in Bucher's opinion torture made following Article V impossible, he soon adopted Admiral Gallery's liar strategy: "Better to confess to the enemy's accusations, the more outrageous the better, showing him up as a liar and a cheat, than to risk torture and death."[96]

Nor should the government's unwillingness to prosecute Bucher be all that surprising; after all, the U.S. negotiators had themselves violated Article V to get the crew released. After publicly declaring it a lie, American officials signed a document which admitted the

Pueblo had been in North Korean waters, apologized for its presence, and promised that this would never happen again. Though successful, this strategy was a strong blow against the Code. "Ironically and tragically," Howard Dunn observes, "a 'confession' had been exacted from the code's promulgating authority—the executive of the United States—to effect release of the crew."[97] If anything, though, John Chafee's blanket amnesty for the *Pueblo* crew had an even greater impact on the Vietnam POWs' homecoming. POWs would apparently no longer be accountable for their actions in captivity—a highly offensive result, because it implied that a civilian administration's failures to follow the Code exempted military men from doing their duty. Most offensive, however, were those distortions arising from a belief that Article V was the Code's heart—what Jim Stockdale called the outsider's most common mistake. The Vietnam POWs *themselves* had decided that men tortured into making confessions should not be charged with violating the Code. Breaking Article IV was the unforgivable crime. The POW who ignored the command chain, renounced his own command duties, accepted parole and special favors, and attended press conferences and met antiwar delegations willingly was the senior POWs' concern. Chafee's *Pueblo* amnesty had however set a precedent, and exposed the government as unwilling to prosecute *any* Code violations. Well before their return, the longtime POWs sensed that America's attitudes about the Code were changing. Because the Air Force had essentially decided by 1969 that "the Code was not a vehicle for enforcement of a PW's obligations," the new shootdowns were almost different beings. To POWs like Jim Mulligan, their "long hair, sideburns, beards and mustaches" made them "a far cry from the military appearance that most of us had been accustomed to during our careers." This "motley looking crew" brought disturbing news about changes in Survival School training. Because getting "their names out to the world press" was their first priority, the 1971–72 POWs began violating the Code almost instantly: "All of them were photographed and most made innocuous statements which we could easily see through. Occasionally one of them would make a tape which would be played over our camp radio."[98]

The "new guys" themselves supply other examples. Captured during the 1972 Christmas bombings, Captain Lynn R. Beens refused to go beyond the Big Four, but relented after a few hours with his wrists tied behind him: "I gave them the aircraft I was from, and some other answers just to satisfy them." Since the North Vietnamese knew that these captives had been trained to get their names out, Beens was then driven to a radio station, where he saw "a whole string of jeeps" carrying new POWs. Though Beens worried about what his captors might want, "there were no pressures. They asked me if I would like to make a statement that I was there. It wasn't propaganda. They wanted me to say I was shot down on such and such a date flying over Hanoi, and how I was being treated, and whether I was in good health or not." When they let him "give any message I wanted to give to my family," Beens took the "opportunity to let someone know I was there."[99] Jeremiah Denton, Richard Stratton, and scores of others had been tortured into making such statements; to avoid such a performance, Jim Stockdale had attempted suicide. Beens neither asked if other POWs had been given the same chance, nor seemed to have considered whether a parade of Americans admitting to bombing Hanoi at Christmastime might create an unflattering impression. Clearly, later shootdowns had a different understanding of Article V.

Beens was no weakling, but the product of changes in training. Nor was he unique. As Stephen Rowan notes, the 131 POWs captured in 1972 and 1973 were "considerably different than the other POWs," because "they never suffered that feeling of terrible guilt which has been so vividly described by others—that period of days or weeks or months after having been broken when each man thought he was the only one who had ever sold out, and when many wished for death rather than have to face family and friends."[100] After meeting these newcomers, the old-timers worried that their own crippling depressions, physical suffering, and hard-line devotion to the Code and each other would be lightly valued when they arrived home. Even Operation Homecoming was disturbing at first. Although Plum 1 had mandated that first the wounded, then the enlisted men, then the officers in order of capture would leave Hanoi, the peace accords erased the enlisted man's priority, and the North Vietnamese violated the order of capture by putting the most cooperative POWs in the first group out. These shifts, however, were relatively minor, and the first planes left on February 12, 1973. The next day, though, twenty POWs were told that as a favor to Henry Kissinger, they would go home on the visiting secretary of state's plane. The resulting encounter between Jim Pirie, highest-ranking member of the reluctant "Kissinger 20," and the U.S. liaisons in Hanoi revealed the distance lying between the POWs and their "rescuers":

> . . . one of the men said angrily, "What the hell are you guys doing?"
> "They're trying to kick us out of here *out of order*."
> "What do you mean—out of order? We've been busting our gut for eight years trying to get you guys home. We're gonna take you any way we can!"
> "Wait just a minute. We have our rules too. We've read the agreement and it says that we leave in order of shoot-down. These guys the V have selected are *not* the next twenty men. Now do you want to take us out of order? It's your decision."
> "OK . . . we'll take you."

The Kissinger 20 were not satisfied, and when POW Norman Gaddis, now the camp SRO, said he would "permit" them to go, they demanded a direct order. As the Kissinger 20 boarded the plane, they therefore knew their own government had forced them to violate the Code in literally their last moments as POWs.[101]

Those men already home were confronting similar paradoxes. Near the end of 1972, when the senior POWs decided that the day of professional reckoning was at hand, they cranked up the bureaucratic machinery, and began "preparing evaluation reports on each POW's performance, which would be a part of his official military record on return home." Though some evaluators disliked Jim Stockdale's policy that it was "neither American nor Christian to nag a repentant sinner to the grave," since 1971 the POWs had also been negotiating with the handful of officers most POWs considered to be collaborators. Only two men refused to rejoin the Wing, and Stockdale would try to prosecute them after returning home. Back in Washington, though, officials were downplaying Code violations and stressing the individual POW's rights. Even before the first POWs had left Hanoi, the Department of Defense had announced that "No charges will be filed against returning prisoners of war for making propaganda statements over North Vietnamese radio."[102] All military escorts were instructed to "act as unmilitary as possible, to avoid the service jargon," and "to change the subject tactfully if a returning American prisoner of war begins discussing possible violations of the military code he might have committed in captivity." The goal was to ease the POW "from a quiet, slow-motion world" to "the military world, with its speed and shine, its customs and bureaucracy and machinery, its rules and regulations and peculiar language"—a world in short that many POWs felt they had re-created in Hanoi. Only after a complete physical examination might the POW be asked about Code violations—and then with "full legal protection, including a lawyer's presence."[103]

For all the euphoria, then, the senior POWs soon realized that their homecoming was neither what they had expected nor what they desired. Instead of "the intimidating battery of intelligence operatives and psychiatrists" who processed the Korean War POWs, each Vietnam captive "was greeted by an escort officer, a man of rank, service branch, background, and experience comparable to those of his charge." The eventual interviews seemed to avoid questions of misconduct. During Jay Jensen's debriefing, "No information about another prisoner's conduct was asked for." Eugene Wilber, one of the officers Stockdale tried to prosecute, "was not given what other men received: an extensive debriefing that usually took several days and covered every aspect of each man's period of captivity." This "apparent unwillingness to listen to *his* story seemed ominous," and so it was—but for Stockdale, who soon realized the military didn't want to hear *anything* about possible misconduct.[104] All POW attempts at legal redress failed. Since their information about the camps had been so valuable, those who had accepted unauthorized parole were never prosecuted. Nor would the military initiate charges against anyone; senior POWs would have to pursue justice as "private citizens." All such actions fizzled. When Peace Committee member Larry Kavanaugh committed suicide, Army Secretary Callaway and Navy Secretary Warner dismissed all the charges Colonel Guy had laid against the men. As for Navy SRO Jim Stockdale's charges against Hanoi POWs Eugene Wilber and Marine Colonel Edison W. Miller, Secretary Warner claimed that "courts-martial would be unduly disruptive to the lives of the other returnees who would have to testify"—even though Stockdale was acting on their behalf. Wilber and Miller were retired.[105]

What many POWs found most outrageous, however, was the government's willingness to trivialize the Code and the POWs' sense of duty simply to avoid unpleasantness. When he dismissed the charges against the Peace Committee, Army Secretary Callaway not only declared that "Army enlisted men had no legal obligation to obey orders from Air Force officers in North Vietnamese prison camps," but also that "the code had no teeth in it." The Army's general counsel then declared that the Code was "not legally an enforceable document." Callaway soon "admitted his former opinion had been erroneous," but the Vietnam POWs still believed that their government was trying to strip their Code, camp regulations, and command structure of all legal authority. Since as Howard Dunn observes, "Many orders were obeyed due to the *misconception* that they were legally enforceable," the returned POWs had to advocate supplementing "moral responsibility with legal authority." Eventually, the Defense Review Committee report stood squarely behind Dunn's position. In the future, POWs must recognize a senior officer's authority, regardless of service branch. The report also concluded that the military had not investigated all the possible UCMJ violations; henceforth, charges would be fully examined, and all POW debriefings "should include reports on possible violations of law, regulation, or policy."[106] Though these recommendations were welcome, many Vietnam POWs remained worried that their time in captivity had been whitewashed or ignored. These POWs had prepared for official scrutiny, and many were disappointed when they didn't get it. This dissatisfaction was one of the most compelling reasons why so many POWs set to work on recording their stories. Within months of Operation Homecoming, biographies, histories, interview collections, and memoirs began pouring from presses small and large—a flood which continues. Public interest in POW narratives and stories of torture undeniably helped to create the market, but the POWs' own agenda was to defend the Code and its followers—to see in short that justice was done. Slighted by their government, the POWs therefore turned to the American people, confessing their weaknesses and crimes, but also proudly describing as well their individual triumphs and many successes as men fighting adversity together.

   Parts II and III of this book explore the many ways that the POWs carried out their task. What remains to be discussed in Part I is the nature of the adversity these men faced—the Vietnamese "Camp Authority," with its own rules and strategies. POW history was also shaped by pressures from without, and what these prisoners struggled within were the institutions created by their captors.

⋆ 2 ⋆

Camp Authority and the Rules of the Game

But what did reality matter, when we had regulations?
MONIKA SCHWINN, POW, Apr. 1969-Mar. 1973[1]

Drawing on the Code and their sense of duty, the senior Vietnam POWs re-established a military hierarchy and a body of law. Though these men would have organized themselves anywhere, in Hanoi it was especially dangerous. As former prisoners of the same cells, the North Vietnamese knew how effective inmate organizations could be, and camp officials worked hard to prevent them. Disorganized prisoners would also be easier to exploit in Hanoi's worldwide propaganda campaign, and a few POWs might be coaxed into supporting the North Vietnamese position. After all, if Americans who had never visited Vietnam were condemning U.S. policy, why shouldn't POWs under Hanoi's control do the same? To carry out these goals, the Hanoi Camp Authority wove international law, Chinese and North Korean detention methods, techniques for running total institutions, and even the Code of Conduct into a set of regulations and penalties as detailed as the POWs' own. If the Code defines in certain ways the POWs as a group, then the Camp Authority's procedures offer a useful starting point for looking at the POWs' captors.

Criminal or POW?

The most fundamental disagreement between the Camp Authority and its captives was over whether the Americans were prisoners of war. Though North Vietnam had signed the 1949 Geneva Convention Relative to the Treatment of Prisoners of War, they referred to it most when explaining to their American prisoners why they didn't qualify. Article 2, for instance, states that the convention "shall apply to all cases of declared war or of any other armed conflict which may arise between two or more of the High Contracting Parties, even if the state of war is not recognized by one of them."[2] North Vietnam argued that because the United States had not declared war, its military personnel could not be POWs, and since the undeclared side was also the one asking for convention protection, the "armed conflict" provision didn't apply either. This argument was however shaky: both countries had undeniably signed the Convention, and were obviously fighting each other. A more sophisticated argument dealt with Article 85, "Prisoners of war prosecuted under the laws of the Detaining Power for acts committed prior to capture shall retain, even if convicted, the benefits of the present Convention." Citing the Nuremberg trials, which had convicted military men for committing "war crimes" and "crimes against humanity," in 1949 the

Soviet Union, North Korea, China, and North Vietnam had filed a reservation to Article 85, arguing that if "I was only following orders" could not protect Nazis, then future war criminals should not be allowed to hide behind Geneva.[3] This reasoning had surfaced in Korea. When General Dean claimed that under Geneva he only had to give the Big Four, his interrogator responded instantly with Article 85, "quoting paragraph so-and-so, that in special cases prisoners could be required to give further information. I was a special case, he said, because I was a war criminal, so he could question me about the 1947–48 acts that made me one."[4]

This argument was of course circular. After isolation, food and sleep deprivation, round-the-clock interrogation sessions, and physical brutality forced their captives to admit they had committed such crimes as bacteriological warfare, the North Koreans and Chinese then used these confessions to justify refusing these confessed war criminals POW status.[5] The North Vietnamese had the same circle ready for their first American captives. Everett Alvarez learned in August 1964 that "you are not a prisoner of war. There is no war," and though Robinson Risner "laughed out loud" when called a criminal in September 1965, the charge was no joke: "I had violated the sovereign air space of the Democratic Republic of Vietnam. I was considered in the same way as those who used to prey on their coasts. 'You are the same as a pirate. You are going to have to talk.'" Jungle officials also trotted out these arguments. When Robert Garwood demanded his rights under Geneva, his interrogator neatly cited both Articles 2 and 85: "We do not recognize the Geneva agreements. We are not bound by any law, simply because U.S. aggressors invaded our country in an undeclared aggression against our people and homeland. Therefore *you* are not considered a prisoner of war, but fall under the policy of a criminal of war." In Hanoi, these arguments became stages in the institutional process leading to torture. When Howard Rutledge referred to the Code and Geneva to support his sticking to the Big Four, back came Article 2: "You are not a prisoner of war," the interrogator responded, "Your government has not declared war upon the Vietnamese people. You must answer my questions. You are protected by no international law." Rutledge still refused, and out came Article 85: "Commander Rutledge, you are a criminal, guilty of high crimes against the Vietnamese people. If you do not answer my questions, you will be severely punished." Rutledge said "no" once more, and was then tortured until he answered another question.[6]

Though most POWs understandably rejected the Camp Authority's arguments, their reasons varied. Jay Jensen actually offered the Nuremburg defense which had provoked the reservation to Article 85 in the first place: "We did not start this war. The men who started it, the leaders of the countries involved, and the men who decided how to conduct the war and the leaders who determined and invoked those orders will be held responsible for those decisions and orders; not the men who carried them out."[7] Other POWs, however, soon recognized that statements like "We were doing our duty" or "We were following the orders and obeying the laws of the country" assumed a split between the political and military which their captors found incomprehensible. What Jim Stockdale called his Geneva convention song and dance got the standard response: "It is true that my country acceded to the Geneva Convention of 1949, but we later filed an exception against those captured in wars of aggression. You are nothing but a common criminal, guilty of bombing schools, churches, and pagodas, crimes against humanity." This interrogator's closing words were however far more revealing: "You have medical problems and you have political problems, and in this country we take care of medical problems only after political problems are resolved." This fact above all made Geneva irrelevant. For the North Vietnamese, the Hanoi Hilton was not a POW camp, but "a political prison" and as Stockdale realized, "Political prisons are not for detention, for imposing punishment, or for preventing certain people from being at large. They are places where people are sent to be used for political purposes, or to have their minds changed, or both."[8]

Here then was the real conflict between the Camp Authority and the POWs. Refusing to abide by Geneva was not a primitive enemy's sadistic act, but more chillingly, resulted from a deliberate North Vietnamese decision that gaining authority over their American captives could advance their goal of gaining authority over their own country. For this reason, while the POWs tried to fight off the Camp Authority's efforts to use them in its propaganda war, concerned Americans back home were learning that they would have to convince the North Vietnamese that following rather than ignoring Geneva would be in their political interest. Or as Sybil Stockdale put it, the National League of POW Families' "simple objective was to educate the world about the Geneva Convention."[9] Otherwise, the POWs' media value would continue to blot out their rights under international law.

What kind of political prison did the Camp Authority run? In Korea and Vietnam, American POWs painfully learned the truth of Philip Holt's remark that "a prisoner-of-war compound, like a prison, an asylum, or a monastery, is a *total institution* whose inmates have little or no control over the ordering of their lives."[10] Such institutions have a single goal—to make the inmates abandon their former allegiances and obey the administrative authority—and in general, rules and procedures contribute more than physical surroundings to this end. In one list of rules which the Chinese gave their Korean War prisoners, for example, the punishments came first—hard labor, solitary, imprisonment with hard labor, life imprisonment, and death. Two kinds of violations—"discipline" and "system"—then get defined. Remaining imperialist, organizing escapes, spreading rumors, or trying "to be sarcastic on the progressive students, and purposely disturb others' study" were "discipline" violations. So apparently was dysentery. Punishment awaited all "who defecate in the pants and get lice on them, or adopt any other method to destroy them." "System" violations could be just as specific—turning books and magazines into cigarette or toilet paper, for instance—but they could also involve more nebulous mistakes in "daily life schedule, lecture, report, discussion meetings, and asking for leave." One principle, however, overrode all specifics. Anything other than what the Camp Authority wanted was a violation, and would lead to punishment.[11]

In another set of rules for British prisoners in Chongsong, the Camp Authority assumed the role of an academic administrator. "Students" must have a doctor's certificate to miss class. Monitors must take notes during discussions following the lectures. All study materials "must be registered and kept in good form." One regulation even seemed to guarantee academic freedom: "The discussion after lectures should be based upon the main ideas of each lecture. Everybody is allowed to voice his personal opinion frankly and straightforwardly, no matter how it differs from that of others. The illegal acts of interrupting other speeches and disturbing the meeting are forbidden." What these rules actually outlined, however, was a process of reeducation—the goal pursued in those political prisons which millions of Russians, Chinese and Koreans had "attended" before the Korean conflict. At Chongsong, the POWs had the same options as those political detainees—conform, or suffer the consequences: "All captured officers and men must get themselves ideologically prepared to observe self-consciously and enforce to the letter all provisions stipulated above. Violators should be punished according to various cases."[12]

When setting up their American POW camps, the North Vietnamese followed these Korean War examples, but they also studied carefully the POWs' own Code. "I have read your Code of Conduct," a VC interrogator told George Smith as early as 1963, "I have it here. Would you like to see it? It sounds noble. If we were attacking your country, I would consider you an honorable man." In 1968, jungle POW James "Nick" Rowe heard that the Code was "a useless piece of paper, opposed by the American people; one which, with many other unpopular laws, will be changed in November by a new government, according to the desires of the people."[13] The Camp Authority's most disturbing strategy, however, was to turn the POWs' own sense of duty against them: "the enemy was familiar with the Code, gave American PWs the hard-line interpretation, and told them that if they had given a single piece of information past name, rank, serial number, and date of birth, that they had already violated the Code (and that they might as well go on to further 'cooperation' with their captors)." For this reason, the Camp Authority extorted precisely those materials prohibited by the Code—"oral or written confessions true or false, questionnaires, personal history statements, propaganda recordings and broadcasts, appeals to other prisoners of war, signatures to peace or surrender appeals, self criticisms or any other oral or written communications on behalf of the enemy or critical or harmful to the United States, its allies, the Armed Forces, or other prisoners."[14]

The most detailed attacks on the Code were the various sets of camp regulations which began appearing in 1965. Most institutions have "a complex of rules (the 'house' rules) whose observance may be enforced by the simple expedient of reward (privilege) and punishment." Total institutions however have regulations that directly attack the inmate's own values. As Philip Holt explains, such rules will "be antagonistic to his sense of logic," and will contradict that "inculcated sense of duty which requires that he continue to resist even after capture."[15] While the senior Hanoi POWs were creating Bounce Back, BACK US, and the Plums to supplement the Code, then, the Camp Authority was composing rules to counter these guidelines at every point. The first printed rules appeared on "the inside of the door of every cell" late in 1965, and stayed in effect until 1969. The Camp Authority made sure that the POWs knew them. According to Jay Jensen, "Each of the incoming prisoners was forced to read the camp regulations, which branded him as a criminal."[16] By March 1966, rules, questions, and abuse were the three stages of initiation for all Americans arriving in Hanoi. Charlie Plumb passed through an even more streamlined version in May 1967. The Camp Authority gave him only the rules demanding answers to all questions. When Plumb stuck to the Big Four, he was "punished" with manacles and ropes. His complete version of the rules arrived while he was recovering from this torture.[17] In 1969, the Camp Authority "revised the regulations so they were not quite so ridiculous," but Jay Jensen recalled that "each POW" still "had to memorize the new regulations." Even though the process had lost most of its menace, Alan Kroboth's welcome suggests that as late as July 1972, interrogators were still going through the motions: "They asked me about a few of the regulations, and I told them I had never seen them. Every time I said that, they'd hand me another set. I had stacks of them."[18]

Virtually identical versions of the 1965 rules governing "*U.S. aggressors caught red-handed in their piratical attacks against the DRV*" appear in various POW memoirs.[19] These rules could be quite specific. Wakeup and bed-time would be "signaled by the gong." Cells must be kept clean, and although "criminals are not allowed to bring into and keep in their rooms anything that has not been so approved by the camp authorities," the POWs must "take care of every thing given to them." Personal safety was mandatory. During camp alerts, "criminals must take shelter without delay, if no foxhole is available they must go under their beds and lay close to the wall." Far more annoying were the rules outlining correct captive-captor relations. Since the "criminals must absolutely abide by and seriously obey all orders and instructions from Vietnamese officers and guards in the camp," the POW was dealing with a hierarchy which he always approached from the bottom. If sick, he "must report it to the guard who will notify the medical personnel"; if in doubt, "he is allowed to say softly only the words 'bao cao.' The guard will report this to the officer in charge." Most galling for the senior POWs were the required daily humiliations. A "cautious and polite attitude" toward all prison officials was essential. If visited by "Vietnamese Officers and Guards," the POW "criminal must carefully and neatly put on their clothes, stand attention, bow a greeting and await further orders."

These requirements had less to do with discipline than with confronting the POWs with their impotence. This strategy was most obvious in those rules which required violations of the Code. Escape was linked to "obstinacy or opposition" as a "punishable" offense. Obeying the rules and showing "true submission and repentance" through "practical acts" would earn a criminal "the humane treatment he deserves"—a direct attack on Article III's prohibition of special favors. Because prisoner unity was a greater threat than any single POW's refusal to talk, a number of rules attacked Article V's emphasis on the command chain. Communicating was entirely forbidden: "All schemes and attempts to gain information and achieve communication with the criminals living next door by intentionally talking loudly, tapping on walls or by other means will be strictly punished." Even the toilets were regulated. POWs were "forbidden to talk or make any writing on the walls in the bathrooms or communicate with criminals on other bathrooms by any other means." As for unity over self, the camp rules promised rewards for "preventing violations," but harsh punishments if a "criminal is aware of any violation and deliberately tries to cover it up." The Camp Authority's 1965 rules thus countered the Code at every point. An American captive was not a fighting man, but an imprisoned criminal who would be punished if he tried to escape, and rewarded if he cooperated. He could not communicate with other prisoners, but was required to report every violation of camp rules, to answer all questions, to provide all required documents, and to remember above all that he was responsible to the Camp Authority. Small wonder, then, that Jay Jensen found the camp regulations "so unreasonable you couldn't help but break several each day," or that Jim Stockdale declared "no normal American" could live by them, or most precisely, that POW historian John G. Hubbell would conclude, "There was no way that an American POW could adhere to them and at the same time abide by his own Code of Conduct."[20]

In late 1969, when conditions generally improved, new regulations appeared as well. Fewer and less detailed, they backed away somewhat from the more humiliating rules. Though prisoners still "must strictly obey orders and follow instructions given them by Vietnamese officers and armymen on duty," the demand for full answers was gone. The POWs' successes in maintaining military discipline also forced the Camp Authority to protect the "progressive" prisoners. Rule Nine reminded POWs that an officer's authority was not recognized: "In the dentention rooms, every detainees are equal with each other. Anyone does have the right to free thinking, feeling, praying etc. . . . and no one is permitted to coerce any other into following his opinion." The most significant change, however, appeared in the Preamble, which redefined the captive and his punishment. Though still not POWs, the captives were now American servicemen, and while the reservation to Article 85 remained—these servicemen had been "perpetuating barbarous crimes"—it was the U.S. administration that was waging "the war of aggression." Consequently, though the captives "should have been duly punished," they would enjoy "a lenient and generous policy" which would provide "a normal life in the detention camps."[21]

These changes mirrored other large policy shifts. Though the Camp Authority could never fully conform to Geneva—truly neutral observers would for instance have heard hundreds of torture stories—the differences between the 1965 and 1969 rules suggest that the North Vietnamese were moving away from a strategy of trying to suppress the Code, and toward a partial accommodation with it. For the first four years, however, the Camp Authority's regulations clearly indicated that the North Vietnamese knew their prisoners' Code and would keep them from following it. For this reason, John Hubbell calls the day the early rules first appeared in the cells the day that "the battle was joined in the prison camps of North Vietnam."[22]

House Procedures in the Total Institution

The regulations and the Code were the rules of engagement, but they gave little guidance for running the camp or passing the time. The Hanoi POWs responded with their command chain, the Camp Authority with the modern prison—that total institution which punished and rehabilitated. Though some commentators felt that Asian institutions were the real models—Philip Holt claimed that "the concept of a totalitarian authority functioning under a law designed not to preserve individual rights but to control the inherent evil in man through punishment dates back to the legalist school of the second century in Chinese thought"—the Camp Authority's methods for running Hoa Lo, the French colonial prison the POWs called the Hanoi Hilton, closely followed those developed in the late eighteenth and early nineteenth centuries for modern Western prisons.[23] In *Discipline and Punish: The Birth of the Prison*, Michel Foucault describes J. Turnbull's 1790s visit to a "modern" prison—in this case, an American one. Like the POWs, the inmate learned the regulations at the moment he was imprisoned. Prison "inspectors," like the Camp Authority, "represent to him the offense that he has committed with regard to them, the evil that has consequently resulted for the society that protected him and the need to make compensation by his example and his amendment." The punishments could be similar as well. In 1775, J. Hanway saw isolation as the key to rehabilitation, since this "terrible shock" drove the inmate "to go into himself and rediscover in the depths of his conscience the voice of good" without fear of contamination from the "bad examples and possibilities of escape in the short term and of blackmail or complicity in the long term" which often arose from "promiscuity in the prison."[24] Almost 200 years later, every detail re-appeared in the Hanoi Camp Authority's own exercise in "spiritual conversion."

The North Koreans and North Vietnamese both called their cluster of rules, isolation, and punishment the "Lenient Policy," or "Humane and Lenient Treatment." As Foucault points out, these prison virtues emerged at the same time that prisons became thought of as places of reform rather than punishment. But as Foucault also observes, "rehabilitating" an inmate could be a more intrusive and devastating process than simple physical punishment. Since "modern" prisons try to change how their prisoners understand the world and themselves, the horrors of the "rehabilitative" and "humane" Soviet gulags or Chinese "reeducation camps" thus arise at least partially from the modern prison's desire to change bad habits, and to socialize the antisocial. American POWs were definitely student-criminals in Korea. As agents of international capitalism they were war criminals, but as exploited individuals, they were also victims of capitalism. Their interrogators offered these men the chance to renounce their evil ways, and to join the war against capitalism. Progress was the key to success. How well the POW accepted "certain rules and regulations, particularly those dealing with 're-education'" determined just how lenient the Lenient Policy would be.[25] Supplying military and biographical information therefore showed a willingness to reform, and so did following all camp rules, studying all assigned reading material, and making public statements in support of his captors' struggle.

The institution's actual methods for producing such "conversions" were however often violent, cynical, and exploitive. According to a 1951 Chinese manual called "The Task of POW Interrogations," questioning an "ignorant, stupid, professional soldier"—an officer, in short—was usually pointless, since changing his behavior was almost impossible. The enlisted prisoners' "fear of death, homesickness, and anti-war tendencies" made them more promising subjects. The manual recommended death threats for the timid, and increasingly rough treatment for the less cooperative. Since these prisoners also lacked "a clear understanding of their aggressive war in Korea," offers of parole would prove effective. Stressing the Lenient Policy's belief in "equality of rank—no officers, no NCOs, everybody equal" was also important, since any hierarchy would be reactionary. Camp officials therefore put "low-ranking enlisted men in charge of officer squads," or selected "inept men or men of low status, in order to undermine group morale." Race was a wedge as well. Black POWs got special attention as capitalism's greatest victims, and thus the men most likely to change.[26] All these strategies reappeared in Vietnam. Well before his July 1965 capture, Jeremiah Denton saw an alleged "Vietcong training paper relating to the understanding and treatment of American prisoners." Its debt to the Korean Lenient Policy was obvious. Though the "American Bourgeois class" had twice tricked soldiers into fighting Asian wars of capitalist aggression, these victims could learn the truth if trained properly. The well-educated, well-traveled, frequently Protestant or Roman Catholic officer POWs would pose the greatest challenge, but all American prisoners had been perverted by material wealth, "military tradition stories," and "blind patriotism." VC interrogators must therefore work with diehards who "never leak out military secrecy, nor confess their criminal deeds, report their personal records; they also refuse to sign peace-appealing documents." For this reason, discipline rather than punishment would be the key, since forcing someone to behave in a desired way was the ultimate captor goal.[27]

Jim Stockdale recognized that this agenda made the Vietnam POW camps modern political prisons: "places where people are sent to be used for political purposes, or to have their minds changed, or both." These "snake pits" may pretend to be "therapeutic rehabilitation centers, places where people get rid of antisocial tendencies," but actually create an "extortion environment," where a "concentrated form of manipulation" takes hold of the prisoner's will. The Hanoi Camp Authority's methods were thus very conventional, since "extortionists always go down the same track: the imposition of guilt and fear for having disobeyed the rules, followed in turn by punishment, apology, confession, and atonement (their payoff)."[28] As in Korea, this payoff would be substantial. Institutionally, the prisons would be trouble-free detention centers. Psychologically, the interrogators could probe into every corner of the captive's mind, inflicting pain for resistance, but rewarding all moves away from past duties. And politically, these efficient modern prisons would produce materials for the worldwide anti-American propaganda campaign on cue.

Jim Stockdale also recognized these goals as the same ones driving all total institutions, "be they academic, business, military, or some other sort." Above all, the Camp Authority wanted "to manipulate us, to get moral leverage on us." As government official Roger Shields further explained, "a lot of the things the Vietnamese did were aimed at harassment and acquiescence, getting a man to say 'All right, I am your prisoner and you can do anything you want to me, and I've got to do what you tell me to do—you own me in effect; I must give you total obedience and acknowledgement that here I am and I am powerless.'" Sometimes this bullying was purely personal. Guards would enter a cell hundreds of times just to make an uncooperative captive bow. The "experienced extortion-ists" who replaced the "ordinary military men" in 1965 and turned a detention camp into a political prison had very different goals. These officials became known as the Camp Authority.[29]

POW life under the Camp Authority amounted to long stretches of boredom and depression punctuated by moments of intense pain and rage. By struggling to control the captive's every waking moment, the Camp Authority placed Hoa Lo among these "com-plete and austere institutions," the modern nineteenth- and twentieth-century prisons. According to Michel Foucault, such a prison "must be an exhaustive disciplinary apparatus: it must assume responsibility for all aspects of the individual, his physical training, his aptitude to work, his everyday conduct, his moral attitude, his state of mind." Even more than "the school, the workshop or the army, which always involved a certain specializa-tion," the modern prison is "omnidisciplinary"—an institution of total control.[30] Regiment-ing time was a common strategy for gaining this control—Foucault cites one prison timetable that broke the day into intervals as short as five minutes. Though the pieces were larger, the time in Hanoi was just as structured. Inmates "were to arise daily about five A.M. at the sound of a gong. If they were permitted to bathe that day, that was taken care of about six A.M. They would eat breakfast usually around ten A.M. and an afternoon meal about three P.M. Most of the day they were confined to their rooms." POW Red McDaniel fleshed this schedule out somewhat. Toilet buckets were dumped around eight A.M. Meals lasted twenty minutes, and the daily siesta extended from 11:30 to 1:30. Though downtime could be filled with "whatever the camp commander had for us"—sweeping the courtyard, washing clothes, or working in the garden—mostly the POWs did nothing.[31]

The Camp Authority's handling of space also drew on the modern prison's methods for controlling inmates. By holding captives for long periods in solitary and severely restricting and disrupting the inmates' contacts with each other, camp officials not only impeded "plots and revolts," but also forced the captives to face the institution alone. As Foucault notes, "Isolation provides an intimate exchange between the convict and the power that is exercised over him."[32] If anything, though, the POWs found the Camp Authority's obsession with administrative procedures even more oppressive. Jim Stock-dale's "ominous, depressed feeling" when first entering the Hanoi Hilton came from its message "that from now on everything was to happen according to party line, by the numbers, with bureaucratic humorlessness."[33] Here too Korea had set the precedent. General Dean for instance noted his captors' "almost pathological" need for records: "I would not broadcast on the radio, therefore I must sign a paper saying that I would not go on the radio. I would not sign a proposed letter, then I must sign a letter saying *why* I would not sign a letter. I don't exaggerate: such things were demanded."[34] Though a few POWs like Ralph Gaither attributed their captors' apparent "awe of paper and writing" to their "primitive minds," or their "small village, rice paddy outlook on life," most POWs instantly recognized that the modern disciplinary institution was at work. In Hanoi, John Dramesi remembers signing for every item he was issued, and this paper pushing even entangled the Vietnamese. German nurse Monika Schwinn recalled the fate of a jungle guard who confiscated a watch, but then lost it. When he was discovered, his fellow Vietcong "were not satisfied until they had written a long report and forced him to sign his name." Schwinn "was struck by the guerrillas' obvious concern to maintain discipline. Red tape had managed to triumph even in the jungle."[35]

Such triumphs, however, were worse than simply absurd when survival was the issue. Three of the four nurses captured with Schwinn died shortly after capture, and almost half of the American POWs in the jungle camp Schwinn went to died as well. Despite these fatalities, though, mechanical rules still ran the compound. "Camp regulations allotted one bottle of water a day to each prisoner," Schwinn recalled, "and no one dared to challenge camp regulations," leading her to ask the kind of question so often posed about bureaucrats: "How can you deal with people who are sympathetic one minute and won't even give you a swallow of water the next?"[36] This paradox permeates all total institutions: strictly following procedures makes the officials themselves timid and fearful. In Hanoi, meeting bureaucratic goals often seemed more important than getting useful information. During one "bullshit session," Jim Mulligan suddenly realized his interrogator "was just filling in squares by talking with me." Ed Flora's monitors "didn't believe anything I put down, because they knew it couldn't be true. But for some reason, it seemed like they were satisfied that they had gotten something." POW Robert Doremus guessed why: "They had to show something to their superiors. . . . And, as long as this guy could save face, and fill his square, and pass that thing on, somebody else can verify it, or believe it, or not, whatever the hell he cares."[37] Self-preservation seemed to drive the interrogators. Red McDaniel for instance found them passionately interested in future Hanoi bombing targets, but indifferent about those at a distance. Careerism motivated the Camp Authority as well. Since carrying out assigned tasks was the road to promotion in Vietnamese *and* American institutions, Jim Stockdale soon recognized that "these political cadres . . . are not ideologues so much as they are just ambitious bureaucrats! After all those months of hearing their impassioned ideological rhetoric, it had somehow escaped me that, like all too many of us, Communists also can get twisted around the axle of chain-of-command bureaucracy, the axle of careerism."[38] This cold regimen made following the set agenda the Camp Authority's highest duty, and violating procedures the most serious POW crime.

This too is typical of modern disciplinary institutions, and Stockdale was very familiar with this concern. Caught fishing for a cigarette passed on by another POW, he soon found himself manacled in solitary while a camp official ranted "on and on about my bad attitude and failure to repent for the crimes I had visited on the 'people of the Democratic Republic of Vietnam.'" What amazed Stockdale was "how seriously" this official "seemed to take this dressing down": "He didn't appear to feel the least bit sheepish about what I'm sure he could see was a patently fraudulent frame-up." Stockdale also "marveled in amazement at the effectiveness of the little device of always basing the infliction of punishment on the technical legalism of having violated one of their legal documents." This "technical legalism" could have its grimly humorous side. When the guards intercepted one of Stockdale's notes, the Camp Authority accused him of violating the camp rule against communicating. Stockdale argued that because his message had never arrived, he had not communicated. Confusion! After a hasty recess, though, his happy interrogator returned to announce, "You are wrong about the camp regulations. They say you may not talk, tap, leave notes, et cetera. This is et cetera!"[39]

The Camp Authority's most elaborate attempt to gain full institutional control was the Make a Choice program, which named POWs' attitudes, set patterns to follow, and punished all resistance. Similar programs were the hallmark of those mid-nineteenth-century prisons that first began classifying inmates by their behavior in prison rather than by their crimes. Prisoners "with intellectual resources above the average of intelligence" and "a dangerous attitude to social duties" were isolated to keep them from infecting others. Because "vicious, stupid, or passive convicts" had been seduced into their crimes—and usually by those in the first group—"the regime suitable to them is not so much that of punishment as of education, and if possible of mutual education." These men worked together, discussed their progress, and earned rewards. As for those "inept or incapable convicts" too stupid to be educated, they were simply watched.[40] Over one hundred years later in Korea, an interrogators' manual would identify the same three groups as the diehards, the progressives, and the enlisted men.

Repeated endlessly over the radio in mid-1966, Hanoi's Make a Choice program seemed to offer only two alternatives. As Ralph Gaither put it, "You can side with the Vietnamese people and live, someday maybe return to your families and loved ones," or "You can side with your government and its policies of war and criminal aggression against the Democratic Republic of Vietnam. That is the side of death." Jeremiah Denton was even more blunt: "Those who cooperated would be allowed to go home. Those who did not might face war crimes trials, with death or postwar incarceration as possible punishment."[41] In practice, though, this program observed the modern prison and Korean War categories. Camp officials told POW Jim Mulligan that they realized only those in group two, the progressives, would accept the North Vietnamese position, and get more food, exercise, mail, and perhaps even parole. The Camp Authority also knew "the vast majority of captured Americans" would never enjoy "the benefits of this education to social responsibility." These group three POWs would be watched, treated humanely, and eventually released. Only the handful of diehards would therefore suffer extreme punishment. Because they would "refuse to listen to the progress to education program" and "lead the others to resist this program," these men "would not receive the lenient and human treatment. They would receive poor food. They would be kept in small dark rooms, alone and in shackles, and when the war was over, they would not be released. They would die in Vietnam."[42] In moments like these, the Hanoi Camp Authority proved itself an heir to the modern European penal institution. The rules and classifications endured, and so did the institution's will to "discipline" its inmates totally. *Plus ça change, plus c'est la même chose.*

Fighting by the Book: The POW Response

The POWs' strategy for defeating the Make a Choice program relied on essentially the same inmate divisions: the difference lay in how they evaluated each group. According to Jim Stockdale, the North Vietnamese "had to think that every American was politically enlightened (willing) or on the way to enlightenment (partial-willing); and that except for a few diehards, a dynamic transformation of partial-willings into willings was imminent," because it was the way communism operated: "Their Party members were the 'willings,' who swayed the 'partial-willings.'" Stockdale simply inverted all the terms. The Make a Choice program itself became the "fink release program," and those POWs called the "willings" were the finks. Though swaying the opinions of the "partial-willings" proved crucial at times for campwide resistance, this huge group was basically left alone. The "diehards," however, became "hard-core resisters," and ultimately the Alcatraz Gang— those 11 isolated POWs whom Stockdale himself commanded. Stockdale saw the Make a Choice program as "the ultimate challenge to our 'Unity over Self.' Get the Americans to compete for early release; only those who come out winners in hate-America speech contests on the radio get into the finals."[43] For this reason, he also recognized that the battle of Hanoi was not just between the Code and the camp rules, but between the diehards and the Camp Authority as well.

As it drove so many other procedures, bureaucratic obsession drove the Make a Choice program as well. Though the Camp Authority certainly wanted Stockdale to provide "a description of how my chain of command worked, who the principals were, how communication was handled, and then a statement of duties performed by each of the principals," the overriding desire to fill in the squares meant that the North Vietnamese "never really captured the secret of what drove our prison resistance system." Whatever the Camp Authority did extort also had to be couched in the proper terms. Since most POW "crimes" violated camp rules, all confessions had to use the rules' terms to prove that the prisoner knew his actions were criminal. This concern with proper procedures and terms affected all stages of a POW's captivity. The Camp Authority felt "social maladjustment" was the basic human problem, and anyone who broke camp rules was "antisocial," "maladjusted," or "criminal." Unfortunately for the POWs, the Camp Authority was not only the sole arbiter of what proper "social" behavior would be, but also the body responsible for reeducation. The POW thus unwillingly had "somewhat the same relationship to his interrogator than an American bears to his psychiatrist. The interrogator understands you better than you understand yourself."[44] And since the POW's duty was to see his crime the way his captors did, his confessions had to adopt the Camp Authority's own overblown and alien vocabulary. The Vietnam POWs often welcomed this demand, since it led to transparently false confessions. "I am a Yankee imperialist aggressor," Howard Rutledge happily wrote, "parroting their text, knowing how little those words sounded like anything an American would write." Jim Stockdale's extorted confessions blended the Camp Authority's rhetoric with his own talent for bad academic writing. The result was "disingenuous pity with a touch of ridicule, liberally sprinkled with obscurantism"; "a flowery piece of 'constructs' with a lot of big words with double meanings alluding to the woeful primitiveness of the Vietnamese people" that no American could read "without knowing it was a spoof."[45]

The POWs also countered the Camp Authority's restrictive timetables with their own iron schedules. "If you can find out the routine, you got a good handle on what's gonna go on," POW Rob Doremus remarked, "If you *know* that every day they have certain times for feeding and you do get out to wash your hands, your clothes or that they do or do not interrogate you a lot—is there in fact torture—if you can find out those things you can at least prepare for them or not worry about them so much."[46] The POWs were of course personally familiar with and fond of highly regimented organizations. The U.S. military was hardly a haven for institutional anarchists, and many POWs felt they could fight off the Camp Authority's attempts "to break our spirit," because of "the strong U.S. military discipline we managed to maintain and the self-discipline which this encouraged." According to POW Robert Naughton, "Planning such common events as exercising, sweeping the floor, cleaning the cell, telling stories, and the time of communication with other cells" gave the men a sense of order and personal control.[47] Ulitmately, this take-charge impulse led to what the POWs considered their greatest triumph: forcing the Camp Authority to recognize them as officers of another total institution—the U.S. military.

This dynamic makes the POW camp different from other modern disciplinary institutions. Foucault's account of the modern prison does not explore what would happen if the imprisoned individuals saw themselves as agents for another authority—if in short *two* total institutions confronted each other. Certainly Korea should have encouraged the Vietnam POWs to think about captivity in this way. One of Kinkead's military sources described how the Chinese interrogators obsessively gathered, filed, and cross-referenced POW personal-history forms, some reaching 500 pages in length—"the largest fund of information about the American soldier ever acquired by an enemy." Once released, though, the POWs encountered American debriefers who produced equally massive and cross-referenced files, leading another Kinkead source to claim that "no group of men in

Army history has ever been so closely studied as these repatriates were."[48] U.S. military officials in Korea also used their own POW camps for propaganda purposes. Like the Chinese and the North Koreans, the Americans released photos of prisoners enjoying medical and dental treatment, seeking vocational rehabilitation, and staging anti-Marxist pageants and plays. In books like William White's *The Captives of Korea* and Kenneth K. Hansen's *Heroes Behind Barbed Wire* "progressive" or "willing" Korean and Chinese POWs become "anti-Communist heroes," and the Americans' humane and lenient camps are contrasted with the atrocities American POWs suffered. The difference between "Our Treatment of Theirs; Their Treatment of Ours"—the subtitle of White's book—thus lay not in the goals, but in the methods and the inmates' suffering.

If anything, the similarities between methods and suffering was far closer in Vietnam than in Korea—so close that most POW narratives prudently don't mention the camps run by South Vietnam at all, even though their population—some 26,000 North Vietnamese and Vietcong POWs' names were handed over in January of 1973—dwarfed the American POW population. Though Philip Holt claims that the chief goal of the U.S. Department of Defense's *Chieu Hoi* (Open Arms) program was "to convert as many VC and NVA as possible into useful citizens through fair treatment, reindoctrination, and training," the "teaching aids" were often at least as brutal as the Hanoi Camp Authority's. The infamous tiger cages and the oft-repeated stories of interrogators throwing prisoners out of helicopters were Southern atrocities, and Amnesty International calculated that "more than 20,000 suspected members of the National Liberation Front were killed as a result of Phoenix Program operations from 1968 until May 1971"—operations backed by the United States.[49]

For American POWs held in Hanoi or in the jungle, though, the moral quicksand beneath their country's own feet was understandably not their primary concern. In memoir after memoir, many of these POWs proclaim that they successfully pitted their own discipline as officers of an American total institution against the prison regimen of the North Vietnamese Camp Authority. Each institution demanded total obedience. Each institution made threats, promised rewards, and had procedures for dealing with insubordination or antisocial acts. At least in Hanoi, though, the most striking and surprising similarity between the Camp Authority and the POWs captured before 1969 was their apparent agreement that one method alone could resolve conflicts between the dueling authorities without compromising either one.

That method was torture.

* 3 *

Torture and War's Body

> It is one of the most difficult things in this world to establish the truth about torture; whether it did or did not take place, and the nature and scale of it. The plaintiff is as unlikely to tell the unadorned truth as his oppressor; for it is so superlative a propaganda weapon given into his hands.
>
> ALISTAIR HORNE1

> Physical pain has no voice, but when it at last finds a voice, it begins to tell a story. . . .
>
> ELAINE SCARRY2

Mentioning Jane Fonda can still make conservative audiences boil with righteous anger, and apart from her midwar visit to North Vietnam, nothing about "Hanoi Jane" infuriated people more than her comments on the returning American POWs. On March 30, 1973, the day the last prisoners left Hanoi, the senior POWs declared publicly that they had been systematically tortured between 1965 and 1969. Fonda's first blunt reaction was to call these POWs "hypocrites and liars," but a few days later she backed off a bit. Though "quite sure that there were incidents of torture," Fonda suggested that the POWs were probably abused by "the people whose homes and families they were bombing and napalming." She still believed, however, the POWs were lying when they claimed that torture "was the policy of the Vietnamese and that it was systematic." Two weeks later, she vowed to "eat her words" if the POWs could prove this claim, and gave reasons for her doubts. The men's physical condition seemed suspicious— "Never in the history of the United States have POWs come home looking like football players"—and the POWs' rank hardly made them credible: "We have no reason to believe that U.S. Air Force officers tell the truth. They are professional killers."[3]

As the tales of torture multiplied that spring, Fonda's remarks seemed increasingly naive and tasteless, and in a June letter to the *Los Angeles Times* she revamped her position once more. Now the political fallout was her greatest concern. Fonda was furious that the POWs' welcome home and tales of abuse were diverting attention from America's fascist Vietnam policies. While military men who revealed atrocities against the Vietnamese were being called "alleged veterans," these "600 strong, healthy-looking POWs," who referred to "the futile Christmas terror bombings as 'the greatest show on earth,' " were treated as heroes. This fact had provoked Fonda's "'hypocrites and liars" charge: "What I originally said and continue to say is that the POWs are lying if they assert it was North Vietnamese policy to torture American prisoners. They are hypocrites because they are trying to pose as heroic victims when they were responsible for killing countless Vietnamese. They are pawns of the Nixon Administration propaganda effort to justify the war." As willing agents in an obscene war that had killed 50,000 Americans and "countless Vietnamese," these "military elite, career officers" did not deserve sympathy, but contempt.[4]

Jane Fonda was misinformed: the North Vietnamese *did* systematically torture POWs. Her attacks are nevertheless a reminder that in 1973, many Americans considered the North Vietnamese a heroic people, and despised U.S. pilots as baby-burning androids. By suggesting that the torture charges were shoddy alibis for making antiwar statements, Fonda also touched on the POWs' fear that they would be judged as having failed in their duties. And perhaps most importantly, Fonda's gross generalizations were matched by equally sweeping, equally inaccurate POW claims. Torture was a common, but not universal POW experience. Few POWs were tortured in the jungle—things were bad enough already—and since torture in Hanoi virtually disappeared in late 1969, those captured later—almost half the POW population—were not systematically abused. Though not "liars and hypocrites," then, the tortured POWs were not the majority either.

Nor were they Vietnam's only torture victims. Although Navy Secretary John Chafee declared in 1971 that "in all the modern history of man's inhumanity to man, there is no example of crueler or more inhuman treatment than that being dealt to our prisoners of war and their families by the North Vietnamese," an even stronger case could be made for the *South* Vietnamese. Amnesty International's 1975 conclusion "that a very large number of Vietnamese civilian and military detainees in the South and a small number of American prisoners of war in North Vietnam have been subjected to torture during the past ten years" suggests something about proportions, and the United States certainly had little success in convincing Saigon to treat its captives as POWs. "Do you know whether we will be treated as prisoners according to the Geneva Convention?" a captured NLF cadre asked journalist Bernard Fall in 1967. Fall's response tells the story: "Obviously, word must have gotten around among the Viet Cong about how badly most of the prisoners are still treated on this side, all promises of improvement notwithstanding, with the Americans reluctant to intervene once the prisoners have been transferred. All I could say lamely was that he was being treated according to the Convention right now."[5]

Most American POWs understandably remained silent about this blight. At least publicly, only a few joined Jay Jensen in denouncing Hanoi for Geneva violations, but denying the VC any right to the same protection. "If you expect to be given the treatment of a captured military constituent you must be wearing a uniform, insignia, and identification," Jensen argued, and since the Vietcong "would conceal themselves as harmless civilians and friends during the day, then be bloodthirsty fighters at night," a captured VC "can be treated as a spy with none of the privileges of a normal POW."[6] Saigon certainly reasoned this way. In 1963, George Smith watched Vietnamese Special Forces "whaling the hell" out of some alleged VC, and realized their next stop would be Saigon, "because that's what happened to prisoners generally—the LLDB interrogated them, put them in barbed-wire cages for a while, and then sent them to Saigon where they got the shit beaten out of them properly because they got professional interrogators in Saigon." Not surprisingly, then, Smith "fully expected to be treated at least that badly if I was captured."[7]

The rest of this chapter deals with appalling crimes against U.S. POWs. I've mentioned South Vietnam's treatment of its prisoners here as a reminder that *all* combatants in Vietnam were at times viciously cruel to captives. Neither their numbers nor the degree of their abuse, but nationality, military rank, and cultural significance account for the American POWs' prominence. If nothing else, then, remembering Jane Fonda can remind us that many more people than Jeremiah Denton and his fellow POWs suffered when hell was in session.

Compliance and the Camp Authority

Though it tends to overshadow the others, torture was only the most extreme torment within the POWs' brutally coercive environment. Take for example hygiene and diet. Though the Camp Authority claimed with some truth that the Hanoi POWs were getting better food and medical care than most North Vietnamese, the inevitable small bowls of rice, and the deadly timetable of watery pumpkin soup for half the year and watery soup greens for the other half led to fifty-pound weight drops and gastrointestinal misery for the meat-and-potatoes Americans. Locked up in filthy cells, the malnourished Hanoi POWs suffered constantly from dysentery, wracking fevers, respiratory ailments, and chronic skin infections. The jungle camps were worse. A diet of nothing but rice and manioc forced the POWs to eat rats, and many died from sicknesses related to profound malnutrition. Nor were the POWs generally in good shape when they arrived. Ejection injuries and abuse during capture left scores of POWs seriously injured, making the Camp Authority's fondness for tackling "medical problems only after political problems are resolved" often a life-threatening policy.[8] Dislocated and broken limbs often had to set themselves. Maggots infested open wounds; rats, mosquitoes, and other vermin swarmed in the cells; intestinal parasites flourished. Brought low by diet, injuries, and disease, frequently until delirious and caked in their own excrement, the POWs at these times posed little threat to their captors.

Overstimulation or isolation pushed the POWs closer to the edge. A light bulb burned through the night in most cells, and loudspeakers blared out Radio Hanoi constantly. For most men, though, isolation was far more demoralizing. In 1966, Jim Stockdale recalled, a POW could live "with a cellmate; in solitary like I was now in Heartbreak Hotel; and in isolation like I lived from December to June in New Guy Village." The largest gap lay between isolation and solitary. You wouldn't see another American in either, but because you could furtively communicate in solitary, "you covered 90 percent of the distance to having a cellmate."[9] The longtime Hanoi POWs knew solitary well. Even though Geneva "set 30 days of solitary as maximum punishment," according to POW Robert Naughton, "A poll of U.S. POW's captured in the DRV before 1969 reveals that 90 percent of the men endured solitary living conditions for periods ranging from a few days to more than 4 years."[10] Isolation, however, was worse. Jungle POW James E. Jackson firmly believed that isolation turned a POW into his own worst enemy: "He gets himself into a certain desperate frame of mind, and before long, one thing brings on another. Before he knows it, why, he doesn't have anything to hold on to mentally." Isolation could drive even the strongest Hanoi resisters into this state. During ten months alone in total darkness, Robinson Risner fought off panic attacks by screaming into blankets, obsessively running in place, and suffering through marathon crying sessions. Even later in his captivity, Alcatraz POW Howard Rutledge "was constantly amazed" at how isolation "could break my own willingness to resist. Physical torture may have ended, but there is still no torture worse than years of solitary confinement." And as Jim Stockdale notes, since "the term of the sentence has nothing to do with the initial 'crime'" in Hanoi, the POW never knew if he would rejoin his community.[11] As the POW waited out his captivity, then, bad food and medical care devastated his body while sensory stimulation and deprivation disordered his mind—living conditions which made him all too vulnerable to abuse.

Torture and the Camp Authority

> A communist is a person who will torture you to write a statement that you have not been tortured.
>
> LARRY CHESLEY, POW, Apr. 1966–Feb. 1973[12]

> If they are not guilty, beat them until they are.
>
> SAIGON POLICE MOTTO[13]

Edward Peters notes in his excellent book on torture that the term itself has drifted in this century toward a "sentimental" definition. Torture now can "mean whatever one wishes it to mean": "the infliction of suffering, however defined, upon anyone for any purpose—or for no purpose." Nothing or everything can be torture—"the electric prod, poverty, frustration, perhaps even boredom or vague dissatisfaction." Arguing against this tendency, Peters claims that torture should be understood as "torment inflicted by a public authority for ostensibly public purposes." Whether conducted "by an official judiciary or by other instruments of the state," then, legally sanctioned, or "judicial" torture is "the *only* kind of torture."[14] Though this may seem like hair-splitting, Peters stresses what is important. Sadism, fanaticism, and rage undeniably lead people to inflict pain; in Hanoi or Saigon, in Baghdad or Johannesburg, however, it has been the institutional sanction for hurting a human being which makes torture a distinct, especially revolting practice.

A few techniques have dominated torture's history. In addition to adopting the Inquisition's compliance practices—"prolonged solitary confinement in dark, festering cells," and "a starvation diet"—the North Vietnamese also used its favorite torture technique: "the strappado, *corda,* or *cola,* called by jurists 'the queen of torments.'" In Europe, the "accused's hands were tied behind the back, attached to a rope which was thrown over a beam in the ceiling, and hauled into the air, there to hang for a period of time, then let down, then raised again."[15] In North Vietnam, "A man's wrists and elbows were firmly bound behind his back with a long nylon rope that was then pulled upward until his arms were raised and his head was forced downward between his shackled legs."[16] On occasion, the Camp Authority followed the Inquisition's example further, and suspended captives from the ceiling. This version of *corda* was called "the ropes"—little had changed in 400 years—and the POWs found it an ensemble of terrors. Binding the arms cut off the circulation, and as their limbs turned blue, then black, the POWs mentally prepared for amputation. The tension was excruciating. Arms and legs often dislocated, men felt like their rib cages were ripping open, and the nerve damage could last for months and years. The "abnormal positions" were also terrifying. Jammed face down into their own crotches, many POWs were certain they would suffocate, and some men became claustrophobic from being folded into their own bodies. POW camp wisdom was simple: no one could resist the ropes.

Other time-honored techniques—braces and shackles, tightly tied hands, enforced sleeplessness, and the distending of joints and muscles—resurfaced in Hanoi. Guards lashed POWs with "fan belts"—rubber strips cut from car tires. Interrogators would question a man constantly, denying him food or sleep until he cooperated—a method Malise Ruthven has called the Russian "conveyor."[17] Many men went onto "the stool." If they fell asleep, they were shaken awake; if they fell down, they were beaten and forced to sit again. As weeks passed, and fatigue and hunger sapped the body's strength, the stool became a nightmare. POWs were also left in shackles, or forced to raise their arms or kneel on stones for long periods. These "punishments" were especially demoralizing because as Elaine Scarry explains, they "make the prisoner's body an *active* agent, an actual cause of his pain." Since he suffers "not only the feeling 'my body hurts,' but the feeling 'my body hurts me,'" his disgust with his body, an understandable reaction for someone living in filthy quarters, eating food laced with dirt and bugs, and sleeping beside their own excrement pails, aroused a hatred almost as strong as the one he felt for his captors.[18]

These then were the methods—but what were the goals? Though torture in Hanoi was primarily a method for maintaining discipline or extorting propaganda, a few other motives surfaced at times. Revenge might seem an obvious motive, and in fact civilians were beating downed American fliers as late as the 1972 Christmas bombings, but even the POWs found it hard to get indignant about these episodes. After all, as one Communist official asked, "What would have happened if we were bombing the United States and one of our pilots was shot down over Pittsburgh?"[19] Nor did the POWs usually call these beatings torture, since they were personally, not institutionally motivated. In fact, North Vietnamese authorities often found themselves rescuing POWs from certain death at the hands of a mob because an even higher official had compelling reasons for torturing them. Revenge did, however, often lead to pain in Hanoi. Certain officials took great pleasure from paying the Americans back, and interrogators would explain a guard's brutality by claiming that American bombing had killed his wife or mother. POW complaints about their treatment could provoke paybacks from the guards, and the vicious punishment that maimed John Dramesi and killed Ed Atterberry after their failed 1969 escape attempt spoke of rage at higher levels. The most violent personal reprisal, however, occurred in September 1965, when the NLF answered Saigon's execution of three anti-American demonstrators by killing jungle POWs Kenneth Roraback and Humbert Versace. Though the executions were purely political—any two Americans would have done—returning POWs George Smith and James "Nick" Rowe have both claimed that Roraback's and Versace's stubborn and combative behavior made them popular choices when the NLF needed scapegoats.[20] But ultimately, revenge was not a major motive for torture, if only because in these cases the pain was not the means to an end, but the end itself.

Gaining military intelligence wasn't a particularly strong motive for torture in Hanoi either. Thanks to survival training and B-movie camp commanders who said things like "We have ways of making you talk," the POWs expected to be tortured for information about military installations and future bombing targets. But since pain gets a response even if the victim doesn't know the answer, coerced information is untrustworthy unless independently confirmed. For this reason, only information about the POWs' own organization could be extorted, because answers could be checked by torturing other POWs. Most Hanoi POWs' experience actually confirmed Elaine Scarry's claim that because "for every instance in which someone with critical information is interrogated, there are hundreds interrogated who could know nothing of remote importance to the stability or self-image of the regime," what often "masquerades as the motive for torture is a fiction."[21] This fiction of intelligence gathering was nevertheless so hard to give up that some POW narratives blamed the Camp Authority's lack of effort on incompetence rather than disinterest. Lance Sijan's biographer, Malcolm McConnell, states that the North Vietnamese "interrogators were not competent to conduct detailed technical questioning with any true military value," and Stephen Rowan claimed that after a POW's first torture session, "the North Vietnamese could have pried loose almost any military secret. But, they didn't know which questions to ask."[22]

Torture was even less important to the Camp Authority's feeble attempts at ideological conversion. This is not surprising, since the "frank use" of inflicted pain is as Philip Holt notes, "just as likely to heighten resistance in the captive and be counterproductive to the goals the captor seeks"—George Orwell to the contrary. George Smith, the most pro-VC of all POWs, actually credited the *lack* of torture or coercive treatment with turning him against his government, and in general, the Camp Authority or VC interrogators found special favors and parole far more effective than torture as tools for reeducation.[23] Robinson Risner's experience as the target for ideological conversion illustrates why any form of coercion was unsuited for changing minds. In a chapter called "The Longest Six Weeks of My Life," Risner described his terrifying encounter with a skilled interrogator assigned to break him. Violent metaphors pervade the account. The man's eyes bored into Risner "like a drill"; Risner couldn't believe how easily this official could "pick my brain." Soon Risner felt "dirty and soiled as though he had been in my mind walking around with filthy old boots on," and the terror only grew: "I cannot explain the apprehension and mental torture each session produced. I dreaded them as much as being thrown into a barrel of snakes. I dreaded them as a person dreads the thing that he fears the most." From a POW who had been tortured several times before this struggle, these are strong words, and they seem even stronger when Risner reveals that his tormentor "was not making me do anything": "There were no ropes, no judo chops, no uncomfortable positions. And yet, it was as if he had a tourniquet around my head and was turning it ever tighter." This interrogator soon had Risner frantically making up answers to avoid disapproval. But if the end was total control, with or without torture, the Camp Authority still hadn't gained it. Risner's interrogator had wanted submission so complete "that not only would I answer his questions as he wanted them answered, but also I would believe them." This however he would not do: "no amount of threats or intimidation" could change the fact that Risner "did not believe what he was saying."[24] Despite scattered attempts like this one, though, ideological conversion was a low Camp Authority priority, and torture was seldom the tool. Americans were frequently tortured for statements of support, but making the POWs *believe* what they wrote was so unimportant that the Camp Authority often let torture increase the POWs' anger in return for the short-term propaganda benefit.

If the Camp Authority did not primarily torture POWs to punish, debrief, or convert them, what then motivated the widespread torture practiced in Hanoi? The history of POW treatment, the modern total institution, and torture in this century provide part of the answer. As Walton K. Richardson observes, most histories of POWs are progressive. In the mythical beginning there were no captives; enemies were killed. With the growth of empires, throwing away labor became less common. POWs became slaves. Medieval Europeans were more interested in ransoming or exchanging prisoners, and especially "those of aristocratic origin"—a practice encouraged by the Lateran Council of 1179, which "prohibited enslaving captives who were Christian." Release without payment at the end of hostilities was a Renaissance notion, but it was the American and French revolutions' championing of an individual's universal and inalienable rights that most profoundly shaped the conventions and declarations composed at the many international conferences on POWs convened over the past 200 years. This story's happy ending came in 1949, when the Geneva Convention Relative to the Treatment of Prisoners of War built on the previous year's United Nations Universal Declaration of Human Rights to descibe how captured enemies should be treated.[25]

However accurate it might be, this account certainly reflects that belief in civilization's successful war against cruelty which fuels most histories of torture as well. These narratives begin with the widespread torturing of slaves or victims in superstitious rituals, but soon pass on to selective uses of pain in civil or ecclesiastical courts, and finally celebrate the recent renunciations of *all* cruel and unusual punishment. Or as Edward Peters sums it up, "The history of torture in Western Europe may be traced from the Greeks, through the Romans, through the Middle Ages, down to the legal reforms of the eighteenth century and the abolition of torture in criminal legal procedure virtually throughout western Europe by the first quarter of the nineteenth century." Unfortunately, this civilizing movement, which brings both histories together in the Geneva convention's total ban on torture, flies in the face of what Amnesty International or any student of human rights must know: that "torture was re-instituted in many parts of Europe and in its colonial empires from the late nineteenth century on, and its course was greatly accelerated by changing concepts of political crime during the twentieth century." Peters links this rebirth to those modern and secular totalitarian states "which exert a demand for total citizenship—that is, total subjection—upon their populations analogous to the spiritual discipline allegedly exerted upon Christians by the medieval and early modern churches." These "infinitely stronger" new religions frequently adopt "the old humanitarian-reformist model that was once occupied by the medieval and Spanish inquisitions and those secular courts that did their bidding." As states supposedly constantly under siege, "extraordinary situations," and therefore drastic measures, are the norm. Hence the modern paradox that "in an age of vast state strength, ability to mobilize resources, and possession of virtually infinite means of coercion, much of state policy has been based upon the concept of extreme state vulnerability to enemies, external or internal." Since institutional hysteria favors speed over deliberation, torture's usefulness as a fast and decisive tool for forcing compliance has caused it to reappear "in other areas under state authority less regulated than legal procedure, less observed, but no less essential to the state's notion of order."[26]

The Americans held in Hanoi would certainly have agreed that torture served the Camp Authority's "notion of order." By 1967, the first interrogation was utterly formulaic. After asking for and getting the Big Four, officials would ask a fifth question—usually "What kind of plane were you flying?" Since they usually had the wreckage, this question was actually the trip wire for the next stage of processing. "They didn't fool around, they didn't try to play games with me, or verbally force me, or go on to another question," Konrad Trautman recalled, "They just repeated that question one time and I wound up in the ropes." The motive here was to display the Camp Authority's power—"not to get information from me, but to demonstrate to me that they were *able* to get information from me," as POW Bill Stark put it. Control, not information, was thus the goal, and once "the POWs caught on that the name of the game was 'answer every question,' they could save themselves from torture by making up answers, or by answering in vague generalities."[27] Of course, no real compromise was possible. Since North Vietnam chose to talk about the war as an elemental struggle between besieged Vietnamese Communists and aggressive American capitalists, a POW was either evil incarnate or a corrupted and exploited victim of his own government. He must therefore repent or be destroyed—and torture ensured that the choice came quickly.

As inmates within a modern prison, the POWs learned that torture also ensured conformity with the Camp Authority's rules, timetables, mandatory confessions, punishments, and rewards. As in so many other totalitarian spheres, torture in Hanoi exposed prisoners' crimes and drove them down the path to correction. In 1965 and 1966, when North Vietnam was threatening to try the POWs under its own laws, the emphasis was on criminality. The Camp Authority extorted statements for Bertrand Russell's international war crimes tribunals, and the government paraded manacled POWs through the streets of

Hanoi to show the Vietnamese people's righteous anger. The international community's outrage over such threats and marches, however, soon led Hanoi officials to shift their focus. Torture then became a method for making the POWs denounce America's war policies. Here too, control rather than actual conversion was the goal. Though the fiction was that rehabilitation had persuaded the POWs to despise their own government, the fact was that torture made such "enlightenment" mandatory.

Michel Foucault has compiled a useful list of the methods total institutions have adopted to produce this illusion of control. Over the past 200 years, prisons have moved away from maiming the captive's body, and toward containing it within power relations which then "invest it, mark it, train it, torture it, force it to carry out tasks, to perform ceremonies, to emit signs." This containment is depressing enough: as Edward Peters remarks, "Foucault's is a theory not without some truth, but also virtually without hope." If anything, though, the North Vietnam POW camps were even more disturbing because of a strategy which Foucault passes over: that marriage in many totalitarian institutions of pervasive bureaucratic coercion *and* the traditional compliance technique of torture. Though Foucault sees "a trace of 'torture'" lingering "in the modern mechanisms of criminal justice," his interest in the shift from breaking bodies to regulating minds leads him to claim that this "trace" has been "enveloped, increasingly, by the noncorporeal nature of the penal system." It is however one of the twentieth century's dark ironies that a "barbaric" practice has enjoyed a rebirth as a widely employed tool for making inmates meet the modern, "humane" disciplinary institution's increasingly broad demands for control—and in Hanoi, the need for propaganda materials pushed things even further. Far from being what Foucault calls "the most hidden part of the penal process," torture in Hanoi was blatantly directed toward modern institutional and ideological ends.[28] Supposedly primitive acts advanced modern agendas, as American POWs were tortured to appear on TV.

Though the Camp Authority's own motives were almost always institutional and political, it often justified its brutality to the POWs by reverting to the concept of "judicial" torture. As the "Queen of Proofs and the Queen of Torments," torture had a role in "the ordinary criminal procedure of the Latin Church and most of the states of Europe" from the thirteenth through the eighteenth century. Torture in these proceedings produced a confession that not only "constituted so strong a proof that there was scarcely any need to add others," but also forced "the criminal to accept responsibility for his own crime and himself sign what had been skilfully and obscurely constructed by the preliminary investigation." Since confession was a sacrament, judicial torture thus blurred the lines between crime and sin, antisocial behavior and heresy, or more generally, law and theology. But having extorted this confession, the Inquisitors then had to get the victim to repent in public, to prove he was acting *of his own free will.* As might be expected, this requirement had its nasty underside. "If the defendant recanted, torture might be repeated," Edward Peters observes, "because the original confession constituted another *indicium* against him." Nor was a successful public confession always sufficient. Because heresy for instance was "a shared offense," Peters explains that "besides the salvation of the heretic's soul, inquisitors needed the names of fellow heretics."[29] In this way, the institution stretched its influence outward, but for each individual the process was the same. After an accusation or transgression began things, pain extorted a confession that admitted personal sin (rebellion), reaffirmed membership in the community (loyalty), and identified other unrepentant criminals still at large (atonement). Last of all, by repeating his confession freely and publicly, the criminal proclaimed that conversion, not coercion, made him reveal his crimes.

It is a commonplace that totalitarian regimes often function like theocracies, and this similarity was especially striking in North Vietnam. The Camp Authority denied it ever tortured Americans. POW Larry Chesley claims that his captors "used the word *torture* only when denying that they had tortured us," and POWs Douglas Hegdahl and Richard Stratton even recalled that the same word "seemed to inflame their captors and often caused prisoners who used it needless additional grief." The Camp Authority talked about "resolute and severe punishment" instead, since "this implied that the 'criminal' had only received his just desserts," but regardless of terminology, the actual procedures for inflicting pain were virtually identical to those of judicial torture.[30] Some violation, however minor, was necessary to start up the process. As Robinson Risner remarked, "The Vietnamese always liked to find an excuse to punish you." Whether this crime was "whistling," "singing," "talking," or refusing to go beyond the Big Four, though, once caught, the POW passed swiftly down the old path of "torture, confession, apology, and atonement." In Hanoi, pain forged the link between crime and "self-criticism" so typical of the modern totalitarian "confession," and like the Inquisitors, the Camp Authority also demanded the names of other "criminals." Perhaps the closest affinity between judicial torture and Hanoi "punishment," however, was the emphasis placed on public and free confession. The North Vietnamese flooded the international media with petitions, letters, declarations, tapes, and films that supposedly displayed the POWs' repentance and atonement. Almost all of these materials were extorted, and often at great psychological cost, for many POWs shared Robinson Risner's experience that making "statements critical of our country and the cause for which we were in prison really tore my guts out." As Jim Stockdale notes, the Camp Authority was more than ready to help with the tearing: "If the inmates are slow to pick up on the 'suggested writings' cooked up by the political cadres, writings such as public confessions of error and guilt, then tourniquet-wielding torture specialists help them clear their minds."[31] Though torture was virtually useless for altering hearts and minds, then, the POWs found it brutally effective at extorting statements couched in the institution's terms.

In Vietnam, the single most important misunderstanding between captive and captor arose over the meaning of this extortion. Since the POWs were most proud of resisting ideological conversion, they saw each torture session as a cry of defeat from their captors. For the Camp Authority, though, forcing these prisoners to speak the institution's words was not the means to an institutional end, but the end itself. Confessions "that can be carried away on a piece of paper or on a tape" are, as Elaine Scarry explains, "only the most concrete exhibition of the torturer's attempt to induce sounds so that they can then be broken off from their speaker." These sounds become "property of the regime"—the theft that distinguishes modern state torture from judicial torture, since secular authorities inflicting pain in the twentieth century seldom actually believe they are converting sinners or revealing the truth.[32] Rather, they are dividing words from speakers, and beliefs from bodies: the Camp Authority wanted ventriloquist dummies, not fellow travelers. If the perspective and the situation could make a POW look like a sinner, an ideological enemy, an antisocial inmate, a student, a criminal, or a heretic, torture therefore made him confess, inform, perform, testify, and betray. As Larry Chesley recalled, "We were being asked to do something contrary to our will and conscience," and "When we refused we were coerced by physical pain and torment until we gave in and did what we had originally refused to do."[33] For at least four years, then, torture forced the POWs to perform the tasks or speak the words that the Camp Authority found necessary—and as a tool for enforcing outward conformity, torture quite simply worked.

Torture and the POW—Another Tale

The POWs had two responses to torture. The "civilized" response arose from that Western progressive tradition which had led most countries, at least publicly, to renounce torture. Since within this history any torturing society was culturally retarded, many POWs thus saw the North Vietnamese as primitive bestial people inflicting pain upon their betters. This civilized response, however, did little but fuel self-righteous hate; the second, "dynamic" response sustained personal and group morale far more effectively. In this scenario, torture was not only the American fighting man's ultimate test, but also *a confession extorted from the Camp Authority*—an admission that the struggle in Hanoi was not between the all-powerful North Vietnamese and their victims, but between equal and worthy opponents. Torture in short was conclusive proof that the POWs' fight was continuing after battle.

Most POW narratives display both responses, with the civilized strongest in individual episodes, and the dynamic most important when campwide policies are the subject. To many POWs, their "uncivilized" torturers often didn't seem human at all. Red McDaniel saw himself in the "monstrous situation" of struggling "against an enemy who seemed to take great satisfaction in inflicting pain, who performed like robots in doing so." Howard Rutledge's torturers were human, but they looked "like criminals off the street," and other POWs just piled on all the ugly traits they could think of. When Charlie Plumb went into the ropes, his guards seemed "drugged," exhibiting "wide and glassy eyes": "They maliciously kicked me in the sides, the limbs, the back, and the head, giggling and having a great time. They picked me up a few feet from the floor and dropped me. Since I was on my side most of the time, they especially enjoyed standing on my head, symbolically victorious."[34] Largely because of the historical and cultural assumptions supporting the "civilized" understanding of torture, many POWs found this "symbolic victory" especially offensive. As military writer Walton K. Richardson concisely puts it, if human history is the story of barbarity retreating before civilization, and if "the most definitive rules for humane treatment of prisoners of war have been developed into international law in the aftermath of World War II," then the POWs' treatment in Korea and Vietnam "has degenerated to the treatments common during the earlier stages"—a retrogression, in short.[35]

But as Edward Peters notes, while "it is easy—and initially tempting—to correlate torture with a temper of brutality attributed to another race, culture, ideology, or particular regime," this is a flawed and dangerous paradigm. Most obviously, such "us-them" thinking not only denies that "they" could ever be humane, but also that such brutality could ever surface among "us." This paradigm also contradicts "our" faith in history's civilizing force, since followers of "the humanist-progressivist model" would presumably have to agree "that in the twentieth century the world became noticeably less humanitarian and less progressive, less rational and more superstitious, although its superstition has different objects and the excesses of its force were often committed in the names of humanity and progress." Since these truths would undermine the myth of progression, however, "civilized" commentators have held firm to "the old humanist-progressivist model" by declaring that the "modern 'religious' state and the 'primitive' unmodernized state" have merely replaced "the powers of the *ancien régime* and the allegedly primitive character of early European culture."[36] In this way, the same antithetical articles of faith cherished by the racist or Western ideologue are preserved. A torturer is always someone else, and always inferior.

Complicating this position in Hanoi was torture's recent history in Asia. Conservatives may have sided with Edmund Burke in claiming that torture was born from the unholy marriage of "Asiatic despotisms" and "the arbitrary nature of colonial rule," and leftists may have seen torture as imperialism's most extreme act.[37] Both, however, have recognized the huge gap lying between nineteenth-century Europe's professed hatred of torture and its methods for administering colonial possessions. As Edward Peters notes, torture in the colonies often *prevented* progress in human rights or national self-determination. When struggling to control "increasingly restive" populations, "colonial administrators" or "police" apparently decided that Europe's cultural, military, and technological superiority now *justified* torture. Undoubtedly, "racial differences, ethnocentrism, the violence of revolutionary movements and actions, and the legal powerlessness of colonialized populations" intensified the antagonism. Nevertheless, "civilized" colonial powers undeniably resorted to widespread torture when dealing with the "savages."[38] One of the many grim ironies that the Vietnam POWs confronted was that perhaps the twentieth century's most influential analyst of torture as a tool for oppression was Ho Chi Minh. In "French Colonization on Trial," Ho had exposed to the world French institutional brutality against the Vietnamese people. Even more unfortunately for the POWs, in the 1920s Ho's interest in the links between American racism and physical violence had led to essays on "The Ku Klux Klan" and "Lynching," which Ho caustically called "A Little-known Aspect of American Civilization."[39] While the culturally superior American POWs were reviling torture as barbaric and un-American, then, their Vietnamese captors saw these Americans not only as close relatives of the colonial French who had built the Hanoi Hilton and tortured many of the current Hanoi officials, but also as the children of racists, sadists, and oppressors.

Torture historians tend to see all racial or cultural arguments as evasions of Elaine Scarry's basic question: "How is it that one person can be in the presence of another person in pain and not know it—not know it to the point where he himself inflicts it, and goes on inflicting it?" Invoking those "two late twentieth-century figures on the darker side of civil society," the "brutal torturer—whether born or created—and the detached torturer," does not get at the real cancer, since these stereotypes can only act out what they are, and therefore cannot be judged. As Amnesty International notes, "Individual perversions are not the cause of a system of torture. Rather, once a system of torture has been created in order to support the political needs of those in power, the rulers' agents will exhibit patterns of behaviour that they would not otherwise be in a position to do."[40] Ignoring this lesson empties torture of any moral significance because it duplicates what was truly hateful about the Camp Authority: its institutional refusal to recognize its victims' humanity. Though torture helped to sustain hatred, and though many POWs undeniably accounted for their torture by claiming "that's what gooks do!", the "civilized" response to torture was therefore ultimately self-centered and counterproductive. The Camp Authority tortured for many reasons, and the POWs had some far more successful strategies for resisting, and even exploiting, their torment.

Their most durable and flexible method, the dynamic response, developed as the POWs learned how torture worked within a total institution. Most POWs began with the most "primitive" notion possible: that torture was a trial by ordeal. In early medieval legal proceedings, ordeals were "physical tests undergone by one contending party, assuming that the success or failure depended on divine intervention."[41] While this version of legally inflicted pain died out hundreds of years ago, the idea that torture is a test which true believers can pass has not. World War II tales of captured but silent resistance fighters and of POW survival in European and Asian death camps added new chapters to the history of trial by ordeal. Jean-Paul Sartre was one of its chroniclers. "Whispered propaganda would have us believe that 'everybody talks,' and this ignorance of humanity excuses torture," he wrote in a 1957 preface to an Algerian victim's account of French colonial torture. Sartre acknowledged that even "the best members of the Resistance feared the suffering less than the possibility of their giving way under torture," and he claimed that "those who talked could not be blamed, even by those who did not give way." But he also declared that "the man who talks becomes one with his executioner" in a ghastly marriage of submission and domination: "Coupled as man and wife, these two lovers made the abject night terrible."[42] Sartre's moral is thus clear. Heroes pass through the ordeal; those who fail swoon into their captors' arms.

Many Vietnam POWs were absolutely certain that God or willpower would carry them through torture. Though scores of men have described losing this faith, Richard Stratton's account is perhaps the most vivid. When the guards first came for him, he was "both apprehensive and relieved": "Now they all could get on with it, the questions, the slapping around (he was prepared for that, expected it), and maybe the black box number [solitary] and all the rest of the survival school skills he had learned." Stratton *knew* he would pass the test: "They would ask, he would refuse to answer, they would trash him a bit, he would roll with the punches, and, that done, he would be shipped off to a tough-guy camp, a stalag." As his tone suggests, Stratton was positively smug: "It would soon be obvious to his captors that they had an American James Bond here, a tough, shrewd, clever chap impervious to insults, threats, or slaps." This self-confidence only made torture's coercive power a greater shock. Stratton struggled at first: "Don't scream. Don't give the cocksucker the pleasure of knowing it hurts. Give nothing. Tough it out. You can tough it out. You can take this, James Bond. You can take anything. They're trying you out. It will be over in a few minutes. Hang in. Tough it out. You can tough it out." But the pain grew, and Stratton failed his ordeal. Within minutes, "He was through."[43]

Stratton later concluded "he had given it a good go," and ruefully admitted that "James Bond died in the ugly room." What also died, however, was his belief that torture was a trial by ordeal. "Obviously I am not James Bond," a battered Stratton decided, "and I am not going off on a sexual orgy in downtown Hanoi right after this adventure, as James is capable of doing. Obviously I had better figure out where the hell I am going."[44] Though Stratton's own "figuring" proved controversial, casting off the Superman self-image was paradoxically a POW's first step toward a strong community, since failing the ordeal forced him to admit personal weakness, and to feel the need for collective resistance. When Edna J. Hunter concluded that "no prisoner of war withstood 'the ropes' without complying in some fashion with the desires of the captor," she was thus recording not simply a fact, but a Hanoi article of faith which the POWs have widely publicized.[45] Ralph Gaither learned this lesson right in the ropes: "Further holding out was fruitless. The experience was like watching destiny come toward me. The end result was apparent, and always the same. Sooner or later after that kind of treatment, you talked." Though sworn to silence until everyone had left Vietnam, a returning Robinson Risner told reporters asking about his recorded antiwar statements to "consider the source of these statements: they were made from a prison in North Vietnam." And Bob Shumaker told Stephen Rowan that any POW statement should be taken "with a grain of salt," simply because torture was irresistible: "Any man can be reduced to a state of irrationality in an hour's time, and never bare scars to prove it."[46] The lesson was therefore always the same. Torture's coercive power was absolute.

This power would on the face of it seem to turn the Code of Conduct into a joke. But while "virtually every American prisoner in Southeast Asia confessed to providing the enemy with more information than that authorized by the strict interpretation of the Code," hundreds of these POWs would disagree violently with an *Armed Forces Journal* statement that "if there ever was a myth that the American fighting man could sustain torture and abide by the Code, it was shattered by the Vietnam War."[47] In fact, the inability to resist torture became many POWs' strongest motive for sticking with the Code. Jim Stockdale saw October 24, 1965, the day when Rodney Knutson become the first POW to go into the ropes, as a crucial date in POW history: "By carrying out a new policy action, North Vietnam had crossed a boundary. Henceforth, Americans were to be allowed to stay within the bounds of name, rank, serial number, and date of birth only at North Vietnam's sufferance." Nothing of course could eliminate the POWs' sense of guilt when the pain stopped. Though very familiar with the "fear and guilt package that any extortionist knows is the key to the breakdown of human will," Jim Stockdale felt an "agony" far "worse than any that could have been generated by physical restraining equipment." He also assumed that after "a return to America that would disgrace my family, my hometown, and my service," he could look forward to a "life of continuous shame without friends or self-respect."[48] That his actual welcome included the Medal of Honor suggests however that Stockdale, and many other POWs, found a way to relate torture's power to the demands of the Code.

They did this by appropriating the pain to their own ends. Since as Elaine Scarry notes, "Almost anyone looking at the *physical* act of torture would be immediately appalled and repulsed by the torturers," institutions usually shift the focus to "the *verbal* aspect of torture." By displaying their captives' extorted confessions, the torturers present their victims as confessed criminals, the stark "lines of moral responsibility" supposedly blur, and sympathy ideally recedes. This strategy, which Scarry calls "The Conversion of Real Pain into the Fiction of Power," closely parallels the mechanics of judicial torture.[49] As Stockdale remarks, "Unlike our courts, spring-loaded to excuse any action to which the general term coercion is attached, prison societies get down into the messy details of degree of coercion and complicity before making judgments."[50] In the modern totalitarian institution, however, control rather than justice is the goal, even though Scarry and many other commentators note that torture actually stimulates resistance. Michel Foucault finds this reaction in nineteenth century chain gangs: "Instead of bringing remorse, torture sharpened pride; the justice that brought the sentence was rejected, and the crowd that came to witness what it believed to be repentance or humiliation was scorned." Small wonder, then, that when some Vietnam POWs became a chain gang during the 1967 Hanoi Parade, they too firmly believed that "the present order will not last forever; not only will the convicts be freed and resume their rights, but their accusers will take their place."[51]

Though the POWs were actually quite proud of this ability "to think like criminals," it was their devotion to other equally powerful total institutions, the U.S. military and the republic it defended, which made the Hanoi "criminals" so good at holding on to the things they lived for. This sense of duty helped set their "standard of performance"; that "expectation which arises from cultural conditioning, social cues, and such dictates as the Code of Conduct and captor-imposed rules." As "a mere accelerator of the basic process of unhinging a victim with fear and polarizing him with guilt," torture tried to make the POWs abandon their standard, and "only the prisoners' comradeship and loyalty to each other can effectively deter this repeated tearing down of a man," Jim Stockdale contends.[52] In Hanoi, "comradeship" not only meant strict conformity to the command chain, but more intriguingly, acceptance of the senior POWs as those who could truly hear confessions, grant absolution, and prescribe atonement. Publicly, the POWs stressed community over command chain. SRO John Flynn claimed that when the Camp Authority "succeeded in breaking a man down," his "fellow prisoners" forgave him, and POW Robert Naughton claimed that the POWs' "willingness to promulgate to all fellow captives personally tragic or triumphant prison experiences" not only "helped others to learn vicariously," but "represented nearly perfect interaction."[53] In most cases, though, absolution clearly came from above. When he finally contacted other POWs, "words poured out" of a battered Howard Rutledge: "I was a traitor. I had answered more questions than name, rank, serial number, and date of birth." SRO Stockdale's response—"Don't feel like the Lone Ranger"—set the protocol for the years ahead. POWs would confess; then the confessor would assure them that torture was irresistible, and that as penitents they remained part of the community. POWs like Ned Shuman cherished this approval. "I just wanted to have somebody else confirm that what I thought was right was, *indeed*, right," he recalled, "And, from then on, I had no problem at all." With acceptance however came weighty obligations. As Kenneth L. Coskey remarked, many POWs gutted out interrogations "because, if nothing else, you've got to go back and explain to your compatriots what went on in that quiz."[54] And years later, enlisted POWs arriving from the jungle camps would find the order to undergo torture before cooperating with the Camp Authority simply insane. Whether individual prisoners liked it or not, though, the Hanoi POWs had institutionalized their own response to torture in ways that profoundly affected their dealings with the Camp Authority and each other.

The problem was quite simple: following the Code was a POW's duty, but torture would make you violate the Code. The senior POWs responded by declaring that any information "not extracted by undue torture or duress was a direct violation of that code." Since some American prisoners had been trained "to give in and at least *pretend* to give the enemy some information of value, before they completely lost the use of their faculties and simply told everything they knew," POW arguments arose over what "undue torture and duress" exactly were. Torture made "adopting a fall-back position" or "setting up a second line of resistance" necessary, but some men "found it difficult to decide when to fall back," and still others "didn't even know they could."[55] Many POWs went through a bitter personal process of trial and error before accepting the fallback policy as their own; the earliest prisoners had to invent it for themselves. Shortly after his 1965 capture, intense pain from the ropes and concerns about his family forced Howard Rutledge to change his tactics in the way that would became common: "I knew my ability to endure any more physical or mental pain was rapidly ending. I determined that before I cracked completely, I would volunteer to answer their questions, hoping that while I still had some control, I could lie and deceive them and so survive." Conclusions very much like Rutledge's became campwide policy in July 1966. "Resist until you are tortured," SRO Risner instructed, "But do not take torture to the point where you lose your capability to think and do not take torture to the point where you lose the permanent use of your limbs." These orders governed Hanoi for the next three years. Upon succeeding Risner as SRO at the Zoo, Jeremiah Denton announced, "We will die before we give them classified information," but then advised that "when you think you have reached the limit of your endurance, give them harmless and inaccurate information that you can remember and repeat if tortured again."[56] Early POW experience thus produced that handful of commands known as the fallback policy: death before treason, torture before confession, and lies before truth.

Falling back, however, could only buy a man time. After regathering his strength, he must resume resisting, and return to torture—fall back, *bounce back*. Here again, Camp

Authority practice led the Hanoi POWs to counter with their own policy. Like confessors, the interrogators would forgive crimes and end the torture only in return for some kind of penance—usually a document or tape. Following this pattern in order to unravel it, the POWs forgave Code violations and offered comfort, but also in return for atonement. And since the forgiven POW had to resume resisting as soon as possible, the only irrefutable proof that he had bounced back was another torture session. Or as POW Larry Chesley explained, the Camp Authority "could break us temporarily and make us do things we would not normally have done, but though we were regretful of having done them we recognized them as an inevitable thing in the circumstances and we were not permanently broken in spirit by the experience. We always bounced back to fight again."[57] The consequences of this policy were both daunting and inspiring. A POW must place his body on the front lines of the clash between the camp regulations and the Code. He could retreat only to renew his strength, and he must return to the conflict as soon as possible. Bouncing back into the ropes was therefore the POWs' most compelling evidence that the fight did continue after battle.

Between 1965 and 1969, returning to torture confirmed a prisoner's worth as an individual, a POW, and an American. For many men, torture and patriotism became indistinguishable. Red McDaniel called the paperback version of his memoirs *Scars and Stripes*, and Jay Jensen watched the ropes turn him into Old Glory: "Although my arms were tied behind me, I would bring them around to the side; and as I watched, they turned red, then white, then blue. I remember thinking to myself, 'Gee, Jay, what patriotic arms you have . . . !'" Jim Stockdale saw torture as Communism's fiercest method for attacking "that tiny vestige of freedom it was in your power to hold." Only the tortured could understand fully Thomas Paine's remark that "those who expect to reap the blessings of freedom must, like men, undergo the fatigue of supporting it."[58] As for George Coker, his reasons for undergoing torture read like the Pledge of Allegiance:

> I believe in the American democratic form of government and the American political system. I believe in this very strongly and am completely opposed to Communism. As a military man, my country expects me to fight when required, and my self-respect forces me to live up to that duty. It seems to me if you are thrown into a situation where suddenly you are going to suffer rather than simply die, this is most unfortunate, but you must be willing to suffer without giving up.

Though the torturer would win the battles, Coker's ideal POW "will continue fighting and resisting the enemy to the best of his ability no matter how long it lasts. No matter how painful it may be, no matter how many times he may fail, no matter how many times he may be broken, he will spring back. He will maintain his will to resist."[59] In Hanoi, this patriotism found its specific outlet in loyalty to the other prisoners. Only torture could make informing on other POWs forgivable—and even then, the guilt was overpowering. "The things that gave me nightmares in prison," recalled Jim Stockdale, "were not the broken bones, but the belief, the knowledge, that I had been tortured and forced to give up knowledge about the prison organization. That was the central truth of my eight years." This guilt was potent because it was self-inflicted. Though ordered "to take torture rather than provide the Vietnamese with specific information about the POW organization, communications, codes, and so forth," ultimately "torture was only what a man required of himself in order to maintain his sense of loyalty to his fellow POWs."[60]

This sense of duty created its own values. A tortured survivor was usually more respected than a martyr, for as POW Thomas Kirk explained, "If you stand someone up in front of a firing squad and say, 'Tell me this or I'll kill you,' and he doesn't tell you and you kill him—that guy's not nearly the hero that a guy is who takes sustained torture for a week." Such heroism was all the more striking because failure was inevitable. "The toughest thing was the battle within myself as to how long I could hold out," Kirk recalled, "because I already knew they were going to get [what they wanted] sooner or later."[61] Not surprisingly, then, the POWs became firm believers in the benefits of struggling against a set outcome. A "truly maximum effort to physically resist torture" was for POW Robert Naughton a Maslovian "peak experience"—a "self-validating self-justifying moment which carries its own intrinsic value with it":

> It may be the first time in [a POW's] life that he musters every ounce of physical strength, mental courage, and determination. The feeling of being totally consumed by this effort is truly unique; and even when this maximum effort, with nothing held back, proves to be not enough, one at least feels pure and satisfied for having done his absolute best. Such an experience usually leaves a POW broken and physically disabled, but is nonetheless of great psychological value to him.[62]

Since Americans often link peak experiences almost mystically to sports, many POWs used playing-field analogies to explain why they fought on to defeat. According to Jim Stockdale, hard-line POWs displayed "the merits of men having taken the physical abuse of body contact in sports." Bob Shumaker found that when torture knocked a POW down, "what separated the men from the boys" was "that you've just got to come off the canvas and come back for the second round."[63] And conversely, nothing could absolve a POW who wouldn't resist or bounce back. "No mas" was no option. "I understand pain, isolation, and degradation," Jim Stockdale wrote in 1981 when discussing Robert Garwood's court-martial, "I've had a lot of all three, and I have cried 'I submit' and done what these punishments were imposed to get me to do more times than I'd like to admit." What he had refused to accept, however, was that a POW's personality could be altered unless he let it be. Terms like "pain thresholds, depression or isolation, interrupted consciousness, discontinuities of judgment patterns" only muddied clear water. Words like "brainwashed" or "broken" were "unfortunate metaphors because they imply that a third force, an unseen hand, somehow enters the jailer/prisoner picture and changes the predilections of the latter." Though Stockdale admitted he had fallen short, "no third force, no unseen hand" erased his guilt. "The charges are about character" when POW misconduct is the subject, and the prisoner who ducked torture, or wouldn't confess to other POWs, or refused to bounce back, was unworthy of "compassion and forgiveness."[64]

As early as 1966, some POWs were using this understanding as the yardstick for separating the sheep from the goats. Upon arriving in a new cellblock, Jeremiah Denton for instance was "shocked" to learn that "while most were putting their lives on the line with bitter resistance, some had been giving written, unclassified information and written biographical material without first submitting to torture."[65] As Denton's experience reveals, some POWs veered away from torture almost immediately, and perhaps the most famous soft-liner, Richard Stratton, quickly learned how unforgiving, and even vindictive, hard-line POWs could be. After his first bout, Stratton "reasoned I would rather make the tape under my own free will and try to screw up the tape than get tortured and do a good job of it." At least with the other POWs, however, Stratton's reasoning proved to be a "mistake": "I was in deep shit in the prison system . . . with a majority of my peers . . . for a number of years with regard to my credibility because of that whole routine."[66] The POWs' suspicions were historical. Evading torture by providing "vague generalities" or lies seemed too close to the "play it cool" approach the Korean War captives had been damned for. With time, though, more POWs joined Stratton in questioning diehard resistance. "A lot of guys went through an awful lot of punishment because they were afraid that once they started talking, a sophisticated interrogator would get to them," 1967 shootdown Glenn Wilson recalled, but this fear proved unfounded, because the Camp Authority "just didn't have any sophisticated interrogators."[67] In his account of a man he calls "Palmer," Charlie Plumb also suggests that hard-liners were sometimes less successful than POWs who lied from the start. Even though his POW commanders permitted him to, in 1968 Palmer refused to answer innocuous questions. He decided to fake insanity instead, but the Camp Authority saw through his disguise, and Palmer was "tortured until he aided V propaganda by preparing tapes about good treatment. He had also written letters to this effect to Senator Fulbright and President Nixon. He had made a mistake. He had been brutally tortured and had caused other prisoners pain. He was sorry for what he'd done, and he apologized."[68]

Neither Charlie Plumb nor Palmer's senior officers were cowards: they simply disagreed with Palmer over what a POW should take torture for. These more moderate POWs refused to suffer in stupid causes, because they knew they would need all their strength for noble ones, and as this attitude spread, so did some unflattering opinions about the diehards. Few POWs were as damning as Dan Pitzer, a jungle camp parolee who told Jane Fonda and Tom Hayden that "it was standard operating procedure to collaborate with the Vietnamese as much as necessary and then repudiate the action by claiming torture when you got home."[69] Other Hanoi POWs did however see the bounce-back policy as a flawed, even masochistic creation of guilt-ridden senior POWs. "They had been broken and they could never forgive themselves," Richard Stratton claimed, and "part of the way they healed themselves was to exhort all sorts of people to do what they wished they could have done." Such hard-liners "used to think every time you saw a gook, you kicked him in the nuts," and Stratton's crowning example was a service academy grad he called "Thaddeus B. Hoyt." After Stratton's first public confession, this senior officer ordered him to stop taping—a command Stratton found "hilarious," since "if anyone should have been sympathetic with me, it was him. He had 'confessed' to 'war crimes' and he had been before delegations and he had made all these statements." But Hoyt had insisted on torture while Stratton had not, and the result was a bad 1973 evaluation which Stratton blamed on mean-spiritedness and mental instability: Hoyt was "a little demented, to my mind, anyway."[70]

Besides creating the hard/soft distinction which pervades the POWs' memoirs, this debate over torture raises once more the question of just what the phrase "American fighting man" in Article I of the Code actually means. If "the fight continues after battle," as the early versions insist, then the Vietnam POW's duty was to remain an American fighting man, and to make the enemy think of him as one. At its most emblematic, then, torture went beyond martyrdom, the ordeal, or the price demanded by loyalty, and became proof that the North Vietnamese Camp Authority and the American POWs were waging war. For this reason, the Hanoi POWs sharply distinguished themselves from other victims of modern torture. As many writers have observed, torture often turns a regime's convenient fictions of subversion into fact. "It is the military repression which creates the need for strategy," Malise Ruthven writes, "and the strategy which in turn creates the need for a secret, centrally controlled organization."[71] But while something very similar happened in the Hanoi Hilton, the POWs felt they were different from virtually powerless captives of a totalitarian authority, or even from the Vietcong abused in a Saigon police station, because as Americans, they felt they served an authority far more powerful than the institution holding them.

The value the POWs granted their pain therefore resulted from a union of ideas about torture *and* war. As Elaine Scarry explains, though inflicting pain is essential to both, "in war, the persons whose bodies are used in the confirmation process have given their consent over this most radical use of the human body while in torture no such consent is exercised." In their policies and narratives, the Vietnam POWs often straddled this distinction. The Camp Authority always appears as a torturing institution, and not just because this view justifies the POWs' moral contempt, but also because torture suggested that the North Vietnamese government was tottering and illegitimate, for as Scarry notes, although bodily pain "seems to confer its quality of 'incontestable reality' on that power that has brought it into being," it is "precisely because the reality of that power is so highly contestable, the regime so unstable, that torture is being used."[72] When however the POWs shift their attention to the victim, a war paradigm takes over. In war, two opponents attack each other, and the Hanoi POWs often commented that their attempts to injure or kill North Vietnamese before capture showed that as American fighting men they were ready to be hurt or killed. Richard Stratton called himself "a highly trained, highly paid professional killer. That is my business, death and destruction. If I think anything else, I'm an idiot." Jim Stockdale seconded General Sherman—"War is cruelty and you can't refine it"—and agreed with Clausewitz that "War is an act of *violence* intended to compel our opponent to fulfill our will."[73]

Torture was therefore torture when the Camp Authority was the subject, but war when the POWs celebrated their own achievements—a conclusion that led to some remarkably circular reasoning. By provoking their own torture, for instance, the POWs claimed they had forced the North Vietnamese to admit that a state of war existed, that the Geneva convention was thus in effect, and that the Camp Authority was therefore guilty of war crimes against American servicemen—torture, for example. A similar logic led aviator POWs like Lewis Shattuck to see "the battle of Hanoi" as a war in which "the only weapons we had were our bodies and our pain," but which the POWs actually won. Jeremiah Denton made the same claim at a March 1973 press conference: "Figuratively speaking . . . we now began to lie on the railroad tracks hoping that the sheer bulk of our bodies would slow down the train. We forced them to be brutal to us. And this policy was success-ful. . . ."[74] Statements like these support Elaine Scarry's claim that the real difference between torture and war is ultimately their narratives. A torturer's "fiction" is "unreal" because the very need to inflict pain proves that the power relations between captor and captive are unstable and misrepresented. In war the ends are also "fictitious," but only because "they are 'not yet real.'" Thus, "in one case, 'fiction' means 'a lie about reality' while in the other, 'fiction' means 'an anticipation of reality.'"[75] The Vietnam POWs exploited this difference. Since the Camp Authority gained confessions through torture, they were lies about reality—transparently false. But since the POWs demanded torture to prove they were still at war, both their demand and their bounce-back policy indicated that as warriors they properly saw pain as something they willingly endured to make their values prevail. Insisting on torture was thus the POWs' way of fighting the Vietnam War, and of guaranteeing they would return home proudly as victors in "the battle of Hanoi."

This fiction became the POWs' official story years before they left Vietnam. Seniority and command granted importance. Those shot down and taken to Hanoi between 1965 and 1968, for instance, generally looked down on POWs held elsewhere or captured after September 1969, when torture all but ended in Hanoi. When Jim Mulligan told the *Washington Post* that "95 per cent of American prisoners were physically tortured," the

Los Angeles Times reported he "estimated that 95% of 589 POWs were severely tortured." The statement was false, but probably because Mulligan was referring to a 1971 survey "made by camp leaders among 351 POWs"—a sample covering only those imprisoned in the North, thus excluding the 250 POWs either held in the South or not yet captured.[76] So many interviews repeated this pattern that both the antiwar movement and the reporters covering Operation Homecoming asked why those POWs speaking up had almost always been tortured in Hanoi between 1965 and 1969. Noting that the POWs themselves "say there were different forms of treatment meted out to different groups of men," peace activist Cora Weiss objected that "those who complain of the worst treatment also claim they provoked it."[77] *New York Times* reporter Steven Roberts responded to the sameness of the stories by pointing out there was "no typical prisoner, or a typical day in prison life. Inmates were scattered in about a dozen different camps at different times: they were treated differently according to when and where they were captured, and according to their will, and ability, to resist." Roberts also reported on a "split between the veterans and the newcomers." While "most of the old-timers kept aloof from the guards," for instance, "some of the younger men developed friendships with them." The old-timers also "were jubilant when the B-52's raided Hanoi last Christmas," while "some of the younger men said that they were merely scared." Roberts accurately reported that torture revelations "dominated" the March 30, 1973, press conferences, but he also recorded that "torture and other forms of harassment declined dramatically after October 1969," and he published one POW's claim that "the older prisoners 'lived on hate' for their captors and the Communist system." Roberts went on to file stories about parolees, POWs who rejected the bounce-back policy, dissidents like Gene Wilber, or the seldom-mentioned, well-treated 1972 shootdowns, who stressed "conscience" and "morality" over the "uniformity" and "discipline" valued by the "embittered veteran prisoners."[78]

Roberts's own agenda was fairly transparent: his version of the POW camps was a microcosm of America, with old-timers insisting on patriotism and pride while young dissidents condemned these values for causing all the suffering. And yet, though Roberts's scenario was if anything even more distorted than the official story, it made him sensitive to the way the POWs were shaping their public history. When he noticed that the hard-liners who had suffered "the worst treatment" in Hanoi were now enjoying "the most publicity" at the press conferences, which "tended to spotlight senior officers, and others with particularly horrifying tales to tell," Roberts had located those bridges between torture and the Code, between torture and war, which the senior POWs had carefully constructed: "Many prisoners feel a deep need to justify the war and the damage done to North Vietnam. And critics wonder whether the desire for justification has also led the prisoners to emphasize the worst aspects of their captivity."[79] Roberts however could wonder; the senior POWs were certain. Long before returning home, they had decided that the essence of a Vietnam POW narrative was that moment when the American fighting man placed his body and will between the Code of Conduct and the Camp Authority. Narratives might differ in details, and personal successes might vary, but the official story memoir was always ethical, always exemplary, revealing those shared values that allowed the POWs to remain true to each other and to their country, even when other Americans were abandoning their duties as free citizens.

Part I has marked out the institutional foundations for the POWs' experience—that working relationship between the Code, the rules, and the body. Part II will explore the official story that emerged from those years of captivity and temptation—a history that assigned praise and blame, highlighted or downplayed events, and ultimately transformed a numbingly boring, routine existence into a rich, significant, orthodox epic.

* * * **II** * * *

THE OFFICIAL STORY
AND THE BIG PICTURE

To make the point as emphatically as it should be made, it is necessary to risk the appearance of immodesty: I do not believe that a more complete history of a prisoner of war experience is likely to be produced.

JOHN G. HUBBELL, author of P.O.W.[1]

★ 4 ★

The Official Story

Larry Guarino was losing hope. Shot down in 1965, he had endured the horrible food, the mosquitoes and vermin, the harassment and beatings, the terrors of solitary, the leg irons, torture cuffs, and ropes for more than two years. Now his strength was ebbing, and though a staunch Catholic, Guarino told his roommate that even God seemed to have abandoned them: "I've prayed ten million prayers, Ron," he said. "We're not getting any help, and I don't think we're gonna get any. I think He just worries about big things, like whether the world is gonna continue or not. I don't think He gives a damn about you and me anymore." Shortly afterward, though, Guarino "lapsed into a brief sleep of vivid dream, hallucinated, or engaged in some other mysterious exercise of the psyche," and a revelation, "one of the most intensely real experiences of his life," proved him wrong.

He was alone in a glassware shop—fine crystal was one of his passions. After slipping some cocktail glasses inside his flight jacket, Guarino spied a Dresden piece which only the entrance of "a kindly-looking elderly gentleman with a white beard" kept him from stealing as well. This gentleman offered Guarino the figurine, but suggested that he put it inside his jacket. Certain the gentleman knew about the glasses, Guarino tried to slip the piece in, but couldn't. As he tried to leave with the figurine in his hand, the cocktail glasses expanded, "grinding against each other, then breaking," and as his breathing became labored, the gentleman, with "real concern on his face and in his voice," urged Guarino to go outside for some air. As he crawled out, Guarino looked back and saw a gong above the gentleman's head. The man told him to hit the gong "before it's too late!"; drawing on his last bit of energy, Guarino heaved a rock. The gong clanged, "a great ray of golden light shone outward from it," and as his strength surged back the gong turned into a rosary. When Guarino awoke, he shared his dream, and both men "began praying the rosary. Neither had ever prayed harder. To both, the message seemed plain: to despair meant to die. Prayer was the only thing they had, a lifeline and weapon, and they had better make the most of it."[1]

Guarino's dream is one of many such vignettes dotting the POWs' histories and memoirs. Usually provoked by suffering, these visions assured the POW that some greater power—God, America, or his fellow prisoners—would sustain him. Such revelations also renew the POW's allegiance to what I will call the "official story," that authorized, carefully prepared account of American captivity in Vietnam. The most detailed published version is John G. Hubbell's *P.O.W.: A Definitive History of the American Prisoner-of-War Experience in Vietnam, 1964–1973*, but even this volume only sketches an outline for that collection of parables, regulations, saints' lives, jokes, and survival tips which the senior POWs presented to new prisoners as the history of Vietnam captivity. However idiosyncratic, each POW's story had its place and value within this narrative. Orthodox memoirs or spiritual autobiographies reaffirmed the common faith. Renegade narratives were just as implicated, since attacking the official story still forced the scapegoat POWs to invoke it.

Nor did agreeing with the official story necessarily drain a memoir of its tensions or contradictions. In Guarino's dream, for example, an orthodox experience nevertheless slips out of the official story's realm. For Guarino, the dream's meaning was "plain." By showing his concern, and by pointing to the gong/rosary, the white bearded gentleman proved that God still "gives a damn." In return, Guarino started praying, since "to despair meant to die." What gets lost here are the dream's vivid and disturbing details. If, for instance, "to despair meant to die" sums things up, why doesn't God simply point to the rosary? Here methods loosely resembling those of scriptural exegesis help to account for the dream's power. Just as a sacred narrative often alludes to others while telling its own, official story episodes will echo or recall Western stories of heroism and valor. Guarino's effort to keep his theft hidden even as the glass shards press into his chest, for instance, closely resembles the actions of Plutarch's Spartan boy, whose friends gave him a stolen fox for safekeeping. When the owners appeared, the boy had it under his garment, but even though the fox ate through the boy's "side to the vitals," he "did not move or cry out, so as to avoid being exposed." This behavior seemed foolish even to those who had put him up to it. The other boys "blamed him, saying that it would have been better to let the fox be seen than to hide it even unto death." The young Spartan disagreed, proudly declaring that it was "better to die without yielding to pain than through being detected because of weakness to gain a life to be lived in disgrace."[2]

Clearly, Plutarch's boy was that diehard resister so many POWs wanted to be—James Bond must have been a Spartan—but how does this hard-line resistance mesh with the kindly gentleman's timely revelation? One answer would be that this apparent contradiction actually freed Guarino from a common source of POW guilt: the failure to remain silent under torture. Only gradually did most men let God or other POWs lift them out of that despair which this failure buried them in. In Guarino's dream, though, the kindly gentleman dispels this guilt in a moment. Since he seems to know what Guarino is concealing, continuing to hide the glasses became a personal decision rather than a moral duty—the kind of choice some POWs made when they refused to say what kind of plane they were flying even after the Camp Authority showed them the wreckage. Nor was the kindly man upset about the theft, even offering Guarino the Dresden figurine as an absolution without demanding a confession. As for bouncing back, though Guarino's collapse in the dream suggests he started down this path, the kindly gentleman saves him by pointing to a far less drastic penance—the gong/rosary, which showed Guarino and his roommate that "prayer was the only thing they had." Guarino's dream therefore not only teaches that "to despair meant to die," but also that God and the rosary stood as a higher authority which could release POWs from the hard-line duty of returning to torture—just one example of how the official story's confident progress forward can mask a tense interplay between orthodoxy and experience.

Part I explored how the POWs understood and acted upon the clash between American and North Vietnamese institutions and values. Part II describes how the Hanoi POWs created an authorized history for this conflict. The early skirmishes between POWs and the Camp Authority produced many short narratives; shared furtively, these stories came to form an oral history that set the standards for evaluating all future events. Just as torture alone justified certain actions, this camp history became the approved means for explaining the longtime POWs' actions to later arrivals, and eventually to all Americans. Neither comprehensive nor democratic, the official story highlighted certain POWs, while downplaying or erasing others. And when the end came, its well-rehearsed historians made certain that Americans would come to know this epic as the first, dominant, and enduring story of their captivity.

History in the Camps: Setting, Character, Plot

Certain constants of location and cast mark the Vietnam POWs' official story. In most narratives, Hoa Lo Prison, or the "Hanoi Hilton," stands at the center of the prison network. New shootdowns were usually interrogated in New Guy Village or Heartbreak Hotel, two sections of the Hilton, then often moved to nearby camps like the Zoo or Plantation. As these prisons filled, POWs frequently went to outlying camps like Briarpatch, Skid Row, or D-1. And in the war's last days, while POWs held in distant prisons and jungle camps trickled into Hanoi, a healthy number of men went to a camp they called Dogpatch, near the Chinese border. Through all these shuffles the POWs kept track of contacts and memorized prisoner lists, thus creating that loose sense of community they called "the system."[3] Directives and news radiated from the Hilton—first to the Hanoi prisons orbiting that stone sun, and then less dependably to the more distant satellites. Since the jungle camps were out of range, those POWs basically didn't exist—a fact many jungle POWs claimed was responsible for the official story's trivializing of their suffering.

As the "Devil's Island of Southeast Asia," the Hanoi Hilton had great symbolic significance as well. Since Hoa Lo had served as a French colonial prison for Vietnamese dissidents and criminals, "many of the high-ranking Vietnamese government officials had been there for ten to twelve years themselves, imprisoned by the French and Japanese." Hard-line POWs like Jim Stockdale actually found it "comforting to know that we were united against the communist administration of Hoa Lo prison just as the Vietnamese communists had united against the French administration of Hoa Lo in the thirties." At that time the "overriding theme" for Pham Van Dong and the Vietnamese had been "essentially the same one" Stockdale had "adopted and promulgated as policy: organization above all—Unity over Self." The senior POWs thus took their captors' successful resistance as a challenge: "We resolved to do it better in the sixties than they had in the thirties."[4]

If the Hilton was the official story's main stage, rank and seniority assigned the principal parts. When Mark Ruhling, a POW since November 1968, told the other prisoners in October 1972 that "today I've been a prisoner longer than any American held in World War II. Don't call me a 'new guy' anymore," he was reacting to a widespread belief that Vietnam POW history was principally about commissioned aviators captured before the summer of 1968.[5] As senior combat officers in the most technologically sophisticated service branches, these career aviators were better educated than other POWs. Many had been test pilots and instructors, and some were academy graduates. Bob Shumaker had been tested for the astronaut program, and shortly before his Vietnam shootdown, Korean war ace Robinson Risner had appeared on the cover of *Time*. These men "had more experience and basic maturity"—a real advantage, 1967 shootdown Doug Clower claimed, because "the older a man was, the better he was able to adapt to the diet, the better he was able to resist a lack of medical treatment, and the better he recovered from normal everyday ailments." As evidence for his claims, Clower recalled how the old-timers agreed to a hunger strike simply to teach some hard-talking new guys something about effective resistance. After only two days, "I've got about 20 who can't even get out of bed, begging me to please break this thing. . . . And I look around at my old and senior men and they're just smiling, and they say 'We think we have shown them our point.'"[6] This "point" went far beyond the moment. Since only the "old and senior men" had truly been tested, only they could set policy or tell the official story.

And yet, despite maintaining the orthodoxy that preserving the command hierarchy had been the POWs' most important task, this narrative also invokes a community of friends and equals by referring to prisoners almost always by first or last names. These claims of excellence and ordinariness, of rank and equality, clash at times. Charlie Plumb for instance may call the Hanoi community a "microcosm," "a petri dish containing its own strains and culture," but he also describes the POWs as "for the most part out of the same mold—that of the professional officer and pilot," and finishes up with superlatives: "We had been exposed to a different selection process and a new era of lifestyles. Gathered together in a dubious fraternity of Hanoi sky-divers we were a group of cocky individuals: we knew we were the best!"[7]

Such pride did not however keep the POWs from arguing that their ordinariness granted them the right to teach other Americans. Though POW Robert Naughton admitted that extracting morals from individual experience was risky, he insisted that the Vietnam POWs were representative enough to draw some conclusions about the "universal" factors of resistance behavior. As for Jim Stockdale, his announced topic when addressing audiences back home was "how a group of middle Americans—average American guys who have chosen military life as a profession—survived in a POW situation and returned home with honor."[8] Patriotism was the POWs' favored method for reconciling excellence and the ordinary. Since all must serve their country to the best of their ability, those with superior talents could exercise them without fear of censure. Their glory was the nation's. This pride in being just another American doing his best appears repeatedly in the POW memoirs, but nowhere more explicitly than in Charlie Plumb's *I'm No Hero*, which claims that captivity had merely added him to "the ranks of millions of Americans who have applied heroic principles in overcoming hardships":

> Every day a disabled veteran steps away from his wheelchair. Every day a life is resumed after a death in the family. Friendships erase loneliness. Addicts throw away the crutch of alcohol or drugs or obsessions. Every day someone discovers how to love life, no matter what the obstacle. Every day someone sees the light at the end of the tunnel.
>
> These ordinary Americans are not held in esteem as heroes, yet they have suffered grave misfortune and have recovered just as I.
>
> So you see, I'm no hero.[9]

The official story thus chronicles an awe-inspiring triumph carried out by regular, modest, and likable "'Jack Armstrong' types." An all-American "aw, shucks" answers all charges of self-promotion, for as POW George Coker explains, while the official story was certainly the "success story of the P.W.," it was most importantly a victory won for "his group, and for the United States."[10]

The official story's own history parallels the Hanoi POWs' growth as a community. As Robert Naughton describes him, the typical prisoner was a loyal military aviator who arrived in Hanoi as "a helpless object vulnerable to the enemy's wrath." Thanks to pride and "a driving desire to prove yourself to yourself and to those whose opinion you respect," James Bond tended to be the POW's first role model. Preserving a sense of self soon however required contact with the familiar—cigarettes at first, but then with other POWs, regardless of the danger. Once within an American community, as he learned about "prison pitfalls," heard "words of encouragement," and followed "the senior officer's policy of resistance, called BACK-US," the POW strengthened his identity through his sense of belonging. Also rekindled was his ethical nature. During the long stretches of solitude, the POW sifted through memories until "ultimately, the question 'Why was that particular event enjoyable or important?'" caused him "to evaluate himself and ask 'What is important? What do I value?'" Answering these questions led to composing an autobiography and latching onto every detail about captivity and his fellow POWs. Passing on life stories and camp information gave the POW community its cohesive force as early as 1965, and Naughton's account of moving into large-group compounds years later suggests just how strong this force had been: "It was rather exciting to meet men whose names and background had been memorized but whose faces were heretofore unseen. New friendships were born; common acquaintances and experiences were discovered; and time was passed listening to new stories and biographies."[11]

But as one POW later remarked, "It is a bit depressing to hear so many tell their stories and not hear one happy ending."[12] Here the official story, a group narrative which fully took shape in these compounds, stepped in to satisfy this desire for a positive narrative. This community history strung together the many episodes and anecdotes that affirmed group values. Like all war stories, with time and repetition, these moments had become "embellished in places, honed down in others until they were perfect tales, even if they bear little resemblance to what actually happened."[13] Some stories endured because of their comforting familiarity. Even though the chances of hearing a new joke were understandably slim, Gerald Coffee fondly recalled a contest held on the POWs' last night in Hanoi. Certain narratives turned long-suffering POWs like Dale Osborne into legends: "Told and retold, the story of his courage was known throughout the various camps as men were shifted and transferred. He was the hero's hero. His was the story of courage that gave new hope to other prisoners." Other episodes became parables—"Denton's Cross," for instance, "which became well known in prison." Sometime in 1965, Ed Davis gave Jeremiah Denton a bamboo-strip cross, but the guards found it and ripped it to pieces. Shortly afterwards though, Denton found a new cross in his cell, left at great risk by some Vietnamese workmen who had seen the guards' cruelty. At that moment, "despondency over my loss turned to glorious triumph and gratitude," as Christ once more revealed his love.[14]

Assembling an epic out of such stories was a complicated but pleasant task. The first stage, getting all the stories straight, began when the POWs arrived in Camp Unity in late 1970. As Jim Mulligan recalls, "We spent our days catching up on what had transpired in all of the various camps," and in the process "filled in the gaps of POW history."[15] Once collected, these stories could then be used for specific purposes. In March of 1971, for instance, Jeremiah Denton "spent three days developing a summary of the prisoner activities and camp structures going back to 1965" as part of his briefing of SRO Colonel John Flynn, who was assuming at last full command over all Hanoi POWs. As "a system of stories or chapters to acquaint new POWs with what had happened in the past, to preserve the stories of bravery and endurance and the facts of injustice and repression," the official story also became the authorized introduction to the Hanoi POW community itself.[16] The senior POWs tuned the official story most finely when preparing for the trip home. Though Robert Naughton's claim that Operation Homecoming created "a unanimity among Americans which had been lacking during the long years of Vietnam conflict" was perhaps more wish than fact, creating the impression of POW unanimity had certainly been part of the agenda. This monolithic front was firmly in place before the first men left Hanoi. When asked if there were "any hostilities or differences between the POWs," December 1972 shootdown Terry Geloneck answered, "None that I was aware of at all. I was tremendously amazed at the organization and the deep feelings—of comradeship—that the POWs had amongst themselves, particularly those that had been there a long time."[17]

Geloneck's comments appeared in the April 1973 issue of *Air Force Magazine*, which predictably gave a faithful account of what the POWs wanted America to know. The sources were high-ranking, long-term prisoners, Denton and Risner among them. Fit and confident, these Hanoi POWs were utterly unlike those held in the South, who "did not fare as well": "A higher percentage showed the strain of years of confinement in a deprived and disease-laden atmosphere. When released to US authorities, many moved hesitantly and took longer to adjust to the new-found freedom." These jungle POWs had apparently lacked "the strong leadership" found in Hanoi—the "very lack of self-imposed military discipline" which had "helped bring about disaster in the POW camps of Korea." The senior Hanoi men also supplied official opinions about the war itself. Asked if it should have ended earlier, in a response "typical of the men interviewed," Robinson Risner diplomatically replied, "I don't for one moment believe that anyone wanted this war to be extended, and therefore, if I believe in my country and in my President and in our military leaders as I do, then I have to believe everyone was exerting their utmost effort to end it as quickly as possible." As for the antiwar movement, many interviewed POWs believed "that the demonstrations helped to prolong the war." Though POW Thomas Curtis among others felt that protecting the right to dissent "was one of the reasons I was sitting in jail there," he also felt the protesters "should have confined their dissension to the home port—the United States." Risner's comments on amnesty for draft dodgers were also "typical": "As a military man, I cannot be in favor of amnesty for anyone who fails to serve his country in time of need." Although *Air Force Magazine* calls this information "sketchy," what it unmistakably sketches are the outlines of the official story.[18] The heroes and villains are fixed, and past divisiveness had subsided into a providential history. The speakers had been chosen as well; all that remained to do in 1973 was to tell the story to America.

The Official Book: *P.O.W.*

Though many interviews, histories and memoirs appeared immediately after Operation Homecoming, the official story's most authoritative version was published in 1976. *P.O.W.: A Definitive History of the American Prisoner-of-War Experience in Vietnam, 1964–1973* was commissioned by *Reader's Digest*. This magazine's interest in POW subjects was on-going and intense. It had printed parolee Robert Frishman's charges of torture in 1969, published Jeremiah Denton's *When Hell Was in Session* in the same year as *P.O.W.*; and it commissioned *Into the Mouth of the Cat,* the biography of Medal of Honor winner Lance Sijan, nine years later. The *Digest*'s commitment to *P.O.W.* was truly remarkable. In the acknowledgments, John G. Hubbell, the history's principal author, thanked the magazine for assigning two senior editors to the project, for placing "all of the *Digest*'s editorial offices, staff, and research facilities" at his service, and for handing him essentially a blank check. The *Digest* also opened large important doors. When Washington bureau head Kenneth O. Gilmore suggested the project to Hubbell, they first contacted Admiral Thomas H. Moorer, chairman of the Joint Chiefs of Staff, whose "support and guidance" were "unstinting," and whose aides arranged "for background briefings and access to vital informational materials." The assistant secretary of defense for public affairs did his bit, and his assistant, Air Force General Daniel "Chappie" James, "was energetic in arranging introductions to and interviews with many POWs." The "military public affairs officers and enlisted men" entitled to Hubbell's gratitude were "too numerous to mention," but he did single out six. Ross Perot arranged a meeting with Bull Simon, leader of the Son Tay raid; anonymous POWs provided "overall background knowledge." In addition to enjoying all the privileges of an officially commissioned historian, Hubbell also had the necessary time as well. After two years of research and "nearly two hundred interviews, ranging in length up to thirty-odd hours," he then went into funded seclusion "to organize a growing mountain of research, to develop narrative insights and tell the story." Nor was profit a concern. As the capstone of *Reader's Digest*'s efforts "to make the nation POW-conscious," *P.O.W.* was a public service, with all proceeds "somehow to be distributed to the returned POWs and/or as they saw fit." The result was a large-format, 630 page volume with no bibliography which claimed to be the ultimate word on the Vietnam POWs: "To make the point as emphatically as it should be made, it is necessary to risk the appearance of immodesty: I do not believe that a more complete history of a prisoner of war experience is likely to be produced."[19]

And yet, what Larry Chesley said about his memoir could with some important revisions be said about *P.O.W.*: "This book concerns only conditions in North Vietnamese prison camps."[20] Its proportions suggest how tied *P.O.W.* is to the longtime Hanoi POWs' official story. Almost two-thirds of the book, 380 pages, chronicle events in Hanoi from 1964 to 1967. The first account of jungle POWs appears on page 383, when Hubbell flashes back to March 1964, then sums up what happened outside Hanoi between 1964 and late 1968 in forty-five pages. (By comparison, thirty pages tell the story of the *first* Hanoi POW from August 1964 to February 1965, when the *second* one arrives.) After this jungle interlude, ninety pages more carry the Hanoi system through late 1969, when the torture largely ended and treatment improved somewhat. Less than a hundred pages thus remain for the three years of captivity which led up to Operation Homecoming. *P.O.W.*'s structure thus resembles an inverted pyramid—or perhaps more accurately, a funnel. The minutely detailed account of early Hilton days gets sketchier and sketchier, until by the end years are flying by in a few pages. This strategy creates two unavoidable impressions. First, a POW's value depends primarily on his date of capture. For example, Mark Ruhling, the flier who disliked being called a "new guy," reached Hanoi in November of 1968. That's on page 463 of *P.O.W.*—or would be. The definitive history doesn't mention him. Second, by discussing the enlisted and civilian POWs held outside of Hanoi only after devoting almost 400 pages to the system, *P.O.W.* marginalizes their experience.

P.O.W.'s dedication creates the same impressions, and adds some others:

> For Ron Storz, Norm Schmidt,
> Ed Atterberry,
> J.J. Connell, "Freddy" Frederick,
> Ken Cameron, "The Faker," Betty Ann Olsen,
> Hank Blood, "Roberts," "Top Benson,"
> and all the others, North and South,
> who didn't make it back.
> I hope I have told it the way it happened.
> J. G. H.[21]

Laid out like a monument inscription, this dedication reproduces the official story's assumptions from top to bottom. The first three men were longtime Hanoi POWs who died after especially horrible treatment. Ron Storz, an Alcatraz Gang member and famous diehard, comes first. Though Norm Schmidt simply disappeared, his sharp anger when heading off to interrogation was assumed to have provoked his murder. As the POW beaten to death for attempting to escape, Ed Atterberry then stands alone. The next four casualties were Hanoi victims of disease or complete psychological collapse—the reason why "The Faker"'s real name does not appear. When however the honor roll leaves Hanoi, the names run together. Betty Ann Olsen and Hank Blood were missionaries who died on a horrific jungle march—innocent victims, in short—and "Roberts" and "Top Benson" are pseudonyms for two enlisted men who died in the jungle camp that *P.O.W.* does describe in some detail. And then, even though the casualty rates were far higher outside the system, the rest of the jungle victims get lumped together as "all the others, North and South, who didn't make it back." America's POWs thus fall into official story formation even in death. The Hanoi POWs are first, on top, and named; the civilians get mentioned in passing; and a mass of anonymous enlisted men brings up the rear.

P.O.W.'s reduction of the Vietnam conflict to infrequent italicized bits of "historical context" also puts the focus on the Hanoi POWs' triumph. The war itself seems to be a hazy, shamefully conducted background for that epic struggle between the early shootdowns and the Camp Authority, and when Hubbell declares that "surely publishing annals will record no worthier venture," he is talking about his chronicling of this archetypic battle.[22] In the pages ahead, "tales of unrestrained savagery are matched and overmatched by tales of towering courage, self-sacrifice and endurance. There was gripping high adventure, inspirational patriotism, the meanest treason, great, belly-laugh humor, tragedy, death, enormous sadness." God plays his part in the Hanoi aviator POWs' lives as well: "The toughest, most pragmatic men tell of the power of prayer, are convinced they are the beneficiaries of miracles, and are convincing about it." In fact, only this "narrative history's" indisputable truth protects it from seeming *too* imaginative or contrived: "The writer of fiction surely would hesitate to submit it for publication—it might have been too much to believe, except that there it was, a history that contemporary Americans actually had lived, and many had lived to recount." Hubbell's fervent belief that the POWs' history was a single "collective experience" aligns him most closely with the Hanoi prisoners' efforts to turn their story into a tool for teaching a post-Vietnam, post-Watergate America what it had so obviously forgotten. Or as Hubbell puts it, *P.O.W.* tells "such a positive story, above all else a story of a great American performance at a time, on her 200th birthday, when America needs badly to know how great she still can be."[23] By calling *P.O.W.* "a definitive history," Hubbell thus not only declares his own ambitions, but those of *Reader's Digest* and the Hanoi POWs as well. By carefully selecting, excluding, proportioning, and orchestrating their materials, the senior officers and their historian wrote both an official defense of the POWs' performance, and a parable for a nation they believed had lost sight of its own greatness.

Secular Scripture: In the Beginning Was Alvarez

The story of a chosen people's struggles and eventual triumph, *P.O.W.* is a providential history. As in the Bible, the first man's first encounter with evil sets the pattern of conflict for the entire narrative. Heroes and leaders emerge as others arrive on the scene. Some become martyrs; some fall, but rise again. When men waver, lawgivers write codes. As time passes, later generations test their elders' authority, and internal dissent and prosperity endanger the community and its values almost more than times of trial. In time, a fiery apocalypse ends the story, sending the chosen people home, but leaving their tormentors in eternal darkness. Within these outlines, events and individual POWs are judged on whether they advance or impede the workings of justice, grinding inexorably on behind the nightmare of captivity.

The official story's Adam is Navy Lieutenant j.g. Everett Alvarez, Jr. Shot down on August 5, 1964, he was hardly Vietnam's first American POW. Among many others, memoirists George Smith and James "Nick" Rowe had become POWs well before. Nor was Alvarez even held the longest. Captured in March 1964, jungle POW and Army Captain Floyd James Thompson left Vietnam in February 1973—at almost nine years, the longest American POW captivity ever. As the first career aviator and the first POW in Hoa Lo prison, however, for the official story's purposes at least, in the beginning there was Alvarez. His capture was historically significant as well. Though U.S. advisers had been in Vietnam for years, and though some had died or been captured, for American fliers the war really began with the *Turner Joy* fiasco of August 4, 1964. Alvarez had been one of the pilots searching for invisible enemy ships that night, and when President Johnson ordered air reprisals the next day, "Ev was pleased to be one of those chosen to make the strike."[24] Because he didn't return, his captivity thus spanned the entire air war, making Alvarez the perfect Adam for an official story dominated by aviator POWs.

In *P.O.W.,* Alavarez's story also introduces the daily tribulations all Hanoi captives would face. His ejection and capture became the assumed narratives for those POWs who drop into the official story with as little warning as they dropped into their cells. Shot down and scooped up by fishermen, Alvarez was handed over to officials who immediately interrogated him. On August 11, he entered "Hoa Lo Prison in Hanoi, a place of dark renown that was to become known to the world as the 'Hanoi Hilton,'" and though conditions then were better than they would become, *P.O.W.* uses Alvarez to begin the process of angering and disgusting the reader.[25] Rats "the size of a large cat" roamed his cell; when he looked outside, he saw "that the bushes and trees were alive with rats, hundreds of them." Meals were even worse:

> Typically, he would uncover a bowl to find a chicken head floating in grease. There would be small pieces of carrot and kohlrabi, and occasionally the hoof of a cow, mule, or pig. There would also be nails, fingernail clippings, strands of coarse animal hair, and shrimp—unshelled, uncleaned, and staring at him through eyes that had not been removed. Once, he was served a blackbird complete with feathers, lying on its back with its feet sticking up—but with its eyes closed.

Such conditions led to "severe intestinal disorders," and thanks to dysentery, diarrhea, and fevers, he could soon "fit his hand around his thigh-bone; he had weighed 155 pounds when he was shot down, and within a few weeks he was skin and bones." Alvarez, however, fought back. He kept his cell spotlessly clean, and though "he would vomit the meals up," he forced himself "to eat them again, even though they were full of blood." Eventually, an unexplained but welcome change to "unseasoned rice soup containing small pieces of chicken" stabilized his sickness.[26] His main weapons for fending off despair were physical and mental exercise, ritual, and prayer. Each day he said Mass before an altar he'd carved on the wall. Imaginary conversations kept him sharp, and as Columbus Day turned into Thanksgiving, and Thanksgiving into Christmas, he thought about his wife and parents to pass the time.

Many POWs suffered through similar periods: by describing Alvarez's methods for fighting off his loneliness, Hubbell frees *P.O.W.* from having to return to the subject, thus keeping the focus on his story's social and political dimensions. Alvarez introduces this political emphasis as well. Even before arriving in Hanoi, the North Vietnamese were exploiting him for propaganda purposes. When some photographers struggled "to make him understand that he was to bow his head and look as though he felt guilty for what he had done, to appear to be submissive to his captors," Alvarez "made no effort to do so," thus forcing the photographers to climb on a table and take "pictures of the Caucasian looking up at them from an inferior position." Alvarez also went through the first POW interrogation. He stuck to the Big Four at first, even though "part of the wreckage of his aircraft lay in a corner of the room."[27] When however his captors reeled off a wealth of personal information they'd gathered, Alvarez decided to lie rather than remain silent. He willingly discussed such neutral topics as football and popcorn machines, and he also agreed to broadcast an innocuous statement. Troubling signs, however, soon had Alvarez questioning this soft-line strategy. As part of its criminal-not-POW strategy, the Camp Authority claimed that "there is no war," and threatened him with a public trial. A chance for parole—"show a good attitude and good behavior, and you will be released and go home"—introduced the Humane and Lenient Treatment policy as well.[28] As uncertainty and depression slowly turned into defiance, Alvarez moved toward the hard-line, and when the bombing of North Vietnam resumed in February 1965, he stepped over: *"The war's on,"* he thought to himself. *"The hell with them. No explanations. No more conversations. No more writing. Nothing."* Alvarez kept this resolution, sitting mute as "three new interrogators" asked him, "Who gives the political lectures on the ship? What about the chaplain? Isn't he the one who gives the political lectures? Where do you learn about your politics? What kind of airplane were you flying?" Alvarez's defiance also led to the first POW punishment. When he said he never could believe in "the purity of the Communist cause," his interrogators exploded—and made him stand in the corner.[29]

Though his resistance and the penalties would escalate, the absurdity of this first punishment introduces another official fact: that the North Vietnamese and their international allies were virtually unarmed for a battle of wits. The camp guards were "elderly and out of condition, or slightly built middle-aged dopes," and the interrogators weren't much better. After telling Alvarez he was not in Hanoi, two officials bungled their senseless lie by pointing in different directions toward the "distant" city.[30] *P.O.W.*'s first antiwar protesters also show up in the first chapter. When an intrigued Alvarez agreed to meet the "American" delegates to a Hanoi imperialism conference, a "Negro couple" appeared. The goateed Mr. Williams soon admitted that he actually lived in Cuba because he "got into trouble with the law" in his native North Carolina, and when he condemned America as racist—"*Oh, hell,* Ev thought, *a nut*"—Alvarez refused to make tapes for "The Voice of Free Dixie," Williams's pirate radio show. Criminal, stupid, and naive, Williams is the prototype for all Hanoi "visitors," and Alvarez's judgment "that Williams was one of the most ignorant people he had ever met" foreshadowed the general POW reaction to such guests.[31]

Alvarez also introduces the highly charged issues of family support and betrayal. Though his parents' homely advice—"Don't be discouraged . . . keep your chin up . . . do the best you can"—served Alvarez "well for many long years," these same years shattered many marriages, including his own. Before leaving for Vietnam, he told his wife, Tangee, "Don't worry. I may not come home right away but I'm coming home." By not waiting, Tangee turned Alvarez into *P.O.W.*'s archetypic betrayed husband. When Hubbell describes

Alvarez clutching his wife's picture in his cell, and taking comfort from Tangee's faithfulness, the irony is almost indecent: "It was the best thing in his life now, the knowledge that she was waiting, and that she would wait as long as it took." If anything, the foreshadowing is even more heavy handed. Concerned that the Communists "would use the fact that he was married," when Alvarez landed in the water after his shootdown, "He stripped off a glove, removed the ring, held it for a long moment, looking at it, then let it go, watching it sink out of sight."[32] Since Alvarez was the only possible source for such details, episodes like these suggest just how polished the official story was even before before Hubbell began his interviews; in fact, though it adds some details, and provides far more information about his family's duties, Alvarez's own 1989 memoir, *Chained Eagle*, presents the central episodes and their meaning almost exactly as Hubbell had recorded them thirteen years before.

P.O.W. thus begins with an Everyman: an "Old Timer," to quote chapter one, whose story lays out the nuts and bolts of captivity. The official story's featured players—aviator POWs, the Camp Authority, and the antiwar movement—all make their first appearance, and so do pride, duty, family, and religion as a POW's sources of strength. As an officer and pilot held in Hanoi by abusive but doltish captors who tempted him with early release, and tormented by ignorant Americans who urged him to betray his country, Alvarez also set the standard for the many POWs to come by vowing that "when he went home, he would go with his head high. He would be able to face his wife, his parents, his friends in the Navy, and to walk in his home country knowing he had done his best, that he had nothing to apologize for."[33] Most importantly, though, Alvarez's lonely early captivity proves that neither peer pressure nor commands, but values already housed in each true warrior's heart, made POW resistance possible. The official story may record a collective triumph, but the community's strength arises from the power of the individual will.

From Self to Unity—Apostles and Patriarchs

Shortly after putting Adam into the garden, God decided, "It is not good that the man should be alone." Everett Alvarez heartily agreed. Though he would not see another POW until September 1965, when he heard the car carrying Navy Commander Robert H. Shumaker pull into Hoa Lo in February, Alvarez *sighed and turned back to his cell. At last*, he thought, *I'm not alone anymore*."[34] Shumaker's arrival began the process that created the POW community. Though Alvarez always had a special status, Shumaker and the handful of POWs who soon followed were the true founders and elders. Shumaker was sterling material. Eighth in his Naval Academy class, he held advanced degrees in aeronautical engineering and electronics. He flew off aircraft carriers, and had been one of the privileged few screened for astronaut training; he was in short the first senior POW. As "the second American pilot shot down in North Vietnam," however, he also followed in Alvarez's footsteps. Shumaker was just as unnerved by how much the Camp Authority knew about him, and just as "amazed at the apparent stupidity of his interrogators, most of whom had introduced themselves to him as army majors." And like Alvarez, he also learned "he was not a prisoner of war but a 'creemenal.'" These parallels suggest that the Camp Authority was setting its own procedures. From this point on, *P.O.W.* only tells an individual's story when it adds a new wrinkle to the routine. Shumaker for instance was the first Hanoi POW to be "paraded before a number of hate rallies": "At one point, he had thought he was to be beheaded; at another, a crowd of about three thousand seemed intent on stoning him to death; and at another, he stood for ten minutes before a firing squad." Since he broke his back when landing, Shumaker was also the first POW to have his injuries exploited: "He began complaining and pleading incessantly for medical attention. These requests were ignored, and the interrogations continued." His need for medical attention—"he really feared the pain would drive him insane"—forced Shumaker to say something, though "nothing but meaningless or untrue information," but like all true POWs, he "suffered a terrible remorse. He felt that somehow he had betrayed his family and country and wondered, desperately, how to retrieve the situation."[35] What he had actually done of course was to become the first POW to fall back, the strategy which SRO Robinson Risner would later mandate for all POWs. As so often happens in *P.O.W.*, then, an old-timer solved a problem in a way which later became camp policy.

As the chapter title "Finding Friends and Making Codes" suggests, Shumaker's greatest fame came from passing the first POW message. His first attempt failed. Though he left notes in the latrine for Hayden J. Lockhart, the first Air Force POW, Lockhart's poor eyesight allowed the guards to find the notes first. Shumaker thus became the first POW to be threatened for communicating: "Nech time, he was told, we shall have to punish you. Nech time, we shall have to tie you up, and maybe put you in leg irons. Nech time, it will be very bad for you." In May 1965, however, when Shumaker saw another POW through a crack, he left more notes, and this time, "in place of the one he had hidden beneath the loose cement he found another, scratched onto a piece of toilet paper with the charcoaled end of a matchstick. It said simply, 'Storz, Capt., USAF.'" The moment is important for several reasons. Since Shumaker and Storz would both end up in Alcatraz, this exchange was the first contact between two legendary diehards, one of whom would become a Hanoi martyr. Most significantly, though, the note itself was the first link in what rapidly became a campwide message chain. Soon POWs were "scratching their names onto the insides of the flat metal handles of their meal pails, and as the pails circulated a limited communications system began developing between New Guy Village and Heartbreak Hotel." With contact came a shared vocabulary, and though *P.O.W.* uses without comment the names given to sections of Hoa Lo prison, the most famous coining of all does get recorded. On June 1, 1965, Shumaker "scratched a greeting" to a newly arrived POW "to let him know he was not alone and, hopefully, to give him a laugh." The message read "Welcome to the Hanoi Hilton."[36]

A "population explosion" that forced the Camp Authority to put POWs together sped up the community's development. After 133 days in solitary, Shumaker actually spoke with other POWs in late June of 1965, when Air Force First Lieutenant Bob Peel, Air Force Captain "Smitty" Harris, and Navy Lieutenant Phillip N. Butler walked into his cell. These four men drew up the blueprints for the Hanoi POWs' future. Since they expected to be separated again, "the first order of business, Shumaker decided, was to devise some efficient communications systems, ways of sending notes, signaling, and so on." Smitty Harris remembered a tap code supposedly used by the Korean POWs, and this code soon became "nearly second nature to most prisoners." Acronyms and abbreviations appeared instantly, and so did "sophisticated offshoots" such as hand gestures or "coughing, throat clearing, and spitting." This code proved to be very expressive. Someone "who wanted no misunderstanding about what he was saying would spell out every word carefully," as in *P.O.W.*'s example "JOAN BAEZ SUCCS" (there's no K in the code). Messages like "Are you okay?" or "Hang tough, ol' buddy, our prayers are with you!" or "GBU" for "God bless you" helped to raise group morale. The official story therefore specially honors Shumaker, Harris, Peel, and Butler as "the apostles of the communications system that became the blood of POW life": "They established it and taught it to each other. Then, as they were separated, each man taught others, who taught still others."[37]

These POWs were predictably the first captives punished for communicating—they went into isolation for trying to contact someone in solitary—and they also formed the first command unit. They swiftly worked out "that Shumaker was the ranking senior officer (SRO)" and "the mantle of leadership, therefore, fell on him"—but not, however, for long, since the triumvirate of great leaders—Jeremiah Denton, James Stockdale, and Robinson Risner—soon followed the apostles.[38] Hubbell faces a challenge here. If the earliest shootdowns were so admirable, how could these senior POWs deserve even greater praise? He solves this problem by using Larry Guarino to distinguish heroic conduct from heroic leadership. One hundred and fifty World War II missions made this 43-year-old career Air Force major stand out even among the high-ranking Vietnam POWs, and so did his performance as the first diehard. Alvarez and the apostles did not start out with a hard-line reading of the Code, and their misinformation seemed to keep the Camp Authority at bay. Guarino arrived in mid-June 1965 breathing fire. He pulled rank on his captors: "What are you, a corporal or something? I am a major in the United States Air Force. I demand some respect and proper treatment. I demand to see the camp commander." He also insisted on his "rights under Geneva," and when one official called him a criminal who would surely hang, Guarino blurted out "Horsecrap!" For all his bravado, Guarino worried about the future. But he still felt certain that God would help him "to abide by the Code of Conduct, to be a good officer, to do an honorable job as an American prisoner of war." Guarino's zeal soon made him the first physically abused POW. When he unwisely suggested that America might be bombing to avenge his shootdown, "in a sudden paroxysm of rage" his interrogator "landed a roundhouse open-palm slap on the American's face that knocked him from his stool, sending him sprawling across the floor." Guarino refused to back down. He staged a hunger strike to complain about the food, and by remaining silent when asked about American planes, he also became the first POW put into leg stocks.[39]

This hard-liner POW, however, soon desperately needed a leader. When he emerged from isolation, Guarino was "surprised, saddened, angered" to learn that the apostles shared a cell, and even though he knew two of these POWs, he decided they had sold out, and "would have nothing to do with them."[40] When combined with declining health and the stocks, this "betrayal" sent Guarino into a downward spiral which only the arrival of Navy Commander Jeremiah Denton put a stop to. Though Denton remembered having to persuade Guarino that a Navy commander outranked an Air Force major, in *P.O.W.* at least, Denton's "strong" whisper, and "firm, authoritative" voice told Guarino that "the man obviously was a leader." A Naval Academy graduate, this "tough guy from Canoe U" so impressed Guarino that he hid his own suffering to keep Denton strong:

> "Tell me, how are they treating you here?"
> Larry looked down at the stocks locking his right foot and at his skinny body. He did not want to say anything that would worry Denton or adversely affect his morale. If he was going to stay tough, he needed Denton to stay tough.
> "Oh, they're not treating me too badly," he said.
> "Well, don't worry," Denton said, "we'll hack 'er."
> "Yes, sir!" Larry said. "We'll sure hack 'er."[41]

If the ideal composite leader would have John Wayne's bravado, Thomas Jefferson's intellect, and Mother Teresa's compassion, as the team star, coach, and cheerleader all at once, Denton certainly leaned toward the Duke. A man "strongly optimistic by nature," he had pursued his career with "verve, imagination, and the enthusiastic support of his family"—seven children at shootdown. Though a staunch Catholic, Denton was prepared to kill himself rather than aid the enemy, an act he would "defend before the throne of Heaven" as falling "on the field of battle in defense of his country." Denton's take-charge approach shook the depression out of the Hanoi camps. After contacting the apostles, who to Larry's chagrin proved to have been resisting all along, SRO Denton issued the first campwide POW policy: " 'Follow the Code of Conduct,' he ordered. 'Think about escape. I want a note about it every day, and I want a map of this camp.' " Denton's optimism could however also lead to impulsive mistakes. Even *P.O.W.* admits that one escape attempt "did not extend beyond tearing a hole in the cell wall; it had not been entirely rational."[42] Though Denton could lift other POWs' spirits, only a cagey, calculating leader could sustain these spirits over the long haul.

This leader hero was Jim Stockdale, the highest-ranking Navy POW and Denton's longtime friend. Almost everything written about Stockdale stresses his intelligence. Another Naval Academy graduate, he had also studied international relations and philosophy at Stanford, where he wrote a Master's thesis on Southeast Asian history. Though he broke his back, shoulder, and leg during shootdown, resisting was his first concern: "How smart, how tough would one have to be to withstand brainwashing?" Unlike the optimist Denton, Stockdale believed "this was going to be a long war. Somehow, he had to buy himself some time and plot a proper course. There could be no leaks, no surrender of precious information." Though his injuries and isolation often distanced him from the other POWs, and though his own memoirs display a philosophic melancholy which could alienate him at times from the other POWs during the days of torture, Stockdale served as the Code's interpreter and judge.[43]

And what Stockdale might have lacked in fellow feeling, Air Force Lieutenant Colonel Robinson Risner possessed in abundance. A Korean War ace, early in 1965 Risner appeared on the cover of *Time* "as the classic example of the kind of dedicated, military professional who was leading the American effort in Vietnam." Arriving on September 16, a week after Stockdale, Risner served as the Hanoi SRO for more than two years. In Risner, heroism and command came together in a pious, domestic nature: "Deeply religious, he was at peace with God, and engaged in activity he knew to be absolutely right. He had no regrets over anything he had ever done and he was not afraid to die. But he could not ward off a deep sadness at the prospect of long separation from his family." Though Denton and Stockdale also had families, in *P.O.W.* Risner is the patriarch—the kind of officer men called "the old man." Though his wife's eyes, "abrim with tears," haunted him, he made the best of things by turning the POWs into his surrogate family.[44]

Although Stockdale's injuries kept him isolated until the days of torture truly began, to new arrivals like Ed Davis, these leaders were "very impressive company." Davis had briefly encountered some men in Heartbreak Hotel, but he received his real orientation in New Guy Village from Jeremiah Denton. Davis had "boundless admiration for this tough, sharp senior officer," who "remained cheerful and kept his attentions focused on the present situation, made it clear he meant to provide strong leadership to any who were junior to him." His "unfailingly and infectiously optimistic" nature raised Davis's fighting spirits—and then SRO Robinson Risner set his future course. Shortly after Davis was moved to the Zoo, a vaguely familiar POW dropped down in front of his cell and "began doing push-ups and speaking, in low tones—but the voice was smooth, confident, reassuring": "Good morning, Ed. I am Colonel Risner. Call me Robbie. I'm senior officer in the camp. We've got things going for us. We've got some pretty good communications established.

I've heard some good things about you, and it's awfully nice to have you with us." Davis was shocked, flattered, and inspired: "*Robbie Risner! Ed thought. Of course I've seen him before, on the cover of* Time! *He was an ace in Korea, he's the Air Force's best, and he thinks it's nice to have me with him!*" Davis listened eagerly as Risner "briefed him on the camp routine and verbally supplied a lengthy operational order, which was a plan to live by."[45] Though Risner clearly believed that "strong leadership was vital if men were to survive and resist effectively," his "orders and thoughts" also made sense. Risner for instance "urged that POWs who had been behaving insolently toward the guards stop doing so; satisfying though such conduct might be, it was worse than fruitless, for it resulted in the withholding of food." Such advice did not however mean he was timid or weak. As SRO, Risner formally requested brooms, beds, lights, better hygiene, and daily exercise. When the Camp Authority ignored him, he ordered his men to ask God for the same things, since "in Risner's judgment, the POWs had few weapons available to them, and far from the least of these was prayer." Such orders had their lighter side—one Catholic POW puzzled over "how to pray in Latin for a broom"—but the result was a union of discipline, loyalty, and devotion that became synonymous with Risner: "Be good Americans," he told his men, "Live by the Code of Conduct. Pray together at one PM each day for unification of effort."[46]

By October 1965, the POWs' steady movement toward unity had spurred the Camp Authority into escalating its efforts to make its captives serve North Vietnamese ends. In the Barn, POWs "deemed especially bad attitude cases"—"Ed Davis, Wes Schierman, Bob Shumaker and others"—were undergoing "prolonged interrogation."[47] Risner and Ron Storz would soon join them, as the Camp Authority prepared the hard-liners for special treatment. Quiz sessions already meant six or seven hours on the stool—a low-grade torture technique that hinted at what lay ahead. But by tightening up their own ranks, the POWs themselves were preparing for the future as well. One striking example occurred when Everett Alvarez's long isolation came to an end. On his first Sunday at the Briarpatch, he repeated the Lord's Prayer, the Pledge of Allegiance, and the Star Spangled Banner, knowing that others nearby were doing the same thing. The sense of community was overpowering: "Like him, they were hungry, unshaven, stinking dirty, and locked up in hot reeking cells a half-world away from the country and people they loved. But none was feeling sorry for himself. In the best sense, they were behaving as American military men should. They were organized, together in prayer, asking for guidance and strength." As the Sunday service ended, Alvarez "wept unashamedly, but not in sadness. He was nearly bursting with pride at being part of such a company of men."[48] Describing how this community would respond to the challenge of torture is *P.O.W.*'s most important task.

The Ropes—Persecution and the Early Church Militant

One hundred pages carry *P.O.W.* from August 1964 to "sometime after dawn on Tuesday, October 19, 1965," when Navy Lieutenant Rodney Knutson went into the ropes.[49] The ensuing "long horror" slows the pace considerably: the rest of 1965 takes forty-five pages, and 1966 takes almost ninety more. As the first Hanoi POW to be tortured, Knutson's importance to the official story can't be overstated. Hubbell devotes thirty pages—more than he uses for all of 1972—to Knutson's suffering between October 19th and 31st. Like Alvarez's "typical" shootdown, this excruciating episode becomes the "typical" torture which all true POWs passed through, and regarded almost as a sacrament.

Knutson seemed doomed from the start. He killed someone while resisting capture, which guaranteed special treatment, and his own combativeness was aroused by his public display before reaching Hanoi: "He was angry, astonished at military men who would expose a captured military man to the populace and behave in such a fashion." During his first interrogation, he was further "appalled that the enemy would so grossly violate the rules of warfare, and that apparently he was expected to casually betray his oath as an American military officer and the American fighting man's Code of Conduct." At this moment, *P.O.W.* prints the Code's six articles, with Knutson supplying the hard-line interpretation. Since as a "military professional" he "still had a war to fight for his country," Knutson adopted the strategy that became official story orthodoxy: "The Code. Those were his orders now. He would live by them and, if necessary, die by them."[50] What followed brought Knutson close to this necessity. His interrogators called him a "piratical air pirate," a "malicious murderer," and an "imperialist aggressor." Though they threatened severe punishment, he still wouldn't answer questions, and soon he was in a cell with rats the size of jackrabbits. When his guards discovered he had thrown some food into his toilet bucket, the Camp Authority demanded an apology to the Vietnamese people, but Knutson refused. This was the trip wire: what follows in *P.O.W.* is the longest account of torture to be found in any Vietnam POW narrative.[51]

His ankles went into stocks, his arms into the ropes. When he still wouldn't apologize, the guards slapped and punched him until his nose and teeth broke. After some forty blows, they turned him over and hit his buttocks with a bamboo club; soon blood was spattering the wall with each stroke. Knutson finally screamed, but the guards just went away, leaving him in the ropes "writhing in an agony he would never have believed men could inflict on other men." Surveillance was now part of the punishment. Whenever he flopped on his side or passed out, a guard burst in and beat him. As time passed, interrogation became the only relief from the ropes—he was questioned at least sixteen times over these ten days—and as the pain perversely became routine, Knutson's hard-line resistance started slipping. A fear, "not of death, but of life," rose in him: "He actually became afraid that his torturers would not kill him, but would keep him alive and keep torturing him." When however he steeled himself once more, the Camp Authority crossed a new threshold of cruelty. Knutson went back into the ropes, but this time the guards tied another rope to his tightly bound arms, ran it through a hook in the ceiling, then hoisted him up into the air. This was his limit: "He needed time, and at this moment his body could buy him no more time. He had to change his tactics, talk, tell lies. He knew that if he were found out he would be tortured again, but he needed more time. 'Wait a minute,' he said. 'I'll talk to you.'"[52] At this moment, he became the first POW to fall back from torture.

As his body recovered, Knutson stuck to his survival training, keeping "his untrue stories simple and easy to remember as the interrogator continued to press him for military and biographical information." If anything, though, guilt was Knutson's greater tormentor: "He had never been so disappointed in himself. They had broken him, made him talk! He knew he had given them absolutely nothing of value; yet he could not dissuade himself that he had let his country down." Nor did regaining contact with other Americans help at first. After Knutson told "his tale of horror" to the men in Heartbreak, he discovered that no one else had been tortured yet. Their "consensus" was therefore "that he had brought the unspeakable treatment upon himself, that his attitude toward his captors had been more belligerent, more aggressive than necessary." Since only a higher authority could redeem Knutson now, he "turned for an opinion to SRO Stockdale," whose reply would set POW policy for years to come: " 'I think you did a fine job, Rod,' Stockdale said. 'I think you took the right approach. Give them nothing; make them take it from you, and make sure they take nothing of value. You did just fine. Hang in there.' "[53] Stockdale's "encouraging words" assigned two new duties. A tortured POW *must* confess what he had said or done, and the other POWs *must* forgive and support him.

Swiftly changing conditions also ended any tendency to blame the victim. Within a few weeks, Knutson's torture was simply the most extreme "rough stuff" going on in the Hanoi camps. Human excrement contaminated the food. POWs went on short rations, into handcuffs, or into contorted positions for long periods. Bob Shumaker was thrown into profound isolation, and Ensign Ralph Gaither, Knutson's pilot, suffered through a time-honored sadistic charade when his interrogator "had a guard hold a rifle barrel to Ralph's temple and squeeze the trigger. It clicked against an empty chamber."[54] The Camp Authority was also paying special attention to POW leaders. SRO Risner almost suffocated on newspaper balls stuffed into his mouth as punishment for communicating. He ended up in leg stocks and isolation.[55] For the official story, then, Knutson's torture was as much of a beginning as Alvarez's capture. Only when the Camp Authority started torturing POWs to make them violate their Code did the struggle begin in earnest—and "by the end of October 1965, the battle was joined in the prison camps of North Vietnam."[56]

Other POWs soon shared Knutson's fate. On November 23rd, Navy Commander Harry Jenkins became "the first senior officer to be thrust into torture immediately on arriving in Hanoi." Jenkins went into the ropes far more quickly after capture; he was also the first victim of that cool, efficient torturer the POWs called Pigeye or Straps and Bars. Jenkins's remorse after submitting and his confession to the other POWs follow Knutson's example precisely. Speaking "compulsively, like a repentant sinner seeking forgiveness," Jenkins described his torture, and admitted he had gone beyond the Big Four. Though the ensuing silence made him fear "that all had been tortured as he had, had suffered it without breaking, and were displeased with his poor performance," Jenkins misread the response. Knutson could perhaps have been a fluke, but Knutson *and* Jenkins pointed to "an organized torture program": "And so in the silence that Harry mistook for censure, each of his fellow inmates was actually wondering how long before he would be tortured and how he would perform."[57] Though virtually all of these men would learn the answer to both questions, *P.O.W.*'s most sustained example of a man who remained dignified, compassionate, and forgiving even under horrifying conditions was not surprisingly one of the official story's hero leaders. Caught trying to send messages from his isolated cell, the self-proclaimed SRO Robinson Risner came in for even more special treatment. The guards taped his eyes shut and for over an hour walked him up stairs, through filthy water, and into trees. Then came the ropes. Risner's shoulder dislocated instantly, but when he groaned, someone punched him repeatedly in the face. Risner did not feel these blows, thanks to the "agony that was in him, a living evil, writhing into every nerve ending." Left alone, he tried but failed to strangle himself. He then started banging his head on the floor—"if he were lucky, he might be able to knock himself dead." Finally, like Knutson and the others, Risner offered to talk, but his fame as a POW—"There is nobody we would rather have captured except Johnson, Rusk, and McNamara"—spurred his captors on to extorting a "complete, unconditional surrender."[58]

When he dropped back into Heartbreak, Risner confessed: "He wanted the others to know that he had resisted to the best of his ability, but that he had been broken, that statements had been extracted from him that he did not believe." As SRO, though, Risner had to bounce back faster, since "men needed strength and encouragement, and it was incumbent on him to provide it." Self-hatred and "private anguish" must give way to duty; like the evangelists, he had to lead, teach, and endure. As the most overtly religious patriarch, he also had to regain full faith in God's love. During his worst moments, Risner had like the Savior wondered about God's plan: "He still was confident that God would let him die before He would allow his country's enemy to extract more from him than he was allowed to give. But where was death? Where was oblivion? Where was anything but the pain that kept mounting toward a crescendo and never reached it?" And yet, though falling back might have shaken another man's faith, in his first orders after torture Risner urged his men to pray "for themselves and each other, for those at home who waited for them, for their country, even for their captors: 'Remember that the Vietnamese are God's children, too. He loves them as much as He loves you and your children. What is happening is all in His plan. Have faith. God loves you. He won't forget you. Everything will work out as He wills it.'"[59] Many POWs felt far less charitable, and more than a few would never forgive those who had trespassed against them. Risner's own pious humanity and modesty nevertheless argued implicitly that God's love could sustain them in their trials.

P.O.W.'s version of 1966 is largely a catalogue of atrocities, as exploiting the POWs for propaganda reasons became the Camp Authority's major activity. Signed confessions or attacks on American policy were mandatory. Stockdale and Denton both went into the ropes; Knutson suffered through two more ghastly sessions. The increasing violence also turned the POWs into more organized resisters. Hubbell uses Navy Lieutenant Gerald Coffee, the first shootdown of 1966, to show how the senior POWs had responded to the events of late 1965. Coffee began his orientation by reading a message carved into his Heartbreak cell wall: "God will find strength. Robinson Risner, September 18, 1965." Risner himself soon contacted Coffee and two other shootdowns, who listened in horror as their new SRO, "who wanted the younger officers prepared for the worst," described his own torture. He then recited "the names of every prisoner he knew had been at Hoa Lo and the Zoo and ordered them committed to memory." After teaching these new POWs the tap code, Risner closes with directions which show just how concise camp policy had become: "Remember, we are only going to be here a short time. Do the very best you can. Go home proud. The Lord will never ask you to endure more than you are able. Remember to pray for the Vietnamese."[60]

This advice was important because around this time some POWs began arguing that provoking torture was self-defeating. *P.O.W.* discounts these soft-liners by refusing to give their names, and by questioning their motives through a vignette featuring Bob Shumaker. When Shumaker ignored some questions, his interrogator produced documents signed by POWs which gave the answers. Shumaker simply assumed they "had been tortured for their comments, and he was girded for torture himself." He was therefore shocked to learn sometime later that these POWs had supplied the documents "without being brutalized," and simply "could not understand why Bob had risked torture over something so trivial."[61] Though this "debate over tactics would go on for years," *P.O.W.*'s synopsis of the soft-liner position clearly sets its value: "Be smart. Play it by ear. Give a little where it doesn't matter. When it comes to information of military or propaganda value, lie. If you can't get away with it, then it's time to clam up." Casuistic and self-centered, this "policy of deceit" was Korea's "play it cool" strategy, and *P.O.W* ringingly presents the hard-line policy as a necessary corrective. Under "a strict interpretation of the Code of Conduct" like the one "SRO Denton" circulated, torture was mandatory: "No writing. No taping. Die before giving classified information. Take torture until in danger of losing mental faculties, then give a phony story. Keep it simple and easy to remember." When the soft-liners raised a host of quibbling objections, their apparent "inability to apply common sense in a situation where communications were at increasingly higher risk" led a frustrated Denton to issue "a blanket, inviolable order: No writing. No taping."[62] The implications of this policy for POW history were enormous. Since the more someone was tortured, the more successful was his resistance, the early hard-liners inevitably became the principal POW heroes. But the official story goes further by crediting the bounce back policy with eventually ending the torture. Though Denton issued the order to undergo torture, in *P.O.W.* Risner and Stockdale get the credit for explaining the policy: " 'Don't sweat it if they torture something out of you,' they told the new POWs. 'We have all been through it. The most important thing is to get back up as quickly as you can and get set for the next round. You're going to get depressed. If it is at all possible to do so, contact someone else. Talk about it. Don't keep it to yourself. Just talking about it helps.' "[63] Though the number of weak, confused, and self-serving POWs supposedly grew over the years, the leader heroes' advice, while compassionate, granted little latitude. Since the clashes between the Camp Authority and the POWs were battles between evil and truth, in the official story at least, demanding torture was quite simply a duty.

The most public battle between captive and captor was the Hanoi Parade of July 1966. Earlier that year, some POWs had been forced into making appearances as part of the ongoing propaganda campaign. The leftist journalist Wilfred Burchett had talked to some men, and an interview with Japanese television reporters gave Jeremiah Denton the chance to blink out "*torture*" in Morse code.[64] What excited the Camp Authority most, however, was Bertrand Russell's proposed "international war crimes tribunal." When the camp radio announced that the "justly wrathful people" of Vietnam were "having meetings and demanding trials for the criminal air pirates," the Hanoi prisoners made their own plans: "POWs who were threatened with war crimes trials were to deny that Hanoi had a right to try them; were to demand legal representation by the United States government; were to stand mute if taken to trial without such counsel; and if forced to speak were to defend the United States' position to the best of their abilities."[65]

Nothing, however, could have prepared the POWs for the Hanoi Parade. Though a U.S. air attack on North Vietnam's fuel supplies was the immediate cause, *P.O.W.* suggests that the government's frustration at the POWs' resistance also had its effect. In any case, "On July 6, fifty-two American POWs tasted the rage" of Hanoi. As they climbed into waiting vehicles, these POWs first thought they were going home. When "the trucks pulled into a big stadium in Hanoi," however, the optimism "dissipated." "Ooooh," murmured POW Ed Davis, "lions three, Christians zero. I've seen this game before!" While sitting in the trucks, the POWs learned captivity's new rules. "The time had come to decide whether they were going to repent their crimes and join with the Vietnamese people in seeking a just end to Washington's 'illegal and immoral' war, or to continue on their belligerent ways. Those who did not repent would be tried as war criminals. The path for them would be the path of death." Having thus introduced the Make A Choice program, the officials then promised a preview of what diehards could expect. "Now you are going to see the hatred of the Vietnamese people," an official told the POWs: "We are going to try to protect you, but we are not going to kill any Vietnamese in doing so. So if the people want to kill you they are going to kill you." Submission would be advisable: "Do not look to the right or to the left, do not look behind you. Do not speak. Walk straight ahead. Show a proper attitude to the Vietnamese people. Bow your head in shame for your crimes."[66]

The POWs were proud and irreverent. Wisecracks flew as they headed toward their unknown destination—"Oh, boy!" joked Bob Purcell. "A parade! I love a parade!"—but the POWs also vowed to stand tall. "Let's hold our heads and shoulders high. Let's look like Americans," Purcell suggested, and when Jeremiah Denton saw cameras ahead, he made this suggestion an order: " 'Keep your heads up!' he shouted, 'Don't bow your heads.' "[67] The POWs then plunged into a furious waiting mob. A scene from hell followed—or more accurately, from Christ's torments on the way to his crucifixion. The obscene, frenzied, yet obviously rehearsed English chants demanded submission. The whole group heard "*Bow! Bow! Bow your head, filthy Yankee son of a bitch!*" which gave way to "*Shoot the Yanks! Shoot the Yanks! You son of a bitch Yankee!*" and then to "*Chonson murderer! Rusk murderer! Mocknomara son of a bitch! Fuck you, Yank!*" Everett Alvarez was personally greeted with "*Alvarā, Alvarā, son of a bitch, son of a bitch!*" Suddenly, the civilians rushed the POWs, and Alvarez realized, "*We might not make it through this thing*": "The crowds were out of control, in the grip of a powerful, unmanageable hysteria. Hundreds of thousands of people had become a lynch mob. The guards were powerless, and too frightened now even to try to retrieve control." And yet, though the "shrieking fury of the mobs, the cursing, spitting, and beating of the Americans never slackened," the manacled POWs kept their heads high, and after surging through the stadium doors to safety, they proudly decided, "We did okay. Great show!"[68]

The night unfortunately was young. If the parade itself echoed the procession to Calvary, what followed was definitely the crucifixion. "You have seen the just wrath of the Vietnamese people," a loudspeaker barked out: "Those of you who have seen the light and want to apologize for your crimes and join the Vietnamese people will receive lenient and humane treatment." Then, presumably to impress this lesson upon the POWs, the guards staged what became known as the "Garden Party." Blindfolded and handcuffed to trees, the POWs were "gagged with towels and socks, stuffed into their mouths and deep into their throats. Then guards strolled about, taking turns inflicting savage beatings and kickings."[69] Jeremiah Denton makes the martyrdom theme explicit. Even though "the now filthy, sweat-, blood-, and dirt-soaked rags that had been used to tie the sandals to his feet during the parade were crammed into his mouth," he coughed out his initials in code, and "back came two answering coughs": "The only one he could make out was 'J.C.' He giggled to himself, *There are three of us here, and 'J.C.' is in the middle—I'm the repentant thief!* Then he realized that 'J.C.' was Jerry Coffee."[70]

As the first test of the POWs' collective strength, the Hanoi Parade was a crucial event. Hubbell in fact suggests that the parade's failure as propaganda altered the POWs' treatment. By foolishly releasing films of the POWs getting beaten in the streets of Hanoi, the North Vietnamese not only embarrassed their American antiwar allies, but provoked dire warnings from Lyndon Johnson and other world leaders about the consequences of putting POWs on trial. There was never another parade; instead, the Camp Authority plunged into the Make A Choice program. The reasons for this frenzied bout of extortion remain vague. Since world opinion was so against North Vietnam putting POWs on trial, perhaps the idea was to generate materials for helpful outsiders like Bertrand Russell. In any case, as 1966 dragged on, the Camp Authority "continued to extract 'confessions' and 'apologies' to be presented to someone, somewhere, sometime." Some of the most embarrassing tapes, letters, and petitions came from this time, and though some men were already following a soft-line position on torture, *P.O.W.* doesn't mention them, preferring instead to let sentences like "There were fifty-six POWs at the Briarpatch, and Frenchy went after them all" suggest that torture scarred everyone worth knowing about.[71]

For almost thirty pages, the Camp Authority drags POWs into interrogation and demands their "choice." When each man chooses America, and thus death, torture forces him to submit. *P.O.W.*'s long list of victims makes the process seem universal. Wendy Rivers, Ray Merritt, Jerry Coffee, Duffy Hutton, Robbie Risner, Larry Guarino, Jeremiah

Denton, Jim Mulligan, John Borling, Norlan Daughtrey, Al Lurie, Darrel Pyle, Larry Spencer, Howie Rutledge, Jim Bell, Jon Reynolds, George McKnight, Rod Knutson, Everett Alvarez, Tom Barrett, Bob Shumaker, Smitty Harris, Jim Kasler, Jack Fellowes, Dick Bolstad, and Bob Lilly pass in turn through the wringer, with Hubbell lingering at times over their suffering. Harry Jenkins also appears as the first example of a "rolling" prisoner—the only kind of POW who could make statements without undergoing torture. Unlike soft-liners or collaborators, who avoided torture by doing what the Camp Authority wanted, a rolling prisoner endured torture until totally disoriented, "rolled" only until he could regain his strength, then returned to torture. One bad session left Jenkins helpless, and he sadly wrote whenever his captors requested. "What he did not understand," however, "was that he was 'rolling'—a term that would be invented later by Jerry Denton—while he searched within himself for the mental and spiritual strength he needed to bounce back from the earlier torture." Jenkins' intense guilt at "violating the Code of Conduct" soon rekindled his desire to resist, and when asked to make his choice, he proudly said, "I'll take uncertainty and death."[72]

As 1966 turned into 1967, the 151 POWs held in the system felt that "a phase of captivity had ended." The Hanoi Parade had been a disaster: "Washington had not been intimidated; the reaction—both from the Administration and from antiwar leaders—had been strongly negative." But campwide torture had failed as well. By trying to "destroy the will of the senior officers to take command, and to destroy the will of all prisoners to communicate," the Camp Authority had hoped to "break and subjugate the entire American prisoner population." Instead, the POWs had "formulated and disseminated a strong resistance policy," and as the new year dawned, the Camp Authority "was satisfied that steamroller tactics were unproductive, and abandoned them." Though its new strategy of applying pressure "on a somewhat more selective basis and for specific purposes" would actually prove more divisive, the POWs considered this shift a triumph.[73] Part one of *P.O.W.* thus ends with the official story's guiding principles fully introduced. Only those who survived the early days with honor and those who followed their example have a full claim to POW history. The official story is *their* story; later arrivals are for the most part students to be initiated, or problems to be solved. As the camp population grew, and the abuse became less systematic, this history increasingly replaced shared torment as the senior POWs' principal authority.

A People Together, A People Apart—
Backsliding, Heresy, and the Purge

The example of Naval Commander Richard Stratton suggests that in 1967, the Camp Authority's policies fluctuated as rapidly as the American war effort. Shot down on January 5th, Stratton was "a Communist propagandist's dream." A "big, heavy-set, dark-visaged, tough-looking American with a deep voice," he seemed "the very model of an arrogant American imperialist." When the Camp Authority tortured him into appearing at a March 6 press conference as the "mad bomber of Hanoi," he responded with his notorious bowing zombie performance.[74] The photograph appeared in the April 7th issue of *Life*, and the North Vietnamese instantly learned they had blundered. According to *Time*, "Stratton's 'Pavlovian performance' had 'Orwellian impact' that 'unsettled even hard-boiled communist newsmen.' " Brainwashing and torture were public issues once again, and the U.S. government was forced to break its policy of silence, as Averell Harriman, who already knew about torture from encoded Stockdale letters and Jeremiah Denton's blinking, tepidly concluded that "from the photographs, videotapes, and descriptions by eyewitnesses that I have seen of the so-called 'news' conference at which Commander Stratton was exhibited, it would appear that the North Vietnamese are using mental or physical pressure on American prisoners of war."[75] After this public relations disaster, the Camp Authority started swinging wildly between abuse and special privileges. Stratton himself was "such an embarrassment to his captors that eventually they would try to fatten him up and send him home early." In late June, an East German crew began filming *Pilots in Pajamas*, a documentary whose "purpose was to depict the American POWs as ordinary mortals, indeed even weaklings, who were being treated leniently and humanely by their Vietnamese captors." Stratton was prominently featured; he was also moved to Plantation Gardens, a model camp shown to sympathetic visitors even though aside from a few spruced-up cells conditions were "actually no better than at Hoa Lo or the Zoo."[76]

Since torture had ruined all attempts to "reeducate" the POWs, the North Vietnamese decided to let other Americans do the teaching. Early in 1967, "the POWs found themselves listening to many of their most prominent countrymen, including high-ranking members of government, not only questioning America's course of action in Southeast Asia, but even condemning it in the most virulent terms." Taped speeches by Wayne Morse, Martin Luther King, Linus Pauling, Benjamin Spock, and Robert F. Kennedy left the prisoners feeling "bewildered, depressed, betrayed": "POWs who had been suffering torture in preference to making such statements could not understand such talk from other Americans, especially from members of their own government, for whose policies they had been committed to combat and were enduring vile captivity." Since however "the large majority of prisoners believed wholeheartedly in the American effort," these speeches seldom led to conversions.[77] A far greater threat to POW unity was the chance for early release. Although parolees didn't leave Hanoi until February 1968, as early as mid-1966 the Make a Choice program was offering the "opportunity to go home even before the war is over." According to *P.O.W.*, the world's "horrified speculation" over Stratton forced the Camp Authority into training some parolees to replace him as "typical" POWs:

> Doubtless, these would be men who had suffered little or no mistreatment themselves, who had been kept so isolated that they knew little or nothing of the enemy's atrocious treatment of the bulk of POWs, or who had been made so fearful by threats of blackmail for statements yielded freely or under minimal pressure that they could be depended upon not to blow the whistle on Hanoi for its treatment of American prisoners.

This "dangerous new approach" pitted "the POWs against each other in a competition for early release." Since "no discipline, no loyalty to any cause save one's own well-being" could survive such a contest, Jim Stockdale reacted decisively: "No one, he ordered, was to accept early release." This is the official story's position on parole. The Make a Choice program was a "fink release program," and almost all of the Hanoi parolees were finks: "12 POWs were to accept early release, 11 officers and one enlisted man. Only the enlisted man, Douglas Hegdahl, was not in violation of Stockdale's order—Hegdahl's release really amounted to a reluctant escape."[78]

Successfully resisting parole did not however rule out more subtle threats, as the 1967 controversy over tape recording suggests. The Camp Authority began coercing various POWs to read aloud news stories and other propaganda materials for broadcast over the camp radio. Although these men often sabotaged these tapes—virtually everyone, for instance, pronounced Ho Chi Minh as "Horseshit Men"—Jim Stockdale detected a slippery slope. Later POWs might not be clever enough to pull such tricks; others might get too cocky and unconsciously collaborate. Stockdale thus declared that "*to read on the camp radio requires a license. The fee for this license is one week in irons. This license is good for only one week and thereafter must be renewed.*" This miniature version of Bounce Back was designed "to hold to a minimum an activity that could not possibly be stopped." The same intent shaped BACK US, that "general policy to give POWs guidance on practical questions not covered by the Code of Conduct" which Hubbell mentions shortly afterwards.[79]

As *P.O.W.* leaps between camps and cells, 1967 becomes disjointed and quirky. Summer 1967, or "The Meanest of Times" was when the Camp Authority went after the POW command. Told in April that "you must choose to cooperate with us and live, or oppose us and die," Robinson Risner lost his cellmate in July, and torture cuffs and a darkened isolation cell put him out of touch until June 1968.[80] It was "the Stockdale Purge," however, that showed how frustrated the Camp Authority was becoming at its failure to intimidate the POWs. Officials knew Stockdale was the "chief of resistance": "He was the most senior, the leader, the chief troublemaker. Stockdale had to be brought down." To this end, the Camp Authority tortured its way up the ranks, laying bare the command structure while keeping its primary goal, to "make a domestic animal" out of Stockdale, always in sight. Stockdale himself stayed optimistic. Though "he and other leaders would be found out and their organization smashed," he assumed "they would be sent to different camps, carrying the gospel of resistance with them, and the process would begin anew." When an interrogator screamed at him that "your instructions have even been understood at camps many kilometers from here" and that "you set our treatment regime back two years," Stockdale was therefore flattered. When torture eventually forced him to write out his "central committee," he responded with a list of 212 names in rank order: "'This is the organization,' Stockdale insisted. 'It is an unbroken line. It is like a living organism. There is no way you can destroy it. Take me away, and Denton will take command. Take me and take Denton, and Jenkins will take charge. . . . Nothing will change no matter who you take. This is the American military organization.' "[81]

The Camp Authority's last stab at ideological conversion occurred around the same time, when a Caucasian interrogator—probably Cuban, and instantly dubbed "Fidel"—arrived with great fanfare. Fidel was not violent at first; apparently his mission was "to make the Americans cooperative without physically torturing them." Instead, through wild emotional shifts, polemics against American imperialism, and gross verbal abuse, Fidel launched a "psychological attack" against a small number of POWs held at the Zoo. When however his guinea pigs easily resisted these mind games, Fidel's own behavior degenerated. Becoming "increasingly impatient and nasty," he began slapping on torture cuffs, hitting the POWs repeatedly, and screaming "*Surrender!*" as loudly as the Camp Authority ever had. As Fidel further descended into sadism and madness, all hope for ideological conversion went with him.[82]

For *P.O.W.*, 1967's most important date was October 25th, when the Camp Authority chopped the head off the POWs' "living organism." Isolating Risner in August had not broken the command chain; Stockdale had simply taken charge. The resulting Stockdale purge had however uncovered the true diehards, those "men to whom the other criminals looked for guidance, for inspiration, for leadership." Following the Korean example, the Camp Authority moved these "eleven American arch-criminals" into an isolated set of cells that the inmates called Alcatraz.[83] In the official story, membership in the Alcatraz Gang stands as the highest possible POW honor. So dangerous that they had to be hidden for more than two years, so hard-line that after fifteen months SRO Jim Stockdale was moved from Alcatraz to break up the command chain forged there, these men were charter members of the Vietnam POW Hall of Fame. Eleven men went to Alcatraz, and all but Ron Storz returned—the POW whose name stands first in *P.O.W.*'s dedication. The Alcatraz Gang is also the most heavily documented group of POWs. Jim Stockdale, Jeremiah Denton, James Mulligan, Sam Johnson, and Howard Rutledge have all published books, and Bob Shumaker and Harry Jenkins gave long interviews after release. These seven men were joined by George Coker and George McKnight, whose joint escape attempt had earned them their place in Alcatraz. Nels Tanner had been responsible for an especially humiliating propaganda failure when the North Vietnamese had joyfully released to the world his confession that Clark Kent and Ben Casey were wavering American pilots. Though isolated from the other men for over two years, the Alcatraz POWs felt their seniority and hard-liner status made it their right and their duty to compose the official version of Vietnam POW history. Their own books and interviews, and their prominence in *P.O.W.*, strongly suggest that they exercised this right.

On December 31, 1967, Robinson Risner was in isolation. He would be there for six more months. His toughest subordinates were in Alcatraz: they would not emerge until December 9, 1969. Conditions in Hanoi were still appalling, men were still being tortured, and Fidel was tormenting a select group at the Zoo. Nevertheless, the Hanoi POWs were hanging on. New heroes were also arriving: Air Force Major Bud Day, for instance, who would eventually win the Medal of Honor, or the grievously wounded John McCain, the future senator from Arizona. These scattered events combine to make a single point. Though the Camp Authority tried to seduce or demoralize its POWs, the Hanoi organization remained strong, as unity stayed before self. The population's steady increase might hint that a silent, unpredictable majority was forming up, but as part two ends, the hard-liners still dominate *P.O.W.*

Brief Interlude: Stories from Elsewhere

After almost 400 pages on how unity before self carried the Hanoi POWs from mid-1964 through 1967, Hubbell finally notes that "in South Vietnam, other captured Americans lived horror stories of their own."[84] Nowhere is *P.O.W.* more "definitive" than here. Introduced at the moment when early release, soft-line pragmatism, and internal dissent are beginning to threaten the Hanoi POW command chain, the jungle POWs act as terrifying examples of what happened to captives who lacked the senior Hanoi POWs' strength, intelligence, and discipline. *P.O.W.*'s narrative radically subordinates these jungle POWs. Part two flashes back almost four years to record the March 26, 1964, capture of Army Green Beret Captain Jim Thompson, "a tough, professional soldier" whose light reconnaissance plane was shot down near Khe Sanh. Thompson knew his duty and did it. Though he broke his back in the crash, he still thought of escape. After capture he refused to give military information and endured the blows. Long marches, illness, malnutrition, and the bush clearing, wood gathering, and cooking that most jungle POWs had to do to survive drained Thompson, but even when threatened with execution he kept refusing to talk. Only after five months in this "overly stressful situation" did he finally fall back and sign a prepared statement.[85] Like Alvarez in Hanoi, then, Thompson first encountered those "typical" conditions and torments that later jungle POWs would confront. The result, however, was very different. If anything, Alvarez prepared the way for even more talented and dedicated men, while Thompson set a standard that few jungle POWs would match.

P.O.W.'s jungle history then jolts forward more than three years. After his helicopter was shot down in November of 1967, Captain Floyd Kushner was taken to a small VC camp holding some South Vietnamese and three American POWs. As an Army doctor, he "correctly gave himself no marks as a military leader."[86] Nevertheless, this high-ranking professional was *P.O.W.*'s primary source for how enlisted POWs held up in the jungle. Though the physical conditions shocked Kushner, "the most depressing thing about the place was the Americans he found in it." The Hanoi POWs' emphasis on patriotism, the Code, and the command chain implicitly damns these jungle prisoners from the moment they appear. Of the two Puerto Rican enlisted men, Luis A. Ortiz-Rivera and Jose Agusto-Santos, only Agusto-Santos spoke English, and by instantly accepting parole shortly after Kushner arrived, they become prototypes for those enlisted men whose desire to go home erased any sense of duty. The third prisoner, a Marine Lance Corporal whom Hubbell calls "Roberts," "had been captured too long ago, and had too long been denied proper treatment or any hope of freedom"—a telling remark, since *P.O.W.* would never offer this kind of excuse for a Hanoi officer. Early suffering could however break a corporal's will: "Roberts insisted escape was impossible. Nor, he said, was there any hope that the war would end soon. He insisted his only chance for freedom was for the Vietnamese to release him. Kushner could not dissuade him." Such desperation had turned Roberts into a traitor. Upon meeting Kushner, he had "launched into a bitter condemnation of the American 'aggression' in Vietnam." Sometime later, he reported their conversation about freedom to the camp commander, and excused this "ratting" by claiming that "the Vietnamese knew everything their prisoners said and thought anyway." In awe of the VCs' "mystical power over us," Roberts was a self-proclaimed fink: "If you don't want them to know anything, don't tell it to me. I want to be released so badly that I'll tell them anything you tell me."[87] Roberts was therefore the exact opposite of the Hanoi POW. By ignoring his military duties (Article I), refusing to resist and pleading for special favors and parole (Article III), betraying his fellow POWs and disobeying his officers (Article IV), providing the enemy with anything it wanted (Article V), and condemning America (Article VI), this enlisted man manages in less than two pages of *P.O.W.* to violate virtually the entire Code.

A cluster of POWs captured during the Tet Offensive soon joined Kushner and the others. Few are named, and like "Roberts," the ranking sergeant gets a pseudonym—"Top Benson." Since Kushner owed his rank to his medical degree, and Warrant Officer Frank Anton to his skills as a helicopter pilot, neither man would take charge. Fortunately, "Benson was a born leader, and his men accorded him a respect that bordered on hero worship." A fire-breathing hard-liner—"Benson's first words to Kushner were 'I'm going to get these men out of here'"—Top was clearly the POWs' best chance for survival. Though badly wounded, Benson began pulling the camp together, and "amazingly, as the days passed, Top improved, and mainly because of him, so did prisoner morale. Even the despairing Roberts responded to the first sergeant's leadership." Nor should it be surprising, given *P.O.W.*'s governing principles, that Benson succeeded by teaching survival skills, organizing duty schedules, and encouraging group patriotism—or in Kushner's words, creating "the climate of resistance necessary to healthy morale and to the development of a community strength of spirit essential to survival."[88]

This weather however soon changed, and the spirit died. Though *P.O.W.* does link this community's collapse to the meager and filthy food, the dysentery that wracked the men's bodies, and a "painful skin disease" which tormented them almost into insanity, inferior personnel and a lack of leadership are the principal reasons offered for the ensuing nightmare.[89] Since Marine Private Earl Weatherman is the only named enlisted man besides the Puerto Rican parolees, he becomes the Kushner camp's representative enlisted man by default. "Nineteen, big, friendly, outgoing," Weatherman "knew and cared nothing about the politics of the war." While in the brig for some mistake, this undisciplined and naive kid heard that the VC would release defectors in neutral Cambodia, so he escaped, surrendered to the enemy—and soon found himself in a jungle camp instead of Cambodia. Weatherman predictably grew tired of this captivity as well, and while on a food run, he overpowered a guard and "disappeared into the jungle with another American." Recaptured in fifteen minutes, his story then ended as pathetically as it began: "A guard walked to Weatherman, placed the barrel of his rifle between his eyes, and blew the young man's head away."[90]

Without discipline, POWs like Weatherman were accidents waiting to happen, but according to *P.O.W.*, what "the young enlisted men in this camp did not get was the leadership to which they were entitled from the highest ranking prisoners."[91] Since Kushner and Anton wouldn't lead, the camp's morale wasted away with Top Benson. Malnutrition had by this point left all the POWs victims of what Kushner diagnosed as acute brain syndrome: "Men were forgetting where they were and who their companions were. Sometimes a man would get up to do something, walk a few steps, and forget where he had been going and what he had intended to do." In Benson's case, the physical changes were bad enough: "His face withered and sank in around its bones. His once steady blue eyes became shifty. With his bald head and white beard, he had the look of an ancient Shylock." His retreat from leadership, however, was far more serious: "The once proud soldier who had cared only for his men showed less and less concern for them. He whined constantly and begged his captors for more food, tobacco, and clothing. He hoarded things and began to steal tobacco from the others. Once selfless, he made it clear that he now cared for no one but himself."[92] By setting Benson up as the day's target for POW group criticism, the camp officials weakened camp unity even more. Though most men "went through the motions and were easy on Top," there was "a trace of bitterness in the tones of some, who told him he was 'obstinate,' 'stubborn,' 'greedy,' 'uncouth.'" As sickness and senility pulled Benson down, his "leaderless" men turned on each other: "There was constant and increasingly vicious bickering over the division of labor. The prisoners divided into factions—cliques. Physical strength became all important." Soon, they began to die—an unnamed POW first, then Top Benson, then a "young Marine," who slipped away as Kushner pleaded, "You've got to try. You've got to want to live." The Marine's last words were "Just tell them where I've been."[93]

On this note *P.O.W* leaves the Kushner camp for a bit, returning forty pages and six months later to report that "another year was dying," and "Army Capt.-Doctor Floyd Kushner wondered how many more Americans would die with it." Roberts starts fading immmediately; like Benson he would die with little dignity. If Top aged into senility, Roberts "regressed to infancy, sucking his thumb and calling for his mother." Hubbell stresses heavily the irony of Roberts's fate. The POW who trumpeted his own unreliability and ruthlessness was now utterly dependent: "He continually dirtied his clothing and the bed, and the others had to clean him and clean up after him. . . . In order to feed him, they had to communicate with him, and in order to get any response at all they found that they had to cuddle him and kiss him and talk to him as though he were a baby. Then they were able to spoon-feed him." According to *P.O.W.*, it was this nightmare that shocked the Kushner POWs into adopting in earnest the plan for survival that Benson had tried to implement, and that the Hanoi POWs had successfully followed from day one. Roberts's death not only taught the other POWs "how bad it could get if a man let go," but also "the lengths to which the others would go to save him—knowledge that made everyone feel better." While tending the dying man, the Kushner POWs had rediscovered their compassion and sense of duty, and in the process, so to some degree had Roberts. As he died in Kushner's arms, his last words were, "Mom, Dad, I love you very much."[94]

With this newfound wisdom, the Kushner POWs turned a corner. Though men continued to fall—"By the end of April, eight Americans had died in this camp"—they had rededicated themselves to unity and survival. As a result, the four German nurses brought to the Kushner camp in May 1969 encountered a transformed group. Although most of the POWs "appeared to be mere shadows of men, weak enough to die" to Rika Kortmann, who would shortly die herself, "yet they continued to work hard at getting the encampment built. She could not imagine the source of their strength. Kushner had no answer for her, nor did any of the others. The Americans knew only that, somehow, they did what they had to do."[95] This redeemed community is still functioning when *P.O.W.* returns to this story five months and thirty pages later, and it obviously weathered two more undocumented years, since when *P.O.W.* returns to this story in 1971, the Kushner POWs are walking North with great expectations after listening "enviously to American pilots who were imprisoned in Hanoi sending broadcast messages home in which loved ones were thanked for packages and told of turkey dinners which had been served on holidays."[96] The system made some of their backbones "firm up" even more. Kushner entered Hanoi "like a robot": "The will to resist had been squeezed out of him. He was compliant. His captors commanded, and he obeyed." Hard-line officers like Ted Guy, however, soon turned him around: "Despite his antiwar views, Kushner was glad to comply, to become part of a team, united behind a strong leader. He told his captors that he was through making statements and reading over the camp radio."[97] Of course, few of these jungle POWs ever attained the highest levels of resistance. "Unlike the American prisoners in Hanoi," for instance, "this leaderless group was not governed by an anti-early release policy. They saw nothing despicable about accepting early release; far from it, each of them, officers included, hoped for it, believed it was the only way to survive."[98] Despite such weakness, though, in *P.O.W.* at least these largely nameless jungle POWs for the most part melted gratefully into that larger Hanoi community which offered them the chance to return home honorably.

P.O.W.'s portraits of other jungle enlisted POWs tend to affirm military stereotypes as well. In a chapter called "Storybook Soldiers," for instance, Hubbell claims that only Rudyard Kipling could do justice to rough-and-ready Army sergeants like Dennis Thompson and Harvey Brande. The "products of poverty and broken marriages," these high-school dropouts had "a penchant for barroom brawling" and no real taste for discipline. Nevertheless, they were "superb soldiers." Thompson was a foul-mouthed, bullish, fearless fighting man. His captors' attempt to break him through a staged execution collapsed when he shouted at the gunman, "Well, shoot, fucker, do me a favor!" Thompson's later dressing down of the camp commander known as Cheese struck the same tone: "Let me tell you something, you little motherfucker, there's only two of us in this room right now. I guarantee it, you insult me one more time, you call me one more name, you shake your fist at me or threaten me one more time, you bastard, and only one of us will walk out of here."[99] Thanks to a detail Hubbell doesn't mention at first, Harvey Brande gets more careful handling. In 1971, the Peace Committee's most outspoken member, John Young, accused Brande of boasting about having executed Vietnamese POWs on the battlefield in 1968. *P.O.W.*'s account of Brande and Thompson in 1968 deftly turns the tables. When they learned that someone named John Young would soon arrive at their camp, they immediately carried out a planned escape, to protect this Young from being held responsible. The attempt failed, however, and Brande and Young became roommates in a jungle camp called Portholes, where "an intense hatred was to develop between the invalid twosome."[100] *P.O.W.* carefully structures its narrative to account for Young's later vindictiveness. Though Brande refused to sign anything, even with a gun against his head, Young hysterically begged Brande to let him sign confessions, then told camp officials that Brande had ordered him to resist. So badly did his captors beat this storybook soldier that "terribly wounded, terribly sick, terribly weak, Brande knew he was dying." But for a number of reasons he held on; "not the least of them, he recalls, to settle accounts with John Young."[101]

Young's later charges were therefore desperate attempts to silence a witness to his own cowardice; they were also perfectly consistent with Young's actions as part of the Peace Committee. *P.O.W.* increasingly narrows its focus to these enlisted POW traitors. Young himself was "grief-stricken" over Ho Chi Minh's death in September 1969. Political convert Robert Chenoweth believed "that communism was the answer to the world's ills," briefed the Camp Authority about his cellmates, and quaked with fear at the idea of American prosecution. Torture had driven Larry Kavanaugh mad: "Never excessively religious, he now announced that he had been visiting with the Lord. He said that he knew himself to be a saint—'the thirteenth disciple.'" As a result, he was now "absolutely opposed to the war," and "to all violence and the taking of life"—ironic principles, since Kavanaugh would take his own life only a few months after returning to America.[102] Taken together, then, the enlisted POWs were an unsteady group. Noncoms and grunts succeeded by being crude hard asses, wandered toward death without officers, and became traitors whenever they rejected Hanoi POW policy or followed their own conscience.

Of all the POWs who returned during Operation Homecoming, however, the least visible in the official story are the civilian POWs. After marveling at the newly redeemed Kushner POWs, for example, the German nurses die or disappear, thus confirming *P.O.W.*'s implicit argument that even the barest vestiges of discipline made the military POWs hardier than civilians. Hubbell's account of agricultural advisor Michael Benge and missionaries Hank Blood and Betty Ann Olsen makes the same point. Captured during Tet, after witnessing mass executions of Americans and Vietnamese, they marched through the jungle for months. Blood and Olsen soon died of disease and starvation; they appear in *P.O.W.*'s dedication between the Hanoi martyrs and the ambivalent "Benson" and "Roberts." Benge also faded, but as captors waited for his death, he suddenly "knew something they didn't know; he was not going to die." Benge at this moment adopted the Hanoi POWs' loyalty and duty to bear witness: "Someone had to survive, to make it known what had happened to Hank Blood and Betty Ann Olsen. It was up to him and he would do it, no matter what it took. He would do it by putting one foot ahead of the other, living one hour at a time, for as many steps and years as it took. He was going to do it."[103] Apart from providing testimony about captor atrocities, and confirming Hanoi POW values, however, Benge has no importance for *P.O.W.*, and after meeting Lieutenant Steve Leopold in another jungle camp, he disappears. Like all civilians, as someone outside of the Code and the command chain, Benge simply didn't count.

Before returning to the mainstream, one further point should be made about how the various civilian and military stories from elsewhere work within the official story. Gathering these profiles together in the way I have misrepresents *P.O.W.*'s actual intermittent and fragmentary treatment—a treatment that creates the overall impression that warrant officers and doctors weren't real military, that enlisted men were unstable at best, and that civilians usually died. Nor should this be surprising. In the official story, unity before self meant officers before enlisted men and civilians, and the system before everywhere else.

Heresy, Dissent, and Endurance:
The Summer of Horror and the End of Torture

From 1968 onward, the official story is largely the story of how the senior Hanoi POWs created an administrative history: the story of how the POW command responded to changes in treatment, and to maverick and apostate POWs. The key dates were March 1968, when Johnson's bombing halt all but froze the Hanoi POW population; September 1969, when Ho Chi Minh died and torture basically ended; November 1970, when the Son Tay raid spurred the North Vietnamese into moving the outlying POWs into Hanoi; December 1971, when Nixon's renewed bombing also resumed the flow of new POWs into Hanoi; and the 1972 Christmas bombings, which were swiftly followed by the January 1973 peace accords and the POWs' return home. *P.O.W.* covers these five years in only 200 pages; in addition, it documents the actions of two groups who seriously threatened camp unity: those maverick POWs who believed that any senior POW who discouraged escape attempts was a coward, and those very different POWs who denied the senior POWs' authority and condemned them, their fellow prisoners, and their country publicly. In some ways, then, the POW command chain became most embattled *after* the days of torture, and the official story was one way that the senior POWs justified their authority over the other prisoners.

By highlighting the suffering of the most senior men, *P.O.W.* shores up this authority. When Fidel "turned to savagery," for instance, his "horrendous torture and beatings" fell upon a "dozen or so" old-timers.[104] Though one of these guinea pigs, Jack Bomar, had plenty of his own suffering—Fidel beat him viciously in front of the guards—Bomar also witnessed perhaps Hanoi's most nauseating case of abuse. In *P.O.W.*, this victim gets called "the Faker," and when he first entered Bomar's cell, his body already bore the signs of beatings, long periods in torture cuffs, and untended infections. So abused that he no longer flinched when hit in the face, the Faker believed his fellow POWs were spies and tormentors, but they nevertheless cleaned him up, forced him to eat, and tended the wounds that Fidel still inflicted. Though the Faker eventually died, his story shows that in Hanoi no one fell so low as to be abandoned—the lesson it took the Kushner POWs a year to learn.[105] Another senior POW was Fidel's nemesis. When Jim Kasler refused to meet an antiwar delegation in the early summer of 1968, an interrogator beat him and put him in the ropes. When Fidel, "beside himself with rage," joined in, however, the suffering reached a new level. Between rope sessions Fidel flogged Kasler, who took "approximately three hundred more lashes" with a rubber whip before falling back. Though left in a semicoma, Kasler did not meet the delegation or write a usable statement, forcing to Fidel to leave in August 1968, his mission a failure.[106]

At a time when despair ruled the jungle camp, then, willpower like Kasler's was surging up in Hanoi. Dale Osborne's was if anything even more impressive. When Osborne woke up on the ground in September 1968 with his left hand and wrist broken, his right wrist shattered, a fair portion of his left calf and thigh missing entirely, and a sizable piece of shrapnel in his head, his chances of granting his wife's parting request, "Please don't make a widow of me," looked very slim. When retreating enemy ground troops left him for dead, he screamed before passing out. He awoke to find himself being lowered into a grave, so he screamed again and escaped death a second time. Osborne's injuries were so severe that his impatient guards heaved him into a ditch on the way to Hanoi, but he managed to crawl to the nearest light and cheated death a third time. It took Osborne seventeen days to reach the Hilton, but once there a cellmate nursed him, thus ensuring that Osborne "was not going to make Donna a widow."[107] Such stories became icons for the cardinal POW virtues. In keeping with the official story's emphasis on rank, such parables often feature the Alcatraz Gang, and its SRO in particular. When these men rioted in January 1969 to get Harry Jenkins needed medical care, the Camp Authority paid Jim Stockdale the ultimate compliment of being removed as a bad influence upon a handful of already-isolated diehards. When a furious interrogator asked him, "Will you be my slave or not?" and Stockdale "was strongly negative," he went back into the ropes. A suspicious order to wash and shave convinced Stockdale that a public appearance lay ahead, and bouncing back, he hacked away at his hair with a razor until his scalp dripped with blood. The Camp Authority erupted—apparently Stockdale was supposed to play an antiwar American businessman in some propaganda movie—but while the North Vietnamese searched frantically for a hat, Stockdale ended his film career by slamming himself in the face with a wooden stool.[108]

Episodes like these fuel the official story's argument that a leader hero's achievements went beyond simple personal courage—or in other words, since a commander's rank and duties made him a bigger target, his triumphs were greater as well. *P.O.W.*'s account of the controversy over planning escapes offers a particularly telling example. Many POWs had tried to evade capture, and some men attempted breaks on their way to Hanoi. Hard-liners like Jeremiah Denton ordered their men to prepare escape plans, and an unsuccessful October 1967 attempt earned George Coker and George McKnight their places in Alcatraz. Nevertheless, a POW's duty "to make every effort to escape" in practice often clashed with his duty to obey "the lawful orders of those appointed" over him. *P.O.W.* sets up its sharply critical account of the infamous Dramesi-Atterberry attempt by presenting the earlier Coker-McKnight escape as the perfect example of a justified attempt. The idea itself came from their SRO, Jeremiah Denton, but a cautious Coker refused to go, since it seemed like "honorable suicide" to him. In October 1967, while imprisoned at Dirty Bird, a Hanoi camp near a power plant, McKnight learned during supervised trips for water that their camp was only a few blocks from the Red River. This escape route meant that the two POWs would not have to slip unnoticed through a heavily urban area, and Coker agreed "that conditions seemed right." Other factors also made the attempt feasible. Since Coker and McKnight could not contact their commanding officers, higher approval was unnecessary. Most importantly, only Coker and McKnight could be hurt by the attempt. Planning took only a week. The moment conditions were marginally favorable, the men jimmied their way out of their cells and got perhaps fifteen miles down river before getting recaptured.[109]

In *P.O.W.* at least, the May 1969 Dramesi-Atterberry attempt lacked all the advantages of the Coker-McKnight attempt. Hubbell recognizes Dramesi's and Atterberry's ingenuity and courage, and calls their escape "a well-organized operation, more than a year in planning and preparation." He even quotes sympathetic POWs who pointed out "that the Code of Conduct called for escape if at all possible," and suggested that if successful, Dramesi and Atterberry could have exposed the Camp Authority's "humane and lenient" treatment to the world. These concessions do not however lift the shadows *P.O.W.* casts on this escape. Other POWs had objected violently to it, arguing that "even if Dramesi and Atterberry got over the wall, chances were nil that a pair of Caucasians would long go undetected in the densely populated countryside." The escapers "would be captured, possibly killed," and if they weren't, the POWs left behind would probably "pay dearly in torture for the leave-taking." These grim predictions all came true during what became known as the "summer of horror." *P.O.W.* spends less time on the actual attempt than it does on the Coker-McKnight escape. Dressed in peasant costumes they had made from carefully hoarded scraps, Dramesi and Atterberry got out over the walls and headed for the river, but "lost track of time." Fearing the morning light, they hid in a thicket, but were discovered: the escape had failed.[110]

The aftermath, which Hubbell calls "the most brutal torture period of the long captivity," gets far more attention. The escapers' careful planning paradoxically became the most damning evidence against them. Coker and McKnight "had simply run away;" Dramesi's and Atterberry's "elaborate props and disguises, homemade knives," and their "expertise to short-circuit a security system" suggested "real planning." For this reason, the Camp Authority suspected a campwide support network, and started digging for it. The two escapers suffered most. Ed Atterberry was beaten to death. John Dramesi spent thirty-two days in irons and went into the ropes fifteen times. *P.O.W.* insists that this treatment "had its psychological effect; he was frightened." Hubbell's last passage on John Dramesi thus describes an anxious, penitent man.[111] For the official story's purposes, though, Dramesi's fate was secondary to what the POW community suffered because of his actions. After declaring that the escape's opponents "were soon proved correct in their surmise that many of them would pay dearly for it," *P.O.W.* then records an orgy of torture that "went on for months." The Camp Authority wanted the POWs' most precious secrets: "Who were the senior prisoners in the camp? Who had been giving the orders? What were the orders? What were the various prisoner committees? How many were involved in the Dramesi-Atterberry escape attempt?" To get answers, "the Vietnamese literally flayed the hides off their American prisoners." Twenty-six POWs passed through this wringer, which left the communications system and the command chain as exposed as the tortured POWs' own flesh. *P.O.W.* blames this purge for another death: James J. Connell, a crafty POW who faked injuries so he could pass messages without suspicion, lost his cover, and like Atterberry, eventually died from the abuse that followed.[112]

Even though the position was less hard-line than some of the official story's greatest heroes, *P.O.W.* supports the senior command's decision never to authorize fully another escape attempt. The Alcatraz POWs were still isolated at the time, but when they reappeared they made Dramesi an honorary Alcatraz member. Hubbell praises this enthusiasm, but uses the story of another hard-liner, eventual Medal of Honor winner Bud Day, to undercut their reasons for championing escapes. Day "was exhilarated when he heard of the escape attempt"; proud of Dramesi's and Atterberry's "imagination and daring," he also felt "that attempts should be made to bring word to the American people of the brutal treatment of the POWs." But since enlisted Hanoi POW Douglas Hegdahl had already been ordered to accept parole for this purpose, Day's justification did not hold water, and in fact, the Dramesi escape *delayed* Hegdahl's release. Though he doesn't personally complain, Day also suffered greatly during the aftermath. Three hundred lashes whipped the names of nonexistent committees out of him, then forced him to implicate his roommates in the imaginary plots he had confessed to.[113]

In the face of such brutality, only a single justification for trying to escape remains intact: that the Code demanded the attempt. In *P.O.W.*, and at far greater length in his own memoir, Larry Guarino provides the senior command's reply. Guarino "had known nothing of the Dramesi-Atterberry escape plan," but as "senior officer in the Zoo and Zoo annex complex, he would have vetoed it." Though he offers "Robbie Risner's years-old order not to try to escape without outside help," as *P.O.W.* admits, this order dealt with a specific instance, and was never meant to set policy. Guarino's own suffering was far more compelling support for his position. The Camp Authority assumed that as the Zoo's senior

POW, Guarino must have approved the escape. Sleeplessness, leg irons, flogging, and the ropes soon had him admitting to everything he was accused of. He also agreed to write for the camp magazine, to "see a delegation and to make a movie."[114] Guarino was obviously rolling, and when he disappeared, his successor, Wendy Rivers, ordered the men "to give the enemy anything he demanded short of security information. He authorized men to read the news over the camp radio, to make tape recordings, and to admit that he, Rivers, was now acting SRO. When the torture ended, he said, they were to resume a normal resistance posture." For some POWs such policies were too late. Red McDaniel's "torture-flogging," involving "approximately seven hundred lashes with the rubber whip" still took place, and as the summer of horror dragged on, each new victim's torment proved once more that the Dramesi-Atterberry escape attempt had created more suffering, and led to more security losses than almost any other POW action.[115]

Whether or not unity before self was actually suppressing individual initiative, the emphasis on the group undeniably became stronger after the Dramesi escape, and the astonishing improvement in treatment which soon followed. The reasons offered for this change vary wildly. Amnesty International has suggested that "perhaps" torture stopped "in response to the halt in American bombing at that time." No one else agrees.[116] Many POWs believed that Ho Chi Minh's death had some impact; the most popular explanation, however, was that world outrage forced Hanoi to change its ways, or as *P.O.W.* put it, "the Hegdahl-Frishman revelations of brutality and torture" became a "rallying point around which the most ardent protagonists on both sides of the war issue could unite, the well-being of the POWs."[117] This explanation gives the POWs some credit. By hanging on until the world learned the truth, the POWs had personally defeated the North Vietnamese. No matter how it happened though, everyone agreed that this moment was the Official Story's turning point. When asked by a camp official in 1973 "what I would say when I got home," Jeremiah Denton states this belief: "I will say that through 1969 you treated me and the others worse than animals," but that "late in 1969 you came off the torture. After that, to my knowledge, you did not resort to extreme punishment. You then acted within your conscience, such as it is."[118] And so did the POWs, who increasingly found that as torture faded from the scene, their fellow POWs became a more pressing problem than their jailers.

Getting the Story Straight:
Camp Unity and Preparing for Home

Hubbell follows the official story most closely in his account of December 1969 to February 1973. These years flash by in eighty pages, with the focus riveted on the creation of the 4th Allied P.O.W. Wing, a fully functioning military unit. The Camp Authority seemed to crumble with Ho's death. When the former system commander known as the Cat took charge of the Hilton, "Stockdale could not have been more amazed": "It was as though the admiral of a fleet were announcing that he had been reduced to command of a single ship. Indeed, the mighty seemed to be falling!" Even more astounding was the Cat's confession to Jeremiah Denton: " 'I have been required to make public self-criticism for my mistakes,' he went on, 'and from now on you will be allowed to follow the Code of Conduct.' "[119] Despite this fading, the senior POWs still found restoring the full command chain difficult. The Camp Authority's early strategy of isolating the hard-liners had at least partially succeeded. When the Alcatraz POWs returned to the Hilton on December 9, 1969, they were "furious" to discover that the command structure had "fragmented." Some POWs "were good resisters but hadn't learned to communicate." Other men "were receiving special favors and weren't participating in the camp structure." Some poor souls "were still rolling from severe torture," and a few men "were just plain collaborating." Torture's end paradoxically seemed to erode morale. By February of 1971, "at least 30 percent and perhaps as many as 50 percent of the prisoners were disillusioned about the war and were becoming increasingly cynical about it."[120]

These feelings grew even as the POWs moved toward full communication and command. On November 21, 1970, American commandos staged a rescue attempt at Son Tay camp. Since the POWs had been moved four months earlier, Hubbell's chapter title—"The Son Tay Raid—A Huge Success"—doesn't quite ring true, but the raid definitely scared the Camp Authority into tightening security. On December 26, 342 POWs from all over Vietnam were gathered together in the Hilton, and assigned to holding areas which contained roughly fifty men. The POWs called this new system "Camp Unity," and it meant that "for most of the Americans in North Vietnam, the long loneliness was over. Compound living had begun." Because Colonels Flynn, Winn, and Gaddis, the highest-ranking POWs, were still isolated, the Hanoi patriarchs all had major command duties. The deputy for SRO Vernon P. Ligon, a late 1967 shootdown, "was Robbie Risner. Jim Stockdale, third ranking, was in charge of plans and policy. And Jerry Denton was current operations officer, responsible for the development of tactics."[121] The rise of "the four wise men" paralleled their captors' steady decline. "Within months, certainly by April Fools' Day, 1971," Jim Stockdale recalled, "in the manner of Oriental theater's swift and subtle scene changes, the Camp Authority would have receded into the mist, and a regime of simple straightforward detention have taken its place."[122] Almost seven years after Everett Alvarez's arrival, then, the POWs found themselves in the kind of POW camp they had anticipated.

But tensions continued to build. America's war policies and the antiwar movement left many POWs "wondering, quite understandably, why they should be different, why they should remain indefinitely in an unspeakable captivity, why they should not at least make things easier on themselves by giving the Vietnamese the propaganda help that seemed so vital to ending the war." Men with this "to hell with it" attitude weren't fond of hard-liners like Denton, who didn't seem to know that "at home, countless numbers of prominent people, including members of Congress, were providing the enemy with all kinds of moral support—and for free, without suffering any torture."[123] Born-again die-hards were another disciplinary headache. Their desire for revenge and "long-smoldering rage" led some longtimers "to bait guards and officers" now that the heat was off, while other men, humiliated by "their own earlier weak behavior," struggled "to carve reputations for themselves, to kick a gook in the ass every night just to show how tough they were." Although self-proclaimed tigers like John Dramesi argued that timid commanders were the real disgrace, everyone agreed the arrival of jungle POWs and new shootdowns, many almost a generation younger than the old-timers, stirred up debates about good conduct. Even the senior POWs themselves weren't always overjoyed at settling back into the micromanagement common in military bureaucracy. After years of solitary, some found it "difficult to come into a room with forty-seven Americans, with a command set up, directives and certain restrictions."[124] General directives on bedtime and toilet duty weren't always entirely welcome either.

The senior POWs met these challenges with a strategy that revolved around how the POWs would go home. "Return with Honor" was the wing motto, and the command goals were to draw all POWs into "a tight, tough, military unit, responsible to their senior officers and accountable for their actions," and to set a good example for "other young Americans" who would "be expected to perform well in future POW situations." For Robinson Risner, restoring "a military organization" required POWs "to act like military men and comply with all directives without quibble. If they had any questions or matters to discuss, they should take them to their flight commander with whom we met daily. He would bring it to the staff, and we would make the final decisions. Once the decision was made, the discussion period was over."[125] This collective sense of discipline did at times surge up in captivity, and most strikingly on February 7, 1971, when Robinson Risner, Howard Rutledge, and George Coker led the first openly held POW worship in Hanoi. After the service, as guards led these officers away to solitary, the cellblocks erupted into what became known as the "Church Riot." The POWs bellowed out "The Star Spangled Banner," patriotic songs, and call-and-response cheers so loudly that Vietnamese riot police burst into the compound. With this event, "the Camp Unity Americans rejoined the war as a unit," as the three wise men left behind—Ligon, Stockdale, and Denton—made discipline the primary POW trait: "The men then started marching everywhere in military formation. For work detail, flights of eight would fall in single column, march out and march back. For the outside exercise, it was being done in formation led by a single individual."[126]

The most contentious part of this systematizing, however, was the amnesty policy the senior POWs wove into the Plums. Since "virtually all the prisoners had yielded something to the enemy, most under varying degrees of duress, but some few under no duress at all," the POW commanders "called on all to rejoin the fold without prejudice, to come into the Wing with a clean slate." This "call to 'come home, all is forgiven'" infuriated diehards like John Dramesi, who felt all the virtuous brother's sense of injustice when POWs who had ducked torture or willingly condemned the war were welcomed back as prodigal sons. Nor can it be denied that as release became more likely, since "squadron commanding officers had full power of awards and courts-martial," some renegade POWs pragmatically confessed their errors and rejoined the Wing. Full forgiveness did however have one large string attached. Only repentent POWs *who accepted the senior POWs' authority* could be forgiven: "Prisoners who denied the applicability of the Code of Conduct and who failed to try to live by it would be stripped of all military authority."[127] Though most POWs accepted these guidelines, a handful of men stayed defiant to the end. Many of *P.O.W.*'s final pages record the senior command's frustrations in dealing with these POWs.

The enlisted status of those in the Peace Committee made damning this group relatively easy. Official expectations were the guiding principle here. When POW Steve Leopold heard Robinson Risner on Radio Hanoi sounding " 'gung ho' on Hanoi's behalf," he "gave it no credence": officers' statements *must* have been be extorted. When however he heard two enlisted POWs making similar remarks, Leopold "was disappointed and depressed": these statements *must* have resulted from weakness. Lieutenant Colonel Ted Guy, the Plantation's SRO from November 1970, shared this opinion. Among his men were "some of the most disgustingly obsequious Americans" he had ever seen; "men who could not seem to snap to attention fast enough when a Vietnamese approached, who bowed and scraped to their captors in the most servile fashion."[128] Nicknamed "the Ducks" at first because of the way they followed the guards around, these POWs ignored their own officers and accepted special favors. Only after describing this gutless brood does *P.O.W.* reveal that its members were Robert Chenoweth, Alfonzo Riate, Michael Branch, John D. Young, and Abel Larry Kavanaugh—men whose poor behavior in outlying camps had already been recorded. Hanoi did not improve these men. Branch and Young declared they were deserters, and Young now took his revenge on Harvey Brande by accusing him in camp broadcasts of killing "fifteen VC with fifteen rounds from his M-16 rifle. These men all had their hands tied behind them and were on their knees."[129]

The senior POWs made sure that the Ducks could never "escape accountability for their behavior by pleading ignorance, by insisting that no one had ever told them what was required of them as American military men." When Air Force Captain Edward W. Leonard confronted the Ducks, however, they confirmed they were hopeless:

> Recognizing only Kavanaugh, he addressed himself to him, speaking loudly enough so that all could hear: "Kavanaugh, you and your men are to stop all forms of cooperation and collaboration with the enemy."
> "We'll do what we want," Kavanaugh replied.
> "Fuck you, Captain Leonard," shouted one of the others, whom Leonard would later identify as Alfonso Riate.

Colonel Guy responded by ordering all POWs to avoid contact with the Ducks, but to watch them carefully, due to the "possibility of future legal action." When three more POWs joined the Ducks, at some point they evolved into the Peace Committee of Southeast Asia.[130]

A "peace committee" had operated in Korea, and when introducing the PCs, Hubbell highlights those traits often blamed for the Korean POW disgrace. One recruit's motive was transparent: "King David Rayford, Jr., twenty-one, a black, had suffered bitter racial experiences while growing up in Chicago's ghetto, and also in the Army." Eighteen-year-old Army Private James Daly was simply naive and incompetent. A Jehovah's Witness and conscientious objector, he "had no business being in any war." As for Marine Private Fred Elbert, he spent his time "sitting alone, daydreaming, almost in a trance"; insisting he was someone else, he was clearly unstable. Naivete, weakness, mental illness, and rage account for these PCs—and by never mentioning that Daly and Elbert had been Kushner POWs, and thus two of the most brutalized captives in Vietnam, Hubbell only heightens this effect.[131] As time passed, the PCs became increasingly extreme. Daly recalls signing a petition which said the PCs were willing "to do anything" to help their captors' cause, "even if it meant joining the Vietnamese Army."[132] The official American response was however equally extreme. After deciding that the PCs' "allegiance was to Hanoi, not to the United States or to their fellow American prisoners," Colonel Guy issued a conditional license to kill: "Should the POWs be observed in any way to be threatening the survival of other Americans, they were to be eliminated." So hated were the PCs that Guy was preventing other POWs from "liquidating" them as late as 1973: "Asserting his faith in the American judicial system, he vowed that justice would be done, that he would file charges and would see that the eight were court-martialed."[133] The official story's judgment is therefore clear. The PCs lacked the intelligence, discipline, and integrity necessary to avoid betraying their country.

The two Hanoi officers who refused amnesty posed thornier problems. An October 1967 shootdown, Marine Lieutenant Colonel Edison Wainwright Miller surfaced in early 1969 on what the POWs called "The Bob and Ed Show." ("Bob" was Navy Commander Robert Schweitzer. His misdeeds get downplayed, presumably because he accepted amnesty.) Though torture had forced many men to tape antiwar messages, when Bob and Ed said the war was illegal, called themselves criminals, denounced the Code, and wished out loud for parole, the "easy spontaneity to the conversation, a quality of sincerity and conviction" infuriated the other prisoners.[134] *P.O.W.*'s thumbnail biography of Miller accounts somewhat for his behavior. An orphan, Miller had passed quickly through the ranks, flew fifty missions in Korea, and became a lieutenant colonel at thirty-five. A degree in political science and his status as a squadron commander made Miller's resume at shootdown look like Risner's, Stockdale's, or Denton's. What set him apart was the huge gap lying between his beliefs and actions. Most Vietnam POWs supported the war, or accepted "the traditional notion that the active-duty military man, regardless of his opinion of the merits of the war, had no business inserting himself in political argument." Even before fighting in Vietnam, the widely read Miller had concluded "that the United States was in violation of the Constitution in that it was waging a war in the absence of a congressional declaration of war."[135] That Miller flew his missions anyway therefore suggests that ambition rather than ethics or duty drove his career.

His Vietnam flight record only raised more red flags. Miller's radio operator, Howe Warner, found "The Bob and Ed Show" especially offensive because he knew that Miller had flown his missions with zeal—so much, in fact, that when their plane's hydraulic system started giving out, Miller's "intense preoccupation with distributing ordnance" had carried him out over the target instead of back to base. A few minutes later, "both men were hanging in their parachutes." Warner also knew that Miller had the worst fault a POW could have—naked careerism. When Warner had asked his pilot why he was in Vietnam, Miller "bluntly advised that he had come to promote his career, to make general." Utterly self-centered and ambitious, Miller showed no real concern for other POWs or for his country. When senior officer in his cell, "he displayed no interest in assuming leadership. He was taken to interrogation far more frequently than the others. He impressed his cellmates as being very frightened. He seemed to exhibit a willingness to cooperate with the Vietnamese." Miller claimed he had been tortured, and had given out only "erroneous information or none at all," but as the evidence of collaboration kept building, he became an emblem for the amoral, careerist traitor.[136]

The second senior collaborator, Navy Commander Walter Eugene Wilber, serves as *P.O.W.*'s sensitive liberal dupe. After his deeply traumatic June 1968 capture—his crewman went down with the plane and Wilber himself probably suffered a stroke on the way to Hanoi—he spent the next twenty-one months awash in "the same endless flood of propaganda that was poured through the radio speakers in all the prisoners' cells." Wilber was never abused, and countless POWs had endured the same flood. Wilber's collapse was therefore self-induced. He decided "to try to educate himself, to try to understand the history that had landed him in a jail cell in Hanoi." Since "as prisoners of war, they remained at war on behalf of their government's policies and were required to support these policies to whatever extent possible," most of the POWs felt that a Hanoi camp was the last place to rethink their politics. Wilber obviously disagreed. Even though "it never struck him that he never was given anything to read in support of the American intervention," after watching antiwar films and listening to Fulbright and Mansfield tapes, he concluded in 1969 that the war was illegal. As someone who also believed that "when he accepted his commission, he did not surrender his right to free speech," Wilber therefore began practicing civil disobedience in Hanoi—but against the POW command.[137]

In the fall of 1970, Wilber, Miller, Schweitzer, and four other isolated but well-treated junior officers were put together in the Zoo. The other POWs called these model prisoners the "Outer Seven," and the group's dynamics were a parody of Camp Unity. Though Wilber was SRO, "he wanted no strong military organization." All problems "were to be resolved in 'democratic meetings.'"[138] The senior men only took the lead in collaborating. During one interview, for instance, Wilber not only condemned the war, but suggested that most

POWs had been treated as leniently as he had. The Camp Unity senior POWs nevertheless worked hard to contact and redeem these apparent traitors. Though Miller and Wilber refused to discuss their behavior, in mid-1971 the four junior officers learned the camp policies and received the order to follow the Code. Eventually, these officers and Bob Schweitzer accepted amnesty, and the Outer Seven turned into the Repentant Five and the Damned Two. Schweitzer's amnesty showed just how forgiving the senior command was. Though his broadcasts made him one of the most hated of all POWs, "Bob" actually reclaimed his rung in the hierarchy: "There being no question about the sincerity of Schweitzer's repentance and his determination to abide by the Plums, he was deemed by the Wing leadership to be worthy of command."[139]

The Damned Two were a different story. Wilber ignored the amnesty offer. Miller "did not feel that he had done anything requiring anyone's forgiveness, and was infuriated at what he conceived to be an attempt to bribe him." Both men vowed to "live by their own consciences" instead.[140] The Hanoi POWs confronted Miller and Wilber in August '71, when acting Wing Commander Robinson Risner "initiated a dialogue" that was as spontaneous as an excommunication. After offering "a chance to rejoin the team," Risner advised them that they were being disloyal to their country, their services, and their fellow prisoners of war." He then "ordered them to abide by the Code of Conduct, and specifically to write nothing for their captors nor make any public appearances nor meet any delegations." Warning the men "that they faced court-martial if they disobeyed his order," Risner then concluded by asking "whether or not they would comply." The men waffled. Wilber said "he would obey all legal military orders"; Miller said he was a true American and Christian who was certain "Risner did not mean to deprive him of his right of free speech." When Risner pressed for a simple "yes" or "no," Miller and Wilber replied "that there was no simple yes or no answer," thus ending the dialogue. On August 11, Miller and Wilber were "relieved of military authority," and though *P.O.W.* mentions the flush toilets, aquariums, writing materials, vegetable gardens, and extra clothing and food that they received for their apostasy, and though Miller and Wilber themselves seemed to delight in mocking or tempting other POWs, most men avoided them like the devil.[141]

Along with the jungle POWs and the new shootdowns, those from the Outer Seven who accepted amnesty entered an organized orientation and education program whose single most effective tool for teaching the Hanoi POW traditions and values was the official story. Though the POWs had shared names, stories, and values from the earliest days, *P.O.W.* claims that the senior captives assembled a group history for training purposes in late 1971, when some longtimers known as the Buckeye 20 came into contact with the Outer Seven. Realizing how confused these renegades were about camp policy, the Buckeye 20 "put together a lengthy oral POW history, each man contributing all that had happened to himself and what he knew had happened to others." Taking "several hours to relate," this story was doubly compelling because of who told it: Everett Alvarez, the only POW who could know the *entire* story, and Gerry Coffee, one of those POWs "with especially retentive memories" who were called " 'memory banks'—historians," and also the first prisoner to hear Risner's New Guy briefings.[142] Though Hubbell claims that "nothing pertinent was omitted," obviously this Official Story could only chronicle events in the Hanoi camps up to the moment of telling. In *P.O.W.*'s last pages, how audiences responded to this history becomes a major subject. The official story bounced off Miller and Wilber, who "in deference to their senior ranks" had heard it separately. The junior men "listened, quietly, intently. They were badly shaken by the revelations, seemed almost unable to grasp the magnitude of the brutality that was described to them or to understand why they had been treated so differently. It seemed to Coffee that, for several days, the four remained unnaturally quiet, morose."[143]

The official story's most important audience, however, soon became those POWs streaming into Hanoi when the bombing escalated in December 1971. Since the Camp Authority now welcomed new POWs with "the blandishments of Wilber and Miller" rather than "the mistreatment the old-timers had suffered," getting the official story to these arrivals was essential.[144] (In fact, six new men at one point did join the Damned Two in condemning the 1972 bombing buildup.) The veteran POWs found these new guys unsettling for other reasons. For instance, these POWs had been taught that "to get their names out they should allow themselves to be photographed and otherwise exercise their own good judgment insofar as participation was concerned in enemy propaganda exercises." This policy suggested that the Hanoi POWs' years of resistance and suffering would seem ludicrous and pointless back home. It was therefore hard for the longtimers "to avoid a sense of betrayal, a feeling that the Department of Defense and the services had broken faith with men who long had been fighting hard on the POW 'extension of the battlefield.' "[145] Countering this threat would require telling the official story not just to the new POWs, but to all Americans—a conclusion *P.O.W.*'s morose "postscript" bears out by reporting that the early releases and parolees, the Peace Committee members, and even Miller and Wilber escaped prosecution.[146]

These disappointments, however, lay in the future. Nothing at the time could dilute the power of the official story's conclusion. Like the providential history it mimics, Hubbell's book ends with a vision of apocalypse and judgment: the Christmas bombings of 1972. The POWs were listlessly following their routines on December 18th, when "suddenly, the whole sky flashed white and stayed white." As B-52 bombs exploded with "a strong gutteral [sic] rumble that went on and on and on," the POWs marveled at the awesome destructive force: "The Americans who shared these cellblocks found themselves looking quickly at each other, open-mouthed and with widening eyes. They were astounded! Elated! Frightened! Depressed!" A series of vignettes display the POWs' various responses to this Hanoi day of judgment. Some men "ran up and down in their cellblocks looking for better vantage points, clapping each other on their backs, shaking hands, shouting encouragement at the skies, shouting to each other about packing bags and making ready to go home." A thrilled Allen Brady "did not want the assault to end until the enemy capitulated," but still worried about a mistake. Red McDaniel approved of the violence, and "hoped the United States would keep applying it until serious negotiations were resumed," but as a "man of deep Christian instinct and charity, McDaniel prayed for the North Vietnamese people." The POWs soon realized the bombers were avoiding them—"Hoa Lo was the safest place in town"—but there was little time for noting much else. The bombing soon stopped, the peace accords were signed in late January, the POWs began heading home on Lincoln's Birthday, and the official story stopped.[147]

Rodney Knutson brings *P.O.W.* to its close. His first words to a welcoming U.S. Air Force colonel were "almost the same as those that Knutson, the first American tortured in Hanoi, had repeated again and again to his inquisitor on an October morning more than seven long years before: 'Sir, Knutson, Rodney Allen; lieutenant junior grade, United States Navy.' " But for the first time in more than seven years, Knutson proudly volunteered further information: "Reporting my honorable return as a prisoner of war to the United States." As the plane lifted off from Hanoi, Knutson realized he was crying: "Then, with the others, he tore off his seatbelt and jumped up into the aisle, exploding with happiness, shaking hands, patting backs, laughing, kissing the nurses, and trying to understand that it was over. It was all over."[148]

The crucifix is the Christian faith's emblem, the Bible is its narrative. A tortured warrior, stretched out between his sense of duty and his captors' wishes, was the longtime Hanoi POWs' emblem; the official story was the history they composed to make this suffering meaningful. Like the Bible, this story's authoritative printed version binds many narratives together to affirm a system of ethics, a hierarchy of superiors, allies, and dependents, and a discipline for life. Also like the Bible, *P.O.W.* omits, conflates, interprets, and allegorizes its materials in light of those larger truths. Though the official story permeates so many POW memoirs, interviews, and histories, Hubbell's *P.O.W.* therefore stands as the most elaborate public attempt to record the POW experience in Hanoi, and to explain what this history must mean for those who consider themselves Americans.

Chapters 1 through 3 have dealt with the tortured warrior; this chapter has outlined the story written by and for this warrior. Two important areas, however, remain to be explored. One is the huge collection of separately published stories that set personal experience in some relation to the official story. These narratives may come from *P.O.W.* heroes like Robinson Risner, Jim Stockdale, or Jeremiah Denton; or from dissenters like John Dramesi; or even from such scapegoats and villains as the Kushner POWs, Robert Garwood, and the Peace Committee. Part III deals with these stories. The second area to be surveyed, however, lies within the official story's own borders. Even if *P.O.W.*'s narrative is totally accurate, how did the POW navigate the long stretches of boredom lying between events? How did captivity affect his attitudes about America, the military, family, and the enemy? And how did he fit his previous experience within that rigid sense of camp discipline he had to live within?

What, in short, went on in the cells behind the official story's names, dates, events, and slogans?

· 5 ·

The Big Picture

Larry Guarino's dream reveals how complex personal experiences could become emblems for the larger community's values. Just as often, though, the official story records moments when the full weight of values or beliefs unexpectedly dropped onto a POW's shoulders. On December 31, 1965, Jim Stockdale found himself in an "eerie" cell in New Guy Village. Its "dirty walls" were covered with "etchings"—"large, crude pictures of hunchback, African-type antelope with long skinny horns, mixed in with big ostriches"—the handi-work, he decided, of African Foreign Legionnaires "taken at Dien Bien Phu in 1954."[1] POWs changed cells thousands of times between 1964 and 1973. On this day, however, a wall became a window into colonial history, as an American stared at pictures of African animals in a French cell built for his Vietnamese captors. Like other European nations, France had used its colonial populations as soldiers: Vietnamese died in Europe during both world wars, and Africans died in Southeast Asia. The ostriches and antelopes suggest how alien these artists must have seemed—how dislocated any foreign national was in Vietnam. As the years passed, the American captives drew planes and sports cars on the same walls.

The Vietnam POW was a character in at least three different narratives. As a prisoner, he unwillingly followed the Camp Authority's agenda. As an American POW, he played his part in that group history that became the official story. And as an individual, he lived his own story within these institutional and collective frameworks. When published, this third narrative became the POW memoir, a highly conventional kind of writing which personalizes larger events. While the official story may for instance credit improved prison conditions to world outrage, successful POW resistance, or the death of Ho Chi Minh, the individual POW actually felt this change when the beatings stopped, or when he finally left solitary. Resistance stories work the same way. In the official story, the American POW community fought the North Vietnamese Camp Authority, while in the memoir, an indi-vidual POW battled daily with a guard he called Abortion. Though forging links between providential history and daily events has traditionally been the theologian's and the legislator's task, biographers and memoirists also make such connections. Saints' lives trace parallels between the saint and Christ to prove sanctity. Confessions like Saint Augustine's reveal how grace transformed a single life; allegories like *The Divine Comedy* or *Pilgrim's Progress* let one traveller's fortunes stand for all humanity's.[2] Spiritual auto-biographies display God's shaping force on one soul, and prison memoirs like from Boethius's *Consolation of Philosophy* to Bunyan's *Grace Abounding to the Chief of Sinners* liken bodily captivity to worldly enslavement.

Though many Vietnam POW memoirs fit within one or more of these genres—the religious fundamentalists for example often wrote spiritual autobiographies—the two most prominent kinds of life writing found in their memoirs are the American colonial and the modern political captivity narratives. An unbroken chain of narratives links the Vietnam POW memoirs to the earliest colonial accounts. "Almost from the moment of its literary genesis," Richard Slotkin notes in his landmark book *Regeneration Through Violence: The Mythology of the American Frontier 1600–1800*, "the New England Indian captivity narrative functioned as a myth, reducing the Puritan state of mind and world view, along with the events of colonization and settlement, into archetypal drama." These immensely popular memoirs—Slotkin notes that "of the four narrative works which attained the status of best seller between 1680 and 1720, three were captivity narratives; the fourth was *Pilgrim's Progress*"—were as formulaic as Bunyan's allegory.[3] Two traits of the colonial narratives reappear prominently in the Vietnam memoirs. First, the colonial captivity narrative insists on its specific cultural identity. Neither some Jungian script, "at once a cultural phenomenon and an organic component of the individual mind," nor some "pancultural ur-narrative, or monomyth" that Sir James Frazier or Joseph Campbell might propose, these "genuine, first-person accounts of actual ordeals" were "a natural, sponta-neous product of the New World experience" which soon became "the first coherent myth-literature developed in America for American audiences." Second, the colonial readers' keen personal interest in the captive's ordeal usually made them a willing audience for the victim's "polemical and theological" convictions as well. For this reason, "Puritan ministers and men of letters" almost immediately "began to exercise direct control over the composition of the narratives, shaping them for their own ends." The result was a "very flexible" genre that could serve simultaneously as "literary entertainment, material for revival sermons, vehicle for political diatribes, and 'experimental' evidence in philosoph-ical and theological works."[4] Chapter 6 explores the explicitly Christian POW memoirs' debts to the colonial captivity narrative. In this chapter, I will discuss the colonial and Vietnam captivity narratives' shared methods for turning personal suffering into an Amer-ican vision of captors, foreign powers, and the home community.

Though the political captivity narrative has deep roots, the years since World War I have been its most formative period. In the hands of authors like Arthur Koestler, George Orwell, and Aleksandr Solzhenitsyn, these narratives mirror modern ideological struggle. Whether set in Russian gulags, Nazi concentration camps, or Korean POW brainwashing centers, these stories describe how the captor tries to suck the prisoner into the state's totalitarian ideology, while the prisoner tries to resist by clinging to certain religious, ethical, or rational convictions. The Korean War POW memoirs predictably had the strong-est affinities with the Vietnam narratives. The larger structural patterns were especially similar. Though published well before Everett Alvarez entered Hanoi, Albert D. Biderman's Korean captivity timeline could with minor alterations serve for Vietnam as well.[5] In both conflicts, an early period of relatively good treatment ended when American forces launched their first major offensive. Men captured from then on endured horrible condi-tions and brutal treatment as the Camp Authority isolated hard-line prisoners and demanded propaganda statements from the rest. When negotiations for an armistice began, the camps slowly improved, and the POWs were gathered into larger groups. These compounds spawned peace committees and other demoralizing behavior. At the peace talks, procedures for exchanging POWs became increasingly crucial to an agreement. In the camps, the captors eventually gave up on indoctrination, and a time of simple detention continued up to release, when the men headed home, worried about their welcome and about America, since it had apparently abandoned them during their captivity.

For the individual Korea or Vietnam POW, this pattern often fell into a "more logical division" of "chase and capture, the battle of ideas, attack by boredom, and attack by luxury" that General William Dean, the Korean War's highest-ranking POW, identified when composing his own memoirs. The proportions found in most Korean and Vietnamese memoirs reflect this division as well. As both unexpected and abrupt, capture and release take up very few pages. The highly charged battle of ideas, which for Dean "has the most importance," takes up the bulk of most narratives, with the methods for avoiding boredom coming in a distant second.[6] In this chapter, General Dean's "logical division" structures my discussion of the Vietnam POWs' common experiences and opinions. If chapter 4 told a story, chapter 5 explores the hatreds, affections, and convictions that determined how the POWs lived and understood this story. Two striking facts emerge from looking at this big picture. The first is its close resemblance to the colonial and political narratives I've been discussing; the second, and perhaps more controversial, is that the most racist, chauvinist, sentimental, and dogmatic attitudes are often inextricably entwined around those values which the POWs credit for their triumph.

The Unfortunate Fall: Entering and Enduring Captivity

Chase and Capture

Whether a frontiersman or an aviator, an American's first reaction to captivity is shock. As Slotkin notes, "like the myths of the fall and the apocalypse," the colonial captivity narrative "begins with man in a happy condition of innocence or complacence." Since "his farm is rich, and the landscape is bright and open," he often forgets that his home "sits on the brink of the abysmal woods, within whose shadows devilish Indians move." As a result, the "sudden violence" of capture catches "the soul unprepared."[7] Thanks to the nature of aerial combat, the Hanoi POWs felt just as insulated. As Robinson Risner explains, "air-to-air warfare is a clean, impersonal type of thing. . . . When people die, you don't see it."[8] During their tumble to earth, then, many POWs felt that like "Alice in Wonderland," they were "falling from one world into another." Malcolm McConnell compares POW Lance Sijan's descent to a time machine: "In the short time it took him to parachute to earth, he would travel from the relative security of the twentieth century's most advanced military technology to a jungle where the rules and conduct of combat had not undergone any major alteration since Neolithic times." According to POW Robert Naughton, the "abrupt" and "disconcerting" events occurring at shootdown aroused "a sense of *bewildering fear* at the alien surroundings and *uncertainty* of one's ultimate fate." The POW "finds himself huddling in a flooded rice paddy—still shaken by the combined effects of his aircraft being hit, abrupt ejection, and an unwanted parachute descent to earth—'skivvie-clad' and tightly bound amidst a crowd of angry, club-waving Vietnamese peasants, screaming in a language unintelligible to him."[9] The time machine is at work here as well—jets turn into paddies, bombs and missiles into waving clubs—but the POW's sense of displacement often went further, as like his colonial ancestor, he often felt he had arrived in hell. This journey has of course its good side: by wrenching the victim out of complacency, the memoir properly functions "not as a crusader's quest but as a sinner's trial and judgment." Whether it begins on the forest edge or over Southeast Asia, though, the story is the same: a free individual loses everything and enters into a struggle that leads to personal salvation and release.

Colonial prisoners had few illusions about captivity. Since their jailors were hell's agents, imprisonment would be an earthly purgatory at best. Many Vietnam POWs, however, had some delusions to explode first. These prisoners often assumed their compounds would resemble idealized European POW camps from World War II. In 1963, jungle POW George Smith looked forward to "a barracks somewhere like you see in the movies—a POW camp with a barbed-wire fence around it, a place where I would have plenty of everything and would be away from the war." Four years later, the same movies were flashing through Frank Anton's mind: "I knew just how it was going to be. A large compound surrounded by a high barbed-wire fence with uniformly spaced wood barracks inside. Watch towers. Guard posts. Searchlights." So powerful was this vision that it could actually survive captivity for a time. "How long would I be here?" Jim Stockdale wondered as he lay injured in a Hanoi Hilton cell, "How long would it be before I got to a real prison camp, with the barbed-wire enclosure, cellmates, and maybe a little campfire at night where we could sit around and talk of home?" That men who knew about Asian POW camps during World War II and the Korean conflict could still expect George Smith's "nice town where we could sit around, visit the public library, walk around, drink coffee, and bullshit," shows just "how easily the imagination can run wild."[10] The same dream however also explains why the longtime POWs resented so bitterly any suggestion that they had an easy time in Hanoi. Accounts of Hanoi captivity like mid-1972 captive Alan J. Kroboth's were especially annoying. After a few days in solitary, he joined some other POWs in the Plantation. Since they didn't think their captors would torture them, "We started singing at night. We made up a Christmas song. We wrote new words to 'The Twelve Days of Christmas.' Of course, the guards would get mad, so we'd sing for the guards now and then, and laugh at them." Then came Kroboth's inevitable, infuriating conclusion: "I'd compare a lot of it to Hogan's Heroes on TV. Very close to it. The morale and the spirit of everybody was like that."[11] When Howie Rutledge complained that many Americans assumed his captivity had been like "that slapstick television series featuring imaginary prisoners in World War II," he was therefore pointing out a fault in the American people, in POWs shot down after conditions had improved, and even in the longtime POWs, until their first days of captivity beat it out of them.[12]

A POW's welcoming committee was usually some understandably upset Vietnamese civilians. "They had been bombed by our aircraft for a long time," Jay Jensen recalled, "they had had their homes destroyed, their crops and animals destroyed, and some of their family killed. It was no wonder that they were very angry." Richard Stratton had been instructed "never to land in an area where you have been bombing or strafing because the reception committee is not going to be too friendly," and Jim Stockdale guessed that one out of every two shootdowns "dies from infection in the jungle or is killed by exuberant mobs of civilians in the capture process." And yet, although most POWs would agree with Tom Kirk that the civilians "hated us—there's no question about that," Richard Stratton had "never heard of any guy ever bitching about the reception of the general populace, because that's the breaks of naval air."[13] The attack itself was a whirlwind of torments. Using knives or machetes, the people cut off the captive's flight suit, and while to POW John McGrath, "It seemed as though they had never seen a zipper," POW Dieter Dengler's remark that American forces did the same thing "to look for a hidden hand grenade or concealed weapon" suggests a more plausible motive. (Larry Chesley offered both explanations: "They cut my clothes off with machetes because they didn't know how to work the zipper on my flight suit. I took some of the clothes off myself, but they didn't want me to touch anything because they were afraid I would pull a booby trap or something.")[14] Looting came next. Ralph Gaither lost "a pistol, several knives, survival gear, an identification card, a watch, and a little money"; Bill Tschudy said good-bye to "my wrist watch, my identification cards, and my box of flip-top Marlboro cigarettes." Some officials made a pretense of honesty. When Norman McDaniel handed over his "watch, wedding band, ID card, Geneva Convention card, and about fifty dollars," his interrogators promised to return them, though of course he "never saw any of those items again." Jungle troops didn't bother to pretend. When looting Ted Guy, "One removed my Seiko, a twenty-one-dollar Sportsman. He pointed at my gold wedding band. I said 'No.' He tried to pull it off. I flexed my finger. He got my survival knife and returned with a big grin. It was best, I decided, to give him the ring."[15]

The beatings that followed the looting often seemed malicious. John McGrath recalled people "beating me with bamboo switches, pinching my skin, and twisting my injured leg. My knee would dislocate and the people seemed to get a kick out of seeing me scream in agony." The air around Richard Stratton was "filled with sandals and clods and words and stones and cooking pots, some of them complete with contents and hot off cooking fires. The barrage was so heavy many of the missiles missed their target and struck other Vietnamese."[16] Though rage and revenge fueled these attacks, some POWs saw other motives at work. Charlie Plumb blamed his beatings on "the almost unbelievable influence" of "Communist officials": "At the snap of a finger, docile civilians could be turned into angry mobs, spitting and screaming and hitting me so vehemently that the guards would have to step in to control the throng in order to avert serious injury." Red McDaniel mourned the spiritual vacuum: "The blows stung me deep, not only because of the pain but in the sudden realization that these short, simple farmers were not one bit willing to show any compassion." Regardless of their cause, these beatings often continued until officials intervened. The "scores of screaming, hysterical peasants" who beat Jay Jensen "with hoes, rakes, and rifle butts" would have killed him "if the military hadn't shown up." Many POWs shared this opinion. Tom Kirk woke up to find a mob "beating me with sticks, kicking me, throwing rocks at me" until some Vietnamese militia fired a gun to stop the abuse. The "four militia types" who saved Konrad Trautman "had to strike their own people with their rifle butts, very forcefully, to keep them off me," and the soliders who captured Guy Gruters were "forced to level their fixed bayonets at the furious crowd of farmers that had boiled out of the nearby villages with the intention of hacking him to pieces."[17]

These rescuers however could prove as brutal, if not as deadly, as the farmers. According to Jay Jensen, the military "hated us every bit as intensely," but had been taught "how important prisoners were for information and especially as barter items for a peace treaty." For this reason, "their orders were to capture us alive and keep us alive—just barely."[18] Many POWs found the shift from civilian to military control a move from the frying pan into the fire. John McGrath's escorts "took turns to see who could hit my face the hardest. After the contest, they tried to force dog dung through my teeth, bounced rocks off my chest, jabbed me with their gun barrels, and bounced the back of my head off the rocks that lay in the bottom of the ditch."[19] Some captives suffered through faked executions like Bob Jeffrey's:

"It's your last chance. Your time is up," the interrogator sternly said. Then turning on his heels—Jeffrey could hear his shoes in the gravel—he gave his command.

The rifle rang out. Jeffrey heard the shots. "They must have shot over my head or into the ground, because I was not hit. They stood me up and took me back to the shack, and that was the end of that. . . ."[20]

These escorts also exhibited POWs in small villages—a dangerous practice, since the townsfolk "seemed to be quite willing to work themselves up to a hysterical pitch." At one event, Bob Craner noted his guards "were showing fear, indicating to me that there was a border-line situation, and they might, in fact, lose control, and that's the only thing I could be scared of."[21]

In most memoirs, then, chase and capture is quite predictable. Many POWs were injured and most were captured instantly, so the chase is brief or nonexistent. Capture involved abuse, but the POWs generally understood and accepted the people's anger. The authorities' arrival often saved the POW's life, but did not end his suffering. He now entered a far more calculated realm of violence and exploitation, as capture turned into captivity.

The Attack by Boredom

Not much happened in the Vietnam POW camps between 1965 and 1970. Some jungle POWs gathered manioc, and walked from time to time to a new compound. In *Bouncing Back*, the best book on how the Hanoi POWs passed their time, Geoffrey Norman explains that between interrogations, "Prisoners were expected to sit quietly in their cells, eat their two bowls of soup a day, come out for a bath and a shave once a week, and otherwise do nothing."[22] Keeping active and alert was therefore a challenge, and the POWs occupied themselves in the ways long-term prisoners always have. In *The Anatomy of Captivity*, John Laffin lists four main methods for attacking boredom: "the physically creative, the physically active, the intellectual, the imaginative."[23] The Vietnam POWs used all four. Except for some half-hearted calisthenics, jungle camp officials discouraged physical activity, even declaring at times that "exercise was against camp regulations." Hanoi's highly competitive aviators, however, needed no encouragement to exercise, and some became obsessed with building strength and endurance. Charlie Plumb's painful first sit-up soon became "twenty-five push-ups and seventy-five sit-ups," a mile of jogging in his cell, and a regimen of isometric and stretching exercises. As endurance grew, challenges flew between cells. "By the time I was released," Plumb remembers, "the push-up record peaked at 1500 and the sit-up challenge was over 10,000!" Waste buckets served as weights; other POWs juggled rag balls or skipped with improvised ropes. These exercises could be a POW's defense against the horrors of solitary. Held in a pitch-dark room for almost ten months, Robinson Risner fought his panic by running in place "as much as twenty-five miles a day. My only salvation was exhaustion—the only time I could stop running."[24]

Since the Camp Authority gave the POW almost nothing to work with, physical creativity was seldom an option. David J. Rollins became known as "Mr. Fix-It" for his ability to turn bits of wire into pens and needles, or to mold food, toilet paper, and odds and ends into chess sets, cookstoves and complete nativity scenes. With charcoal and improvised paints, Danny Glenn and Ronald Mastin drew and painted so skillfully that the North Vietnamese displayed their work at the Paris talks to show how well the POWs were being treated.[25] Most POWs, however, fulfilled their creative urges imaginatively. Elaborate house-building fantasies were very popular. Since killing time was the goal, Jay

Jensen, a self-declared "nut on house plans," would "plan the house, all the dimensions, down to the square inch; then I would remodel it and furnish it, putting every piece of furniture in every room, and planning the color schemes and all the accessories." Though the German nurse Monika Schwinn "would gladly have done the filthiest work in the camp in order to keep busy," she too resorted to building fantasies. She began with "real houses, using the tiles, bits of wood, and the sand in my yard," but soon decided her buildings "would be much larger and more beautiful if I simply sat down in the yard, smoothed out a patch of sand with my hand, and drew the floor plan with a small bamboo stick." Eventually, she threw away her stick, and erected "purely imaginary houses": "Freed of my inhibitions, I worked away for days and weeks and months."[26]

As this progression suggests, the mind was the POWs' greatest ally against boredom. Though "much of the actual knowledge" faded after they returned, Stephen Rowan claimed that many POWs seemed "to have expanded their mental capabilities." Jungle POW Donald Rander and his companions went through "all sorts of mental exercises to keep our sanity": "We tried to name all the cars we knew, the states and their capitals, dogs with names beginning with each letter of the alphabet, and all the other things you've read about." Dr. Floyd Kushner "explained mathematical formulas as if they were all that stood between him and madness," and Jim Stockdale considered the Taylor expansion for exponential functions, which provided "the key to natural logarithms that could be calculated to two decimal places in four or five iterations with a stick in the dust," as "one of the greatest gifts" he ever received. Complicated and endless games were a comfort. Alone in the jungle, Nick Rowe scratched some baseball symbols on his cup, and "using a spinner I had devised from a piece of wood, I played two entire seasons with the National League." One golfer spent "two hours a day playing a course he remembered hole by hole"; Al Stafford sailed boats he designed and built in captivity.[27]

Some POWs acted out these fantasies. Charlie Plumb played on a piano keyboard drawn on the floor, and Gerald Venanzi had an imaginary motorcycle, which he "washed, polished, and repaired" regularly. During exercise periods, Venanzi "would wheel his cycle out, start it up (complete with sound effects), and ride it wherever he went." Only an equally creative camp commander ended this game: "Because they didn't have motorcycles to give to all the prisoners, he explained, it was unfair for Gerry to have one. So Gerry started walking."[28] Any imagining that could counter the boredom was valuable. John Dramesi devoted a whole chapter of his memoir to the day he learned how to daydream, and the Kushner POWs kept busy by thinking up alternative versions of Vietnamese propaganda. "I learned a lot about the four-thousand year history of the Vietnamese," recalled Ike McMillan: "I thought it was stupid as hell. They should have given up a long time ago. After class we joked about how we wished all the Vietnamese had been killed when the Chinese or French or Japanese were there." Jim Stockdale imagined another self. When he blew up one day at his interrogators, their fear and confusion told him instantly that they wouldn't dare let such a madman talk to reporters: "Ergo, for self-protection, I should construct a subtly unstable personality and climb into it—climb into it like a wetsuit and internalize it."[29]

Others' words also strengthened the POWs. As Elaine Scarry observes, although language usually fails to represent suffering, the "isolated cases" when words succeed "provide a much more compelling (because usable) form of reassurance—fictional analogues, perhaps whole paragraphs of words, that can be borrowed when the real-life crisis of silence comes."[30] Only the Bible and the Code were more carefully memorized than the songs, poetry, and proverbs that passed between POWs' cells. Larry Chesley lists patriotic texts like "This Is My Country," "The Battle Hymn of the Republic," and "What Is America to Me?" as POW favorites. Show tunes like "My Favorite Things" moved Jay Hess, whose wife revealed that when he first phoned home after leaving Hanoi, he said, " 'I don't want you to talk for a minute,' and then he recited to me the beautiful words of the song 'You'll Never Walk Alone.' "[31] Poetry ennobled the POWs' experience. John Gillespie Magee's "High Flight," which compares the thrills of flight to communion with God, was a natural favorite among so many aviators. Purple Shakespeare—the "To be or not to be" soliloquy, Polonius's advice to Laertes, Antony's funeral oration, or "Shall I Compare Thee to a Summer's Day?" and "Let Me Not to the Marriage of True Minds" from the *Sonnets*—was prominent on Jay Jensen's list. Because Norman Wells's parents had "asked him to memorize a poem every year to recite at their Thanksgiving reunions," he became the source of long ballads. Though the themes of bondage and loyalty made "The Highwayman" popular, the POWs loved Robert W. Service's tall tales as well. Closer to home were Rudyard Kipling's "Gunga Din" and "The Ballad of East and West," which Charlie Plumb tellingly mistitles as "The *Battle* of East and West." The most cherished poems, however, dealt with adversity and suffering. While Kipling's "If," that hymn to imagination, coolheadedness, and the will, is often mentioned, the POWs' favorite poem was probably W. E. Henley's "Invictus," which several memoirs mention, and even reprint. Henley's "bloody, but unbowed" speaker's faith in his "unconquerable soul" allows him to triumph over "the bludgeonings of chance" in a "place of wrath and tears," and the closing declaration—"I am the master of my fate; / I am the captain of my soul"—practically versifies the Code of Conduct.[32]

Others' words led some men to think about writing their own. Among the talents he wanted to develop, Jay Jensen listed "communicative skills, such as writing a diary, biography, family history, POW experiences, genealogy, travel books, or other types of books." Everett Alvarez held in his head an epic yarn about an Hispanic boy in frontier America.[33] There were also POW poets. Gerald Coffee smuggled out a sizable collection of POW verses on cigarette wrappers, and the *Los Angeles Times* devoted an article, "POW Poets Wrote of Love, Home and Mice," to the subject. Porter Halyburton, Ralph (Tom) Browning, William Lawrence, James Hutton, and Quincy Collins generally wrote love letters, songs of freedom, verses of suffering, and hymns of thanks for life's blessings, and "if the rhyme was sometimes uncertain or the flow irregular, the feeling was always sincere, often eloquent." The POWs shared this opinion. Jim Mulligan said his Thanksgiving poem for 1971 "wasn't much, but it came from my heart and each man took my hand and said thank you when I had finished." Jeremiah Denton's Easter poems urged others to pray beside Christ's tomb or reminded them that clouds can hide the sun. They also confirmed his status as "president of the Optimist Club." And such titles as "My Plight," "Anniversary Poem," and "God is My Pilot" suggest that for poet Norman McDaniel at least, suffering, family, and God's love were more important concerns than imagery or prosody.[34]

The self-proclaimed POW poet was Ralph Gaither. With a separate table of contents for the fifteen poems printed, Gaither's memoir traces the growth of a Christian poet. A devout Baptist, Gaither claims his story is "about Christ"—and poetry made him feel closest to his Savior. Gaither's favorite subjects—God's presence in his life, and the love of a distant, idealized woman—came together in his first lyric, "Lovely Sonya." A poem written with Mike Cronin "became a tradition. Each Christmas I repeated it as part of a Christmas program, and I included it on Christmas cards that I made for other rooms." His creativity really caught fire in late 1969, when more contact with other POWs meant he could learn from men "who knew meter and rhythm." Gaither solemnly records his moments of inspiration. "When I held a picture in my hand, and when I watched the faces of my buddies as they looked at their pictures, a poem began to form in my mind," and the result, "Your Face," predictably described how photographs made the POWs think of "freedom, home, and God." With the move into Camp Unity, Gaither "began to write poetry in earnest." That winter, "a creative one for me," he wrote a number of poems "either romantic or religious in nature." He also played the role of "the poet": "I woke up one night during the summer, about midnight, with a poem boiling in my head. I couldn't sleep as I thought of that girl. As I lay awake, this poem forced its way out of me." In time, Gaither's verses "not only developed around my own thoughts, but also around those of the other guys in the building." True to his artistic vision, his memoir's last words blend poetry, country, freedom, and religion: "Every American must be free to sing whatever song he wants to sing. That's how God wants this country to be."[35]

That same move to Camp Unity also made large group activities possible. For longtimers, simply meeting more POWs was very comforting. After years with the same cellmates, some POWs left Hanoi "like men who had been in an encounter group for five *years*." Camp Unity's breathing room had its downside as well. "As the treatment got better," Red McDaniel recalled, "our discipline seemed to vanish. It was the old story about adversity drawing us closer, prosperity making us independent and more selfish." In response, the commanding officers became recreation directors—or as Red McDaniel recalled, "It was because of the growing unrest of being thrown together, where diverse personalities could play more easily on each other's nerves, that we had to organize more games."[36] Though some men played cards and chess compulsively, such intense games weren't always the best recreation for highly competitive types. Trying to divert the POWs without provoking fights led to some novel activities. Since longtime roommates often knew each other far better than their spouses, playing "The Newlywed Game" let them joke about this fact. Red McDaniel's friends "would get together as a group," and have one man "host the rest of the room for the evening. We would fantasize going to his house, and there he would serve hors d'oeuvres, then the meal—a menu we would all lovingly concoct in our imaginations." As "excuses to bolster morale," the POWs "celebrated anything and everything—birthdays, anniversaries, religious holidays, Groundhog Day, Jewish Independence Day." One POW recalled fondly a "Mummer's Day" parade: "Imagine guys flailing their arms and legs in Mummer fashion. . . . The guys in prison really enjoyed it."[37]

Gifted storytellers entertained other POWs with Hemingway and Faulkner stories, or versions of *Gone with the Wind*, *Advise and Consent*, and *The Caine Mutiny*. Men would ask, "Have you heard the latest movies?" and at year's end, the POWs gave out their "own form of Academy Awards." Some story tellers "filmed" their own scripts, as "scene by scene, the POW performed his histrionics until the plot was so complex and confused that a denouement was impossible." With time, " 'Low-cost' productions, lasting about fifteen minutes in 1967, became full-blown spectaculars six years later." Ratings ranged from PG to XXX. Descriptions of the heroine—"her low-cut gown, her seductive smile, her inevitable trip to the bedroom"—forced Charlie Plumb "to quit listening" because the films "hurt more than they entertained." Sometimes New York alternated with Hollywood. Al Stafford "became known for telling the Broadway musicals that he had enjoyed so much." Larry Chesley reports that the POWs actually staged " 'South Pacific' and 'The Sound of Music,' with costumes, 'girlies' and everything," and George Day fondly remembered the 1971 POW production of *A Christmas Carol*.[38] Choirs and glee clubs met regularly, and so did fraternal societies—toastmasters, for instance, the perfect club for men wanting to work on their postrelease speeches. The POWs' most comprehensive response to the "atmosphere of growing tension, and the real fear that some of the men might try to organize an escape or even storm the walls" was "Hanoi University." Courses in "history, political science, biology, astronomy, literature, poetry," mathematics, and a broad range of foreign languages were available, and so was instruction in auto mechanics and dairy farming. Classes "in a lighter, less academic vein" included "hunting, gun classes, camping, stereo, photography, book reports, music, art." Basket weaving, meat cutting, and wine appreciation were popular, and so was Jay Jensen's skiing class: "Just imagine fifty prisoners standing on their cement bunks and trying to do jump turns and stem christies and hot doggin' while the Vietnamese stared through the windows and bars, wondering what in the world was going on." On a more somber note, marriage and family life seminars had large enrollments.[39]

Though all POWs were bored at times, their memoirs stress the battle of ideas so heavily that virtually no one captured after late 1969 has published a memoir. "It was the guys who had been there longer who really suffered," 1972 POW William Angus explained, "I didn't want to detract from their stories."[40] Together, these stories were of course the official story, and to the later arrivals, the old-timers seemed nostalgic at times about their early suffering. The longtime POWs' prominence thus split Hanoi history into two unequal parts and populations. The epic struggles of 1964–69 petered out into the annoying, uneventful waiting of 1969–73, just as those grizzled veterans of the battle of ideas saw themselves as different from those later arrivals whose only challenge was fending off the attack by boredom while waiting for certain release.

The Battle of Ideas: Their Fight Continued

At first glance, the POWs' chances in the battle of ideas looked grim. The Camp Authority controlled their captives' food, surroundings, and contacts with other POWs. Stripped of their weapons, the POWs had only their background, their politics, and their faith to fight back with, and while POW Robert Naughton argues that "past survival school training and the ingrained knowledge that the Code of Conduct is the order of the day embody the spirit of resistance and give a man an instinctive *modus operandi* from the outset of captivity," even the highest-ranking POWs believed that personal attitudes and talents had to supplement military training.[41] For instance, an early love of competition often gets mentioned as a source of strength. One chapter in Red McDaniel's memoir is called "Fourth Down—and Goal to Go," and he also describes how a vision of his high-school coach saved him from despair. As his captors tortured him, McDaniel wondered, "Why was the game spirit coming up again in such a ridiculous place and in such a setting?" Coach Frank L. Mock, whose "kindly, rough-hewn face floated before me like a balloon," was the answer. Mock's chief lesson had been Vince Lombardi's: "To win isn't everything—actually, it's the only thing." For this reason, "every game, every challenge of life" fueled McDaniel's fire. Other POWs had similar role models. John Dramesi relied on his wrestling coach; Jeremiah Denton's "athletic mentor," football coach Ed Overton, told him that "to be a champion, you have to pay the price every minute, day in and day out."[42] Those attitudes linked to "age" and "cultural experience" had however a far greater impact than contact sports on the POWs' resistance. In their toughest struggles with the Camp Authority, the POWs commonly drew most upon their beliefs about the family, about male-female relationships, and about the merits of civilians versus soldiers, Asians versus Americans, and communism versus capitalism. Many other Americans, and sometimes other POWs, did not agree with these attitudes; nevertheless, the mainstream memoirs repeatedly claim that a set of shared values guided the senior officers as they founded the POW community, and then plotted out the course for an official story that would slowly encompass all POW history.

The Matter of Race

Admiral Daniel V. Gallery prefaced his book on the *Pueblo* incident with the following remarks:

> Throughout this book I use the word "gooks" in referring to the North Koreans. Some people object to this word.
>
> By "gook" I mean precisely an uncivilized Asiatic Communist. I see no reason for anyone who doesn't fit this definition to object to the way I use it.[43]

With the simple substitution of "Vietnamese" for "Korean," Gallery's preface could open many Vietnam POW memoirs. These prisoners often blamed Vietnam's poverty and cultural differences on their captors' "Asiatic" inferiority. The "uncivilized" Vietnamese gook seemed stuck at a stage of cultural development which Americans had supposedly passed through generations before. And the label "Communist" only added insult to injury, since it suggested that the Vietnamese had become Marxists *because* they were poor and primitive Asiatics.

Assumptions like these have a long history in America. A broad racist streak came in the cultural baggage of the earliest European settlers, and as Richard Slotkin observes, missionaries in Puritan New England "demanded that the Indian give up all his Indian ways and become thoroughly Anglicized before he could gain acceptance as a church member." No compromise was possible: "Far from accepting and joining in Indian customs, the English demanded their total extirpation." This harsh attitude was relatively tolerant by New England standards; when the Puritans' "assurance gave way to self-doubt, they thought of exorcizing the Indians through physical extermination." In either case, though, the Puritans did not "perceive the Indians' humanity."[44] This state of mind set the New Englanders against those from their own community who adapted to the frontier. During the witch trials, infection by Indian customs was proof of Satanic possession. Nor did the gap between good white settlers and evil brown savages close much over the next three centuries. As Slotkin and Richard Drinnon both argue, what Herman Melville called "the metaphysics of Indian-hating and empire building" accompanied America's march west from Massachusetts to Montana, and later from Manila to the Mekong.

In the twentieth century, Indian hating has merged with the practice of colonialism, which for Jean-Paul Sartre grew out of Europeans' belief in "two complementary and inseparable truths. That they have the divine right, and that the natives are sub-human." This "mythical interpretation of a reality" is also an economic one, and not simply because "the riches of one are built on the poverty of the other," but because colonialism "puts the exploiter at the mercy of his victim."[45] A modern POW's outrage often arises from this inversion. When captured by the Japanese, some World War II POWs found it hard to get past their first reaction: "To think those little bastards beat us!" Communist POW camps in Korea provoked the 1955 U.S. Advisory Committee on Prisoners of War into making similar responses. Even if American POWs had been given the same food as their captors, "the Chinese were inured to a rice diet. The average American could not stomach such fare." As "products of a semi-primitive environment," some of the "North Korean officers were bullwhip barbarians," and the notorious Colonel Pak was "a sadist, an animal who should have been in a cage," and thus "symbolic of the institution" he ran. Even some Western POWs held in Korea recognized how counterproductive such attitudes were. Before his imprisonment, reporter Philip Deane [Philippe Deane Gigantes] noticed that "no American seems to call the Koreans, friends or foes, anything but Gooks." Deane's guards and interrogators told him that being called " 'dirty yellow bastards' to our faces," and reading signs like the one outside of the Seoul PX—"No dogs—No Koreans"—had led them to join the Communists. General William Dean also discovered what "terrific harm" such "thoughtlessness" had done: "Again and again I was told that this man or that one had come north because he had decided he never could get along with people who called him a 'gook,' or worse, among themselves; because he resented American attentions to Korean women; or because he hated to see foreigners riding in his country in big automobiles while he and his family had to walk." Dean's conclusion was adamant: "Use of the term 'gook,' or its many equivalents, by Americans," should be grounds "for military punishment."[46]

Nor did exposing racial hatred end the matter. Though William J. Lederer and Eugene Burdick denounced cultural arrogance and isolation as America's fatal weaknesses in Southeast Asia, the alternative vision offered in *The Ugly American* seems to be a population of grateful children who abandon Communism in return for help and instruction from decent American folks. In *The Quiet American*, Graham Greene had heaped abuse on this benign parent paradigm well before the first Vietnam POWs were captured. Alden Pyle, a caricature of CIA operative Edward Geary Lansdale, at one point attacks cynical British correspondent Thomas Fowler for his attitudes toward the Vietnamese. Pyle however is the real target, as the resulting dialogue shows:

> "You talk like a European, Thomas. These people aren't complicated."
> "Is that what you've learned in a few months? You'll be calling them childlike next."
> "Well—in a way."
> "Find me an uncomplicated child, Pyle. . . ."[47]

The Americans heading into Vietnam could thus be bringing with them not only that tradition of violent racial hatred which stretches back to colonial Indian hating, but also a well-intentioned, humane, but equally dismissive racial condescension. Between them, these twin impulses cover the range of racial attitudes that Edward Said has organized under the term "Orientalism." To the mature, civilized, and modern American POWs, their captors were physically and psychologically like children—tiny, petty, immature—culturally like savages—uncivilized, inhuman, sadistic—and historically like primitives—underdeveloped and anachronistic. They were in short nonentities even in their own country, or as jungle POW Frank Anton put it, "Sure, we called them slopes, dinks, and gooks. But those were simply slang words. It was strange to think of the Vietnamese as foreigners, because they were in their own country, but to us that's exactly what they were—foreigners."[48]

The Vietnam POWs were especially likely to fall into such attitudes because they were virtually ignorant about the enemy. Often confined to air bases or aircraft carriers, many of the fliers "had never seen a Vietnamese face-to-face until they were captured," and bouts of harsh treatment and torture immediately after capture did nothing to encourage sympathy or tolerance.[49] It's small wonder, then, that many POW memoirs could serve as textbooks for Western racial stereotypes. The adult-child opposition is pervasive. Red McDaniel, "six foot three inches, now about 160 pounds, with red hair, fair-skinned and round-eyed," described "the average North Vietnamese" as "about five feet two inches tall, with black hair, yellow-skinned, slant-eyed." (Five foot eight inch Larry Chesley found his captors proportionally smaller: the "tallest" Vietnamese are "5 foot 1" or so.) As he stared down at the troops who captured him, McDaniel was "conscious of how little they seemed in their floppy, pajamalike clothes, not sure of themselves even now that they had me. This was 'the enemy,' I thought, but looking at them, all I could think of was that they appeared to be more like a bunch of kids out in the jungle looking for something to do." McDaniel thus saw himself as a Gulliver: "I did not feel any fear they would or even could deal me any great harm. They seemed as much awestruck by my size and what and whom I represented as I was of their smallness."[50]

The immature bodies inevitably led POWs to assume childlike minds. Though Charlie Plumb begins his pseudoanthropological chapters on his captors by stating that like "any ethnic group, the Vietnamese make an interesting but complex study," his overview, "based on thousands of hours of observation," displays a people who "frequently seemed childish and immature." The guards teased animals, threw rocks, and beat birds' nests with sticks. Vietnamese anger resembled infants' tantrums, for "try as they would, these peasants were so small that they were unable to express their fury effectively." "Vietnamese pastimes" were equally infantile. Plumb gleefully describes two guards bouncing up and down and making engine noises in a disabled jeep, until "after half an hour, their interest spent, these 'distinguished wardens of enemy captives' climbed out and, arm in arm, walked away kicking at rocks." Fond of preening—"more evidence of adolescent behavior"—the Vietnamese treasured personal belongings, but were careless with issued equipment.[51] Their art was wretched. Plumb found "nearly all Vietnamese music was a strain on my nerves," reminding him "of a basement full of grade school horn-blowers trying to imitate the cry of a panther." Their paintings "were mostly in watercolor, charcoal, or red brick, and they were a far cry from the artistic achievements in China or Japan. They resembled exhibits of grade school children." As for ethics, "punishment for stealing was token" and "lying was also a Vietnamese way of life." For all of Plumb's talk about "a kaleidoscope of the mundane, the tragic, the humorous, the paradoxical—a conglomerate of human emotion and response," his portrait of the Vietnamese strongly resembles many earlier American sketches of childlike frontier Indians, pre–Civil War slaves, South Sea islanders, or Filipino plantation workers:

> The Vietnamese seem more content than Americans, often smiling and laughing at work and play. Frequently they were childishly giddy and irresponsible. They also carried strains of an unpredictable sadism. They were excitable. They were stoic about pain. Although generally not sentimental, they mourned the death of Ho Chi Minh. They lied and stole from each other but rarely came to fisticuffs. They were vain and ostentatious, but they were afraid.[52]

Other traits that the POWs linked to race were far more damning. When his captors seemed to ignore his injuries, Red McDaniel decided that "the Oriental attitude toward Americans in war" would make the Vietnamese no more sympathetic than the Japanese had been. Richard Stratton and Robinson Risner also worried about "the legendary cruelty of Orientals," and many POWs confirm this fear by describing their captors' treatment of animals.[53] "The guards made horrible sport of butchering their food," Ralph Gaither recalled: "When they killed a pig, they first punched its eyes out so that it would stand still, then they beat it to death." Dogs fared no better. POW James Daly remembered vividly the day his guards "brought a dog to camp, tied his hind legs, and strung him up to a pole." The dog started "howling for dear life" as they "beat him with sticks," and when the interpreter said they were "making the meat tender," Daly skipped dinner. In a section entitled "Man's Best Friend," Jay Jensen also bemoans this "strange, cruel" custom. His captors "would all get in a circle around the puppy so he couldn't get away and then stone and beat the dog to death," and "even after it was dead, they beat it some more, I suppose to make it tender."[54] Other animals simply died for amusement. "Soldiers would catch a baby bird just learning to fly and pull the feathers out of one wing," Charlie Plumb recalled: "Released, it would become an easy target for rock throwing." Ralph Gaither's guards would "catch a mouse, douse him with gasoline, set him on fire, and turn him loose to run and writhe until he died." Plumb also saw this "most sadistic practice of all" used on puppies: "Guards would douse them with gasoline, set them on fire, and turn them loose to squeal and scurry in search of relief from the heat. Then the soldiers would chase them with sticks, playing polo with their live fireballs until the little animals blackened and died."[55] Guard bestiality was a staple of POW humor. "Spike" Nasmyth said Hanoi's "funniest fuck story" came from a POW who claimed he "saw, 'with his own eyes' a Gook guard fuck a duck. His detailed description of feathers flying, wings flapping and painful quacking brought the house down." Equally damning was George Day's account of a "young female worker" who "was masturbating a male dog with enthusiasm": "The dog was also enthusiastic, until the young woman lighted her cigarette lighter and put the flame directly against the animal's penis!"[56]

Obviously, the North Vietnamese held no monopoly on such cruelty. Some bored American layabouts set fire to a dog in *Huckleberry Finn*, and the napalm released from the POWs' planes notoriously had the same effect on people. Nor was pleasure at such suffering restricted to the North. When monks began immolating themselves in 1963, Diem's brother Nhu quipped that "if the Buddhists wish to have another barbecue" he would "be glad to supply the gasoline and a match," and his wife, the infamous Madame Nhu, said "I shall clap my hands at another suicide." The animal atrocities had a special meaning for the POWs, however, because they "could not expect much better treatment than they gave their animals"—and according to Ralph Gaither, "that's about what we got." Red McDaniel agreed. Blinding pigs and incinerating rats may have been "peculiar" to his captors' "own kind of life," but such actions "got to us, because we did not know how far that 'sporting' streak in them would carry over to us in the torture room. If life, even animal life, was no more to them than that, was our value much higher?"[57]

This supposed "satisfaction in inflicting pain" sits uncomfortably with another common POW claim that their captors showed "no pity, no compassion, no emotion at all; in fact, there was nothing in them to indicate they were dealing with human beings." Larry Chesley claimed that "the consensus among the prisoners" was that their guards were basically "computerized robots doing what they were programmed to do." Also famous as "Asian inscrutability," this impassiveness led Ralph Gaither and his friends to "quit trying to figure out why the Vietnamese did what they did. Their logic was completely unfathomable." Better conditions in later years did not make things clearer. "We never knew how to read the faces of our guards now," Red McDaniel recalled, "When they laughed, we thought it meant things were better; but we found that the opposite sometimes was true. Smiling might mean things were going well for them in the war. When they were frowning, we would get more food, so we realized there was no reliable way to read them."[58] As it happens, though, the POWs themselves often behaved in very similar ways. Robinson Risner mentions "an unwritten standing rule never to let the Vietnamese know if we were interested" in radio broadcasts, and he proudly reports that when the POWs did not greet the October 1972 peace negotiations with "back flips and handsprings," or fall into despair when the talks collapsed, the camp commander told him, "You are all very good actors. You yourself are a very good actor. That's the reason we don't trust you." The POW maxim that "the only thing consistent about the Vietnamese . . . is their inconsistency" could thus be one side of a coin that Charlie Plumb describes: "They don't understand us, and we don't understand them. That's part of the whole problem."[59]

The reason POWs gave most often for this gap was a historical one. As citizens of an advanced and progressive society, the POWs felt the Vietnamese were culturally retarded—an attitude McGeorge Bundy caught perfectly when he responded to Curtis LeMay's famous remark, "We should bomb them into the Stone Age," with "Maybe they're already there."[60] Though the POWs laughed when Charlie Plumb yelled out, "These people are a thousand years behind in blind-folds!" such comparisons were common. George Day called his captors a "polyglot of extremely diverse-appearing throwbacks." Konrad Trautman "felt like I had been through a time machine, from the year 2,000 back to the year maybe 1,000, perhaps 1,000 B.C. The people were that primitive and crude, both in appearance and their dress, their conduct especially, and the tools that they used to beat us with." For Richard Stratton, a self-proclaimed "political hostage held by an uncivilized, brutal, petty people," the North Vietnamese were "an armed group of paranoid children that have a national inferiority complex and are trying to overcome four thousand years of backwardness by working one day a month." Captivity itself seemed to violate natural order. As he looked at the "little brown guy" guarding him, Robinson Risner was amazed that "he could lock me in, put me in stocks, and seemingly could decide if I should live or die. I was no longer a proud American from a rich and powerful country. I was nothing . . . at their disposal." For many captives, this amazement turned quickly into anger. The *New York Times* reported that many POWs had been "outraged at being captured by a backward, Communist country they considered socially, militarily and morally inferior; they habitually referred to their captors as 'sleazy gooks,' and worse."[61]

The "worse" includes the entire range of racist abuse. Fury at being treated like animals led the POWs to return the favor. "Two kinds of rats infest Hanoi," wrote parolee Robert Frishman, "the four-legged rodents that swarm the camps where American servicemen are imprisoned, and the two-legged sadists who operate these hellholes." To Ralph Gaither, a very troublesome mosquito symbolized "the Vietnamese, my tormentors": "I wanted to smash him all the more then." Some POWs concluded that living conditions were horrible because "personal hygiene was not important to the Vietnamese." Or as Charlie Plumb claimed, "The V seldom bathed and saw no reason why we should."[62] Vietnamese feeblemindedness was part of Richard Stratton's defense for avoiding torture: "Obviously, there was a certain superiority complex here. Here's a bunch of dumb bastards and I can outwit them, you know? I am smarter than they are, better educated than they are, traveled farther than they had, and no one is going to believe their crap on the outside anyway." Other POWs blamed their wretched treatment on their captors' raging sense of inferiority. Though Red McDaniel granted that "cultural sensitivity" might explain some camp rules—no leg crossing, no turning your back on an interrogator—he felt that many punishments arose from this rage: "Maybe that was only natural, since we did represent a superior war machine in terms of technology. It might have won some respect from them for us. Instead it built in them a kind of ruthlessness that became more and more sadistic: it bred a heavy-handed superiority and made them sensitive in odd ways."[63]

Observations like this one explain how the POWs could see themselves as victims of racism without altering their opinions of their captors. Richard Stratton felt he had "experienced the other end of racial prejudice" because of "a backlash against the humiliation" the Vietnamese "have felt at the hands of the French for a hundred years." Now "it was their turn to be in the saddle; hence the insistence on the ninety-degree bow to everybody, to see the white man cry, to see the white man bow, to see the white man dirty, to see him urinating in his pants."[64] The familiar racist paradigm—*we* are diverse and complex; *they* are simple and transparent—shaped *both* sides' opinions of the other. "Most POWs thought the Vietnamese were stupid," POW Tom Davis recalled, because they "couldn't understand that we all had somewhat different attitudes because one guy was reared in the West, one in the East, and one in the South; that one was white and one was black; one was Jewish, another Baptist or Catholic." But as Davis also notes, "we probably understood them less than they understood us. Most of the time we underestimated them because guys thought, 'Oh, he's just a gook.' In irritation you called them gooks, as a white guy might say he's just a nigger, or a black man he's just a hunk. Racism shows itself in anger. You must understand a man's culture before you can understand his race; and we knew nothing about the Vietnamese."[65]

What further complicated matters in Vietnam was the POWs' woeful ignorance of just how volatile Vietnamese reactions to Western racism were. One of Ho Chi Minh's many pseudonyms was Nguyen O Phap (Nguyen Who Hates the French), and his earliest writings in Bernard Fall's opinion "reflect the personal humiliations he must have suffered at the hands of the colonial masters—not because they hated him as a person, but simply because, as a 'colored' colonial, he *did not count as a human being.*"[66] Racism and colonialism were the enemies that drove Ho to communism. When he asked his French Socialist comrades, "Which International sides with the peoples of colonial countries?" someone gave him Lenin's "Thesis on the National and Colonial Questions." Ho found the "political terms" difficult, but by "reading it again and again," the message eventually hit him with the force of a religious conversion: "What emotion, enthusiasm, clear-sightedness and confidence it instilled in me! I was overjoyed. Though sitting alone in my room I shouted aloud as if addressing large crowds: 'Dear martyrs, compatriots! This is what we need, this is our path to liberation!'" Leninism thus became Ho's key to Vietnam's racist dynamics, and anticolonialism became the "central issue of all his public statements at Communist Party congresses, to the almost total exclusion of any other consideration."[67] The POWs' ignorance of Vietnam, and their understandable hostility toward an enemy treating them so brutally, thus made them resemble those portraits of colonial racists that Ho had been drawing years before many of the POWs had been born. In this version of U.S. history, America forced its way into Japan, occupied the Philippines, aided Chiang Kai-Shek, intervened in Korea, and restored French colonialism in post-war Vietnam as part of a racist and imperialist agenda. Both Hanoi officials and Western antiwar groups met any claim that the Vietnam War was a battle between freedom and communism with this racist interpretation. Ho himself could have written Bertrand Russell's remark that only racism "allows the U.S. press, the Senate, and many public figures to remain absolutely silent when 'Viet-cong' prisoners are summarily shot; yet at the same time these bodies demand the leveling of North Vietnamese cities if the pilots are brought to trial for their crimes."[68]

And yet, although Philip Holt guessed in 1968 that Vietnamese indoctrinators "would meet with more success pushing an 'Asia for the Asians' line than by presenting theoretical ideological exhortations," the POWs generally ignored appeals "cast in terms of oppression by the wealthy or of race discrimination," simply because the prejudice so obviously went both ways. Though Monika Schwinn and Bernhard Diehl were opposed to the American policies in Vietnam, these two German nurses soon learned that "because the people hated all whites, it was not safe for us to travel in the daytime." Among the common people, this racial antagonism often grew out of an ignorance as deep as that of the POWs. After learning Vietnamese, jungle prisoner Robert Garwood discovered that many people "regarded the Americans as men of legendary strength who did not feel any pain, and were like machines in operation."[69] Officials familiar with the party line on colonialism often seemed obsessively enraged. When a new cadre not only showed the manner "of a man who could give the order for his child to be beheaded and smile as it was carried out," but also a doctrinaire racial "arrogance," Nick Rowe knew he was in trouble: "The impression was that we were the Caucasians who had dominated his country, in the form of the French, and had felt superior to him as a Vietnamese. Now he, as a Vietnamese, was in complete control over us." The simplest actions could suddenly bring POWs face to face with anticolonial fury. When a prickly guard kicked a stool over to a badly injured Jim Stockdale only after he had struggled to reach it for some minutes, Stockdale tried "to make the best of an already bad relationship," and said "Attaboy." Instantly, "Dipshit stormed up in front of me and surprised me with pidgin English"—"I am not boy—I am mister"—and Stockdale drew the proper lesson: "Enragement over colonialism's racial slights was very close to the surface in this country; I was to be paying a lot of French debts."[70] Perhaps the most naked example of this racist dynamic occurred between Robinson Risner and his virtually omniscient interrogator. When asked, "What do you think of the Vietnamese people?" a terrified Risner answered, "Well, they seem to be very highly motivated and industrious—and very determined fighters." The official then nailed the POW to the wall—"You do not believe that. You think they are ignorant, duped by their government, and not far removed from savages"—and Risner confirmed the charge: "That was exactly what I thought, but how did he know?"[71]

The North Vietnamese also tried to exploit racial divisions among the POWs—divisions that certainly were there. The interrogators threw whatever they could think of at the POWs to break up their sense of unity. Camp radios broadcast reports on American civil rights marches. Officials eagerly met with Martin Luther King and other leaders to discuss early releases for minority POWs. For propaganda reasons, blacks and Hispanics were more likely to be paroled. When Willie Watkins was released for the November 1969 Washington antiwar rally, for instance, his broadcast speech "thanked the Liberation Front for releasing him and talked about racism in America. They played Aretha Franklin's 'Respect' along with his talk."[72] For all these efforts, though, the Vietnamese generally failed to drive a racial wedge between the POWs. Population was part of the reason. Fewer than twenty black POWs returned home in 1973, and black Hanoi POWs were so rare that one man was mistaken at times for a Vietnamese. Tensions were thus almost nonexistent because black POWs were as well. Camp conditions also affected racial conflicts. Like sexual desire, prejudice lost much of its heat when simply eating was the problem. The experiences of one Hanoi and one jungle prisoner, however, provide the best insight into the black POWs' imperviousness to racial appeals. In the official story, Air Force Major Fred V. Cherry embodies American racial solidarity. After describing how sadistic Vietnamese doctors operated on him without anesthetic, Hubbell then discusses Cherry's feelings about his race, his profession, and his fellow POWs. Though he witnessed "racial indignities" as a child—a white boy knocked over his brother's bicycle—"by and large, life had been good." The career "opportunities that had been granted him and the confidence exhibited in him" meant that "he had done well in the Air Force, and the Air Force had done well by him." After his capture, he owed his life to the care of cellmate Porter Halyburton, a white Southerner, and Cherry's feelings toward other POWs were also positive. When the Camp Authority attempted "to zero in on his blackness, to find and exploit his resentments," he just "squelched them. He had made clear that he was first and foremost an American military officer, and expected to be treated as such."[73]

In the jungle camps, where black POWs were more common, and racial tensions more intense, officials still hardly ever converted someone to their cause. The story of Army Sergeant James E. Jackson, Jr., suggests why. When he and two other POWs—one black and one white—were released in November 1967 "in response," announced Hanoi, "to the American Negro's struggle for peace in the United States," Jackson returned home to give an excellent description of the racial appeals. His interrogators told him his race entitled him to special treatment. They asked "why the American Negro wanted to come to Vietnam," when he was treated so badly at home. They told him about race riots and assassinations of black leaders, and played him tapes of Stokely Carmichael condemning the war. And above all, they insisted that blacks should sympathize with the Vietnamese people. Why did this strategy fail? To begin with, Jackson never believed that his captors felt any solidarity with black POWs. For all the propaganda, Jackson's guards "largely followed the official line: all Americans are bad and hate Asians." Second, the Vietnamese themselves occasionally revealed some strongly racist attitudes toward blacks. Richard Stratton remembered his guards coming "around one time with a picture of Wilt Chamberlain, laughing and saying, 'He looks just like a monkey. Where does he ever find a woman to satisfy him?' Extremely prejudiced." Third, the Vietnamese often showed that they knew little about American blacks. Jackson's guards "would ask me whether it was true that Negros in America don't go to school, whether all Negros are poor. . . . You'd be surprised at how many people I ran into over there who told me that there were no Negro officers in the U.S. Army." The most compelling reason most black POWs refused to collaborate had however little to do with racism: prison conditions were simply so bad that offers of special treatment leaked like a sieve. "I could readily see that they were only making promises," Jackson recalled, "All I had to do was look around me and see in what miserable shape the other Negro prisoners were in." Though Jackson admits that the racial appeals made him and "some of the other Negro prisoners think," and though the Kushner camp split disastrously for a time along racial lines, if given the choice—which they were not—most black POWs found being ill-treated in America with their families and friends a more attractive option than rotting away in the jungle. Despite the racial tensions within American society and the military, the mistrust and bigotry in the camps arose most strongly between captor and captive.[74]

Speaking and Naming

The most telling indicator of the differences between POWs and their captors was language. A POW tapping furtively on a cell wall is perhaps the most common image in Vietnam memoirs because it suggests how hard both sides struggled to control who could speak, to whom, and how. Robinson Risner, for instance, noted that the prison staff "would not tell us their Vietnamese names," nor, according to Jim Stockdale, did they ever "wear badges of rank in front of prisoners." The POWs' own names disappeared as well. " 'Don' was my Vietnamese name," Stockdale recalled, "they give every prisoner one that is pronounceable by the guards." To keep the POWs bewildered and out of touch, the Camp Authority put them through frequent and pointless room changes—a tactic Stockdale linked to the language policy: "No wonder they wouldn't allow us to learn any Vietnamese words. How could they run complicated evolutions like this and still keep us in the dark on what they were up to if we could make out what the leader was saying?"[75] The POWs chose to fight back by pulling the blind down on their side as well. Prisoners didn't simply resist learning Vietnamese; it became in fact POW command policy not to. The Camp Authority therefore had to address the POWs in English, and POW Bill Tschudy recalls that "mocking the captors' fractured English" became "a great morale booster": "Whenever they would say something like, 'Don't change horseshoes in the middle of the stream,' or that somebody had 'let the cat into the bag,' we'd spread it around and get a big kick out of it."[76] Such fumbling led POWs like Charlie Plumb to speak confidently about the primitive and impoverished nature of Vietnamese, even though he could not speak the language. Plumb claimed the first Vietnamese dictionary appeared only during his captivity, replacing the U.S. pilots' "pointie-talkie" dictionaries. Plumb was grossly misinformed, but his mistake is consistent with his claim that the Vietnamese cannot "express their knowledge succinctly, especially during philosophical arguments," because their language "lacks 'sophisticated' words which describe abstract concepts, and entire paragraphs are needed to express a thought which can be conveyed with three or four words of English." One result was clutter: "A Vietnamese word root is often loaded with parasitic prefixes and suffixes in an attempt to enhance meaning." Another handicap was a lack of subtlety. Charlie Plumb claimed that "everything we said was interpreted literally," because their captors "simply could not comprehend our use of humorous sarcasm or irony."[77]

The question however remains: Why did the POWs *deliberately* avoid learning Vietnamese? Though he mentions that "our captors did not try to teach us," Larry Chesley reveals that by refusing "to pick it up" the POWs were "maintaining our separate status, making no concessions that would even hint of collaboration with the enemy, and forcing our captors to address us in English."[78] Like their Puritan forebears, then, though unavoidably clothed and fed like their captors, the POWs resisted anything, including language, that could suggest spiritual assimilation. As Richard Drinnon notes, since colonial days, for American authorities "all white renegades, from Thomas Morton to John Winfrey, were freaks of nature, *white* savages who had, as John Quincy Adams said of Arbuthnot and Ambrister, disowned 'their own natures.'"[79] The Hanoi POWs also tended to mistrust *any* American who spent long periods in distant camps, even though jungle POW Donald Rander claims that mutual incomprehension was the law of the jungle as well. Some guards may have "wanted to learn a few words of English—like how to greet someone," but "they didn't speak English and were virtually not allowed to learn. It was beyond their purview—and you don't overstep your boundaries in their society."[80] All these linguistic barricades tended to make anyone who could erase them suspect. Robert Garwood's jungle skills and fluency in Vietnamese seemed to arouse as much hatred in the other jungle POWs as any real evidence of treason. In Garwood's case, bilingualism was evidence that he had become that latter-day freak of nature known as the White Cong. But even a totally innocent figure like jungle POW Douglas Ramsey, a Vietnamese-speaking civilian captured in 1966, threatened the prevailing us-them rhetoric by remarking that his captors "ranged from saintly to something out of Marquis de Sade." Such a comment, which raises the possibility of real diversity among the Vietnamese, wouldn't fly in Hanoi, where language also divided the POWs' captors as well.[81] Since "none of the guards knew English," Charlie Plumb found that "countless beatings would be forthcoming because of my inability to communicate to the guards the many promises the officers made." The guards' mute ignorance led many POWs to think they were subhuman—a belief that could survive almost any evidence to the contrary. When one guard suddenly revealed he knew some English, and therefore must have understood the abuse POWs heaped on him, Charlie Plumb's "mouth dropped." This shock did not, however, stop Plumb from ridiculing the guard's fractured pronunciation—"Molly Cleemas. You zrink coffay?"—or from reporting that from then on the POWs called this guard "Francis the Talking Mule."[82]

This christening points to one of the most racially charged qualities of all POWs' memoirs. Since camp officials concealed their identities, like Adam the POWs had to coin names for locations within the system, and for the guards and interrogators. These names often reflected the earliest POWs' anger and contempt, and therefore profoundly affected POW history. Camp and cellblock names came early—the second POW dubbed Hoa Lo the "Hanoi Hilton"—and later names like Rockpile, Skidrow, Dogpatch, Heartbreak, Calcutta, and Alcatraz spoke about conditions. The Zoo, the Stockyards, and the Pigsty were known for inhumane treatment. The sarcasm found in the Hanoi Hilton also oozed out of Plantation Gardens and that area called Las Vegas, with cellblocks named after casinos—Stardust, Desert Inn, and Golden Nugget. A very few names were positive. Camp Faith lay just outside of Hanoi, and the large group compounds inside the Hilton became Camp Unity.

Captor names reveal a remarkable range of hate, ridicule, and contempt. POW Norman McDaniel explains that names were chosen "by the first prisoner or prisoners exposed to the North Vietnamese in question, and then would be passed around to all the other prisoners for purposes of common recognition and reference." McDaniel claims that most of these names "were not vicious but rather comical," but since he also says that *The Tales of Uncle Remus* was a primary source, it's debatable how funny the guards would have found them. Certainly the POW memoirs often read like *Uncle Remus* or Aesop's Fables.[83] The senior Hanoi officials were Rabbit, Eagle, and the Cat, and other names cover the entire animal kingdom. Monkey Man, Monk, Dog, Fox, and Bear were the mammals; the birds were Owl, Hawk, Parrot, Goose, and Duckling. There was one Fish and an Eel. Pig, Pigeye, and Chihuahua were especially hated, as were those Vietnamese who became vermin—rodents like Bunny Boy, Mole, Rat, Rat-face, Zoo Rat, and that extended family of Mouse, Mousey, Killer Mouse, Miss Mouse, and even Mouse III. Frog and Snake dropped things lower, and with Flea and the infamous Bug, the names sank into the animal kingdom's dregs.

The POWs drew names from many other realms as well. Nasty, Sadistic, and Mr. Bad need little explaining, and neither does simple abuse such as Shithead, Dum Dum, Moron, and Sot; Anus, Bastard, Useless, and Piss Ant; or Fubar, Dipshit, Cool Jerk, and Drut (that's "turd" backwards). Stag was not an animal, but an acronym for Smarter Than the Average Gook—a rare backhand tribute to brains. Camp function defined some guards. The Clanger woke the POWs each morning; the Turn Key let them out. The Sheriff, the Gunner, the Searcher, the Pro, the Artist, the Engineer, the Professor, the Doctor, the Intern, and the Thief all performed as expected. Some guards became the punishments they inflicted—Slug or Slugger, Straps and Bars, and Switches—and other names reduced the person to a striking mark or feature. Toothpicks, Needles, Buckles, Sun Hat, Blue Shirt, Short Sleeves, Man with Glasses, Flower, Steel-Helmed Baron, or Colt 45 were typical, and Cig, Cig Stealer, and Smoke Stack reflected the POWs' own passion for smoking. Seal Beams had thick glasses. Vegetable Vic wore helmet camouflage in downtown Hanoi. Names referring to appearance often mirrored American racial stereotypes. The few large guards were Jumbo, Big Man, Big Moon, and the Tall One, or more cuttingly, Big Ugh, Big Dumb, and Big Stupe. One guard even became WTG, or World's Tallest Gook. On the other hand, Shrimp, Little Ox, Little Sau, and Shorty were predictable. The common opinion that Vietnamese men either looked like teenagers or geriatric cases accounts for Kid, Kid Crazy, the Machine Gun Kid, the Music Kid, the Quiz Kids, Teenager, Johnny

Longrifle, Sonny Boy, Buck's Boy, and Babyface, and for Old Dad, Old Moon, the Old Man, Father Hundred, and Grampa as well. Some names alluded to Vietnam's colonial past—Frenchy, Pierre, and Monsieur—or to other inferior peoples—Jap, Spook, and Chink; Pepe, Chico, and Pancho; or Savage.

When the abuse became more idiosyncratic, so did the names. Tan, Slim, and Husky were fairly neutral, but Scruffy, Skinny, Pudgy, and Hanoi Fats moved into the insulting. With facial features things got rougher. Slopehead was inevitable, as were Cross-Eyes or the eye-rolling Roly-Poly. Stoneface and Old Stoneface were Asian inscrutables; toothiness inspired Fang, Goldie, and Marty Mouthful, with Jawbone and Lantern Jaw as close cousins. Since they made identification easy, facial deformities or disease were favorite sources. Pock and Pox, Scarface and Scar-under-the-eye joined Mark, Spot, Pimples, and the infamous Hanoi official known as Lump. Personal quirks also suggested names. Unless the names were ironic, Happy, Jolly, and Court Jester were among the few pleasant guards. Nice Guy and Smiley made the POWs uneasy, and Smoothie was a close relative of Slick, Greasy, Crisco, and Slime. Mr. Precision, Prima, and Dude were too fastidious, Yes Yes too agreeable, and Blasé and DILLIGAF—an acronym for Does It Look Like I Give A Fuck?—too detached. Volume and noises explained Loudmouth, Vocal Cords, Squeaks, and Hack. Ashley Asthmatic wheezed.

Famous historical and fictional figures soon had namesakes. The Three Stooges guarded one camp, although another Moe also worked in the system. Samson had long hair. Doctors and medics included Ben Casey, Dr. Zorba, Kildare, or even Dr. Spock, whose antiwar activities added another barb. Pure whimsy seems to have suggested a few names—Plato, Elvis, Frank Lloyd, and Walter Brennan. Others were ham-fisted: when POWs dubbed guards Clark Gable, Jeff Chandler, Jack Armstrong, or Sam Spade, the humor supposedly arose from the contrast, and Frankenstein and the Cyclops were simple monstrosities. Media characters were very popular. Mickey Mouse and Alvin the Chipmunk were fictional rodents; Cheeta and J. Fred Muggs were monkey men. Ferdinand the Bull, Winnie the Pooh, and Jack-the-Beanstalk all came from childrens' books, while the funny pages supplied Mr. Magoo, Andy Gump, Amos Hoople, B. O. Plenty, Oil Can Harry, and the Little King—another size attack. Sad Sack and Sarge were cartoon enlisted men. American popular culture provided Clem, for Red Skelton's hayseed; Nicely Nicely, famous from *Guys and Dolls*; and Ichabod, a nervous English speaker worthy of Washington Irving. Radio accounted for Lamont Cranston, his alterego the Shadow, and Digger O'Dell, the undertaker from the "Life of Riley." The underworld provided Mafia. As for American history, Abe was a Lincoln lookalike, and Asia's frontier status might account for Crazy Horse, Wild Bill, and Tonto. The war against communism naturally turned the POWs' Hispanic interrogator into Fidel, but they also discovered Ivan the Terrible, Mao, and Uncle Ha patrolling the cellblocks. Domineering types became Little Hitler, Little Caesar, and Young Ho Chi Minh, and some jungle POWs commented on camp conditions by calling their guards Frank Buck and Frank Buck II, after the author of *Bring 'Em Back Alive*. Gunga Din needs no gloss. The only taboo seems to have been blasphemy. Though calling someone Buddha was no problem, some Christian POWs objected when a self-centered guard got called JC. He was rechristened Dum Dum. And one final note: though most POWs claimed they had Vietnamese names because the guards couldn't pronounce the real ones, a few narratives suggest that Dipshit and Anus at times were returning the favor. Since his father was commander of naval forces in Europe, the Vietnamese called John McCain "the crown prince," and that thorn in his captors' side, John Dramesi, claimed his given name meant "Pain."[84]

What ultimately makes Vietnam POW memoirs at first so unsettling, but soon so numbing, is not however the fact of nicknaming, but the effect of repetition. The reader enters a Roger Rabbit world of real Americans surrounded by deformities, cartoon characters, deviates, and beasts—by Vietnamese, in fact, whose nicknames arose from those feelings of technological, cultural, and racial superiority which the POWs drew upon for strength. Though many passages could serve as closing examples for the skewing effect such naming had on memoirs, one deliberately stands out. Jungle POW George E. Smith, an unpopular parolee and outspoken critic of American policy, was apparently so obnoxious that his guards called him "the White Wise Guy."[85] Like most POWs, Smith returned the favor, but as he came to believe that America's Vietnam adventure was a mistake, he also decided that his own racism had led him to give demeaning names to patriots and admirable human beings. Smith makes this point outrageously but effectively in his memoir's dedication, which can without comment end this section:

> To Walter Brennan, Anus, Oil Can Harry, Suave, Gidget, Pussy, Little King, and all the others, with sincere appreciation from myself, my wife Maureen, and Robin, Leslie, and Trent, our three children.[86]

Real Men, Real Women: Captivity, Sexuality, and Gender

At first, harsh treatment, illness, and near-starvation reduced POW libidos to little but a memory. For John Anton, sex "receded so quickly as a point of interest that I could hardly recall how it used to be." Nick Rowe, another jungle POW, claimed that "even the thought of sex was exhausting and not really involved in our survival, although it was another reason to survive."[87] Whenever the hunger or pain abated somewhat, however, sex became interesting once more. The Vietnam POWs present themselves as militant heterosexuals who were therefore celibate during their captivity. Just as predictably, these same men claimed that their stunted, childlike, and backward captors were effeminate, homosexual, and aberrant as well. Civilian Alton Newingham recalls that the POWs "had a saying" about their captors: "Ninety per cent of them are perverts, 5% of them are homosexuals and the rest are no-good bastards."[88] This belief had a history as well. That Asians were erotically stimulated by wielding power over Caucasians had been a Korean War commonplace. Philip Deane for instance remembered how "the little major in charge of the British prisoners, got up during the night. In front of Commissioner Lord and proconsul Owen, who were not sleeping, he proceeded to masturbate, after which he announced that it was time to leave for Pyongyang."[89] P.O.W.'s account of Bud Day's torture is only the most explicit of many such scenes in Vietnam narratives. Through "eyes blurred with blood," Day saw that the "strikingly handsome Vietnamese officer in a new, well-pressed uniform" who was whipping him "seemed feverish, as though in the grip of some sadistic insanity." Only when his "impeccable uniform was soaked through with sweat, and perspiration poured from his face," did he stop, "out of breath and exhausted by effort and excitement." The next day provided an explanation. As a bound Day dangled from the ceiling, he glanced over at the Vietnamese official, whose "arm was moving vigorously beneath the desk." Though "Day had paid no attention" at first, "now he could see that his tormentor was massaging his genitals, masturbating!" Day then knew "he was in the hands of a pervert, a genuine sadist, one who achieved sexual satisfaction from inflicting pain on others."[90] Such moments account in part for that perceived link between torture and homosexuality which led Jim Kasler to claim that he "knew" one official "to be a sadist, and judged him to be a homosexual," or led Leo Thorsness to state that "there are a lot of queers in that society" who "enjoyed their job and did it more thoroughly than necessary." (Nineteen years later, Thorsness announced that his guards had raped him.)[91]

As names like Sugar Plum Fairy, Soft Soap Fairy, or even Peaches suggest, many POWs felt they were surrounded by Vietnamese homosexuals. Charlie Plumb observed that the men "puffed effeminately, holding the cigarettes between their thumb and fore-finger and extending their 'pinkie.' " Though they "seemed to have little use for female flirtation," they often showed "an especial affection toward their male comrades": "It was common to see two V guards or officers holding hands, walking arm in arm, reaching hands under one another's clothing, or lying in the undergrowth with their bodies inter-twined." Other scenes were less amusing. Since complaining was against camp rules, jungle POW James Daly "never bothered to say anything about what I saw the assistant guard commander do to Ti Son's little boy. How he pulled out his penis and stuck it in the boy's mouth!"[92] The most chilling stories for the POWs, however, involved senior Vietnamese officials who were both sadistic and perverse. "Cheese," the D-1 commander, would "reach deep into the prisoner's eye sockets, fasten his small fingers on the eyeballs, and would squeeze and roll them for long, agonizing minutes, sweating, salivating, and telling the prisoner in wheedling tones, 'You must trust me. You must rely on me. You are mistaken in your beliefs, and I will help you.' " "There was something terribly wrong" about this "tiny brute" that made Steve Leopold's "skin crawl." Cheese "walked mincingly, from the knees down, like a woman wearing a tight skirt, and often holding his hands shoulder-high, palms out." In addition to these "effeminate mannerisms" though, Leopold saw "something in the eyes, the set of the jaw, the weak mouth, some furtive malevolence of expression that chilled the blood."[93]

One of Larry Guarino's failed experiments suggests how stereotyped the POWs' homophobia was. Zoo Rat's "less-than-forceful personality" and "girlish, limp-wristed manner" convinced Guarino that the man was a homosexual. In a very uncommon move, though, Guarino decided to lead Zoo Rat on, then blackmail him by threatening to expose his "sexual weakness" to the camp commander. Though not entirely for reasons Guarino seems aware of, as it appears in *P.O.W.* the episode is embarrassing:

> One morning when Zoo Rat came to his cell, Guarino gushed, "Oh, come in! It's so nice of you to visit me! I've been so lonely." Folding his blanket, he placed it on the bunk, sat down next to it and patted it. "Sit down here, near me. What do you want to talk about?"
>
> Zoo Rat giggled like a little girl. "I want to talk about you, Guarino," he said.
>
> "Oh," said Larry, "let's talk about you. My, you're a little fellow, aren't you? Just look at how small your hands are."
>
> Zoo Rat laid a hand alongside Guarino's to compare them. Larry lifted the interrogator's wrist, as though to measure it, saying, "Oh, your wrist is so fine compared to mine!" Zoo Rat giggled and squirmed delightedly, and Guarino told him, "Gee, you're really a nice fellow; one of the few Vietnamese I can understand."

If nothing else, Guarino's performance here reveals how caricatured POWs' notions of homosexuality could be. Even more revealing is the message he then tried but failed to send to the other POWs, one apparently designed to explain his plan and assert his masculinity: "*If I've ever seen a queer, Zoo Rat is one. I'm going to suck him in, and when he makes a move for me, I'll nail him. . . . Don't sweat me, I'm doing fine. YKB.* "[94] (YKB meant Yankee Boss.) The word choice of course could hardly have been worse; in fact, when writing his own memoir fifteen years later, he would change "suck" to "sucker him in," and "nail him" to "chop his pork off."[95] But Guarino's message also hints at other POW fears which had little to do with their captors. Although historians like A. J. Barker have concluded that "a certain amount of homosexuality is inevitable" in POW camps, the Vietnam prisoners vehemently disagreed. In "our camp, I don't know of one man who had any homosexual tendencies at all," Ed Flora reported, "It surprised me, because I figured over that length of time there would be guys who would turn homosexual. But, after we all got together in 1971, I talked to all the rest of the NCOs [noncommissioned officers] and most of the officers, and they also had no problems with homosexuality." While held in the jungle, David Harker heard from his guards that the Hanoi POWs were "all of them very bad. Masturbation and homosexuals." Harker himself, though, "never saw any evidence of homosexuality," and only years later did he learn that "one homosexual approach" had been made and rejected in his jungle camp.[96]

Heavily charged activities in other POW camps remained innocent in Vietnam. A. J. Barker claims that "dressing up as a woman turned out to be a perilous pastime" in European POW camps. POW Larry Chesley fondly recalled staged "musicals such as 'South Pacific' and 'The Sound of Music,' with costumes, 'girlies,' and everything," but he solemnly insisted that as far as he knew, in Vietnam "the revolting sin of homosexuality . . . simply did not exist among the prisoners." Service attitudes intensified this proud denial. According to Gerald Coffee, the Hanoi POWs were "all products of a military community in which homosexuality was flat-out illegal, punishable by court-martial"—and the higher the rank, the smaller the chances, for as Bob Shumaker explained, "the American military has been very quick to weed out any homosexuals from normal service life." These same officers, however, were certain that such weeds grew plentifully among civilians and the enemy. POW and psychology major Steve Long, who "had worked around the state prison in Oregon," told his fellow POWs that homosexuality usually "started out either among the extremely low educated people, who were depraved in their minds in some way or other before they became prisoners, or else it was among the super-intellectuals, who wanted to go the other way."[97] This theory confirmed several POW opinions. Ignorance accounted for the guards, and stupidity or intelligence for the senior officials. Perhaps most comforting of all, Long's theory also explained the "super-intel-lectual," and thus effeminate, American college students and professors who opposed the war and dodged the draft. Similar reasoning convinced the POWs that maintaining sexual potency was almost a patriotic duty. Wet dreams were thus happy occasions—Ed Flora said "most of the guys were pretty proud of them"—and when a POW medic "suggested masturbation, monthly, because of the danger of sterility," most men "took it seriously, and, even though there was really no desire, they'd do it." Frequency depended on age. Flora knew "some guys who masturbated twice a day. Other guys masturbated once a month. Very seldom did I ever masturbate." In a chapter called "Embracing the Good Fairy," Gerald Coffee remembers how he "speculated—with some trepidation—about my future sexual prowess after so long a layoff," and as a result, gave "the Good Fairy a hand off and on, not only to release the tension but also to maintain the function."[98]

Things became more complicated when the POWs wrote about the female cooks, food carriers, and floor washers who worked in Hanoi and the jungle camps. Whether credited to homosexuality or simple contempt, in Vietnamese culture there was an "apparent high morality between male and female" that compared favorably to the "American moral indecency" which Charlie Plumb sadly found embodied in the "bars and brothels of Saigon." The American POWs, and especially "the guys who were captured at 18 to

22 years of age," definitely felt obligated to see the women around them as sexually stimulating. Even Charlie Plumb confessed that although he personally found "nearly all" of these women "most unattractive," and although the radio announcers known as Hanoi Hannah "really 'turned us off'" at first, "the longer we listened, the better they sounded— not because of *what* they said, but because they were *female voices*."[99] The names the POWs gave the Vietnamese women set them into those categories of moms, whores, dogs, baby dolls, and bitches which the men brought with them into captivity. Older women were Momma Son or Charley's Mother. Plain women became Piggy, Dusty, Tuffy, or Tank; shy pretty women became Pia, Ponytail, or Little Moonface. Dragon Doll and Queenie seemed threatening. Other names blended racial and gender stereotypes; John Dramesi christened four water girls the Gungas, then he and the other POWs coined Gunga Dinnie, Gunga Baby Doll, Gunga Bitch, and Gunga Damn to tell them apart.[100] Such names pointed to a common tension felt between the POWs' masculinity and their generally patronizing opinions toward women—attitudes at work when for instance the POWs named three male guards Pussy, Abortion, and Afterbirth.

The problem was an old one: should POW desire override their contempt for females, enemies, and Asians? When nothing was at stake, many POWs went with their manhood. While shaving one day, a naked John Dramesi noticed that a water girl known as Dusty was watching him. Soon it became "more and more difficult to shave as I realized what Dusty's presence was doing to me," and Dramesi saw himself "smile in the mirror. If Dusty could do what she was doing, then I would have no trouble adjusting when I returned to the good old U.S.A. Finally, perhaps satisfied with her own woman-hood, she climbed down off the rim of the lye bin and walked off."[101] Other POWs' memoirs report that as prison conditions improved, even the hard-liners developed crushes. Alcatraz POW George Coker supposedly became obsessed with a water girl, although John Dramesi claimed he couldn't tell whether Coker "was in love with Zorra," or her "flared blouse and black silk pajamas."[102] After returning from Alcatraz, Jim Mulligan also noticed Jeremiah Denton was "acting strangely." Certain that "a dumpy short Vietnamese water girl we named the Tank" would help him escape, he courted her by smiling and bowing. They began communicating through coughs, and soon "all Denton was doing was coughing" every time he thought she was near. Though Mulligan idolized Denton, this was "the damndest time of our living together. Jerry was driving me nuts. I in turn, with my negative responses, was completely frustrating him. For a while I thought he was actually losing his mind and one day when he was at quiz and I was alone, I tapped this feeling to Shumaker." Tank however eventually rejected Denton, and "the saga of Jerry's water girl escape plan ended, sailing off into oblivion as he had more pressing business to attend to running the camp."[103]

At their most melodramatic, the POWs describe brief encounters that seem like revisions of *Madame Butterfly*, with themselves as blameless Pinkertons. Apparently fascinated with Dramesi, one woman would pound on his door, then gaze at him silently when he peered out. She threw some litchi nuts into his cell, and he threaded the seeds into a necklace, leading to a kiss in the shadows straight out of *The King and I*:

> When I opened the window, she turned and we looked at one another for a short moment. I motioned for her to come close to the bars and she did. As she came close, I lifted the necklace that I wore so that she could see it. . . . She came closer, bowed her head slightly, and I put it around her neck. Then, without releasing the string, I moved very close to her face and through the bars our lips touched. There was a slight smile as she turned slowly and left, fingering one of the polished seeds with her left hand.[104]

Operating silently beneath scenes like these is a widespread assumption that Vietnamese women would instantly recognize an American POW's total superiority to their own cold and brutal men. Monika Schwinn, the only female POW who survived to return during Operation Homecoming, actually offers some support for this assumption. As she staggered through the jungle, her guards just laughed: "After all, I was only a woman. A woman was nothing; a woman was even less than a prisoner." These same guards also left Schwinn in dangerous situations as apparently not worth the rescuing, and while she was never abused or molested, it was only because touching "a female prisoner, a creature without rights or honor, would have been an unpardonable crime." According to Everett Alvarez, this protection did not extend to Hanoi. When in 1965 he heard "the lash of whips and the cries and screams of female prisoners," supposedly prostitutes, he couldn't help but conclude that these "torturers were moved neither by the gender nor by the pain of their victims."[105]

Clearly then, Hanoi Butterflies fell for POW Pinkertons because they weren't Vietnamese, and in Jeremiah Denton's memoir, this story has its tragic end. All the camp women were "fascinated by the American prisoners, and each appeared to have her favorite," so Denton soon had an admirer he called Greta. Since "prisoner-women relationships were usually confined to an exchange of meaningful glances, more sympathetic than sexual in nature," and since he also showed Greta a family photo, then gestured to his "heart and then to Jane" to indicate his love for his wife, Denton does not believe he had encouraged his admirer. Nevertheless, as he sat waiting in October 1967 for the vehicle that would take him to Alcatraz, Denton "heard a shrill voice nearby":

> It was Greta, arguing with Sarge. I heard her approaching at a fast pace, heard more arguing and a slap as Sarge struck her. But she kept coming, and in a moment I could feel her hand on my shoulder. I remained still and quiet. This was a serious loss of face for the guards, and the consequences could be disastrous.
>
> I heard Sarge moving away, apparently to report Greta's actions. While he was gone, Greta stood there with her hand on my shoulder talking to me in soothing tones, as a mother would talk to her child. After several minutes, the guards came and dragged her away. Then I was pulled up by the ear and pushed into a truck with the others.
>
> I never saw Greta again.

Here at his most overt is the POW as redeemed Pinkerton. Though Denton was an innocent, "still and quiet" bystander at a suicide, Greta's sacrifice was somehow both poignant and understandable.[106]

Two vignettes can together sum up most POWs' sexual attitudes toward the Vietnamese, male and female. The first episode was a "sweet diversion" during the horrific summer of 1969, when the "strikingly beautiful features, long, light brown hair, and tall, willowy figure" of one of the "female peasants" caught the attention of Everett Alvarez and some other POWs. Because of her "tight thighs," "whispering hips," and womanly walk, the POWs decided "she must have French blood," and called her Frenchie. She became immortal on the day she disrobed and bathed without knowing she could be seen from one of the cells. "Breathlessly" the single POW observer gave a "graphic rundown" to his cellmates, "who immediately transmitted it to us for relay down to the others." The POWs' response lay somewhere between voyeurism and almost religious adoration. The Americans were "electrified with anticipation"—"She's taking her clothes off! Oh my God, she's got nothing on! She's bathing herself!"—and they screamed in tap code for more information: "Describe it!" "C'mon guys, tell us what's happening!" The "play-by-play" itself "was full of the minutest sensuous detail—a guess at her vital statistics, the tone of her breasts, the slope of her back, the shape of her buns, the swoop of her legs." Given the circumstances, Frenchie could hardly be more than a parts list, with race, personality, and head all missing. But this same dismembering allowed each POW to reconstruct Frenchie as a personal goddess. "We imagined her standing like a supple Venus, soaping her slender limbs and stretching her elegant neck skywards," Alvarez recalled, and when the moment ended, "as abruptly as a hazy mirage dissolving into thin air," each POW had a memory that "lingered like a whiff of perfume." Nowhere else is the link between the POWs' highly conventional masculinity and their relentlessly conventional fantasies about the women around them more clear. Though only one POW saw her, "Not a man forgot that day when Frenchie bared her elongated body beneath the azure summer sky."[107]

The second vignette records a very similar event with a radically different conclusion. In the summer of 1967, Charlie Plumb heard "a lilting song originating from outside our cell wall." The "voice was tender and beautiful," and "as a sweet fragrance drifted into our stale cell," the POWs "sprang to the window." Though the angle was poor, soon "a pair of dainty feet stepped into view":

> We gasped. It was too much. I thought of those teasing knee-on-down camera angles of a 1960 movie—and in color. Bright-red bikini panties fell to her feet!
> The siren song continued. We breathed harder. "Closer! Closer!"
> She came closer. Her knees, her thighs, her . . . her . . .
> His! . . . how utterly disgusting!
> Yes, there he was, a Vietnamese soldier, waltzing around with nothing on but perfume.[108]

Though self-mocking, this anecdote displays the POWs' anxieties about their captors' and their own sexuality. The feet, the voice, the perfume, and the (imagined?) panties add up to the effeminate Vietnamese male. The peeking through cracks and the grasping at any straw for arousal show that the Hanoi POWs remained red-blooded American males. When however one set of genitals replaced another, POW desire turned into a revulsion dictated by homophobia. Gender lines were therefore never crossed. Vietnamese women, even when desirable, were children, headless bodies, or victims, while the Vietnamese men were sadists and homosexuals. And as U.S. military, the POWs were neither.

The Women Who Wait

American women were different. On a pedestal, in a rocking chair, with the children, or in bed, they were sources of anxiety, gratitude, reverence, and despair. They were also intensely discussed. "Women certainly were a topic with us," Rob Doremus remarked, "There were no restraints. Jokes were quite often about women, or the relationships between men and women." John "Spike" Nasmyth was less diplomatic: "We screwed every woman known to man. Each man described in incredible detail probably every episode he'd ever had and some he didn't have, but would like to have had." The result was "some of the greatest 'pussy' stories ever heard," with some episodes becoming so famous that POWs would request "that night with Marie" from a new roommate. In a closed community like a POW camp new material was especially welcome. In late 1971, "When was the last time you got laid?" would be "one of the first questions" a shootdown would hear, followed immediately by the command *"Describe in detail."* As graduates of the school yard, locker room, and barracks, many POWs believed that sharing graphic accounts of their sex lives was "the normal, typical American reaction to the thing; nothing unhealthy about it at all."[109] At times, though, the "healthiness" seemed simply pathetic. A new POW's story "about what he called 'flavored dishes,' a new kind of treatment a woman used in her vagina to give it different flavors," led to a Hanoi survey "on how many of the guys 'ate a woman' when they had sex. When the results were tabulated, they showed most did." And James Daly sadly remembered that when a Kushner POW doing the laundry for Monika Schwinn or the dying Rika Kortmann "would get his hands on a pair of panties, anyone would have thought it was the most exciting, valuable piece of cloth in the world. He'd hold it up, wave it in the air—even pass it around to be smelled."[110]

The POWs' fantasy women were the ones to be expected for the mid-1960s. Though he personally favored Rhonda Fleming, Red McDaniel reports that a 1968 POW poll selected Elizabeth Taylor as the most beautiful movie star. When John Dramesi's "training, discipline, and physical strength were on the verge of failing" in 1967, a record by a famous blonde played over the camp radio saved him: "It was the woman, Nancy Sinatra, at that critical moment who kept me loyal to my purpose."[111] Calendars, magazines, pulp novels, and movies supplied other fantasy figures. On the day Dramesi "learned to daydream," he created "Tutter," a golden-haired and crystal-eyed beauty with "almond skin as smooth as satin, scented lips, pink and delicate as rose petals, more intoxicating than a hot spiced wine, proud breasts yearning for attention and a lethal flair accentuated by a wide band of gold around a waist you could clutch with both hands." Motionless and silent, Tutter was the prize for a chariot race straight out of *Ben Hur*—a Roman example of how high-performance vehicles and beautiful women went together in many POWs' minds. George Day for instance declared that "fighter planes are a little like cars and women" because "they all do about the same job, and look somewhat the same, but each performs with significant differences," and during a fantasy birthday party, even straight arrow Charlie Plumb sat the honored POW between Gina Lollabrigida *and* Marilyn Monroe, then gave him a Harley Davidson *and* a Mercedes Benz.

This POW's next present, however, a girl named Susie who jumped out of the cake "in a scanty orange bikini," raises a vexing issue for many POWs. Susie was someone the birthday POW "had wanted to marry but never had the courage to ask."[112] Since he had obviously mentioned this wish, Susie had become a fantasy woman for other POWs as well. That someone actually knew Susie, however, made her very different from Liz, Tutter, or Marilyn. Though the POWs "made a pact that when we crossed the International Date Line, we had sealed lips," it's clear enough that at least some POWs offered up women close to them as fantasy objects.[113] Even Charlie Plumb mentions "a sister's measurements" as an example of the "mundane" information POWs exchanged, and Spike Nasmyth told his sister in a 1970 letter that he spent "a lot of time talking about you, and my roommates are all hot to see you." Spike then asked for "pictures of you showing the new fashions, from mini skirts to swim suits," a request he repeated two years later.[114] Photos were a popular imaginative aid—"Leo, my boy, me and Fast Eddie have almost forgotten what real women look like. Can we borrow your wife again?"—and in their joint memoir, the Nasmyths reproduce a modest photo of Virginia that had been "worn out by being passed around to his buddies." One Nasmyth cellmate would "look at her picture, get that crazy look in his eyes, then recite poems to her. Then he said he started having wet dreams, poor Virginia his victim." One of the "poems" gives some idea of the general tone:

> I burned my little finger
> Now it has a blister
> The only way to fix it
> Is stick it in your sister.[115]

Another vision of the women at home, however, clashed fiercely with this aggressive horniness. For some men, such raunchiness seemed a defilement, as the well-meaning flight crew who distributed copies of *Playboy* on the Operation Homecoming planes soon learned. Charlie Plumb was "astonished," Jay Jensen denounced the "lewd display," and Richard Stratton blew up: "If that is the best you can do, shove it up your ass! I don't need beaver shots, for chrissakes!"[116] Stratton fittingly calmed down when the attendants gave him a Sears Roebuck catalog—a tribute to that domestic sense which the POWs associated with the women back home. Though capable of radiating sensual heat, when worshipped as mothers, wives, and children, these women glowed with an innocent, holy warmth. Even the bachelor POWs meditated on such fantasy women. When Ralph Gaither decided that someone back home must be married by now, he "wrote a last poem to her, then erased her from my thoughts." But the poem itself declares his love is eternal—"So long as God gives me the breath of life, / So long will I want you to be my wife"—and when Gaither learned sometime later that "Lovely Sonya" had not married, he insisted in various poems that her "Lovely brown eyes and kisses of gold, / Gentle shy ways and warm hands to hold," meant that "My past, my world, my dreams, my heart and soul, / My love for thee is all that life can hold."[117]

An emblem of sentimental and domestic bliss, Sonya obviously had little in common with Tutter or Marilyn Monroe, and since actual wives and lovers waited for the married POWs, for them this holy glow often burned more intensely. For the career officer POWs, returning home was a familiar moral duty. These men often had years of experience with absentee matrimony—and so did their loving, understanding, patient, and faithful wives, who held the family together while their ambitious husbands chased the assignments that would carry them up the command chain. Though captivity raised the anxiety level, and Hanoi was certainly a longer tour than usual, the POW's duty was still to return, and his wife's duty was to wait. Fears of captivity, for example, almost made Richard Stratton stay in his damaged plane. But his wife's last words—"Don't you dare die and leave me with these three little kids"—made him decide that "for the old lady, I'd pull the curtain." POW Doug Clower's poems fantasize about how *three* generations of women were grieving but dutiful. His wife would support his mother—"I hear your words of comfort now to one: / 'This duty calls my husband and your son'"—and his daughter would learn to be strong: "Our Ginny has now grown to womanhood, / But I am confident she understood / Just why for freedom's cause I wasn't free / And why both Mom and Dad you had to be." Even this blending of resignation, regret, and duty could not however shake Clower's professionalism from the closing lines, which even he admitted seemed outrageous: "And, though my love for you will strong remain, / You know, when duty calls, I'll go again."[118]

Despite their radically different domestic roles, the POWs often insist on their responsibility to lead, instruct, and if necessary command their wives. Few, however, were as adamant and deliberate as Jay Jensen. When he learned that his wife had divorced him, he composed a "Prospective Wife Analysis Chart" to help him when searching for a new one after he returned home. Though the Lord would provide "decisive confirmation," Jensen's "rating and weights system" ensured his choice "would be based, at least in part, on intelligent evaluation and not just emotions and physical attraction." Still, his "very detailed statistical method" did lean heavily toward appearance: "prospective future weight" came before intelligence, and Jensen suggested looking at a candidate's mother, since the wife "may look like her after a few years and babies." Because devotion and fidelity were complementary, religion and romantic love counted more than sex, and obedience was worth more than intelligence. Though Jensen granted his wife might "even advise me on some matters," he did not "want her to be too much smarter or *more* intelligent than I, or if she is, to display this attribute flauntingly." Instead, she should hit a "happy medium," making suggestions and expressing wishes, but realizing that "sometimes, in some matters, the final decision should be left to the man, as long as he respects and considers his wife's viewpoint in a righteous manner."[119]

So strongly did the POWs believe in male authority's importance to a family that men like Ernie Brace "rather hoped, especially after the second or third year, that my wife had remarried to provide a father for my four boys." (She had.) At one low point, Jeremiah Denton felt the same way, and gave Jim Stockdale "a message for Jane in case he got home"—"I wanted her to get married again. My love for her was so great that I could even love the man she married." (Jane waited.)[120] This sense of command made reunions difficult even when the couples agreed about marriage. A week before his return, Marjorie Jenkins talked about the family vision her husband's letters contained. Harry was clearly dreaming about their daughter Karen as "his delicate little girl," even though "she hasn't worn a dress since we've moved here." Another letter painted a "beautiful picture of us sitting around and arranging flowers," a fantasy which "struck us as so funny because Karen is definitely not the flower-arranging type." Marjorie concluded that "he only remembers the good things, which is a terrific attitude to take, but it could be a huge problem." She assumed however that the problem would largely be hers, and was "ready to turn myself inside out to please him." An interview with the reunited family suggests what actually happened. Harry had a new respect for his wife: "When I was shot down I didn't give her due credit. She made an occasional error in the checking account, or put air in the radiator of the car. That sort of thing. She was just a woman." "Credit" did not however mean a different relationship. Though she had bought a house and car and put their son through school, Jenkins was still "glad to put my wife back in skirts. I think a woman should be a woman and not whatever they're trying to be with these movements." Marjorie herself was "very eager to give him back the reins. I have no desire to keep running everyone and telling them what to do. He's ready to take over . . . He can have it."[121]

When difficulties arose during this change of command, the POWs tended to see their wives as the problem—or as POW Norman McDaniel put it, "For many of the wives, the harmful effects (though in some respects different from those encountered by the men) of the POW experience were and are more serious and lasting than those suffered by the men themselves." When captured in 1965, McDaniel had worried intensely because "my wife and I had been so close that I felt she'd be completely lost without me." Their reunion confirmed his fears. Though "overall" her efforts with the children pleased him, "it was necessary for Daddy to impress upon them the need to be obedient." His wife posed a bigger problem. Before captivity, there had been "no divergence of views between Carol and me on religion, the war, women's liberation, and attitudes toward other people." Norman returned "not substantially changed," but Carol had "changed significantly" and "cultivated rigidity in her views as a source of strength." This obviously would pose "a serious problem of readaptation," but for Norman the only solution would be Carol's return to her proper role.[122] In Hanoi this same dogged conviction had helped POWs deal with news of adultery and divorce. The Camp Authority was fond of delivering or making up such news, and the POWs struggled to keep from showing their despair. When for instance one interrogator told civilian Charles Willis the name of someone his wife had dated before their marriage, then asked, "Did you know your wife is running around with this man and having an affair?" Willis replied, "That's all right as long as they are old friends."[123]

The POWs did however discuss their fears with their cellmates. Norman McDaniel reports that "satirical stories were told, such as a situation in which you'd return home and your children would start talking about Uncle Bob (whom you'd never heard of), who used to visit very often while you were away, play with them, and spend the night with them." While "strictly for laughs," these stories were "a pre-conditioning exercise to air, in a lighthearted fashion, situations that in some cases could become reality." And in some cases, it had. "I'm sure there will be a lot of divorces," an unidentified wife said in early 1973, "Some wives are no longer in love with their husbands; they're in love with the men they met later." A casualty himself, Jay Jensen estimated "the POW divorce rate at fifty to seventy percent," and Bob Shumaker stated that "most of the other early guys have lost their wives."[124] As Norman McDaniel's opinions suggest, however, a straight divorce was not necessarily as intimidating as a change in a wife's understanding of what her role should be. "After so many years of forced independence, few wives remain subservient homebodies," Steven Roberts reported in 1973—a point hammered home in an interview with POW wife Alice Cronin published just before Operation Homecoming. "Mike married a very traditional wife," she admitted while "puffing on a series of cigarettes," but her "ideas and values" had changed. Thanks to "the whole thing about relationships not necessarily being wrong outside of marriage," Alice knew herself "really well sexually," while Mike had obviously "missed out on a good deal of that," and though she didn't know what to expect from his return, "I do know that I have to do it my own way. I can't sit home and cook and clean house. I'm very career oriented, and I just hope he goes along and agrees with that."[125]

For 1973 readers, Alice Cronin would have embodied a movement that the POWs had small use for. "He asked if I was a women's libber," Delia Alvarez told reporters after her brother Everett's return: "He seemed kind of turned off by it and said 'That's one thing I don't want to talk about right now.' "[126] "Turned off" put it mildly. Many POWs fervently believed that military failure in Vietnam, antiwar protests and social unrest, and their own family upheavals were related symptoms of a moral collapse represented by the figure of an unfaithful, defiant, or simply different woman. The case of Al Brudno suggests how disturbing this figure could be. Married only a short time when shot down in 1965, during the next seven years he wrote an epic poem for his wife—a "complete" but "wonderful obsession" with "127 verses of eight lines each" that took ninety minutes to recite—"a very moving, personal, perceptive and emotional story." Since Brudno was arguably the POW who idealized the woman who waited most, the end of his story was the saddest as well. At the funeral following his June 1973 suicide, the rabbi said, "Brudno had been depressed about American reconciliation with China," but devastated by marital problems. Returning to a wife "he had known in her youth and immaturity," he found she "had developed into a very strong person." Brudno in short "wanted to be her strength and she became his strength, and he couldn't stand it."[127]

By POW standards, this assessment was fairly evenhanded. Usually a wife's new-found "strength" or independence was damned as weakness or dishonesty. Fred Cherry came home after seven years of silence to discover that his wife was living with another man, that a baby had been born in 1969, that his children believed he was dead, and that his entire salary had been spent. When Cherry then filed for divorce, his wife contested it—a move he said he understood: "You been gettin' a nice fat check all these years, and all of a sudden, you ain't got it. Who's gonna take care of this and that?"[128] *P.O.W.*'s archetypic betrayed husband, Everett Alvarez, elaborates on this same theme in his 1989 memoir. His 1971 Christmas present was news that his wife was no longer waiting, and though he hadn't heard from Tangee for years, the news still hit "like dynamite. I read and reread those few lines and reeled. Each time I read the words '*Tangee has decided not to wait*,' they seemed to spring out of the text and impale me." When he learned the details—a Mexican divorce, a remarriage, and a child, expected or born—Alvarez plunged into a deep depression. His bitterness came from the same sources as for other divorced POWs. "With the advantage of freedom and distance," Tangee had "uncoupled" him, leaving him "stranded and bewildered in a godforsaken land far from home." That woman with "the mind of a child," his "light at the end of the tunnel," had changed utterly: "The Tangee I loved and left behind was warm and openly affectionate, completely without guile or malice. But the woman who divorced me, who took off with someone else and had his child, was heartless and coldblooded."[129]

Charlie Plumb's *I'm No Hero* contains the most calculated and relentless POW account of marital betrayal. Since in chapter one the returned Plumb describes attending tributes with "my dad, three uncles, and my date," warning bells go off in chapter two, when he recalls meeting his wife, Anne. Things were never exactly promising. When dating in high school, Plumb accidentally learned Anne was already engaged, and when this problem was solved, she began breaking out in hives whenever she and Charlie reunited—a problem her psychiatrist called being "allergic to a Plumb." They were married anyway. Plumb remained a devoted husband while a POW. "Anne was on my mind day and night," and in his poems, he hoped for a passionate return "not today, not tomorrow, but someday." Anne responded at first, telling him she "had planted a garden for my return," but her letters became evasive, and Charlie "could not see her face" in the photo she sent. When the first POWs left, a very worried Plumb sent some uncensored letters with Everett Alvarez. Ev mailed them, but "a few days later he found them unopened in his mailbox. I didn't know it yet, but Anne was no longer interested in my letters . . . or my love."[130]

Plumb was doubly hurt because his own wish "to be the perfect husband to Anne and father to our future children" had been encouraged by Anne herself, who as late as 1972 still "sent her love and said she hoped that I would soon be coming home." Operation Homecoming exposed the fraud. Plumb's escort officers, the chaplain, and his parents all tried to avoid telling him that Anne had filed for divorce. Though each stage of travel involved painful farewells with POW friends now reunited with their families, no "little blonde with tears in her eyes" greeted him in Chicago. Anne's recent behavior made things worse. Charlie's "desertion" was her grounds for divorce, a charge that "was of course not applicable," and her plans to remarry hinted at adultery. Anne's greatest crime, however, was against the woman who did wait—his mom. In their first phone conversation, Mrs. Plumb attempted to break the bad news by saying, "Son, I'd give ten years of my life not to have to tell you this." Plumb was crushed: "I could tell right then that the biggest casualty of the divorce was going to be my mother—wrinkles in her brow, gray in her hair, and years already stolen from her." Charlie nevertheless decided not to "become an obstacle" to Anne's happiness, and told reporters he "did not want her maligned in any way." Even more nobly, when Anne asked for a meeting "to get it all settled as soon as possible," he agreed.[131]

They met in a cafeteria—a compromise between Anne's tactless suggestion of her place, and Charlie's unwelcome offer of his parents' house, since Anne "was not on particularly good terms with them." Anne seemed the same: "I was immediately engrossed by her personality and was particularly surprised that, instead of wrinkles and time and worry and loneliness, she was as beautiful as the day I had left her." As she reached for the papers, though, Plumb saw the engagement ring, and knew that loneliness had not been a problem. Their "final comments" settled the blame for all eternity:

> "Are you bitter toward me?" Anne asked.
> "No. I . . . guess I still love you."
> "I'm sorry, Charles, but I don't feel I did anything wrong."
> "You broke your vow."
> Anne started to cry. "Do you really believe that?" she beseeched.
> I didn't want to believe it, but my pride left me no alternative.[132]

A similar pride led many other POWs to feel the same way about wives, friends, dependents, and total strangers whose wavering added to the suffering. Captivity's trials had convinced the POWs that they deserved the steady support of those at home. No excuse was good enough, no hardship serious enough to justify betrayal. Though a POW could choose to forgive, those who had not waited should always feel a guilt. He had done his duty; they had not.

Though many POWs' families waited for them, even the most successful reunions often displayed signs of how totally notions of command and proper place shaped the POWs' understanding of male-female relations in Vietnam and in America. POW Jim Mulligan wrote that in Vietnam, "women were free like the freedom that the beast of burden enjoys," working "like pack animals under the harassment and haranguing of their male overlord." Americans knew better: "We put our women on a pedestal so that they can help bring out the best that's in each of us males."[133] This pedestal, however, could be raised or lowered. When perched on a higher moral plane, this woman supposedly found her greatest reward in serving, pleasing, and inspiring her man. Whether the girl he wanted to marry, the girl he had married, or the girl his father had married, the Vietnam POW often kept gilding this quiet, loving, and faithful woman until by 1973 this fantasy seemed too good for this world. Nothing however could redeem this woman if she fell off the pedestal. After all, if a tortured, starved, and isolated POW remained true, what possible excuse could a woman surrounded by America's luxuries give for betraying her trust? As the POWs meditated upon the women who did or didn't wait, therefore, adoration and concern often went hand in hand with a righteous, enduring rage.

The Matter of Belief: Communism and Home

Color and gender can be seen; patriotism, ideology, and faith appear through their effects. POWs like Konrad Trautman knew what drove their captors: "All the North Vietnamese were hard-core, dedicated Communists. They were loyal to their immediate superior and to an ideology." The battle with this ideology began at capture, when the POWs learned they were political prisoners, not military men, and they won this battle by relying on "some kind of personal philosophy." "For many it is religion," Jim Stockdale recalled, "for many it is patriotic cause; for some it is simply a question of doing their jobs even though the result—confinement as a POW—may not necessarily seem fair." Regardless of philosophy, the struggle itself was always the same: a battle between American personal opportunity and Communist slavery. The Vietnam POWs had some vivid fears about communist contamination. Charlie Plumb's greatest worry was becoming "a different person." He feared for his mind: "Would it be so twisted that I would change my values and become a Communist . . . or a vegetable?"[134] This Manchurian Candidate scenario suggests how profoundly the hard-line version of the Korean conflict affected the Vietnam

POWs. The supposed collapse of American POWs during that war placed a great burden on later captives. "You can argue about such things till doomsday, but the Communist challenge has got to be met," Hugh M. Milton II, assistant secretary of the Army for manpower and reserve forces, told William Kinkead, "And it's got to be met in an American way—no compromise with evil." Though the POWs may have to suffer "emotional pressure," "psychological pain," and even "physical torture" for "the good of the country," Milton insisted that "any deviation from this, in the Army's opinion, would only delay our ultimate victory."[135]

Though they modified their torture policy somewhat, the Vietnam POWs basically stayed true to the strategy Charlie Plumb adopted as he parachuted down: "I'd simply have to sustain, to perpetuate my values by continually summoning and applying all the things I'd ever known. I would hang onto my faith in God and my love and respect for my country." The most doctrinaire men gamely believed that the South Vietnamese also saw the war this way. Even though he'd never set foot in the country before his capture, Jay Jensen somehow "knew there were millions of South Vietnamese who didn't want to live under Communism. I knew we were helping them to gain and defend their freedom." Most POWs, however, divorced the people from the politics. "I believed that what we were doing in Vietnam was right, that we were trying to contain Communist aggression," wrote Red McDaniel, "And even if the South Vietnamese didn't particularly care whether democracy or a dictatorship ruled their lives, the point was that the United States was trying to draw the line here for the Free World." This personal/political split offered the only hope for the POWs' captors. Though Larry Chesley despised "their governmental system which prohibits freedom of thought and controls one's every act," he felt "no hatred in my heart for the North Vietnamese people nor for any individual I met there." John McCain considered the North Vietnamese "the enemy from a technical standpoint, just like we thought of the German people as our enemies," but "communism, the take-over of southeast Asia, and the leaders of North Viet Nam" were the *real* foes.[136] It was only a short step from here to seeing the Vietnamese as food for voracious communism. "The most powerful free nation in history could not idly watch the Communist world gobble up and dissolve sovereign nations," Charlie Plumb declared, and the North Vietnamese had already been swallowed: "We compared our lot with that of the guards. While POWs were behind bars, the V were captives inside their own bamboo borders. We considered ourselves more fortunate than they. One day we'd leave *our* cells." Donald Rander simply "pitied" the Vietnamese people: "I was a prisoner for 5 years. They're prisoners for the rest of their lives."[137]

At its most schematic, the battle between captor and POW was a theological one, arising from what Jeremiah Denton saw as the "infinite difference between the heartless, mindless, and Godless nature of the Democratic Republic of Vietnam and the United States of America." Such theology has been part of what Stockdale calls "the totality of our American heritage" since the mid-seventeenth century.[138] The Puritans, as Richard Slotkin notes, did not see Indians "as real, individual beings, but rather as symbolic 'masks' of the demonic wilderness." Since this struggle was "between the Puritan and the 'invisible world' behind the Indian world," whatever "happened to the mediating Indian world in the course of that interaction was of secondary importance." Early New Englanders in fact complained they could hardly distinguish the Indians from the wilderness. These guerillas of the 1690s "appeared and disappeared at will in the heart of 'safe' settled territory," as "without demonic agency," they penetrated "almost any part of the colony and on several occasions, in the very suburbs of Boston, assassinated particular individuals who had especially offended them." Reeling from this New England version of Tet, the colonists' "ignorance of the Indians' ways produced an irrational fear of them culminating in the belief in their demonic power." Since however the devil could not be Indian, the colonists looked for white masters lurking in the background, and found them in captivity narratives like Mercy Short's, who found herself "in an Indian camp, and French Canadian priests are using the threat of the Indians to force her to take their communion."[139]

Many have written about the military's fondness for casting the Vietnamese as Indians. Frances FitzGerald's *Fire in the Lake* describes how U.S. forces turned the conflict into a mythic Western, and Richard Drinnon's study of the "metaphysics of Indian-hating" ends in Vietnam.[140] No one, however, has argued more chillingly that the Vietnamese were unconscious agents for evil—Typhoid Marys for communism, much as mosquitoes carry malaria—than the notorious Lieutenant William Calley: "We weren't in My lai to kill human beings, really. We were there to kill *ideology* that is carried by—I don't know. Pawns. Blobs. Pieces of flesh, and I wasn't in My lai to destroy intelligent men. I was there to destroy an intangible idea." Though such "leprous innocence" raises the question of who truly served Satan, this vision of the Vietnamese fighter pervades many memoirs and histories.[141] Lederer and Burdick may blame "the legions of official fatheads and timeservers" for the successes of the Red Menace in Southeast Asia, but as Richard Drinnon notes, the liberal "ugly American" still casts "the natives as counters in the battle between the huge empires of the West and of the East," and thus stands poised to take that "short step between overt and covert racism." And while Malcolm McConnell claims in his 1984 biography of Lance Sijan that "the little guys in rubber sandals were some of the best trained, best equipped troops in the world," everything but their size came from elsewhere.[142] Their indoctrination started early, for as Charlie Plumb sadly observed, "The children were not at all hostile until the guards taught them how to react properly: they must shake their fists and throw dirt clods and rocks. The mystery thus became the monster, and little hands groped for the nearest stone or stick." By adulthood, the people were zombies: "At the snap of a finger, docile civilians could be turned into angry mobs, spitting and screaming and hitting me so vehemently that the guards would have to step in to control the throng in order to avert serious injury." Personal injury, national pride, a hatred of colonialism, or even the napalm dropped twenty minutes earlier therefore played little part in motivating the Vietnamese enemy. He was instead a victim of "the almost unbelievable influence" of "Communist officials"—and not necessarily Vietnamese ones. According to George Day, "the entire Communist world ganged up on South Vietnam," and Malcolm McConnell claims that by November 1967 "the reality of the Russian ELINT trawlers, their command center in Hanoi, and the radar-controlled flak guns along the Ho Chi Minh Trail" had pushed America "almost unawares, into a proxy war with the Soviet Union." POWs suffered because hidden masters and latter-day Russian priests had enslaved a primitive people. The North Vietnamese didn't know what they were doing.[143]

To fight this enemy, the POWs often turned for strength to truisms apparently as bald as the ones driving the Vietnamese mobs. Underpinning everything was the certainty that Americans were "not only bigger, stronger, and healthier than most other humans," as POW George Coker wrote, but "also far better educated, better trained in all manner of individual and team pursuits," and with "moral goals loftier than most of the rest of the world." Or as Jay Jensen put it, "Oh, I know our country isn't perfect, our government isn't perfect, but it is the *most* perfect in the world."[144] Superiority was thus a given: POWs only differed over what accounted for it. History was the answer for some. Charlie Plumb and other POWs memorized the Preamble to the Constitution, the Gettysburg Address, the

Bill of Rights, and any stirring speeches they could recall. Other men valued American institutions most. Nick Rowe foiled all attempts at reeducation by refusing to "accept our system as being at fault; instead, I attatched blame to individuals within the system." Still other men loved America for not being Communist. As "an average product of Middle America and its values," Jeremiah Denton believed his "heritage, training, and background" made him "the very antithesis of everything my Communist captors stood for." At their most fervent, though, the POWs equated their patriotism with theology. For Jay Jensen, "the spirit of God is in America and always has been," and as frontline American warriors, the POWs were therefore captured while doing God's work. According to Jeremiah Denton, "over 99 per cent of us" credited "faith in God, and second, faith in country" for their survival.[145]

This faith served as a parallel Code of Conduct. If Jim Stockdale was the POWs' constitutional lawyer, Robinson Risner was their chaplain-commander, who bound what he considered the four essential articles of POW faith "into a pretty simple package." The POWs were first "American fighting men, fighting the enemy of freedom and of our way of life—international Communism." This battle, which Jeremiah Denton called America's "classical" struggle, overruled any claim that the United States had trespassed in another nation's affairs. "We were fighting," Risner insisted, "not only the North Vietnamese but also to maintain the freedom of all Southeast Asia." The second article, "duty to our country," gave the POWs "something to focus on in prison." They did this duty by remaining true to "the most visible and obvious symbol of our country," the president, and by defying "the nuts and the kooks" back home who had made "honest-to-goodness patriotism a dirty word." The third article—"we believed the American people were behind us"—also responded to the antiwar protesters. The Camp Authority made sure the POWs knew about "the pouring of blood in the files at the induction centers, the burning of flags and draft cards, and protest marches"; Risner denied these protesters were Americans: "We knew the American people to be honest, stable, and in general supporting the Administration in time of need." Article four made faith in God camp policy, for his will sustained the other three. Risner's articles thus reminded the POWs that "1) We were fighting the common enemy of freedom—international Communism. 2) We were fulfilling our duty to our country. 3) I was sure the American people were behind us. 4) I believed God would bring me out of prison—better for my stay." These were the basics, and in Risner's opinion "one of the reasons we all spoke so similarly when we came out."[146] Howard Rutledge reports the POWs honed the articles into an acronym. By 1971, "We always ended our communications in code throughout the wing sending R.W.H.S.W.D.G.B.U!, which translates: RELEASE WITH HONOR, STICK WITH DICK, GOD BLESS YOU!"[147]

Behind such maxims, however, lay an even more fervent belief that Americans were superior because they had *no* ideology, fighting only when their freedom was threatened. For some POWs, this belief paradoxically explained why enlisted men supposedly fell victim to propaganda. Since America's "democratic society does not indoctrinate military personnel as to a political theory or system," Larry Chesley explained, "our young men going to war do not understand what they are fighting for." And yet, this same ignorance stood as further proof for America's superiority. Ideology is the tool of governments that must trick people into fighting; the North Vietnamese, for example, who "have been pumped up with propaganda to the effect that they have a great cause, a cause worth dying for." Though the Hanoi POWs saw themselves as several steps up from the apolitical grunt, they too preferred simple pieties to political analysis. "We believed in our commanders, in our President, and in the cause, no matter how marginal or confusing at times," Red

McDaniel recalled, "and every military man since the beginning stuck by that and delivered the goods as best he could."[148] Religious and patriotic platitudes were therefore just outward signs of a Hanoi POW's certainty that his single duty was to obey. Education, reflection, and debate were valuable only as aids for standing steadfast. Put another way, while the enlisted POW had no ideas and followed orders, the officer POW had many ideas, and proudly followed orders.

Believing that only your side has a reason for fighting is of course nothing new for soldiers. As Elaine Scarry notes, Mouloud Feraoun's paradigm of "defending a just cause, killing for a just cause, and risking an unjust death" has been "the universal self-description of all participants in war."[149] Pervading the Vietnam POW narratives, however, was a fraternal sense that was stronger even than patriotism or piety. "Perhaps I wasn't so proud of letting go with bombs on targets," confessed Red McDaniel, "no combat man is. There is nothing to be proud of in inflicting pain and death." Pride therefore had to come from helping the South Vietnamese, from serving his country, or above all, from flying "formation with my fellow pilots." Cynicism played a part here. Vietnam aviators knew the missions that McNamara's civilian whiz kids cooked up were often ill-considered or overly ingenious. Like their doomed ancestors in the Light Brigade, though, the Vietnam flyers banded together in Red McDaniel's "fraternity of men who stuck by the spirit and the rule, Ours not to reason why, ours but to do and (sometimes) die." Flying in formation was even more important after capture, for "as prisoners of war, they remained at war on behalf of their government's policies and were required to support these policies to whatever extent possible." This spirit doomed all efforts to make the POWs think about the justice of the Vietnamese cause. Though they "represented both liberal and conservative political philosophies," POW Robert Naughton notes, "there was universal agreement that the POW camp was not the place from which to air those views to the world."[150] This agreement also affected the POWs' opinion of their enemy. Political tampering with the military was in the POWs' opinion one of North Vietnam's ugliest traits. During one brutal period, for instance, manacles had cut so deeply into Jeremiah Denton's wrists that his guard couldn't get the cuffs off. But when one revolted Vietnamese officer apologized—"'Denton,' he said anxiously, 'I am very sorry about this'"—political retaliation was swift. One of the guards, "an enlisted man, turned on the officer, snarling, and delivered a severe dressing down. It seemed clear to Denton that the guard was a party member and that the officer was not."[151]

The POWs' own military bearing reinforced their racial and cultural attitudes. As Elaine Scarry observes, one of power's greatest appeals is "its ability to oblige observers to redescribe it as a moral superiority," and as agents for America's military might the POWs often claimed their actions were by definition altruistic. This position could be hard to defend at times. Though POW Jay Hess gamely "tried to explain" to a Vietnamese political rally "that I was just trying to help them, to show them a better way to live," his bombing of the countryside only hours before meant that his words "even seemed silly to me at the time." What never seemed silly, however, was the POWs' belief that Vietnamese issues were secondary to that larger clash between the American warrior and the North Vietnamese Communist, "an enemy whose values, behavior, and logic are completely different from those we know in America." As Stephen Rowan notes, the returning POWs "found themselves out of step with the rest of the nation" on precisely this issue. The POWs saw the war as "a contest between communism and democracy, a contest in which Viet Nam, as Ed Flora put it, 'just happened to be the country where we had to put our foot down.'" Ned Shuman agreed with Harry Truman that "the only way to talk to a

Communist is with one foot on his throat," and Rob Doremus insisted that "many of the POWs were so eager for a victory over the Communists that they would gladly have died in a nuclear explosion in Hanoi."[152]

While this absolutism motivated many POWs to resist, it could also be a vulnerability that the Camp Authority at times exploited. Pitting national sanctity against the world Communist conspiracy tended to amplify the effect of any action which didn't fit the paradigm, and also led to defiant behavior that could be suicidal. Take the issue of ideological conversion. Army Colonel Ben H. Purcell believed that in all POW camps "the aim was the same in every case": "The Communist 're-educators' wanted to coerce the prisoner into breaking with his past and to convert him to their cause." POW George Coker also insisted that the enemy wanted to "warp your thinking," "destroy your confidence in your moral values," and "confuse you and start you believing in some of his values." And Red McDaniel seemed almost relieved to report that Rabbit, the camp's "master psychologist," told him that "we will control you even if you ever do get back to the United States."[153] And yet, though polar opposites politically, George Smith and Nick Rowe agreed that two of their fellow jungle POWs were selected for execution largely because their outspoken devotion to American values had become simply tiresome. Smith couldn't believe that Sergeant Kenneth Roraback was "trying to do the impossible—trying to indoctrinate Man with Glasses with the same silly reasoning we'd been given at Bragg," and while Rowe's poem presents Captain Humbert "Rocky" Versace's integrity far more nobly, it still caused his death: "for such a man, standing firm / defeated them on their own ground / and for him to live and tell of this / was a thing that could not be." Rowe's own experience shook his faith in the usefulness of such absolute dichotomies. He soon realized that his captors played on American self-righteousness by tugging the POWs into that grey area between U.S. infallibility and Communist evil. "I began to realize that what we heard over Radio Hanoi wasn't total lies," Rowe recalled: "In this propaganda effort, the mixture of truth and distortion was in such proportions that the desired image was conveyed without completely destroying the veracity of the source." Many POWs noted this strategy. Rowe, however, was almost alone in suggesting that hardline attitudes didn't serve him well in this case. When "confronted by an enemy who stressed the interrelationship between military and political, both serving to achieve a political goal," Rowe couldn't "cover myself against the oncoming attack." Though he had learned some "political theory at West Point," Rowe therefore came to wish "that as a member of the military I hadn't been encouraged to disregard the desire for political awareness."[154]

Rowe was hardly a fellow traveller—twenty years after his escape, he was assassinated in the Philippines while helping with government counter-insurgency efforts—but he did locate the POWs' most common Achilles' heel: "knowing what I was against, but failing to define clearly what I was for." The Hanoi prisoners generally chose to "stand firm" by refusing to entertain doubts. "In my mind, if you establish a guy as a liar, you can discount everything he says," Bob Shumaker explained: "This is the way I treated their propaganda, and I think others did too." This strategy urged the POWs "to go to the extreme right and discount what the Gooks were telling us. Certainly, if you didn't question the war before you got in trouble, you weren't in a good position to change your mind in Hanoi." This same strategy also reflected the POWs' understanding of how their captors worked. "There's two ways to go," the Camp Authority told Allen C. Brady, "Over here, you completely surrender, and over here you resist. Now which do you want?" Brady's facetious answer—"Well, how about in the middle?"—was unacceptable because "this is the way Communists are. You're one of two ways. You either do everything they say, or you are in complete opposition to them. There can be no in-between, and it's really frustrating."[155] What many POW narratives make obvious, however, was that the senior POWs themselves not only believed in the same two options, but publicly insisted that their men had all chosen the right one. In February 1973, at the very moment when the Camp Authority was forcing the frightened PCs to go home, Robinson Risner was telling welcoming crowds that "I'm speaking for all of the men because we've discussed this many times. I would like to say that, as far as I know, every man that has been in prison in North Vietnam supports and has supported our President and his policies."[156]

This allegiance to POW orthodoxy in the face of facts also explains the military's actual preference for brainwashing over differences of opinion. When parolee George Smith was threatened with a court-martial in 1965 for making antiwar statements, *Newsweek* posed the rhetorical question, "If it wasn't brainwashing, what then was it?" and let the Marine Corps commandant declare that brainwashing was what it was. Two years later, when three enlisted POWs were supposedly released for showing "sincere repentance over the crimes they had committed against the Vietnamese people" and "in response to the American Negro's struggle for peace in the United States," once again "some eager U.S. official in Saigon spread the word that the prisoners had been 'brainwashed.'"[157] This reaction arose from America's own "rhetorical ammunition," which saw POW actions that apparently aided the enemy as "treachery" or "brainwashing"—"There can be no in-between." Once again, Korea accounted for the rigidity. During that war, brainwashing became the officially favored "rationale" for altered behavior, because the brainwashed POW could "define his defection in terms acceptable and compatible to role expectation of his own country," which then "consciously or unconsciously" helped "in this diversion, in part, because the propriety of national values is put in question."[158] What tends to emerge from the real and imagined ideological struggles between captor and captive, however, was not a climactic showdown, but an ongoing clash of mixed motives. The Camp Authority seemed uninterested in changing its captives' opinions, and by using torture to produce tapes and public statements, it treated the POWs like pawns without heads, to be moved despite their resistance. Though deeply engaged in an ideological struggle, the North Vietnamese did not feel that it was primarily with their captives. The POWs countered these pragmatic and cynical actions by demanding to be treated as worthy ideological opponents—a demand the Camp Authority found trivial when they even noticed it. The proud claim of many POWs that they *forced* the Vietnamese to torture them thus suggests how seriously they wished to be taken by the enemy, their brothers in arms, and their fellow Americans.

Civil War: Protesters and Bureaucrats at Home and Abroad

Like their colonial ancestors, the Vietnam POWs had little patience for Americans who disapproved of military retaliation or sympathized with the enemy. Both sets of hard-liners found themselves railing at their own children for foolishly slipping through a carefully erected "stiff 'hedge' of religious dogma and rigorous government." In colonial America, "the younger generation, seeking land beyond the 'hedge,' are equated with the Indians for the breaches they make in good order and filial piety." Such rebellion and dissent was fueled by "heretical" citizens like the pacifist Quakers, whom Cotton Mather accused of aiding "Satan's grand design of conquest" by opposing the seizure of Indian lands, and by feeling compassion for the forest devils. Community leaders who would not press the war against evil forward also shared the blame. Eventually, all these failings and fallings away affected a "change in the New England mind" which left the Puritan "no longer sure of his ability to conquer the wilderness in a righteous manner; instead he felt himself weak enough to be debased by the wilderness to the level of the depraved natural man, the Indian." Responding to this anxiety, Cotton Mather tranformed "the myth-structure inherent in the captivity narrative into a coherent vision of his culture's history." Since these captives knew the savages and their masters at first hand, yet had also felt the joy of release, their stories could "harrow the hearts of those not yet awakened to their fallen nature," yet offer "a similar salvation" to "the faithful among the reading public."[159]

In cold war America, the supposed failure of the Korean War POWs was one of many proofs that America's postwar generations were going soft as well. Because the Vietnam POWs were terrified about being mistaken for the weak-willed Korea captive, they themselves often vented a Mather-like rage at the same antiwar backsliders and government officials who had sapped colonial America's will to triumph. The POWs' dislike of the peace movement grew with the movement itself. Just as the colonists had hated the Quakers for defying community standards, the Vietnam captives hated those Americans who met with the North Vietnamese, served as unwelcome liaisons between the POWs and their families, or even screened extorted statements. Many POWs blamed the antiwar movement for much of their suffering, and even for South Vietnam's eventual collapse. Jeremiah Denton believed that such protesters became "almost as grave a problem as the military forces of North Vietnam." Red McDaniel remembers his faith "faltered badly" in 1968, when some "really bad antiwar statements" made by two other POWs started a barrage of anti-American propaganda. The Camp Authority "used every statement, projected every film they could about the antiwar business at home," and all the POWs could do was "face the reality of the antiwar movement and defend against it as best we could, because to allow ourselves to be put down by it was only one more means to break us." Richard Stratton told his peace activist sister that "the antiwar people prolonged the war." He also credited captivity with showing him America's true enemies: "I think seeing the communist movement eyeball to eyeball, seeing what a very vocal minority, basically, did to this country in terms of tearing it apart, I can no longer sit back quietly."[160]

The POWs developed a number of methods for dealing with the fact of antiwar protest. Simple denial was the most basic. For POW Alan Brunstrom the protesters were "just a bunch of loud-mouth radicals" spouting "bull": "They weren't saying what the American people really felt." Another common response was amused contempt. In July 1968, the Camp Authority tried to make Jim Kasler more cooperative by showing him "pictures of large antiwar demonstrations in the United States." In most of these photos, "protesters held high placards inscribed 'End the War,' 'Stop the Slaughter,' 'Get the Troops Out,' even 'Communist Party USA.' " When however he spied "two elderly gentlemen wearing American Legion caps" who "smilingly held up a placard inscribed 'Drop the Bomb'" in "the middle of a howling, antiwar mob," with a grin Kasler refused to help out. Over a year later, a public showing of "a movie about the antiwar movement in the United States" boomeranged just as badly. The POWs "roared at the film with unrestrained, gleeful derision. The movie struck them as hilarious, full as it was of scenes of unkempt crowds waving placards inscribed, grossly, 'Spiro Sucks,' and 'Pull Out Dick Now.' They laughed, hooted, and shouted catcalls in a display of contempt that earlier would have resulted in brutal reprisals." Another defense involved taking the higher moral ground. Though "antiwar sentiment" had prolonged the war, and its leaders had helped the North Vietnamese, POW Ralph Gaither vowed he "would suffer every blow, every handcuff, every leg bar, every indignity, every horrendous moment of my captivity all over again to protect the right of those people to speak their minds."[161]

This offer did not however extend to protesters who visited North Vietnam. "Westerners who showed up in Hanoi were on the other side," Alan Brunstrom declared: "They gave aid and comfort to the enemy, and as far as I'm concerned, they were traitors. It's just cut and dried." As in colonial America, "unwilling captivity" was "the only acceptable excuse for going into the wilderness," and most Vietnam POWs were as a result extremely hostile to American delegations. Though Red McDaniel granted that these visitors might have been "well-meaning," and though some POWs had naively hoped that these visits might improve conditions, "as we listened to their statements, condemning the war and the U.S. role in it," McDaniel and his friends "realized that we were being tortured to get us to say the very things being said by our own people right here in Hanoi." According to McDaniel, "These statements crushed some prisoners completely, and they never got back up—as we called it, they 'let their balloon go.' " Most POWs however only became outraged and revolted. During a meeting between POW Douglas Hegdahl and visitors Tom Hayden, Rennie Davis, some unnamed women, and a "purported" Episcopalian minister, for instance, Hegdahl furtively gave Hayden the finger, and Hayden, who "thought it would be a gas" to visit Hanoi, returned the favor. Hegdahl found the women especially offensive: "There were four girls, all of them dressed in worn, patched blue jeans. Disagreeable body odors emanated from them. It was Hegdahl's distinct impression that the Vietnamese were ashamed of these allies; there certainly was no question that the Vietnamese women who served them tea found them repulsive—their eyes were full of contempt."[162]

For long periods, these unwelcome delegations were the only way for POWs to contact their families. Some relatives felt getting the letters was their only concern. On the eve of her son's return, Mrs. Peyton Mecleary thanked his commanding officer, her neighbors, the Navy, President Nixon, and the Lord for helping her through his captivity. But she also thanked Cora Weiss and her antiwar organization: "The Liaison Committee has been marvelous," Mrs. Mecleary said, "They carried out 17,000 letters and they never asked for money or contributions." More orthodox POW narratives, however, compare the antiwar movement's treatment of the families to the Camp Authority's treatment of the POWs. Joy Jeffrey told herself that she "really didn't care who took my letter to my husband, as long as he got it," but she still "found it very difficult at first to deal with the peace groups." Right with Bob's letters "there were enclosures, which were very much like the propaganda we listened to in Paris," and much like what "Bob was getting in prison every day." Receiving letters from peace groups was thus "a torture treatment they used on the families of prisoners." Sybil Stockdale agreed. In her opinion, the Vietnam War's real zombies were "the Women's Strike for Peace crowd who were welcomed in Hanoi by the North Vietnamese and then came home and babbled the North Vietnamese propaganda line about treatment of prisoners like so many windup robots." These women "seemed not to care whether we ever got the mail as long as they got credit for the North Vietnamese in the newspapers"—and Sybil denounced the American government for letting these "delegates" visit North Vietnam—"I thought they were giving aid and comfort to the enemy, but there was just the usual silence from our side."[163]

This "silence," when coupled with years of mounting impatience, led some family members to join the antiwar forces themselves. Family dissent could be muted. In 1972, POW mother Mrs. Loyal Goodermote told reporters she had "felt more frustrated in the last year or so," as her family "began to feel strongly that our involvement was a mistake and could see that nothing good was going to come out of continuing the conflict." Other family members, including relatives of such POW legends as Stratton, Risner, and Alvarez, became antigovernment activists. Everett Alvarez's status as the first shootdown drew a great deal of attention to his family's firm belief that his "sacrifice of eight and one-half years in a North Vietnamese prison was a waste of time." According to the *New York Times*, his parents had "turned against the government," and his sister Delia was "virtually a full-time war activist" who called POW family life "rough" because "if you spoke out against the war, people would think you were unpatriotic, or were being unfaithful to your brother." As Delia herself admitted, though, antiwar relatives were far removed from the more conservative POW dependents she called the "Pentagon princesses." As events would show, these promilitary relatives correctly guessed that "most of the old guys were pretty loyal" and "didn't appreciate any antiwar statements made by their wives." Or by other relations—Alvarez himself was not happy when he learned about his family's actions.[164]

These threats, however painful, could at least be seen. As is so often true, the POWs actually worried more about American enemies they *didn't* know. After his extorted denunciation of "Clark Kent" and "Ben Casey" became "the biggest joke of the war," Nels Tanner went into leg irons for so long that Jim Stockdale could barely believe the "staggering" and "unbelievably thin" POW was his old friend. Despite the Camp Authority's obvious cruelty, and the transparency of Tanner's confession, Stockdale was most furious at the "American leftists" who "wrote the North Vietnamese exposing Nels" for his suffering—a reaction that suggests how strong this fear of outside exposure was. When tortured into writing to U.S. military officials in early 1966, Stockdale's own anxiety increased because he knew "that a visiting left-wing American could blow the whistle" on his waffling.[165] No one, however, felt more betrayed by invisible Americans than Nick Rowe. Early in his captivity, Rowe had concocted a pseudobiography which he then stuck to for the next four years. When one day a visiting official told Rowe "that the peace- and justice-loving friends of the South Vietnam Front for National Liberation in America have provided us with information which leads us to believe you have lied to us," Rowe was therefore terrified. "Oh dear, God, I'm scared. God, I'm scared," he thought, "cringing inwardly" as his "carefully constructed cover story came crashing down." Soon however his fear gave way to bafflement and rage: "He had to be lying about someone at home sending the biographical data on me! An American wouldn't do that to one of his own people. God only knew, it was tough enough being a POW without someone in the States dumping a load of crap like that on your head. Could anyone be misguided enough to actually help these VC?" Rowe thus came to the same conclusions as the Hanoi POWs about the antiwar moment: "I could understand opposition to a war and a strong desire for peace. . . . Dissent was a part of American life, but to support the enemy at the expense of another American was inconceivable. There was no other place the VC could have gotten some of that information except from the United States and I suddenly felt very sick."[166]

The POWs saved some of their bitterest comments, however, for those military and civilian leaders responsible for the war's wavering conduct. This contempt had deep roots; letting concern for hostages dictate government policy had been an American problem for at least three centuries. After the Indians' Tet-like attack on Salmon Falls, for example, colonial officials stopped trying to overpower the enemy: "The dominant theme of the war would be the captivity of New England settlers." The problems with such a theme are of course numerous. To begin with, since negotiating itself compromised that Puritan "principle of resistance to the forces of superstition, paganism, passion, nature, and unreason symbolized by Catholicism and tribalism," simply having to redeem the captives was not only "a sign of New England's total humiliation," but a source of "intensified Puritan self-doubt" as well. With compromise came corruption. Talking with the enemy could weaken officials' hatred of primitivism and Catholicism, a softening the doctrinaire Puritans called "Americanization."[167] In response to such weakness, captives have traditionally demanded a "violent retribution in the name of a transcendent and inhuman justice," even if such retribution buried the prisoners as well.[168] "We didn't think we would get out of there on the strength of antiwar sentiment," Jeremiah Denton recalled, "We would get out when a real settlement had been reached through the application of significant force." As the years passed, and no such force was applied, Washington increasingly appeared to the Hanoi captives as a nest of politicians who lacked the nerve to act. The POWs called these weaklings "Nervous Nellies," Lyndon Johnson's term for domestic critics who would "turn on their leaders and on their country and on our own fighting men."[169] For the POWs, though, Robert McNamara, his defense whiz kids, and eventually Johnson himself were the real Nellies.

Perhaps the most concise summary of POW opinion about responding to Americans in captivity actually appeared in 1981, when Jim Stockdale commented on the recently resolved Iran hostage crisis. Hanoi had taught him why three common assumptions about dealing with a hostage-holding enemy were false. Seen "from within that band of brothers behind barbed wire," False Assumption No. 3, that parolees should be welcomed, was pernicious. Groveling before the captors or encouraging citizens to ignore their duties as POWs could only undermine America's moral strength. False Assumption No. 2 was that captives valued any contact with home, including with visiting delegations. Stockdale saw Americans who willingly crossed battle lines as disruptive traitors, since "the tremendous ennobling and uplifting effect the overcoming of shared hardships has on a band of prisoners over time" could only be shaken by unprincipled Americans wanting to "mediate." If parole and mediation were both mistakes, what then should be America's strategy? The answer is implicit in False Assumption No. 1—"We must not hammer the captors or they'll take it out on the captives." For Stockdale, significant force was the *only* agent that ever improved treatment. The POWs were treated best after the Son Tay raid and during the Christmas bombings. The worst days were "during America's sporadic bombing pauses when we were showing national 'good will.'" "Being nice to the enemy so he'll be nice to your captives" is therefore "a bush-league idea." Instead, "this country has to get itself in hand, get its actors off the stage and get our audiences ready to shed not tears but rotten eggs and at least a credible threat of bombs and bayonets the minute the next bunch of punks tries to pull our chain by taking prisoners."[170]

The vehemence here points to one last explanation for the flood of POW interviews and memoirs. Though the first priority was to end all suspicions of collaboration by exposing the North Vietnamese as torturers, an equally strong need to be recognized as moral authorities drove the POWs. Because they had seen the enemy's true nature while Americans back home were protesting the war or avoiding their military and legislative duties, the POWs saw their captivity as a kind of election. The battle of ideas must continue, but the enemies were now those who had betrayed the POWs, and more generally, those contributing to the steady decline of American values. Here the ties to colonial America were very strong. Though the Indians act as "instruments of God for the chastisement of his guilty people" in the New England narratives, the captive is often the only person fully aware of the guilt. Through his narrative, the captive therefore "hoped to ingratiate himself with his society by portraying himself as its symbolic martyr and scapegoat, yet at the same time he wished to express his sense of alienation and to release his hostility and contempt for his society and its smug ignorance of his true plight." Similar feelings rise up in many memoirs, POW or otherwise, written by those who served in Vietnam. These veterans also believed "their fellow citizens could have no conception of the ordeal or their response to it, and thus their experience alienated them from their fellows."[171] For this reason, the POWs emphatically declared they were neither broken and confused victims, nor Rip Van Winkles waking from a seven-year sleep. Instead, the senior men emerged from Hanoi like Moses from the mountain, carrying with them divinely sanctioned values for a divided nation. Jay Jensen's words rang with the certainty of a prophet: "How many aliens are among us? The Communists are making us aliens in our own beloved land, killing our love of liberty, and raising the standard 'Better Red than dead.' They are destroying our respect for law and order, our love of harmony and beauty, and destroying our patriotism so that we would rather be slaves than protect our rights as free men and women."[172] I'll be discussing the POW memoirs' links to theology in chapter 6. What needs to be mentioned here is that many POWs believed they had suffered for their country's sins, and that America needed to know and learn from this fact.

Struggling with their captors led the Hanoi POWs to two conclusions. First, that by doing their duty as American fighting men, they were proving themselves superior to those at home who ignored their own responsibilities, or undermined the nation's will to fight. Second, that as torture ended and the treatment improved, the battle of ideas was increasingly fought between the POWs and their fellow citizens. By refusing to press the war forward or curb the liberal media, and by welcoming early releases despite the Code, the government had proved unworthy of its captured servants. The battle of ideas thus had two stages and two fronts. In Hanoi, the North Vietnamese were the foes, and the POWs' weapons were military discipline, covert communication, and shared beliefs. Once home, though, the released POWs attacked their American enemies in the pages of newspapers, magazines, and books, where they told their grim stories and proclaimed their faith in those ideals that had once made America great. During and after their captivity, then, for these POWs their fight continued.

The Attack by Luxury—Operation Homecoming

In BACK US, the K stood for "kiss." Stockdale had assumed the Camp Authority would try to exploit "the euphoria all would feel at release time," by staging some "'let bygones be bygones' scene" for the world. Since the North Vietnamese could hardly pull back from a release after agreeing to it, Stockdale ordered the POWs to stay out of this propaganda "booby trap." In other words, "Don't kiss them goodbye."[173] This fear of scripted farewells was legitimate. Parties and photo sessions were so much a part of early releases that at the Kushner camp, even the men who remained behind looked forward to parole ceremonies: "Grissett was excited, practically dancing around. He kept saying, 'We're going to have a lot of rice tonight! Maybe they'll kill a pig tomorrow!' He sounded as though he was celebrating his own release." In a few notorious cases, the 1973 farewells did involve great fanfare. The PCs spent their last days in Hanoi going to theaters and museums, and attending good-bye dinners, where they "spent several hours drinking beer and wine and singing songs."[174] It was precisely this kind of send-off that Stockdale wanted to avoid, but most POWs easily resisted the temptation.

Nor were the reasons hard to discover. To begin with, such charades had been an insulting part of captivity for years. When forced to meet delegations, the POWs were always placed beside large spreads of food, or photographed in clean and spacious "typical" cells. These last days were just more of the same. "Officials wanted wide coverage of POWs playing volleyball, chess, or eating 'good' food," Charlie Plumb recalled. Even more amazingly, the North Vietnamese apparently "wanted to make us feel that this improved treatment was representative. They felt they could make us forget all our suffering, but we had better memories than their peasants." Resisting this attack by luxury was also fairly easy because even the most extravagant bribes paled next to the rewards waiting at home. A bottle of beer or a trip to a theater hardly measured up to the back pay, career advancement, and accolades most POWs expected. In fact, the softening treatment actually made some POWs *more* abusive of Vietnamese officials. These born-again tigers tended to be junior officers whose "hard-line beliefs did not surface until prisoners lived in large communities where the visibility of toughness had a larger audience." Such "antagonistic behavior" from POWs with no "final authority or responsibility" was as a result insubordinate, since it "conflicted with the 'live and let live' policy issued by senior officers during periods of relative calm." In any case, though, "Beware of Gooks bearing gifts" remained "a popular expression" among POWs until the end.[175]

The loving attacks of their fellow Americans were far more pleasant, and far more difficult to fend off. The POWs came back to one of the largest out-pourings of goodwill America has ever lavished on a group of its citizens. This welcome was something of a surprise, because Operation Homecoming was supposed to be a low-key operation. Two weeks before the POWs' release, one official vowed "there will be no brass bands, or any banners to welcome the returned prisoners," because "we want to try to keep this on a dignified plane." When the first aircraft touched down in the Philippines, though, thousands of American military dependents were waving banners and cheering, while back home millions of people were watching by satellite. At the base hospital, the POWs plunged into showers and cafeterias, where cooks prepared any meal a man wanted. *The Chicago Tribune* described this time as "a whirlwind of tests," punctuated by "giant bowls of ice cream" and chances to ogle "mini-skirted nurses." *The New York Times* reported the POWs' trip "to the base exchange to buy gifts for their families, stereo equipment, civilian clothing and other things." For the ex-prisoner who walked out "puffing a cigar and carrying a box that appeared to contain a portable television set," and presumably for many other POWs as well, Clark Air Force Base was the first stage of a happy return home.[176] Some somber facts did however temper the hoopla. "Bad news along with good news seemed to be the situation for most POWs," as men "received news for the first time of deceased members of the family, of marital problems, and of financial difficulties." Norman McDaniel found he took "the sad news of the passing of my father and sister more in stride by having it come at a time when my joy was so great about being free again." Other POWs had a harder time. Charlie Plumb nervously recognized that the upbeat attitude around him sagged whenever he asked about his wife: "They wanted to observe me a few more hours before I was hit with a sledge hammer." And Jim Stockdale detected behind the smiles a concern about the POWs themselves: "Although we did take some medical tests, it was soon apparent that all the authorities were trying to do was decide whether we were nuts or not before they put us on other airplanes heading east."[177]

Though POW memoirs usually mention the welcome at Clark, they move quickly to that moment when the husband, father, or son embraces his family, and his story ends. Few POWs describe the following months, when corporations, private citizens, and federal and local governments practically fought with each other to supply the POWs the biggest welcome or most impressive gifts. Some gestures, like the return of POW-MIA bracelets, deeply moved the POWs. Other gifts seemed more like game-show prizes. Baseball comissioner Bowie Kuhn awarded each POW "a gold-plated lifetime pass good for any professional baseball game." Businesspeople chipped in for hometown heroes. Clothing store certificates and other vouchers were common. The POWs generally saw these gifts and honors as legitimate rewards for service. Career military for the most part, these men were comfortable with a system of benefits and securities that increased with rank and seniority. In addition, many POWs believed that their achievement soared beyond military standards, and into ideological and even theological realms of excellence. It was probably for this reason that the most detailed versions of the attack by luxury appear in the memoirs of Mormon and fundamentalist Christian POWs. *From the Shadow of Death*, a group history of the Mormon POWs, presents the gifts, the celebrations, and above all the recognition by famous Americans, as rewards granted to righteous servants of God. The governor of Utah and an assistant to the Twelve Apostles of the LDS Church welcomed Jay Hess back to Bountiful. Governor Wallace in Alabama and Governor Reagan in California held POW dinners. At H. Ross Perot's banquet for the Son Tay prisoners and their would-be rescuers, "movie star Ernest Borgnine was master of ceremonies, Red Skelton entertained, and John Wayne was the guest speaker. California Governor Ronald Reagan sent a message to the POWs, which was read by his wife. The former prisoners mingled with the stars and special guests, chatting and being photographed." At another Perot celebration in Dallas, 70,000 people joined Bob Hope and famous friends in the Cotton Bowl "to cheer and honor the repatriated POWs." And at May 1973's White House gala for all the POWs, John Wayne, Phyllis Diller, Joey Heatherton, Jimmy Stewart, Sammy Davis, Jr., and politicians up to and including the president were the POWs' dinner companions. Thus "surrounded by stars and celebrities, the men and their partners were hosted in a gracious way."[178]

As a guide to how heroic service brought material reward, nothing can match Jay Jensen's *Six Years in Hell*, the story of a proud American who was rudely separated from affluence and comfort, but regained all his former wealth and more after years of suffering. Jensen's opening description of his last day of freedom makes Korat Air Base sound like a country club. After a shower and shave in his large, air-conditioned room, he rode his new bicycle to the dining hall, reminding himself as he pedaled to get fitted at the base exchange for some custom-tailored suits. Some silk he planned on mailing to his wife led him to think about the jewelry, bronzeware, and "Oriental" memorabilia he had already sent home. The variety excited Jensen—"there were so many more gifts and bargains I wanted to buy for my family"—and so did the base's recreational activities, such as paddleball, tennis, and the nightly movie. Jensen inserts the first of his "Thoughts to Ponder"—in this case, the domino theory rationale for America's presence in Southeast Asia—right in the middle of this narrative; clearly, the American way of life he was defending had a lot to do with the comforts surrounding him in Thailand.[179]

After six years of captivity, his return to such comfort was thus a restoration, a reward, and a right. Jensen takes two full chapters, "A Nation Gives Thanks" and "That First Year Home—Overcrowded with Joy, Excitement, and Adjustments," to list the various gifts he was offered as a returning POW. Beginning with those he *didn't* accept—a Caribbean cruise, a Florida vacation, and air transportation within California—he then moves on to the $500 clothing voucher from the Men's Fashion Association of America, "the loan of an LTD Ford for a year including insurance and all repair costs, Mattel toys for my family, slides of the Apollo II [*sic*] moon landings from movie newsreels, a lifetime pass to all major league professional baseball games, and complimentary lifetime memberships to AMVETS and European Health Spa's." This was "by no means a complete list," since gifts kept popping up during his first six months home. As a Mormon, Jensen was always turning down bottles of champagne or giving them to friends. Remarried within two months of his return, his extended honeymoon created endless opportunities for people to display their thanks. Jay's entire new family went on a ski trip, "all compliments of

Snowbird, Alta Utah." The newlyweds then headed off on a "second honeymoon"—the second in three weeks—which "was part of a free Suncoast Vacation package provided the POWs by station WFLA in Tampa, and included a rental car and $75.00 for food and expenses." Discount tickets, hotel rooms, rental cars, and free food made trips to Disneyland, New York, Washington, and Florida possible. Then off to Europe, with an Aegean Sea cruise ("half price fare for POW families") and royal treatment in Germany. These gifts were so numerous that when Jensen mentioned a Nassau vacation, he felt honor-bound to say that "this trip we paid." Nor did returning home stem the flood. House painters and wallpaperers worked for free. Old friends didn't "charge half enough" for wiring the house; new friends sold him furniture at below cost. His new in-laws gave the Jensens a television and antenna.[180]

No one could sum up the effect of these chapters better than Jensen does himself— "People are wonderful, and the list goes on"—and no one could be more convinced that such bounty was the most appropriate way to thank him for defending America's prosperity. When explaining "What America Means to Me," Jensen speaks of "the many *freedoms, blessings, traditions, opportunities,* and the *highest standard of living* in the world America offers us," and in a thank-you letter sent to Disneyland for the "America the Beautiful" show in the AT&T Circlevision Theater, Jensen draws patriotism, bounty, religious faith, captivity, and major corporations together into an American credo:

> Six years, yes, six years to the day, of my life—and my former wife, my three lovely children—all this I gave up forever. And many others like me have done much the same and more. For what? For America, democracy, freedom, and our way of life. So that other people, all over the world, the universe, might enjoy the same freedoms. Yes, it *was* worth it—well worth the sacrifice. All our prayers have finally been answered. So, thanks, dear God, thanks Disneyland, thanks American people and America the beautiful. And thanks, AT&T, for showing me and my children so vividly why I had to serve so proudly in Vietnam. That's what it's all about, Sherrie, Roger, and Carrie. That's America the beautiful![181]

Charlie Plumb had a similar epiphany on the night he threw out the first ball at the brand new Kansas City Royals baseball stadium—"the prelude to vacations, an automobile, gifts, and the general red-carpet treatment of a 'hero's welcome' that returning POWs have received." Charlie "felt out of place" as he watched the game from the owner's suite, a room "softly lighted by crystal chandeliers," and "filled shoulder-to-shoulder with VIPs—senators, governors, mayors, the baseball commissioner etc.": "Drinks, hors d'oeuvres, diamonds, expensive gowns—the affluence was overwhelming." And yet, he also firmly believed these people embodied the best in America. Far from being "ogres or mechanical robots bent on persecuting the poor," Charlie's hosts that night were "congenial, down-to-earth-human beings" who radiated "warmth and compassion," leading him to conclude that the privileges of the powerful were among the most precious things he had suffered for:

> ... it was gratifying to know that, because I had tied my raveled drawstrings and had paced in battered sandals, I had in some small way helped protect this system wherein worthy individuals could attain material success. The influential people who were gathered in this suite were depicted by North Vietnamese propaganda as dangerous capitalist warmongers who exploited the poor. But as I observed their kindness and mutual respect, I knew that they were the same people who had worked hard for accomplishment and who were instrumental in programs and projects beyond their own immediate interests. As any citizen in America, they had the right to excel and to enjoy the fruits of their labors.[182]

Luxury therefore could not corrupt a POW, because it confirmed the righteousness of his cause. Most POWs felt they had served those institutions that not only ensured America's moral and economic strength, but also linked the nation's will to God's. When a POW compared returning to the riches of the United States with returning to paradise after years in hell, he wasn't exaggerating much. Nor as Larry Chesley suggests was this reunion unrelated to that yet more important reunion to come:

> . . . when I met my mother and father at Travis, they hugged me and kissed me and we cried. They told me that they were proud of me. I have thought many times since that day, "How great—how great it will be if I should live righteously enough to meet my Father in heaven at homecoming."
>
> And he will throw his arms around me, and say, "I love you Larry, and I'm proud of you." I am working toward that end.[183]

My account of the official story ended with a Christmas apocalypse and clear signs that the Hanoi POWs were worried about returning to a weakened America. Their main concern was justice, but as the grim postscript to *P.O.W.* reveals, their government refused to prosecute the guilty, thus betraying the POWs' trust. Half expecting this result, they composed the official story as an elaborate defense for the senior Hanoi POWs' actions and beliefs. The big picture laid out in this chapter is hardly so neat. Only by exploring the myriad of prejudices and convictions lying behind the official story's providential narrative, however, do some of the puzzling, even contradictory opinions many POWs held begin to make sense. Two simple yet absolute beliefs lie deeply embedded in the official story: that the senior Hanoi POWs embodied the right values for waging their battle against the enemy, and that those who ignored, disobeyed, or disagreed with these POWs always drifted perilously toward corruption or crime. Gender, race, and language assumed fixed values within this crucible, and so did certain political attitudes, religious beliefs, and opinions about the war. The senior POWs' greatest leadership challenge was to forge these convictions into a code of duties and behavior. That most POW memoirs reflect the official story is a sign of their success.

For all its expansiveness, though, this official story unavoidably distorted the stories of individual POWs—and especially those who weren't career officer aviators shot down in the mid-1960s, held in the Hanoi system, and tortured by the Camp Authority. Part I of this book evaluated how different POW interpretations of the Code stimulated great debate. Part II has described how the senior Hanoi POWs lived and shaped a narrative that affirmed a broad range of attitudes and beliefs, and which eventually stood as the true and final word on the Vietnam POWs' captivity. Making sense of how each POW related himself to this group narrative, however, requires a closer look at some of these stories as tales, histories, polemics, or fictions in their own right. Part III will explore how nuanced and diverse even the most orthodox POWs' strategies for retelling their own stories often proved to be.

★ ★ ★ III ★ ★ ★

ONE MAN'S VIEW

May he be damned who, after regaining freedom, remains silent.

From a latrine wall, Kotlas prison camp, Russia[1]

★ 6 ★

A Prophet Returns to His People

I am Lazarus, come from the dead,
Come back to tell you all, I shall tell you all.

T. S. Eliot[1]

Peace. That's why I am in the Navy.

Ralph Gaither[2]

The POWs were first asked for their life stories by their captors. In the early days "each man was required to write an autobiography detailing his background," and refusing to cooperate often led to the first torture session. But the POWs had their own reasons for reliving their lives as well. For one thing, it passed the time. Each day Charles Willis would "reminisce over the years, like a continued story of a soap opera. I would start remembering what had happened to me when I was six years old and would take it up with myself for that morning."[3] Fueled by knowing that they could be separated forever at any moment, roommates shared their lives in sessions that could take weeks. And since knowing who you were meant knowing what you believed and why you must resist, composing autobiographies also helped the POWs endure their captivity honorably. In time, these stories formed the biographical mosaic I've called the official story, that important tool for orienting new captives, and later, for passing the POWs' insights on to the American public.

Though Stockdale and Dramesi play with chronology, the Vietnam POW memoirs tend to follow traditional narrative patterns: beginning with capture, then briefly sketching in the POW's early history before recording his captivity. The tone is also fairly uniform. Occasionally the POW writing can be academic, flowery, or clever, as in this passage from Jim Mulligan: "I think that in each person's life as he passes blissfully through this world's vale of tears there comes a time when the fickle finger of fate rears its ugly head at him and he finds himself in a terribly uncontrollable situation which marks the lowest point of his existence."[4] For the most part, though, understatement, sports metaphors, and truisms move the story forward. This homely quality grates at times. Larry Chesley for instance found combat "a bit scary," and he also wrote this bit of pseudoprecision: "I was losing weight. I had gone into prison at about 160 pounds, but by March 1967 I weighed only about 100 pounds—a loss of approximately 60 pounds." Chesley also struggled to keep the metaphorical and literal straight: "My feet were uncovered the whole winter because they felt as if they were on fire. They were so hot that they burned the hair off my leg halfway to the knee."[5] This fiercely colloquial writing, however, also reflects the captive's need to speak the unadorned truth. What Richard Slotkin says about Mary Rowlandson could be said of most Vietnam POWs. It was not "artistic skill," but "the fact that her experience, training, and state of mind were accurate reflections of the experience and

165

character of her culture as a whole," that made Rowlandson "the originator," and the POWs the inheritors, "of a major stream in the American mythology."[6] As titles like *I'm No Hero* suggest, the POWs saw themselves this way. Chesley claimed they did "only what we were supposed to do for our country, only what others would have done if they had found themselves in our circumstances." Being typical was the goal: "I was really a symbol, a representative of a group of men who had done their best to keep faith—with God, with country, with the American people."[7]

And yet, this ordinariness also grants returning captives a privileged perspective on their homes. As someone who has "experienced a thing that his fellows have not," the "captive is not initiated into an entirely new way of life; rather, he is restored to his old life with newly opened eyes." A. J. Barker observes that "nearly every ex-POW will claim that he learned more of human nature in a couple of years of captivity than he could have done in two decades of normal life," and that this knowledge prompts his writing: "Whether it is simply a wish to record their experiences for their family, or for history or an innate desire to justify themselves, the fact is prisoners of war compile more voluminous diaries and records than other servicemen."[8] The Vietnam POWs fit the pattern. "Because of the years that I spent analyzing life, determining the things that should and should not be important," Norman McDaniel felt his "assessment of my countrymen" was not just "quite different," but also more accurate. As "a detached uninvolved observer," McDaniel could "evaluate a situation better than someone who is an active part of it." Robinson Risner also felt that isolation had allowed him "to sift out those things that were most important —to reduce a lifetime to what really matters." His memoir just passes these treasures on. When asked "why I was writing this book," Risner's "honest answer" was this: "I believe that today's young people are searching for a dragon to slay. I want to help them find the right dragon. I want our young people to be proud of the things that count. I want to show that the smartest and the bravest rely on their faith in God and our way of life."[9] Many other POWs join Risner in presenting their captivity as a source of inspiration and instruction for the country they served. This chapter examines a number of these narratives.

Alcatraz and the Hard Line

According to Albert D. Biderman, roughly 80 percent of the Korean War POWs "performed no singular acts of resistance or collaboration that were corroborated." The remaining 20 percent split almost evenly between collaborators and resisters; a 1955 report on British prisoners further notes that the tigers, "men who had distinguished themselves by their heroic resistance to all Chinese brutality," were isolated in Camp 2, which then further subjected some of these hard-liners to "long sentences of solitary confinement for attempted escapes and 'reactionary' activities."[10] The Hanoi Camp Authority followed this model. Diehards who resisted and ordered others to resist went into solitary, and the cream of this group was skimmed off in October 1967 and isolated until December 1969. These eleven POWs were the Alcatraz Gang. In an interview published in late March 1973, Jim Mulligan described the Alcatraz Gang as the hardest of the POW hard-liners: "The V's got nothing. They tortured people but they got nothing. Everyone of us hung in out there. They were all tough nuts. Ten of us came back and one didn't." Though senior officers and diehards tend to dominate most military accounts, the Alcatraz Gang's impact is still startling. Of the ten survivors, Jeremiah Denton, Howard Rutledge, Sam Johnson, and Jim Mulligan have written books, and Jim Stockdale, the camp SRO, published two—a collection of essays and a lengthy memoir with his wife Sybil. Bob Shumaker figures prominently in *P.O.W.* and in Stephen Rowan's book of POW interviews, and Harry Jenkins spoke out frequently after his return. Seniority accounts for some of the attention. Since the POWs held longest came home first, Shumaker, Denton, Stockdale, Jenkins, and Rutledge were on the earliest planes out, and served as spokesmen for the other POWs. It was their singling out by the Camp Authority as true diehards that contributes most to the Alcatraz POWs' habit of seeing the official story as their own. The most representative of their accounts is Jim Mulligan's *The Hanoi Commitment*. When a bruised and spit-covered Mulligan decided shortly after capture that "if there was an ugly American in North Vietnam I knew it must be me," the shoe fit for at least two reasons. Mulligan certainly felt that like the novel's "ugly" but noble American, he had come to help the Vietnamese people resist communism and build a better future. But Mulligan also champions those beliefs identified with Americans at their most jingoistic and ugly. *The Hanoi Commitment* describes a "we-they" world. "We" were all the diehard Americans, and the Alcatraz Gang especially. "They" were all who opposed or differed from "us," whether Vietnamese, Americans, or fellow POWs. Mulligan's memoir is therefore the story of an ideologue who won't soft-pedal his convictions.[11]

His comments on race are typical. Ignorant of Vietnamese culture before his shoot-down, Mulligan "had never developed any feelings for or against the Vietnamese as a people." In Hanoi, though, he "started to build up a personal hatred for the Vietnamese that grew worse during the remaining years I spent as a POW, and which I am ashamed to say, still persists down deep in the recesses of my heart and mind." Mulligan admitted he "did not understand the ways of Orientals," but he "made no effort to remedy this deficiency." The result was racial stereotypes—"Damned inscrutable Orientals, they're hard to figure. They don't think like Westerners"—and a refusal "to have compassion about someone I didn't know and whom I couldn't understand."[12] "Bastards" was Mulligan's favorite term for his captors. Shooting him down made them "lucky bastards"; firing rifles as he parachuted in made them "little bastards." When they slipped his belongings "into their dirty pockets," they became "corrupt" little bastards. Mulligan's "typical" Vietnamese men and women were extreme versions of the POW stereotypes. Though many narratives claimed that the men were homosexual, Mulligan is the POW who heard a "Yank" yell out, "Lieutenant, tell that queer guard of yours to keep his hands off my balls, or the next time I'll belt him!" and Mulligan is the POW who woke up to find a guard "manipulating" his testicles, leading him to conclude "these bastards are all queer."[13] Though Vietnamese women slaved "like pack animals under the harassment and haranguing of their male overlord," Mulligan also confirms the repulsive yet sexually agressive stereotype. Some women who "scrutinized" him shortly after capture began "laughing and giggling at this broken down male American, clad only in torn skivvies and socks standing before them." Suddenly a bold one "put her hand in my fly opening, grabbed my testicles and massaged them and my penis," but when his "body failed to respond to her ministrations, she spat in my face, let go of my genitals, and said 'Ancien! Ancien!' in disgust."[14] All the components are here—the women's randiness, and emasculating tendencies, but above all, the POW's certainty that American males would naturally interest Asian women.

Race and cultural backwardness became linked when Mulligan looked down during his last flight at the "primitive meanderings of cart trails unknown in America except in the wilderness and depths of rural underdevelopment." From the air these trails seemed "barren of traffic," but once on the ground, Mulligan learned he had been fooled—"My Lord, these little bastards have themselves one helluva fine system for moving right under our noses down Route One." This discovery did not however change his mind: "Clever people, these North Vietnamese. In their own primitive way they were dealing quite effectively with our supposedly sophisticated air threat to their ground supply system." At his most caustic, his captors became animals. "These little monkeys aren't even smart enough to know how to use the clutch properly," Mulligan thought as he lurched down the road which stymied U.S. air power. The building of a bakery filled him with contempt: "These damn North Vietnamese are barely out of the trees, I thought as I recollected their primitive efforts in the brickyard. They are rushing ahead to full progress like leaping head first from the tenth to the eleventh century. My God, who the hell are we fighting and what are we fighting for?"[15] Language became Mulligan's standard for intelligence. Vietnamese itself was "gutteral [sic] jibberish" or simply "babbling," and most of his captors spoke "broken English" like bit players from World War II films. "You no die today, Yankee," someone said at one point, and someone else refuted Geneva like this: "Yoo our no pryson er of wah—yoo our crimeinal of wah." When however a well-educated doctor who spoke "perfect English with an American accent" dressed down a guard for his "barbarity," Mulligan felt that justice was being done.[16] English and intelligence were synonymous. Mulligan's low opinion of the Vietnamese fueled his hard-line attitudes about the war's conduct: "I wonder when in hell LBJ is going to use the B-52's, crank up a blockade and really hit these guys where it hurts?" Mulligan asked himself in 1966, "When that happens, I'll be going home soon. The only thing these little bastards will ever understand is brute force." Mulligan of course understood a great deal more. Survival training had taught him to "remember you are better educated, have more experience and are much smarter than your captors will be." Mulligan laughed at how quickly his inter-rogators "swallowed the bait," and when one official pretended to understand some aircraft mumbo jumbo, Mulligan gleefully thought, "You dumb bastard, if you swallowed that one I can get you to swallow anything."[17] The racial paradigm was therefore complete and precise. Most Vietnamese were all but animals, and their tiny elite was no intellectual match for the POWs.

How then did Mulligan explain North Vietnam's military successes—or even his own captivity? His answer was communism, which he sometimes discussed in an almost scholarly manner: "I am convinced that the world's greatest material development has been achieved not by political direction but by the economic results of human effort in a free society. I feel that history shows that in free societies economics dominates politics, whereas in totalitarian societies the exact opposite prevails. Hanoi is living testimony to the latter's inadequacies." At other times, though, Mulligan just blew up. "Bullshit!" he cried when ordered to bow at a people's rally, "Screw you! I don't bow down to anyone, prisoner or not!"[18] Regardless of the tone, however, Mulligan always believed that com-munism pulled his captors' strings. What little compassion he felt for the Vietnamese came because they "had never tasted true freedom and most certainly never would. I hated Communism for what it did to the human spirit, but I prayed for the people in this Communist country." Life in Hanoi was a nightmare which called out for American intervention. The morning bell that "summoned its Vietnamese victims to their required rising on a new people's work day" called them to a state of "national enslavement": "Damn these Communist bastards. They are all the same. They have no respect for the rights of the individual. Ultimately that's what this damn war is all about, even if the world press calls it a war of national liberation." Such collectivism left individuals helpless in a crisis. Seeing a guard mourning Ho Chi Minh's death, Mulligan could only think, "Poor little bastard, Uncle Ho's dead. The center piece of his country and life is gone and, he doesn't know what to do or what will happen. You poor leaderless bastards." Like so many

POWs, Mulligan also believed that state-enforced atheism was perhaps communism's greatest sin: "Where the hell did their humanity go to? I surmised that when North Vietnam replaced a Divine cause with a human goal, it had doomed itself to oblivion forever, or at least until it got out from the yoke of Communism." This belief also pervades a prayer that crystallizes his hard-line beliefs: "The benevolent Communist state will protect you all and give you all your worldly possessions. But the price you pay is your own humanity. Poor little North Vietnamese. Poor little Communist bastards. 'Our Father who art in Heaven . . . help them see the light.' "[19]

Mulligan's disgust with POWs who didn't measure up was almost as strong. In his opinion, the Make a Choice program created two groups—the weaklings who sold out and the band of diehards. The Alcatraz men were the stars of the second group, and their hatred for those in the first pervades his narrative. A tape spewing "bullshit about the war" over the camp radio was Mulligan's first hint that "some men were not following the Code of Conduct." Furious at such "fink behavior," the Alcatraz POWs vowed to investigate the two "moral pygmies" responsible and "prosecute them when we got out." As for parolees, any fink who would leave behind "other POWs who were critically injured, ill and who had borne the brunt of captivity for seven years or longer" deserved the worst fate Mulligan could imagine: facing up "to this reality for the rest of their lives."[20] Almost all the POWs, however, hated the collaborators and parolees. What set the Alcatraz POWs apart was their annoyance with that "vast majority" of POWs who didn't collaborate, but didn't rock the boat either. Hard-liner memoirs often vent frustration at this passivity. As Barn SRO in 1966, for instance, Mulligan ordered his men to shout "bao cao" if they heard another POW being beaten. At the moment of truth, though, Mulligan "was the lone participant." Obviously "disappointed at their lack of involvement," Mulligan "assumed they were all afraid of what the gooks would do to them in retaliation." As he stood exposed, abandoned and frightened, however, he took comfort in knowing that *he* at least had done his duty: "What the hell, there are certain times when you just have to put your ass on the line and stick up for your rights and the rights of your men."[21]

Three years later, when the Alcatraz Gang returned to find that POW morale had sagged badly in the system, Mulligan's disgust rose to its highest. Most POWs "were rolling along. That is, the Vietnamese had, by threats and torture gotten them to go along with the camp propaganda program. Many of them were reading over the camp radio and writing articles for some camp magazines." Though no real conversions had taken place, such outward conformity sharply contrasted with the Alcatraz POWs' reaction when they realized they were back in the Hilton, instead of on the expected plane home: "We thumped until the noise reverberated throughout the building. We hacked and coughed in our secret way until we had pinpointed each man's location in each cell. We were all angry! We didn't give a damn about the Vietnamese! We didn't give a damn about their stupid regulations or their stupid guards or officers!" This anger first washed over those POWs who had caved in to the Camp Authority, then over the newly arrived POWs. A "motley looking crew if ever there was one," they "seemed so young" to Mulligan, and their "long hair, sideburns, beards, and mustaches" were "a far cry from the military appearance that most of us had been accustomed to during our careers." In addition, the "changes in American morals and life style" these newcomers "described were almost too unreal to believe," suggesting to the Alcatraz POWs that America itself had drifted off from the course which they had so proudly followed.[22]

The same concern drove Mulligan's attacks on some of the folks back home. The "massive invasion" heading south as he traveled to Hanoi worried him. He "knew Vietnam was the right place for the right war," but he "also felt that the free world and our own people wouldn't have the guts to fight it properly." Soon Mulligan was grieving over the 1964 election. Though Americans had "crucified Goldwater as a war monger and elected LBJ as a responsible leader," captivity had taught Mulligan, even though he himself had voted for Johnson, that Goldwater "had the right idea, blow Hanoi off the map. The only thing those Communist bastards understand is force." Johnson's policies for this "lousy war" were doomed—"arm twisting won't work on the Communists, and by the time he finds this out he'll have lost his hat and ass in Vietnam"—and Mulligan thus vainly prayed, "Lord, save me from the politicians who have the nerve to engage me in a war but who don't have the guts to let me win it."[23] Those Americans Mulligan considered traitors received even less sympathy. He simply pitied "all the do gooders and well wishers" whose Pollyanna vision of communism left them Hanoi's dupes. The media he found stupid, treasonous, or both. The North Vietnamese soldiers he had seen streaming south made Mulligan think about "how naive those reports were that bombarded the American people with the idea that the hostilities in South Vietnam were just an internal revolution fired by the efforts of a dissident peasantry." When reporters who swallowed this myth then "spent most of their effort defending and building up the reality of this grand hoax," naivete spilled into malice. Though it claimed to hold "all the news that's fit to print," even Mulligan's "favorite American newspaper," the *New York Times*, published Harrison Salisbury's reports from Hanoi, but seemed uninterested in coming up "with a bit of news about the true condition of the American POWs" who "were being tortured, starved and dying from medical neglect."[24]

Mulligan was also shocked at how easily "the Communists are able to fool the intellectual elite of this country and the world." Many "intellectuals" visited Hanoi, and while he claimed he "honestly felt sorry" for Ramsey Clark and Jane Fonda as "well intentioned do-gooders who were being duped and exploited at every turn by the fawning Vietnamese Communists," Mulligan also "hated them for their phony concern for the poor and downtrodden. I was convinced that neither of them had wanted for anything their entire lives, and, in fact, had been raised smack in the lap of luxury." Clark and Fonda therefore "would ultimately have to account for behavior which, if nothing else, aided and abetted our enemies, and caused us by their visits more mental and physical anguish than was our usual want." Women who left their pedestals and joined the antiwar movement especially annoyed Mulligan. When an "American female" visitor suggested in some "casual vocal meanderings" over the radio in 1972 that the POWs should see the Hanoi War Museum, Mulligan sensed trouble: "The next thing you know the Gooks will be dragging us downtown to the War Museum. What a great idea for a propaganda stunt, and just think they got it from some dumb American broad who was shooting off her mouth." Some POWs actually were wrestled into the museum, and Mulligan assigned the blame. When "On 27 September 1972 the three latest fink releases left for home," he "was glad that they took with them the American bitch that had caused our museum troubles." This "big-mouth American" was only one in a series of "dumb American broads" who "had caused us to be mistreated." Only one group could have been more depraved, but while the Camp Authority "often threatened the safety of my wife and children by action from American anti-war activists who would carry out Hanoi's orders," nothing ever happened.[25]

Where then to look for inspiration? As someone who felt he was one of the minor members, Mulligan pointed proudly to the major figures of the Alcatraz Gang, "the greatest team I would ever be on." Mulligan himself was famous for being one of Hanoi's stubbornest and most abused POWs, but he personally "admired the POWs in Alcatraz more than any other men I would ever know. Each man there was a dedicated American who paid a terrible price in physical and mental torture for what he believed in. I considered it a high honor and special privilege to be one of them." The shared "agony of solitary confinement, leg irons, torture, abusive treatment and inhumane living conditions" welded these POWs "into one steel chain with each link connected to the others and a part of the whole." Under Jim Stockdale's and Jeremiah Denton's influence, Alcatraz became a model of how the entire system should have functioned: "We might have our own personalities and individual differences, but when it came to living up to the Code of Conduct and resisting the brain-washing and torture efforts of the Vietnamese, we were united as one man."[26] Mulligan found the Alcatraz spirit embodied in his superior officer and best friend, Jeremiah Denton. Though Denton had impressed Mulligan when they served together in the early 1960s, this "okay guy," assumed heroic proportions in Hanoi. In late 1966, Denton was Mulligan's SRO in the Pool Hall. An "inspirational leader," Denton "ran a good show" by putting out "resistance policy" and setting up "an intelligence-gathering information bank." Mulligan especially admired Denton's courage: "He never gave any quarter to the Vietnamese and he never asked any POW to endure any physical abuse which he himself had not already endured." What made Denton "truly the POWs' POW," however, was that he always "went first, heading the line of resistance and paid the full penalty for his dedication to the moral principles he believed in and lived by." Always at his absolute best when the treatment was at its absolute worst, Denton was the "strongest voice of resistance when torture was rampant and others in command had been broken and had assumed docile resistance profiles." Deep affection came with this admiration. The day Mulligan became Denton's roommate was "the best day I'd ever have in Hanoi save one"—the day he went home. This first stay was so brief that Mulligan called it "the three day honeymoon." The men embraced and pounded each other on the back; after washing, they prayed over dinner. Through these simple actions, "Jerry and I became the closest of friends. I knew that no matter what outcome our incarceration would bring that this friendship would last as long as we lived." Alcatraz drew them tighter, and years later in Camp Unity, "Jerry and I put our sleeping gear next to each other so that we would remain close."[27]

Jeremiah Denton is not however simply a good officer and friend. In his greatest moments of torment, Denton surpassed all other POWs. Though many POWs have quietly suggested that undergoing torture for trifles made hard-liners like Denton fanatics, Mulligan insists that the POW he first saw on January 22, 1967, was a persecuted American saint. Denton's pitiful physical state—"Look at what they have done to Jerry Denton in a year and a half. My God it's unbelievable!"—turned Mulligan's gaze on the torturers: "I'd never felt this way before in my life. One and at the same time I was filled with love and compassion for Denton and with hate and contempt for Lump and all the North Vietnamese he represented. The hate was etched deep in my heart, where even today it festers and gnaws at me when I recollect the conditions of those days."[28] The hard-liner's habit of seeing captivity as a struggle between antithetical forces is powerfully at work here. In his book's epilogue, Mulligan presents these oppositions as a hard-liner catechism. America's failings are always corruptions, not faults, and since "Permissiveness is the corruption of Freedom," "Anarchy is the corruption of Democracy," and "Immorality is the corruption of Morality," the nation's course is clear: "A free democratic moral society has the right as well as the obligation to resist the incursions of those perversions which would lead to its destruction." Though Denton's example is important to fostering this sense of duty, ultimately Mulligan's stubborn resistance makes him the fiercest POW diehard: "Man is an imperfect creature living in an imperfect world but he should always strive to be better than he is. In this struggle he should never, never, never, give up!"[29]

The Aptly Named Jeremiah

When Hell Was in Session, Jeremiah Denton's memoir, combines Mulligan's zealotry with the spiritual leader's self-assurance. As the man who blinked out T-O-R-T-U-R-E during an interview, and who first spoke to America after release, Denton was the most famous returning POW. "Who can ever forget that night," Ronald Reagan asked in his 1982 State of the Union address, "when we waited for television to bring us the scene of that first plane landing at Clark Field in the Philippines—bringing our POW's home. The plane door opened and Jeremiah Denton came slowly down the ramp. He caught sight of our flag, saluted, and said, 'God bless America,' then thanked us for bringing him home."[30] His Naval Academy background, master's degree in international relations, high rank, and maturity—he was 41 when captured—make it hard to disagree when Denton claims "the North Vietnamese had made a good catch." A sense of election pulses through his memoir. On July 18, 1965, his last takeoff was delayed so that a visiting Robert McNamara could watch. The thirteenth POW held in Hanoi, Denton was also unlucky enough to be chosen for the infamous Hanoi Parade. (He identifies himself as the one who shouted out, "You are Americans! Keep your heads up!") Denton's hard-line resistance also made him one of the most frequently tortured POWs. Like *P.O.W.*, *When Hell Was in Session* blends the personal, patriotic, and religious together. Denton describes his captivity as long periods of endurance punctuated by moments of abuse, and whether by following the Code's advice, or by sharing W. E. Henley's gratitude for his "unconquerable soul," Denton remained certain that an implicit contract with God would give him the strength to endure if he remained true to his values.[31]

Especially when operating in concert with military prejudice and performance evaluations, however, this deifying of personal fortitude and duty could lead to blaming victims for their fate. The hard-liners often found POWs almost more responsible for failings, and in some cases their own deaths, than the Camp Authority, and Denton was famous for being harsh, even in Alcatraz itself. After Jim Stockdale's January 1969 removal, Denton found himself SRO over a dispirited group: "Everyone was extremely nervous and irritable, and while we remained united, the mood in the compound was growing black and sometimes not quite rational." Through petty arguments and short bouts of despair, though, the Gang held on—all that is but Ron Storz, the POW who never left Alcatraz. Stockdale tactfully recalls that largely because of sickness, "our spark plug, our hero Ron Storz" in early 1969 "became depressed, lost interest in eating, and failed rapidly." *P.O.W.*'s account is more detailed, but credits Storz with a strategy: "He had decided that the most effective way to combat his captors was to fast, to confront them with the prospect of losing a prisoner for whom they would have to account, or at least of releasing one whose horrendous physical condition would give credibility to his reports of incredible mistreatment."[32]

Though sympathetic, Denton takes a harder line. Homesickness, pessimism, and a rising fear that no one would ever leave Hanoi sapped Storz's toughness, and soon "the young Air Force major who had resisted gallantly, was beginning to pay the final price." By May 1969, only his cynicism remained strong: "There's no way the war's going to end soon. We'll be here forever." When his weight dropped to 90 pounds, Denton ordered Storz to eat, "threatening him with court-martial upon release if he failed to comply." Storz also asked about the difference between amnesty and parole, but Denton's reply—no POW would be punished for accepting early release *if* he was dying, and *if* he made no propaganda statements—was essentially a death sentence. Storz became "more and more irrational as the summer of 1969 wore on." When he started yelling to other POWs rather than covertly communicating, the guards didn't bother to stop him. He broke with the other POWs on the day he cried out, "Well I know who my *real* friends are." Too weak to rally after Ho's death in September, his behavior when the other POWs left Alcatraz in late 1969 showed how far he had fallen: "Ron Storz actually became violent. He screamed at Frenchy. 'You lying son of a bitch, you're not going to do anything.' While Storz tapped on the wall, 'Don't believe him,' Frenchy stood outside his cell shaking his head and shrugging his shoulders." Denton's epitaph is brief and tactful: "We hadn't been allowed to say goodbye to our friend, and we never saw him again. He died in April of 1970."[33]

For Denton, this story was a parable that showed how even diehards could fail without faith, unity, and a defiant will. The other Alcatraz POWs survived, but Storz didn't: weakness must therefore have led to his death. Such blunt reasoning was a Denton trademark. Collaborators he damned outright. When "voices were too steady, the tone too sincere" on the camp radio, "some in Alcatraz would have happily cut the throats of the speakers." Undisciplined POWs were poor military men. Once back in the system, Denton instantly realized that "despite the best efforts" of some senior POWs, the organization had "fragmented." Some men were accepting special favors, reading over the radio, and ignoring their commanding officers; others "were good resisters but hadn't learned to communicate." As the Alcatraz POWs struggled to restore "camp-wide resistance and unity," their "fury" often boiled over. "You rotten sons of bitches," George McKnight screamed at some backsliders. Denton also yelled at some POWs he thought were collaborating. Improved conditions and new arrivals only increased these tensions, as even the Alcatraz POWs started squabbling. Simple conversations "led to trouble and we engaged in violent arguments that on occasion nearly resulted in blows." Without the threat of pain and death, the POWs started losing their sense of duty and purpose. "Like the Children of Israel," Denton recalled, "we were having trouble with our own people as we neared the Promised Land and the frustrations created by years of imprisonment and torture surfaced."[34]

Resistance gave way to bureaucracy with SRO Colonel John Flynn, whose talents as a "judicious leader and excellent administrator" suited the times. The resulting micromanagement approach to captivity, however, produced what Denton calls an "administrative nightmare": "The sophisticated command structure was run on a flood of to-from-subject memos which sometimes included numbered paragraphs and subparagraphs as the instructions and policies grew more complicated. I had nine staff men working for me alone as we developed a hierarchy, and I became swamped with paperwork." This bureaucracy also explained why old-timers didn't tend to take POWs who arrived after the bombing halt very seriously. After a brief struggle on the ground, most of these shootdowns entered Camp Unity, and a POW community that resembled a "new Pentagon Southeast Asia."[35] This drift into top-heavy bureaucracy threatened to erase the hard-liners' early sacrifices. Denton and other hard-liners responded by making rigorous performance evaluations, by drafting and refining the official story, and by carefully planning their return home. Denton's write-ups adhered to a hard reading of the Code; just as predictably, more moderate POWs objected to such evaluations, and sometimes saw the evaluators as fanatics, lunatics, or hypocrites. Richard Stratton was very bitter about a devastating performance evaluation from a senior Naval Academy man he renamed "Thaddeus Hoyt," and some sources claim Jeremiah Denton was dangerously impulsive even before his capture. According to Stephen Rowan, POW Bill Tschudy had been Denton's flying partner because he "could be counted on to be level-headed in a crisis situation, and Denton needed that kind of person in the cockpit with him." Even this precaution, however, had apparently not been enough: Rowan praised Tschudy for not second-guessing "Denton's decision to leave the airplane, even though it was still flying level when the Commander ejected, leaving Bill with no choice but to bail out."[36]

Such dissent did not however shake Denton's faith in rank and seniority's privilege to pass judgment, and even on the America he returned to. Though pleased by the cleanliness, the "greater sense of commonality of purpose and respect among members of different religions," and the greater "respect between black and white people," Denton was also outraged by the "dark corners"—"group sex, massage parlors, X-rated movies, the drug culture," and other products of "the new permissiveness." A familiar "alien element" had clearly infected the American scene, leading to apathy, disunity, and that "weakness in the national character" he had seen after returning from Alcatraz, and which he now saw in those attacking Richard Nixon. America's defenses against communism were obviously collapsing, and as a returning prophet, Denton offers a restorative:

> I thought at one point that the title of this book should be *Under God Indivisible*, because that was my view of the performance of most of the prisoners in North Vietnam. It was difficult to achieve because imprisonment tends to breed resentment, suspicion, jealousy, hatred, and disunity, and in Hanoi our captors fostered these emotions. But most of the prisoners, finding themselves in desperate circumstances, quickly rediscovered God and became indivisible in their resistance and with the understanding that our way of life, with all its imperfections, is incomparably greater than anything offered by Communism.[37]

As the POWs who zealously enforced their country's values in Hanoi, men like Jeremiah Denton and Jim Mulligan felt obligated to offer the same services to America itself. The claims of success in Hanoi have their self-congratulatory side, their tinges of *noblesse oblige*, and even their echoes of Captain Queeg. Nevertheless, these claims give the official story much of its power as a righteous mythology. Even the scapegoats and renegades report that few things were more familiar in captivity than the stories of those held in Alcatraz.

God's Witnesses: Spiritual Autobiographies

Though many POWs gave religious faith some credit for their survival, for men like the one who told a public relations officer "You know, Dick, I couldn't have made it if it wasn't for Jesus Christ, and being able to look up and see Him in some trying times," captivity's spiritual dimensions dwarfed all others.[38] These POWs were grateful for their military training, their fellow prisoners, and their national heritage. Having rendered to America what was America's, however, they then declared that God had been their greatest support, since he granted nations and peoples whatever moral strength they had. This distinction is a crucial one in spiritual autobiographies. Though the captive may represent "the whole, chastened body of Puritan society," the "archetypic drama" of a single life spent "awaiting rescue by the grace of God" is the most important story. Because the perils of the frontier and the colonists' own reasons for being there made drawing a line between the literal and the spiritual difficult, the New Englanders were fascinated by such archetypic stories. Sermons drew parallels between Indian captivity and hell, and returning prisoners cited scripture to explain their literal imprisonment. Politically, as Richard Slotkin notes, the captive's experience not only paralleled "the bondage of the soul to the flesh and to the temptations arising from original sin," but also "the self-exile of the English Israel from England." If captivity was "likened to the regeneration of the soul in conversion," then the captive's "ultimate redemption," thanks to Christ and the Puritan magistrates, anticipated the soul's "ultimate salvation."[39]

These Christian analogies were still in place as America began fighting the cold war. William Lindsay White ends *The Captives of Korea* by declaring that "if, in our almost two millennia of Western Christendom, anything remains worth saving from the brutish materialism of Karl Marx," it is "that Man is more worthy of respect even than those governments which, in his folly, he creates," and "that Man, even in defeat and humbled as a prisoner, has a dignity which should be inviolate." Similar pieties appeared in memoirs written by the crew of the *Pueblo*. Stephen Harris ends with the claim that "if one person should read this book and be challenged to trust in God through Jesus Christ, then all the dreary months I spent in the North Korean 'socialist paradise' will have been worthwhile."[40] Nothing, however, accounts for the sheer number of Vietnam spiritual memoirs. *When Hell Was in Session*, *With God in a P.O.W. Camp*, *Six Years in Hell*, and *In the Presence of Mine Enemies* announce their intentions in their titles. *Before Honor* alludes to Proverbs 18:12, "Before destruction the heart of man is haughty, and before honor is humility"; a Mormon POW history, *From the Shadow of Death*, invokes the 23rd Psalm. *Yet Another Voice*, *The Passing of the Night*, and *Seven Years in Hanoi* are all standard spiritual autobiographies, and so are *Captive on the Ho Chi Minh Trail*, the story of two missionaries captured in Laos who ended up with American POWs, and *No Time for Tombstones*, an account of how missionary POWs Hank Blood and Betty Ann Olsen were martyred for their faith.

The traits common to Puritan captivity tales—"sermon-narrative form, each beginning with a biblical text and prefaced by a doctrine section in which the moral principles demonstrated in the narrative were defined and offered to the reader as a lesson and a warning to reform his life"—resurface in many Vietnam POW memoirs.[41] They often begin with personal disclaimers. Ralph Gaither "had not planned to write a book. The other prisoners had so much more to tell. But I knew I had a story to tell about Christ." Norman McDaniel solemnly promises "the account of the way a man's deep belief in God and in the promises of the Bible somewhat prepared him beforehand, and then sustained and strengthened him while undergoing a test of mental, physical, and spiritual strength at the mercy of a cruel enemy." McDaniel also insists that his story's greatest value will be for those who may never actually imprisoned, but who will definitely face the same threat from evil: "The writer emphasizes throughout that God is able and willing to stand with us through any trial, no matter how difficult, if we will only believe in God's power, trust in him, and honestly seek and obey his will."[42]

This belief rejects both pride and guilt. Although some POWs had difficulties seeing their story not "as a crusader's quest but as a sinner's trial and judgment," Cotton Mather's warning that "redeemed captives should not judge themselves better than those who were not rescued by God, nor should they be considered as great sinners for having been captured themselves" was just as appropriate for POWs held centuries later.[43] Charlie Plumb's *I'm No Hero* is only the baldest example of a memoir that shuns the heroic so it can compare the POW's sufferings to Christ's without presumption. Even before being tortured, Jay Hess was also forging links between Christ's anguish and his own: "The time he spent alone, those first forty days, were days of preparation and seasoning for what was

ahead. He thought of the Savior's forty days in the wilderness, as he himself was experiencing all kinds of temptations, alternately with hours of meditation." Torture predictably
brought the the Christ analogy to a POW's mind. Jim Mulligan saw Jesus as a fellow
victim: "Lord, give me the strength and the guts to see this thing through to the end, one
way or another. No one else knows, Lord, but you and I know, and that's all that's
necessary. You suffered for your beliefs, and I must suffer for mine." George Day called
a chapter about a particularly gruesome session "Crucifixion." Other POWs identified with
Christ's later temptations. After leaving his own "blood, sweat, and tears on the torture
room floor," Jay Jensen felt he understood "the story of the Garden of Gethsemane, where
Christ prayed and sweat blood from every pore." Red McDaniel saw his entire captivity
as an emblem: "Now I sense the purpose of my own Gethsemane there in Hanoi—I had
to be humbled before I could know the perfection Christ had in mind for me."[44]

Release similarly paralleled Christ's resurrection, and ultimately the welcome promised all good souls on Judgment Day. This analogy was in one instance quite literal.
Because Hanoi had never provided prisoner lists, POW Ronald L. Ridgeway came home
to learn he had been "buried" in 1968 with the patrol members who died in the ambush
that had led to his capture. (Though his mother had attended his funeral, she later told
reporters, "I always had a feeling my son would turn up.")[45] Most examples, however,
were more like Howard Rutledge's claim that captivity "had been a kind of tomb for seven
years, and now I felt resurrected from the dead, driving away to life again." Hours after
his release, Jay Jensen declared that "I have spent six years in hell and that I have been
resurrected and I'm going to start a new life." Norman McDaniel simply called chapter
three of his memoir "Resurrection." Families sometimes drew the same comparisons.
Though POW Jack Rollins's wife Connie found many similarities between the scriptures
and her own situation, "the best one was the analogy to Christ's second coming and Jack's
coming home. No one knew what day the Vietnamese were going to humble themselves
and sign the peace agreement. So, we likened it to the second coming of the Savior."[46] A
humbler but equally joyous parallel ran between the POWs' return to America and the
Last Judgment. Jim Mulligan called his arrival in Norfolk "a day of days. It was the
Judgment Day and Day of Resurrection when I would be born again into a free world to
be reunited with my wife and family, with my relatives and friends." Like fellow Mormon
Larry Chesley, Jay Jensen found in his reception glimmerings of God's eventual judgment:
"Dad said 'Son, welcome home. A job well done. We're all proud of you.' That touched
me deeply and made what I had been through seem worthwhile. And it helped me imagine
how wonderful it will be, if when I return to my Father in heaven, I can hear Him say,
'Welcome home, son. Well done. I am proud of you.' How much joy that reunion will
bring!"[47]

Nor was this joy confined to the future: many POWs proudly recorded examples of
Divine Favor in captivity. In keeping with Larry Chesley's argument that "those who took
God to prison will have brought God home with them, while with a few exceptions those
who did not will have left him there," the most devout POWs stressed that earlier instances
of grace made them confident: "He had answered my prayers then and would do so now."
Such POWs usually began their prayers as they parachuted down. "Dear God, help me,"
Jay Jensen cried, "It is all up to you now; it is all in your hands. I cannot help myself
much, and I certainly cannot help my family at home. Please watch over my wife, my
children, my parents and family." Charlie Plumb and Larry Chesley asked for the same
protection for their wives, and though some knife-twisting is going on here—all three men
ended up divorced—this selflessness is common. For many POWs, a personal prayer of

thanks soon proved appropriate. Since many POWs "should, by all elements of human reasoning and understanding, be dead," even the most "severely injured" were "greatly aware and appreciative of their blessings." Some men's survival was truly miraculous. After ejecting at treetop level from a disintegrating jet traveling at 200 miles per hour, Jack Rollins survived *even though his parachute never opened.* A "flooded rice paddy" saved his life, but Rollins understandably believed "the Lord also had something to do with it." Those surviving only slightly less hazardous shootdowns thanked God as well. Trapped in his burning plane until the last possible second, Robert Jeffrey credited "Divine help" for his escape: "I knew there was a reason I didn't die. I was not quite sure what it was, but there was a reason."[48]

Near misses like Jeffrey's could actually begin a POW's spiritual progress. Howard Rutledge ejected just "as another shell burst under the cockpit itself," and as he watched "with horror as my plane exploded into a ball of flame before me," his thoughts turned elsewhere: "'Thank You, God!' I prayed for the first time in twenty years, dangling 1,000 feet above North Vietnam." God continued his help on the ground. Rutledge shot a man during his capture, but an old man held back the crowd. Rutledge later decided that "the hands of God were gesturing through the hands of my enemy to save my life, and I am grateful." On his way to the village, Rutledge also glanced over his shoulder to see someone "running at me full-tilt, carrying a three-foot-long rusty harpoon." After avoiding the attack, Rutledge asked the obvious question: "What made me feel the danger and turn? I believe it was God at work again." God also worked through the medic who appeared with morphine and a tetanus shot, and later, when "alone for the first time since my capture," Rutledge realized that although he "had not thought about God much since dropping out of Sunday school in my late teens," he "had felt the hand of God" all that day. The conclusion was inescapable: "I was a prisoner of war. I had no idea what my fate would be, but the Lord had made Himself abundantly clear. He was there with me in the presence of my enemies, and I breathed my second prayer of thanks that day."[49]

Nor did God only intervene at such critical moments. When for instance his captors took away his boots, Larry Chesley prayed for them back, and "about one minute later my boots were returned to me." When his arms were tied, Chesley told God, "I can't travel very far this way." The knot came loose. Then, when a brutal guard started beating him on the way to Hanoi, Chesley prayed once more, and sure enough, "I had a different guard the next day and this one did not hurt me."[50] Though these examples may seem more like coincidences or card tricks than revelations, their frequency suggests how fervently many POWs believed in their divine origin. When Larry Guarino "prayed for strength and guidance" shortly after capture, for instance, he "pondered the strange, indeed mystical things that had been happening." He had somehow anticipated his shootdown, but had been just as certain "that he would be all right, that he would survive." One incident confirmed this belief. When his captors tied him up in blankets, Guarino "sweated, he struggled for breath and life, he waited for death and he prayed." All of a sudden, "there were breezes, cool, sweet, refreshing, swirling gently all about him. He breathed deeply, easily, gratefully. He had never been more comfortable in an air-conditioned room, on a beach, anywhere. He kept on praying, in thanksgiving. When the troops returned and unwrapped him, he felt cool and relaxed. Outside there seemed not a breath of air in the whole world." In May 1968, when the Alcatraz cells turned into hotboxes, Jim Mulligan offered a prayer. Cooling rains poured down, and in giving thanks to God, Mulligan tossed down a challenge to all skeptics: "When I get out and tell this story someone will say, it was just coincidence, the mere arrival of a fast moving tropical cold front. But You and I know it was more than that. In my direst need I begged for Your help and You answered me. Thank you Lord."[51]

Nothing was too mundane for God's interest. He lanced boils—Larry Chesley had one in his armpit, but "after much praying," it eventually "burst, giving me relief from its pain." Jeremiah Denton arguably received the most remarkable sign of God's grace. Though manacled, filthy, hungry, and thirsty, for some reason all Denton wanted during one bad period was toilet paper. He "prayed, almost apologetically, for a small favor," then looked up to see "a large leaf, swirling and fluttering in the heavy air and heading my way": "I watched fascinated as it took a sudden dive and landed practically at my feet. It was large, about 9 inches long and 6 inches wide, and pleasantly furry on one side. Perfect!" An equally fine sense of Divine timing freed POW Ed Davis: "Ed found a nail and was able to manipulate it with his fingers into the lock of the cuffs behind him. He tapped to Denton 'A miracle!' He had been saying a rosary, and on the last 'amen' the nail had found the lock release and the cuffs had broken open." A POW's ears could also move God to act. When a nearby loudspeaker began blaring out propaganda and "discordant Oriental music," Robinson Risner "went immediately, almost angrily, into prayer: . . . *God, you are going to have to help me! You have just got to get that thing turned off. . . .*" This wish for "some sort of lasting, Almighty damage" was granted: "The speaker never came on again."[52]

Prayer was also the POW's weapon when facing the harsh spiritual challenge of sustaining his belief in God's love as captivity stretched on for years. How could a POW's faith endure when experience suggested that God had delivered a devoted servant into the hands of the Devil? Jay Hess felt his family's prayers were more effective than his own: "He knew that someone was working for him. 'It was the simple faith of my children,' he said to himself, feeling close to that divine guiding Spirit." Other men faced captivity as a personal challenge. Red McDaniel drew his strength from his mother's stubborn certainty—"She believed in what God could do and stuck by it"—and from Norman Vincent Peale's *The Power of Positive Thinking*. Perhaps most ingeniously, Larry Chesley believed that through captivity God had ironically *answered* his prayers. Before shootdown, Chesley had prayed for the pilot's wings which made his Vietnam tour possible: "What would have happened had I prayed differently back at Webb AFB—if I had asked that God's will be done in the matter? Perhaps I would not have become a pilot, in which case the years 1966–1973 presumably would have been very different." The same ironies dogged Chesley in captivity. When the POWs moved from Camp Hope to Camp Faith in 1970, he believed their prayers for better conditions had been answered. Unfortunately, Camp Hope was the camp raided by U.S. commandos four months later, and realizing "we probably would have been liberated 2 1/2 years earlier than we were," Chesley wondered whether the move had been "the best answer to our prayers, or should we have left the details to the Lord?"[53]

Desperation forced other POWs to ask for Divine help. As three POWs withered away before him, jungle POW Nick Rowe found that "partially from a strong sense of self-preservation, partially from a sense of responsibility to the other men, because I could offer them no solutions if I could find none for myself, I turned to the one positive force our captors could never challenge, God."[54] Though shootdown and capture had surprised Howard Rutledge into praying for the first time in twenty years, it was during a bad torture session in early 1966 that he "made God a promise. If I survived this ordeal, the first Sunday back in freedom I would take Phyllis and my family to their church and at the close of the service confess my faith in Christ and join the church." Neither a deal nor a bargain, Rutledge's promise was a simple confession of powerlessness: "It took prison and hours of painful reflection to realize how much I needed God and the community of believers. After I made God that promise, again I prayed for strength to make it through the night." As in the Puritan narratives, for Rutledge this need endured even those times when God seemed to be the one tormenting him. Arriving home only to learn that an accident had paralyzed his son, Rutledge wondered but held fast: "God had been so real to me in Prison. This time when I prayed, there was no clear answer. I don't understand these things. I don't know why God seems to intervene so plainly in one event and seems so absent in another. But I refuse to let my questions overpower my faith in Him. To not believe there is a God at work in the world is a grim and unacceptable option."[55] Rutledge's last sentence is therefore the spiritual autobiographer's credo. Not believing is no option at all.

Significant Scriptures: The Story of Job

Since Christian captives must accept their fate as a necessary part of God's plan, they predictably turn for comfort to Biblical narratives dealing with tribulation and suffering. As the ultimate role model for those facing martyrdom, Jesus inspired the colonial captives most, but they also meditated on Job and the Prodigal Son as figures who fell deep into torment, but eventually regained favor.[56] The same stories inspired the Vietnam POWs. At one point for Howard Rutledge, "the boils got so bad I felt like Job." During these miserable nights, he wondered "why God answers some prayers with relief and others with silence." Like Job, however, he "could only go on trusting him. The alternatives are too bleak to consider." A desperate Ralph Gaither worked his way up to Job. He prayed for better conditions and for patience, "but nothing changed." He tried to strike bargains, promising to tithe, to become a preacher, to sell his Corvette, to date only nice girls, to obey God's laws—"everything I could think of"—but "nothing changed." Then he recalled "Job and what he went through," and an inspired Gaither "gave God everything I had, every bit of faith in my heart and soul, all the faith I could muster and all the faith God might give to me in the future." No sign appeared, "no trumpets or angel chorus, no white lights, just an absolute certainty of God's presence." And for Gaither, "that was all I needed."[57]

Learning simply to submit was not however Job's most challenging lesson. When Jeremiah Denton made his "vow of surrender" to God, "with an admission that I could take no more on my own," this act had an immediate, "profound and deeply inspiring" reward: "Strangely, as soon as I made the vow, a deep feeling of peace settled into my tortured mind and pain-wracked body, and the suffering left me completely."[58] The far more difficult task was to follow Job's example even though relief might never come. Though a number of POWs discuss this challenge, Red McDaniel draws the line most sharply between duty and reward. For McDaniel, "the crucial test to my own faith, to the sense of optimism I had tried to maintain all these months," came during the summer of horror following the Dramesi-Atterberry escape attempt of 1969. Though manacled, whipped, denied sleep, and forced to kneel on the floor, McDaniel was at first defiant, refusing to cooperate until the pain became unbearable. To buy time, he then lied a bit, but when the pressure resumed, he turned to his competitive instincts: "In all of the exhaustion, when my mind wouldn't function, when the pain beat a steady rhythm through-out my body, I still rose to the occasion with an insane desire to beat them." Soon, however, that high-school advice which the military "picked" up and "socked" home—"To win isn't everything—actually it's the only thing"—collapsed as well, and McDaniel decided that "with death knocking at the door, a man has time for only one thing: to go out with some kind of honor." For some hard-line POWs, this "thing" was the ultimate value, but for the spiritual autobiographer, honor failed ultimately as well. McDaniel's captors jammed a rag down his throat and hung him upside down. When electric shocks began the next morning, he realized that "he wasn't going to come through this after all." At this moment, everything fell away: "Suddenly I was not a U.S. Navy flyer at all; I was not a patriot at this point, and being an American meant nothing in the reality of the moment. I was simply a human being sliding further and further toward death, and there was nothing at all to reach out for anymore, within and without."[59]

Like many POWs, McDaniel had assumed that "Christ was in me, making of me a kind of model person in morality, good citizenship, love of country, family, and all the rest of it." As he faced his end, however, McDaniel realized he "had not entered into the sufferings of Christ in all that time. I had lived on the 'good times' of Christianity, but I had never been tested by pain, as He had been, and the dimension missing in my life was tied directly to that." McDaniel in short was now seeing through the eyes of Job, and even though God promised no relief, McDaniel abandoned his pride in a prayer he called a "surrender": "Lord . . . it's all Yours . . . whatever this means, whatever it is supposed to accomplish in me, whatever You have in mind now with all of this, it's all Yours. . . ." In this moment, McDaniel threw off all the standards he had set for himself, including God's own: "I was totally willing now to accept whatever He had in mind, whereas all the time of my life up to this point had been spent reminding God that I was measuring up to Him and therefore He would make sure I never got beyond my depth." Such unqualified surrender was possible only for a time. At the end of his captivity, McDaniel even used Job as his text for a sermon about how the POWs were returning to wealth and family greater than what they had lost. Having fought their "greatest battle," they could begin "to enjoy our greatest victory."[60] This happy ending however no more trivializes McDaniel's submission than Job's textually suspect reformation solves the problem of unmerited and unrelieved suffering. In captivity's darkest moments, Job's example helped some POWs remain devout and obedient without expecting rescue, or eventual reward.

The Prodigal Son

When POW Brian D. Woods reached his critically ill mother's bedside on February 13, 1973, he "told her the prodigal child is home. There's no reason now she shouldn't get better." Her response was a simple one: "God has rewarded my prayers."[61] Whether returning from the wilderness or a Vietnam prison, American captives have often taken this parable to heart. Just as the Prodigal Son demanded his inheritance and left his sheltering home, the New England colonists looked for ways to test their spiritual mettle even after their often guilt-ridden departure from England. Mary Rowlandson lived "in a state of relatively complacent ease" before her captivity. As a "good Puritan," however, she longed "for some 'affliction' of God to be visited upon her, in order that her sinful will might be overborne by a stronger and purer force of holiness than her own."[62] Many Vietnam POWs shared something of this longing. Already part of the military's elect, these aviators had further distinguised themselves by flying combat missions. When shot down, then, they fell almost as far as anyone could. Nor did they feel entirely guiltless. Though they obviously hadn't wanted to be captured, they had pursued a very dangerous profession that had created hardships for the families they so often said good-bye to. Though they too lost a great patrimony through pride and circumstance, like the Prodigal Son, they were also chastened through suffering, and returned to a joyous homecoming.

Hanoi's most insistent Prodigal Son was Robinson Risner. A famous air warrior even before his capture, Risner's eight confirmed MIG kills in Korea made him that war's twentieth ace. As one of the most experienced pilots flying missions in early 1965, he participated in news conferences "to help explain to the American people why we were in Vietnam." He even made the cover of *Time*. A happy family life complemented these achievements. His memoir begins with his last hours at home, when a "strange premonition" made him go over "insurance policies, investments, and obligations" with his wife, Kathleen. He also taped a message for his family, though he never had before: "I don't expect anything to happen to me ever, but you never know. If anything should, you all will know that I was prepared and you all will know, also, that I have had a rich and rewarding life."[63]

Given Risner's military credentials, and this very standard narrative structure—the POW leaves home in the first chapter and returns in the last—it's therefore somewhat surprising that Risner credits his captivity with forcing him to accept the blame for a mottled life. Like the Prodigal Son, Risner was guilty of "riotous living" before his Hanoi ordeal. His backwater World War II posting was to Panama, and what he and his fellow pilots did there to fight off boredom "did little to endear ourselves to the local populace." Blowing "the roofs off the little native huts" was a favorite pastime, "and if the huts were not available, sailboats were fair game."[64] Though Risner mentions no repercussions here, his high spirits definitely had consequences as he moved through the ranks. When stationed in Oklahoma, he flew off one day for Brownsville, Texas—to pick up shrimp for a party. The plane's navigation tools were poor, the radio was virtually useless, his own knowledge of the jet stream was nonexistent, and a hurricane lay off the Gulf Coast. Soon lost and low on fuel, Risner landed on a secluded beach and weathered out the storm. The first people he met told him he was in Mexico, and three days passed before he got to a phone. By this time his friends and his seven-months-pregnant wife believed he was dead. Nor had his Mexican adventures ended. Told to stay out of trouble while embassy officials tried to explain to the Mexicans why a fully armed fighter plane had violated their air space, Risner was almost killed by a gang in a bad section of town. Risner finally got home—but at a cost. The friend who flew him back "told me that my wife was in the hospital and that she had lost the baby."[65] Here Kathleen and the unborn child were the victims; in Korea, Risner's high spirits endangered, and even killed, those flying with him. Seeing his first MIGs made Risner so excited that he forgot to look for other planes; he only barely escaped. Sometime later, a superb MIG pilot lured him across the border and right over a Chinese air base. Though Risner made it home, his wingman was hit and forced to bail out into the ocean on the way back. Through a freak accident, he drowned. Risner's malfunctions and miraculous rescues were part of his Vietnam tour as well. He first went down when he inexplicably circled back over a target; like his Korea wingman, he bailed out over water and only barely survived. Risner's luck ran out on September 16, 1965. Hit after dropping napalm, he ejected, and thus made his "reservations for a seven-and-a-half-year stay in the Hanoi Hilton."[66]

P.O.W. and other memoirs present Robinson Risner as a strong yet humble and compassionate leader. In his own memoir, he describes how captivity turned him into the figure the other POWs saw. Though a family man and famous pilot, Risner saw himself as a daredevil who had not properly valued the treasures he possessed. Hanoi changed him. If anything, the distance between his exciting career and prison life in Hanoi was wider than that lying between the Prodigal Son's home and his pigsty in a far country—and of course, Risner couldn't simply decide to go home. Certainly Risner was shocked at the contrast: "With all the power of America behind me, all the technology, all the brains and the riches, here I was in a seven-foot cell, eating food hardly fit for consumption . . . in dirt and filth that we would not have raised our pigs in."[67] As Richard Slotkin notes about Mary Rowlandson, however, "The throes of the soul's regeneration begin with a sense of separation, a perception of the distance one has fallen from grace," and Hanoi definitely helped Risner see "sin and sinfulness as a total environment, a world like hell, in which one breathes, gnaws, drinks one's own spiritual filthiness."[68] His own progress began in early 1966, when he prayed in isolation for his family, confessed his loneliness, and opened up a seven-year dialogue with God. The following two years of torture and solitary led to the four principles of faith discussed in chapter 5, although Risner's paraphrase of the fourth principle, "faith in God," should be mentioned here, since his belief that "God would bring me out of prison—better for my stay" shows how Risner valued personal rehabilitation over service or martyrdom.[69]

"Better" did not however mean vindicated or rewarded. Like the Prodigal Son, Risner returned humbly and without expectation. Events had also made a full restoration impossible. Since his mother had died in 1971—a heavy burden, since "it was from her that I had learned to pray"—no parent welcomed this Prodigal Son home: "There is no way to express how much I wished she could have lived to see my return." When he did arrive home in 1973, Risner learned that his brother had also died; nevertheless, his memoir ends triumphantly with an image of Risner surrounded by his wife and sons. As in Christ's parable, he who had been dead was alive again, and he who had been lost was found, a condition the penitent prodigal describes through a series of contrasts steeped in gratitude and humility:

> The musty, dank smell of small enclosed cells was forever gone. The air was fresh and free for the taking.
>
> I could go where I wanted, talk to whom I wished, read—with glasses—whenever and whatever I wished. I was being treated as a man again and not as a caged animal. . . .
>
> My dread was gone. The future was before me. The doors that were locked and closed were now unlocked and permanently open. The darkness of that long unbelievable night had finally passed.[70]

Job was a more flattering model for POWs to follow. Past wrongdoing was not an issue. Though working God's will, the tormentors were still devils. Job submitted only to God, and was ultimately rewarded for his goodness. As Robinson Risner's memoir suggests, however, the parable of the Prodigal Son generally came closer to the POW's experience. Because torture forced them to submit, or because their former lives contained shameful or thoughtless moments, many Vietnam POWs felt intensely guilty. By presenting adversity as a time for spiritual reformation, the Prodigal Son parable not only offered humility as a cure for their guilt, but also accounts for Robinson Risner's success as those admirable paradoxes: the humble leader or Christian hero.

Christ, Disciples, and the Saint's Life

Since the Christian captivity narrative passes from suffering to redemption, allusions to the Savior himself were inevitable. Such parallels had to be modest, for even the most pious shied away from claiming they had successfully followed his path. Nor were Vietnam

POW martyrs all that common either. Though the murdered escaper Ed Atterberry was a notable exception, because the POWs credited their survival to unity, they were more likely to see casualties as despairing victims rather than as Christian martyrs. The strongest case for POW martyrdom is Malcolm McConnell's biography *Into the Mouth of the Cat: The Story of Lance Sijan, Hero of Vietnam*. Published by Norton in 1985, it too was commissioned by *Reader's Digest*, and like *P.O.W.*'s John G. Hubbell, McConnell claims to be definitive: "I am confident my dramatization of Sijan's astonishing performance is as accurate a record as it is now possible to write."[71] McConnell also offers this story as an aid for dealing with the war's legacy. His sources urged him to record truths they felt were fading. Some men asked McConnell to express "the deep bitterness they still harbored toward former antiwar activists like Jane Fonda and her husband, Tom Hayden, who, they reminded me, had defied their country's laws by giving public aid and comfort to the enemy in his own capital yet now seemed to have become born-again capitalists, beneficiaries of America's short memory and overdeveloped popular-culture industry." Other men wanted McConnell to smash Frances FitzGerald's *Fire in the Lake,* that "ridiculously dated and simplistic paean to the National Liberation Front"; still others wanted him to attack *Apocalypse Now*. Though McConnell does end with the hope that his book will remind Americans that Vietnam vets paid the same price and deserve the same gratitude as World War II vets, he ultimately decided that "Lance's story and its underlying statement on America and North Vietnam's strategic motives would tell itself without blatant interlinear commentary."[72]

McConnell makes it abundantly clear that Lance Sijan will definitely be a *Hero of Vietnam*. His childhood credentials for martyrdom were impeccable. "Physically stronger than the other kids," in high school his many academic, athletic, and social commitments forced him to "function with less sleep than other people." He stood out at the Air Force Academy as well. Fellow POW and academy man Guy Gruters remembered him as one "of the biggest, strongest, and certainly the best-looking cadet in the 21st Squadron, probably in the whole damn academy." This Adonis of the early 1960s "projected a warm, guileless vitality, a kind of physical optimism, an unspoken assertion that his strength and beauty were invulnerable, that he was, indeed, one of those knights of the New Frontier who had been well prepared to fight any battle in the defense of liberty." The academy also gave Sijan his first real challenge. Though he still tried to juggle many activities, the combination of varsity football and academics was hurting his grades. Because he equated "athletic ability and competitive drive, when linked to intellectual flexibility and mental toughness, with the vigor that John Kennedy and his family had so epitomized for Sijan's generation," the Academic Review Board's request that he "voluntarily give up varsity athletics" came as a shock. No one was questioning Sijan's work ethic; the board was testing his ability to make sacrifices and submit to authority. Sijan passed. Showing "unusual maturity," he gave up football, and after graduating from the academy, in time he was sent to Vietnam.[73]

The events that turned this Adonis into the "mangled, dying scarecrow" Guy Gruters knew in captivity began on November 9, 1967. After bailing out, Sijan lay semiconscious on the jungle floor for thirty-five hours. His injuries included deep forearm cuts, a mangled right hand, a compound fracture of his left leg, a serious concussion, and a fractured skull. After he made hand radio contact, at least six U.S. aircraft were disabled trying to rescue him. The air team had to give up at nightfall on November 11, and as Sijan crawled around below he fell into a sinkhole, thus losing radio contact and injuring himself even more. Then, *for the next six weeks*, Lance Sijan dragged himself through the jungle, looking for a place to signal rescue aircraft from. On Christmas Day, he tumbled onto a road and lost consciousness. What the North Vietnamese found was "a long skeleton in muddy rags, bound together with twisted straps and metal buckles. White skin near the head and raw, bleeding expanses of flesh showed everywhere." When his captors put him in with two other POWs, Guy Gruters and Bob Craner, Gruters was certain he "had never been near a *living* person in such horrible condition." Sijan's face was "a battered skull," his skin was a mass of sores, and his limbs were like sticks. Though taller than six feet, he felt like less than 100 pounds when lifted. He had also been physically abused.[74]

The level of suffering put Sijan in the company of the strictest diehards. What carried him beyond was his unbelievable sense of duty. The Code of Conduct appears in full before McConnell's story begins, and Sijan followed it to the letter. Take for instance the obligation to evade capture. Sijan had vowed that if enemy forces shot him down, "They won't get me alive"—and they almost didn't. Three hard-line reasons account for the gravely injured Sijan's desperate, even suicidal decision to stay hidden. He worried first about his welcoming committee. Sijan knew what "marine and army grunts did to NVA or VC prisoners they flushed out of tunnels and bunkers after ambushes where the Americans had suffered heavy casualties," and since "soldiers were a lot alike," he assumed the troops looking for him would not be "any more disciplined or understanding." His fear of "being captured, of becoming a POW to be brainwashed, tortured, broken, and paraded around like a goddamn zombie," was Sijan's second reason for evading. Korea's legacy was at work here, but it was the photographs and taped confession of Richard Stratton and other POWs that frightened Sijan most. Though Stratton later insisted that his strategy had countered brainwashing more successfully than the hard-liner's methods, Sijan was unyielding: "They won't turn me into some kind of zombie like that poor son of a bitch." The third reason for avoiding captivity was the simplest of all. Even though "he was probably condemning himself to life as a cripple, very possibly as a double amputee who would never again fly an airplane, run, or enjoy any sport," Sijan's "job, his military duty, was to escape, to evade capture, even if he died in the attempt." He would in short obey the Code.[75]

Guy Gruters and Bob Craner set the baseline for measuring Sijan's outstanding fidelity to the Code. Though in far better shape physically, for instance, they couldn't match Sijan's determination to make "every effort to escape." A Vietnamese official told them that despite his hideous injuries, Sijan had actually overpowered a guard, taken a weapon, and staggered away from a rest station. Recapture had not discouraged him. Whenever conscious, between his cries of pain he grilled Gruters and Craner about camp security. They "stared at each other behind Sijan's bobbing skull. He was talking about *escape*. Incredible, absolutely unbelievable." His behavior when delirious was even more telling. Sijan scratched at the floor and pushed at the bamboo walls, seeking a way out. His unbending attitude toward Article V set Sijan even further apart. When first interrogated, Gruters had followed his survival training, which basically duplicated the Hanoi POWs' fallback policy. Gruters knew that he "was to resist answering all military questions, that he should stick to name, rank, service number, and date of birth, as delineated in the Code of Conduct—until he was tortured. Then, after an undefined period of torture, he was to start giving the enemy false information *slowly*, as if the pain and shock had broken his will." By admitting that going beyond the Code would be necessary, this strategy offered an escape route. Sijan refused to take it, thus hastening a death that his fellow POWs felt was virtually certain anyway. He greeted all questions with silence, and soon "Gruters heard thuds, harsh cracks, the sound of a bamboo club striking bone, the awful crunch of a boot striking the man's body." This abuse only angered him—"The new guy actually *roared* with pain now, as loud as any tormented animal. 'I'll get you, you fucker!' he screamed. 'I'll kick your ass.'"—and when his body failed him, his voice, but not its message, was weak: " 'I'm not . . . going to tell you anything. . . .' The guy's voice would phase in and out like a badly tuned radio receiver. 'I can't talk to you. It's . . . against the code. Can't you understand?' "[76]

Such performances turned Lance Sijan into an icon of resistance for the two POWs who knew him, and for the hundreds more who would hear his story. It was his late January 1968 death, roughly a month after his capture, however, that turned Craner and Gruters into disciples and sole witnesses to a martyr's death. Bob Craner felt at first that Sijan "was too damn brave for his own good. If he kept up this amazing defiance very long, these people would kill him." When Guy Gruters heard the beatings, he just "threw himself to the far side of his cell and began to pray for the injured skeleton thirty feet away." When the official told them about Sijan's escape attempt, however, "Gruters realized that he had just heard an account of resistance and heroism of historic proportions." His own experience with Sijan confirmed there was something mythic about his last days. On the way to Hanoi, for instance, some Vietnamese peasants gave a "truly spontaneous moaning sigh of shock and compassion" when they saw that "tableau of the bruised, filthy, but powerful American pilots crying with uncontrollable grief as they cradled their dying comrade"—a tableau "so emotionally awesome" that it "transcended the cultural and political barriers separating the Asians and Americans." Gruters soon felt fortunate he knew Lance Sijan: "If there was any single person who epitomized the qualities a prisoner needed to survive and return with his honor intact, that model now lay in the three-man cell across the courtyard."[77] Sijan's example steeled his cellmate's own will. When "two guards tried to reach up and force down Gruters' head in a bow of respect," he "easily resisted them, a small act of defiance in sympathy with Lance's unbelievable, stubborn resistance." Just as importantly, since "Sijan might well die before he could tell his own story," as they tended his wounds Gruters and Craner asked for and received the details of his shootdown and jungle tribulations.[78]

All these details prepare the way for McConnell's account of Sijan's last hours. The Christian parallels here are overwhelming. Timing their shifts by the bells of a nearby church, Gruters and Craner tended their cellmate. Though Sijan never lost his sense of humor—smiling, he asked at one point for a burger and french fries—his condition deteriorated, the bouts of delirium increased, and finally his captors came to remove him. After covering his lower body with a blanket, they placed him on his wooden pallet. Saint John reports that Christ's last words were "It is finished"; Saint Luke says that "when Jesus had cried with a loud voice, he said, Father, into thy hands I commend my spirit, and having said thus, he gave up the ghost." Lance Sijan did both:

> As the soldiers hefted up the pallet, Lance's face flashed with savage intensity. He *knew* they were taking him away to die.
>
> Suddenly his loud, clear voice filled the cramped cell with a force that shocked them all. "Oh, my *God*," he called. "It's over . . . it's *over*." His face rippled and clenched with terminal emotion. "*Dad* . . ." he cried in the same powerful, commanding voice. "*Dad* . . . help me. Dad, I *need* you. . . ."[79]

At this moment in Milwaukee, Syl Sijan, trapped "in a vacuum of despair" since Lance's disappearance, heard his son's cries:

> Suddenly his fist pounded the cold plastic of the steering wheel.
>
> "Lance!" he screamed. "Lance . . . where *are* you?"

Shocked by his outburst, he felt a weird certainty that Lance was trying to reach him, that Lance was calling for his father.

"Lance . . . *Lance*," Syl Sijan moaned as his eyes washed with tears and he struggled to control the car.[80]

Gruters and Craner were devastated as well, "utterly spent with despair, their faces sticky with tears." When however "Bug turned his smooth face" a few days later, and smiling sweetly, told Craner that " 'Sijan die,'" sorrow gave way to duty: "Sijan was dead. But Bob Craner resolved, as he stumbled along before the prodding enemy, that he would do his best to commit to memory and spread the incredible story of Lance Sijan's heroic resistance—his protracted struggle against pain and overpowering adversity—among his fellow prisoners and, eventually, to the nation Sijan had served with such distinction."[81]

This promise was kept. The last two sections of *Into the Mouth of the Cat*, "Honors" and "Requiem," describe how Sijan became a legend in the POW community, and still later, for many dedicated Americans. Fellow Medal of Honor winner Jim Stockdale called Lance Sijan "a hero to every American prisoner of war in North Vietnam. In spite of broken limbs, lacerations, concussion, lack of food and drink, he did it all: Evasion, Escape, Stoic Resistance under torture. What he did was truly above and beyond the call of duty. As the story of his heroic performance inspired us who were in prison with him, it will inspire future generations in our country's combat personnel."[82] Plans for the first written version of this story began before the POWs' 1973 release, when Bob Craner told SRO John Flynn that Lance Sijan deserved the Medal of Honor. Flynn asked for a written recommendation, thus initiating a process that led to the White House. By the time of the ceremony three years later, Sijan's metamorphosis from man to myth was almost complete. President Gerald Ford served as celebrant in a military mass. When he presented the medal to Lance's parents, "There was a certain liturgical quality to this part of the ceremony, the passing of a sanctified object among a circle of anointed leaders." Ford then called Sijan a martyr and visionary: "He deeply regretted, he said, having the duty of awarding this medal posthumously. Lance Sijan was a man of 'uncommon courage who gave the country a cherished memory and a clear vision of a better world.'"[83]

McConnell's greatest task, however, remains: to show that America's desire to deny or forget the Vietnam War had not made Lance Sijan's struggle "a futile effort, a one-man Charge of the Light Brigade, tragically flamboyant but ultimately meaningless."[84] McConnell responds to the challenge with an account of two visits—to the Air Force Academy and to the Sijan family home. In Colorado, he found that the Academy's first Medal of Honor winner was "an inspirational model who now stood in America's military pantheon alongside Nathan Hale, Sergeant Alvin York, and Audie Murphy." Of "the seventeen thousand young people" who had attended the Academy, "Sijan had become the best known and most revered." Cadets memorized his story like a catechism. A building bore his name, and some cadets considered his portait inside "a talisman and saluted the canvas for good luck before examinations or important athletic events." At the academy, then, Lance Sijan had become what his father felt America needed—"a symbol for the true meaning of our involvement" in Vietnam.[85] McConnell grasped the domestic significance of his story in Wisconsin. The Sijans "seemed an eminently *normal* American family," which of course was the point: "It was exactly the family's decent, predictable stability, their spirit of community service and leadership, their uncomplicated and traditional values, and their unquestioning bonds of love that had molded Lance's adult character." This is McConnell's answer to skeptics. "There were no mysteries about Lance Sijan's indominable character"; he had simply remained loyal to those values which many Americans abandoned during the war.[86] At a time of dissent, confusion, and apathy, Lance Sijan had lived and died a true American.

Into the Mouth of the Cat thus presents Lance Sijan as a typically American saint. Because the unique circumstances of his life and death made all charges of fanaticism ridiculous, in Hanoi Sijan could serve as a pristine symbol for those ideals which the senior POWs tried to instill in the other prisoners. Like Jesus, Lance Sijan was both an anomaly and the essence of an official story. And also like Jesus, his suffering, death, and virtual deification were so uncontaminated by self-interest that his blood can be offered as evidence to all who question the justice of his cause.

Fighting the Good Fight: Witnessing to Others in War

One of religion's greatest benefits in captivity was its value as an inexhaustible subject for meditation and debate. Jay Jensen recalls trying "to remember all the scripture that I could, all the Bible and Book of Mormon stories. I tried to remember all our thirteen Articles of Faith and managed twelve. I sang all the hymns I could remember. . . . I did much praying." Four years of solitary had Howard Rutledge trying "desperately to recall snatches of Scripture, sermons, the gospel choruses from childhood, and the hymns we sang in church" as well. When POWs made contact, they exchanged religious texts or meditations as frequently as poetry, batting averages, or camp news, and though "this talk of Scripture and hymns may seem boring to some," Howard Rutledge insisted "it was the way we conquered our enemy and overcame the power of death around us."[87] For evangelical Protestant or Mormon POWs, this sharing was also personal ministry. Some men felt this duty was the real reason for their captivity. After meeting the badly injured Bill Metzger, for instance, Red McDaniel "suddenly realized the selfishness of my question of God when I was shot down: 'God, why me?' Now, looking at Metzger, so helpless there, with wounds open and gaping, I said, 'God, why *not* me?' " McDaniel "somehow sensed" there was a Divine reason for his captivity: "It wasn't perfectly clear, but I had to grab onto the possibility that I probably had something I could give to the others that was needed here." Such notions appealed to a POW community whose Code declared it would trust in "God and in the United States of America." Larry Chesley called this phrase the "great reaffirmation": "It is that under God's blessing the United States of America is the greatest country on earth."[88] Even happy marriages of religion and politics could of course pose dangers. Chesley's fellow Mormon Jay Hess noted that the North Vietnamese "did things so much like the Church that it scared me. They have their kids sing about Ho Chi Minh; we teach our children to sing about Joseph Smith. They sing about their armies; we sing 'Hope of Israel, Zion's army.' In the Church we try to motivate people; the Vietnamese are masters at motivation."[89] For this reason, most POWs treasured simple religious beliefs that strengthened their community, but they shied away from doctrinal absolutism.

This tendency neverthless left some spiritual questions unanswered. For example, how should the devout POW feel about his captors? Though Christianity had a history in Hanoi, the rare Roman Catholic services held for the POWs were propaganda shows, and the Vietnamese shunned all POW attempts at saving them. Moments of compassion did of course occur. When Howard Rutledge noticed the guards were being gentle with Ron Storz, at least for a moment he stopped seeing them as robots: "I'm sure the enemy had families who bled and died. I'm sure the enemy cried when loved ones went away and did not return. I'm sure they, too, were tempted to give way to anger and hatred. But revenge is God's business. Anger and hatred can destroy us all. When it's over, we must try to forget and to forgive." Red McDaniel shared this opinion with his cellmates. Sensing "the burden deep within" all of them, he announced, "I'd like to pray for our Vietnamese guards": "Nobody said anything. Maybe it was a bit of a shock. After I'd taken everything they could throw at me in torture, shouldn't the guards have been the last recipients of prayer I would consider? But then again, as I prayed, I knew the other men were entering in with me. I had lost my hatred for my captors."[90] Such concern however did not mean that the POWs had any real hope for the enemy's salvation. At best, they pitied their captors for their ignorance and evil, and some devout POWs seemed almost relieved at having their overtures rejected. As Mormon POW Larry Chesley explained, "It's very difficult to convert someone who is determined his beliefs are right and yours are wrong, especially when he has no objective basis for evaluation." Whether the issues were religious or political, then, when it came to changing minds, "We couldn't convert them any more than they could convert us."[91]

Since evangelism was a militantly Christian POW's spiritual duty, he therefore turned his attention to the other POWs. Not surprisingly, the most zealous POW proselytizers were the Mormons. In their Utah-published memoirs, both Jay Jensen and Larry Chesley present themselves as active Latter-Day Saints. As a Camp Unity chaplain, Jensen asked each POW in his Sunday School class to talk about his church. The Catholics took two weeks, the various Protestants one apiece. When Jay's turn came, though, "for the next twelve weeks they learned about Mormonism!" Jensen admitted that "maybe it was kind of a dirty trick," but the men seemed interested, and his intentions were good: "I don't believe I converted anyone, but perhaps I helped increase their understanding. Maybe I even got some of them interested so that they will look into the gospel of Jesus Christ a little deeper later on."[92] In his classes, Larry Chesley outdid even Jensen: "It took me a year, teaching mainly on Sundays, but I finally exhausted my knowledge of the Bible." Chesley also made a number of good-natured but unsuccessful attempts at aiming men toward the Mormon church. After orienting Chesley to captivity by explaining the command structure and resistance policy, Robinson Risner prayed with Larry, who then asked Risner "to promise me that when we get out of here you'll look up the Mormon missionaries and learn about our Church." Between October 1967 and November 1968, his "most spiritual year in prison," Chesley taught his Catholic roommate, Gerald Coffee, "what I knew about the Gospel": "I remember the night I left Jerry. I said, 'Well, Jerry, you may not be a Mormon but I know you can never quite be a Catholic now.' " Though Larry had the humor to report that Coffee "just laughed," no one could accuse Chesley of neglecting his ministry, which even extended to his Operation Homecoming debriefer: "He's not LDS, but I got him some dates with nice LDS girls, with the thought that in that way he might get interested in the Church."[93]

For most POWs, what in religion could promote unity and frustrate the Camp Authority was valued. What did not was ignored. Norman McDaniel's choirs, for instance, brought music and ministry together, and Red McDaniel's spiritual advice was taken seriously because of his familiarity with torture. When POWs asked him "how it was, how I took it," McDaniel "never let the others forget what God had done for me in the torture, that I had come out with an entirely new dimension in faith and commitment."[94] Because the POWs therefore judged faith by works, they directed their faith toward specific ends. The goals could be quite mundane. By getting "past such things that separated us to the common faith we felt in Christ," for instance, Protestant Howard Rutledge and Catholic George McKnight found they could help each other stop swearing at the guards. With the shift to compound living, such support greatly increased. "One of the first things we did in Camp Unity was to begin regular church services in every cell block," and Howard Rutledge recalled how "almost every prisoner entered into worship wholeheartedly." Because "Asians, friends and foes alike, use singing and speeches in group gatherings like our church services for political purposes," the Camp Authority saw such services as "a dangerous rallying point"—which they were of course, since for most POWs, their nationality, military bearing, and dedication to prisoner unity were inseparable from their religion.[95] The link between faith and country was most obvious during the 1971 Church Riot. When the Camp Authority led away the POWs conducting the services, the "apolitical" worshippers began a patriotic hymn sing. One cell belted out "The Star Spangled Banner"; others answered with "God Bless America," "America the Beautiful," "My Country 'Tis of Thee," and many state songs. It took armed troops to break up the concert.[96] Norman McDaniel also claimed that the POW leadership embodied a productive union of secular authority and spiritual devotion: "All of these men were acutely aware of the great strength and constructive results of sincere belief in and worship of God, and to the best of my knowledge most of them, if not all, are genuine Christians."[97] Whether they claimed their patriotism and professionalism grew out of their spirituality, or whether they claimed their faith was one of many sources of strength they drew on to do their duty, most POWs therefore sang "Onward Christian Soldiers" with feeling.

Reaching home meant new duties for the spiritual memoirists. Since witnessing to those not yet tested in God's crucible has always been a returning captive's duty, many POWs felt intense pressure to declare while they were still celebrities that the doctrines of their home churches had helped them endure captivity. Heslop's Mormon POW history, and Larry Chesley's, Charlie Plumb's, Ralph Gaither's, Howard Rutledge's, and Robinson Risner's memoirs all appeared in 1973, Jay Jensen's in 1974, and Red and Norman McDaniel's in 1975. Though church obligations had their influence, many of these POWs also seemed driven by a personal need to write. Chances for writing in captivity were so limited that Charlie Plumb would dream about "leaving the Hanoi Hilton, going home, looking for and finding a brand-new yellow pencil, and bringing it back to my cell. Or I would dream of entering shops containing nothing but rows and rows of pencils. I've never since taken a pencil for granted."[98] Pencils for Jay Hess became emblems for the greatest of gifts:

> . . . When you live in a world where you have no means of writing, you learn to appreciate a pencil. It was big loss to me not to have a pencil.
>
> If my children can appreciate being without means of writing things down, then maybe it will help them understand the significance of the loss of eternal life. I will put on those pencils an "EL" to remind them of eternal life as they use the pencils. I will tell them about eternal life when I give the pencils to them.[99]

America's own evils, sometimes hiding within their own families, also drove the POWs to write. Though he did not mention it, for instance, Norman McDaniel's wife "had worked for the McGovern camp and, in her words, become a peacenik": "I didn't care anything about national honor. I wanted Mac home." A firm believer that the fundamentals *never* change, in his memoir's last paragraph McDaniel describes himself as affirming the truths running through all Christian captivity narratives:

> All of the religious references I've made in this book and all the words on how to live a meaningful and fulfilling life have been expressed many times throughout the ages, sometimes with words and at times in actions, by various individuals. Wise men of the Old Testament have conveyed the message; men of God in the New Testament have borne

the same message with further enlightenment; Christians for nearly 2,000 years have continued to bring the message; and I am yet another voice. May our Father in heaven open our eyes and grant that we, individually and collectively, heed his call lest we remain in the dark beyond the point of no return.[100]

Other POWs were less measured. Jay Jensen hurled fire and brimstone. His belief that cars, trips, and gifts were America's reward to worthy servants did not keep him from damning everything he found subversive in the nation he returned to. Though "a beacon of righteousness, freedom, and happiness," America was sliding into "perilous times" similar to those the apostle Paul expected before "the last days": "For men shall be lovers of their own selves, covetous, boasters, proud, blasphemers, disobedient to parents, unthankful, unholy, without natural affection, trucebreakers, false accusers, incontinent, fierce, despisers of those that are good. Traitors, heady, high-minded, lovers of pleasures more than lovers of God." In the 1970s, pornographic movies and magazines, higher prices for food and clothing, the loss of pride in good work, undisciplined children, vulgar language, drugs and alcoholism were simply the outward signs of communism's grim marriage of Satan and Marx:

> How many aliens are among us? The Communists are making us aliens in our own beloved land, killing our love of liberty, and raising the standard "Better Red than dead." They are destroying our respect for law and order, our love of harmony and beauty, and destroying our patriotism so that we would rather be slaves than protect our rights as free men and women. We allow pro-Communist groups to promote acid rock, bright lights, and drugs. This subversion is bringing people down to a subhuman level at which they are easily led away from good, wholesome values.

The aliens found easy targets in those "lazy, good-for-nothings, who contribute nothing to their society except sin, trouble, crime, problems, disrespect, and are a drain on our economy."[101] Though these parasites may claim to be antiestablishment, actually they "cannot hack it in competition with others." When led by traitors, this "society of misfits" becomes a Communist Army:

> This type of people have abandoned their own personal standards of integrity, culture, loyalty to flag and country, democracy, tradition and religion upon which our civilization has rested, and instead, they attack, and are hypercritical of everything good and worthwhile. But is it constructive criticism? What do they offer in return, to improve or replace that which they would destroy? Nothing but sin and degradation, lawlessness, chaos and disaster, and take over by minority groups, Socialism, or even Communism, which is really at the root of much of this rebellion.[102]

Jensen's own response to this threat is to cry out "Wake up, my America!" and to spout homilies about America's providential destiny. We must elect good leaders and realize our major concerns must always be "Duty, Honor, Country." Above all, we must do God's bidding, for Hanoi taught Jensen "that God is inseparably connected to our country. Let us keep 'God' in 'America.' "[103]

Like the colonial captive, then, Jay Jensen came home with newly opened eyes, and denounced those who had stumbled since he had left. Though few POWs were as comfortable as Jensen in this role, many sincerely believed that captivity had granted them an authority they were obliged to use. This too was a time-honored response, for as Richard Slotkin notes, "like the regenerate convert," the New England captive "has experienced a thing that his fellows have not. . . . He has perceived that life is lived on the brink of an abyss, and this perception stays with him as an acute and continuing anxiety for the state of his soul and the wrath of God's judgment on sinful people." Whether consciously or not, the Vietnam POWs followed in this long tradition of American citizens who were imprisoned by evil, but confronted it, vanquished it, and returned to speak of their struggle. The most devout POWs declared that a loving God, present even in America's historical and military traditions, sustained the captives' own will. The more secular memoirs, and the official story itself, however, often still follow the "common pattern" of America's captivity myth: "a devilish visitation, an enforced sojourn in evil climes under the rule of man-devils, and an ultimate redemption of body and soul through the interposition of divine grace and the perseverence of the victim in orthodox belief."[104] If therefore the official story was the Vietnam POWs' providential history, then whether believers, atheists, or agnostics, the POW memoirists have been that story's evangelists.

* 7 *

The Story's Other Sides

The official story was lived, written, and enforced all at once. Fashioned by the early shootdowns, it is the history most POWs set their stories within. The same heroes and traitors appear, and the same POWs remain virtually invisible—too late, too junior, or too minor. Insignificance came in several forms, and some men—most notably those who clashed with the Hanoi POW command—cherished their anonymity. Some scapegoats did however respond—a few Hanoi POWs, and several from outside the system, whose rank, service branch, and behavior created tremendous tension when they straggled in to Hanoi. Regardless of perspective, these stories both enrich and temper the official story by revealing what has been passed over or revised. Not all POWs in short saw the big picture.

The Diehard Scapegoat: John Dramesi's *Code of Honor*

John Dramesi is the only POW who claims that the POW command scapegoated him for being *too* hard-line. His difficulty lay in reconciling Article IV of the Code, which required him to obey his superior officers, with his belief that those officers were ordering him to disobey the Code's other articles. Though many memoirs and the official story agree with Kinkead's claim that "the Communists were never more lenient with or less demanding of those prisoners who did not resist them; actually, the opposite was true," Dramesi accused many POWs of caving in when actually put to the test.[1] Angered and insulted, these same POWs then denounced Dramesi as a self-righteous maverick who weakened other prisoners' resistance by indirectly subjecting them to needless punishment. This conflict arises within any POW hierarchy. As Albert D. Biderman observes, men pursuing "a highly successful military career" knew that sticking out was usually impolitic. Team players like these have "tremendous difficulty accommodating the man who, as a POW, is a real 'tiger'—the person of such fierce independence, high self-esteem and stubborn convictions as to be completely unbending in the face of enemy pressures." For this reason, Biderman acidly suggested that officers who claim they want heroes "should examine pathologies of their own organization that favor the timid over the 'tiger,'" and John Dramesi believed he suffered under the same institutional assumptions in Hanoi. His own obsession was Article III—the one about escape. If escape was the most contentious issue in Hanoi, as many POWs claim, then John Dramesi was the most divisive prisoner. The dispute was over motive. Dramesi claimed duty drove him, but as A. J. Barker notes, "This never has been and never will be the fundamental reason for man refusing to resign himself to life behind barbed wire." Instead, the "true escaper" is simply "rebellious by nature, and objects to his liberties being restricted by a lot of bastards whom he despises." His

193

real spurs are adventure and risk, placing "escaping into the same class as big-game hunting under difficult conditions."[2]

Dramesi was definitely this kind of escaper, and many prisoners felt he threatened their unity and survival. Senior POWs gave two major reasons for discouraging almost all escape attempts. First, since the chances of Caucasian fliers slipping unnoticed through Hanoi were slim, Robinson Risner's order "that no one should go without outside help, meaning someone like a friendly guard" seemed to shut down almost any escape attempt. In practice, though, this reason proved no obstacle for confident or high-ranking POWs. Jeremiah Denton assumed Risner would "agree with me that God is our outside help," and George Coker and George McKnight relied on the same aid.[3] The second, far more controversial reason for discouraging escapes was their potential effect on the POWs left behind. The "fantastic reprisals" following the 1969 Dramesi-Atterberry attempt led to Atterberry's death, Dramesi's own brutalizing, and a vicious battering for many uninvolved POWs. Red McDaniel was an especially extreme case. Though many POWs considered him a hard-liner, in a chapter called "Escape and My Darkest Hour" he blasts Dramesi's attempt. When he heard about the break, McDaniel felt "we were going to be in for it," and he almost died from the torture that followed. This session convinced McDaniel that preventing impulsive men like Dramesi from endangering group unity was the POWs' greatest challenge. Though McDaniel "admired John for always seeking to fulfill the military code of taking every means to escape," McDaniel insisted that "we had learned in 1969 that there was no way to go out without outside help. The only way we would do it again was when we were sure we had no alternative, that the VC maybe were coming to exterminate us." When Dramesi drifted into planning escapes again, McDaniel therefore decided he "wasn't about to be put through torture again for another one of his attempts to break out," and told a senior POW about Dramesi's threatening "mental masturbation." Even God had become fed up with Dramesi. According to McDaniel, when Dramesi ignored a direct order of "No escapes," and thus began opening "another horrible chapter in human suffering at the hands of the VC," the Lord stepped in: "At that precise moment, when Dramesi was one eyelash from making the attempt, the VC had showed up and knocked a hole in it! With moving us around, the whole cadence of the escape was thrown off. Dramesi could not risk it then. I could only thank God, because it would have been a disaster if he had, and everybody knew it."[4] The battle lines are therefore clear. While POWs who thought unity and the command chain were the keys to survival saw Dramesi as a suicidal renegade, he in turn denounced as hypocritical sheep all those who impeded his fight with the Camp Authority.

In a chapter called "The Mold and the Casting," *Code of Honor* describes a tiger's formative years. A South Philadelphia boxer's son, Dramesi grew up fighting bigger kids and black gangs. Gymnastics and wrestling kept him busy in high school, and he entered the military by common means: no academy trained him. Dramesi's self-confessed "biggest fault" was a "constant mistake—expecting too much from others." When for instance he asked his Vietnam flight commander why some pilots seemed so negative, Dramesi received a harsh lesson. Because "all officers are not leaders," being negative is "a way they justify their own weakness. If they can't do it, they will explain very quickly it can't be done."[5] Even before captivity, then, Dramesi perceived two military hierarchies—one administrative, in which rank determined who commanded whom, and one heroic, in which leaders earned their men's loyalty and respect by example. Dramesi offers his own shoot-down and early captivity as evidence that "given the opportunity, I will attempt to be a hero, for I most certainly prefer to be a hero, dead or alive, than to live the life of a coward."

The scale is epic. After parachuting down in the spring of 1967, his skill at radioing in air support killed twenty Vietnamese. When captured, Dramesi passed swiftly through the torture, submission, remorse, and renewal sequence so many other POWs had suffered through. What set Dramesi apart, however, was his belief that he had made "a terrible error. It was not honor that had caused me to tell the truth, it was stupidity and fear." Instead of adopting a soft-line strategy, then, he vowed that he "would have to do better," revealing nothing, "even if I lost my arms." He corrected a "more subtle" error the next day. Though the subjects had been trivial, he decided he had "talked too much." This too would stop.[6]

The next two years made Dramesi's reputation as a diehard. On the way to Hanoi, he escaped and eluded capture for a day. In the Hilton, stocks and solitary followed eight days of torture. Though apathetic or antagonistic, his eventual roommates learned that as SRO Dramesi demanded group resistance and escape planning. His fateful May 1969 escape attempt with Edwin Atterberry earned him months of torture in isolation until he reentered the POW community in late 1969, at the same time as the Alcatraz Gang. Dramesi not surprisingly admired these hard-liners, and they returned the favor. Jeremiah Denton mentions making Dramesi "an honorary member of our club," and Dramesi himself records that when asked if he would accept this membership, "With honor" was his reply. One of Dramesi's chapter epigraphs advises "Be not ashamed to look to those who elevate themselves above all others, for it is they who, knowing that indecision is the burden of men, guide the confused minds of the masses. It is they we recall when we speak of leadership, genius, the great." Given this philosophy, Dramesi predictably considered the Alcatraz POWs Hanoi's real leaders, and Jim Stockdale as the real SRO. Though "at least five Air Force officers in Little Vegas" outranked him, "for some strange reason they were not available for command," while Stockdale "was willing to lead, to live by the code of conduct as much as he was physically able."[7] Dramesi's standards were however so high at times that even an Alcatraz man fell short. Jeremiah Denton's orders to fast seemed "a form of self-induced punishment" to Dramesi, and in some incredibly wooden conversations, Dramesi presents Alcatraz POW George Coker as his own apprentice:

> . . . "How did your quiz go?"
>
> He told me that the Cat had told him that the United States has made many, many mistakes.
>
> George said, "I agreed with him, of course, the United States had made many mistakes."
>
> Irritated, I said, "No, George, that was not the right thing to say. They will attempt to confuse a man about the facts of the war. That done, they dictate what is right and wrong, and it always adds up to the United States being wrong."
>
> George said, "Yes, I know what you're saying now."

Nothing here even hints that Coker had already spent his time in Alcatraz. Neither do his closing words: "John, you have helped me more than anyone else since I've been here. I think I'll be doing a lot better when I talk to the Cat next time."[8]

The teacher-student relationship suggested here is even more remarkable when juxtaposed with an article Coker wrote after release that totally rejected Dramesi's notions of duty. The Code "states that a prisoner will make every attempt to escape and aid others to do likewise. It also states that a senior will take command. All P.W.s will support the senior man in every way." Coker then posed the obvious problem—"If a senior officer says escape is not feasible and should not be attempted, there is a contradiction"—but offered a solution that explains why John Dramesi was a maverick: "What takes precedence? The obvious answer is that a military man should always follow orders. Thus, the orders of a senior officer should take precedence over general guidelines."[9] This policy put Dramesi on a collision course with his commanders, and his intense hatred of passivity further accelerated the process. Shortly after shootdown, Dramesi saw a water buffalo with a ring in its nose. Though "he looked so powerful, it seemed as though nothing could hold him if he decided to move," the animal just stood there. Dramesi then supplies the moral: "How many people, I wonder, are willing, like this bull, to give up their freedom."[10] When disgusted by a POW officer's timidity, Dramesi thought about that bull. Furthermore, his belief that real leaders gained respect through deeds made Dramesi one of the few POWs who felt he was fighting worthy opponents. When Ho Chi Minh died, Dramesi opened his window, "and in full view stood erect and saluted. . . . I thought that as a soldier I should render my salute and that, as a soldier, I should try to defeat my enemy."[11] This same love of action unfortunately struck other POWs as offensive and self-righteous. George Coker must have been thinking of Dramesi when writing that "often the person who thinks he is the greatest is also the most hard-headed. It is impossible to get across to him that he is wrong." And certainly Dramesi was hard-headed about the virtues of personal resistance. When passing Stockdale's BACK US on through the system, Dramesi couldn't help tacking on his own acronym "R.S.R."—"Through Resistance, you can come out of here with your Self-Respect as a soldier and a man."[12]

The same personal emphasis led Dramesi to contrast Robinson Risner's method of resistance—"in difficult times, he looked to God for help"—unfavorably with his own four spurs: "ambition, discipline, loyalty to purpose, and physical strength." Even in the abstract, this radical self-reliance insulted other POWs. Take the question of religious faith. Though Dramesi toyed in solitary with asking God for help, his reasons for rejecting the idea could only offend devout POWs like Risner: "If I stood there and then knelt, perhaps I could later tell the story of how I looked to God to gain my strength, but there was no God in that cubicle. The only people who could help me were myself and those attempting to defeat the North Vietnamese." Nor did Dramesi's mention of "discipline" mean simply following orders, for he drew a line between "self-discipline," which is "complying with the best of two philosophies, your own and society's," and "discipline," which begins with "fear of something, but, later with increased understanding there is a recognition of that which is best for you and your group."[13] It was Dramesi's belief in background and personal character, however, that most frequently led him to trivialize other POWs by pointing out flaws in their casting. Don Heiliger for example was a trombone-playing former accountant who "went through pilot training, not because he was really suited to be a pilot but because he felt he had to do it to be 'one of the boys.' " (He also "had originally flunked the pilot training exam" by answering incorrectly the question, "Would you prefer fast cars or listening to a symphony?") This sketch is actually quite mild for Dramesi. He was far harder on those who openly disagreed with him. Invariably, these POWs were as fear-driven or conformist as Heiliger. When one man bitterly complained to Dramesi that "You think you know everything. You won't listen to what any of the rest of us have to say. . . . God speaks and we must listen," Dramesi saw the charges as signs of insecurity: "His concern was not really the escape, anyway, but whether he was acting properly as a kind of elected representative of the majority. He is not trying to lead, I thought, but is trying to be everybody's 'nice guy.' " The same insecurity lay behind the other POWs' reasons for refusing to escape with Dramesi and Atterberry. "I am not going to risk my life for nothing," one honest man explained, "They are feeding me, and sooner

or later I'll get out, and not feet first." Another POW demanded the "proper equipment"—
"a two-way radio," for instance—and still another man hid his fear by attacking Dramesi
as "a medal-hungry glory-hound in combat who cared for nothing except how to become
a hero," and therefore refusing to "contribute to Dramesi's hunt for glory." The SRO just
shrieked—"You! You! What the hell makes you think you're always so right. Nobody here
wants anything to do with you. We all regret the day you walked through that door."
Dramesi's reaction to these examples was always the same: "All I could think of was the
sleek black water buffalo I had seen right after my capture—with a ring in its nose."[14]

Dramesi is most heretical when he shows many senior POWs, including some
"princes of the realm," wearing the same ring. Though he "was still looking for that
common fiber that good men possess" as late as 1971, by then he knew that neither family
background, nor university education, nor time at a military academy, nor skill as a pilot
guaranteed integrity. Only those with "the awareness of a purpose and the willingness to
make sacrifices to uphold that purpose" brought "leadership and example" together, and
since "the purpose" was resistance, Dramesi's most disillusioning period of captivity began
on Christmas Day 1970, when the POWs moved into Camp Unity.[15] Most narratives rush
through this last period. Since Dramesi devotes over a third of his memoir to it, *Code of
Honor* is one of the most detailed accounts of what Dramesi considered Camp Conformity
or Camp Surrender. Leadership in a POW compound is always a touchy matter. According
to A. J. Barker, "Strict 'military' discipline cannot work because it is too easily equated
with the enemy—Japanese, Korean, Chinese, Vietnamese—orders," and Dramesi certainly
accused many POW leaders of doing the Camp Authority's work for it. He had always
been impatient with what POW Tom Kirk described as his earliest wish: "All I wanted to
do was to sit in the corner of the cell, and I didn't give a damn if that door never opened.
All I wanted them to do was to leave me alone." When senior officers who in Dramesi's
opinion had behaved in this way during the bad times started to reclaim their commands
and privileges in Camp Unity, he was furious: "Here we were in prison, forty-seven strong,
still being intimidated by the North Vietnamese, now doing to ourselves those things they
had failed to force upon individuals. Could it be that those who had failed so miserably
were now to determine our conduct?"[16] A few senior officers resisted the shift. When the
POW command rejected Dramesi's escape request, Jim Stockdale sent him the message
that "I have done everything I could to help you. Sorry I could not swing it. I know you
tigers deserve the opportunity." For the most part, though, the highest-ranking men im-
plemented what John McCain called "a whole new concept for resisting" which strongly
suppressed agitation or individual initiative. The effect on escapes was so devastating that
Dramesi could only agree when George McKnight remarked that "when we get out of
here, if someone were to ask me, 'What was the greatest obstacle to escape?' my only
reply can be, 'our own leaders.' " These same commanders also seemed dedicated to
erasing before returning home all distinctions between POWs' performances. Soft-liner
Richard Stratton predicted to his hard-liner friend Dramesi that "you'll be surprised who
the good soldiers are going to be. *Everybody*'s going to be a good soldier. And everybody
will be so tired of the Vietnam War and the P.O.W. issue that the question of resistance
won't even be brought up. We'll all be part of one big group."[17]

Many memoirs and *P.O.W.* do of course highlight sterling performances, but except
for accused collaborators Ed Miller and Gene Wilber, senior POWs who didn't measure
up usually get the silent treatment. John Dramesi's *Code of Honor* is the major exception.
He remembers being worried when John Flynn, Hanoi SRO for more than five years, took
full command over Camp Unity in March 1971. Other POWs had earlier told Dramesi,

"Don't trust Colonel Flynn with camp secrets," and Dramesi found his policies "totally unfamiliar as far as my experience in the military is concerned." Dramesi especially hated the Amnesty Policy: "'Forgive and forget, live and let live!' Why was it necessary for us to forgive? Were we so lacking in our leadership? And why was it necessary to forget? Unless you wanted the other person to forget what you had done also." In a chapter sarcastically called "The Return of the Prodigal," Dramesi offers up Bob Schweitzer as a test case for amnesty—and amnesty fails. As "Bob" from the infamous "Bob and Ed" tapes, Schweitzer was almost universally despised. Nevertheless, under the amnesty policy he rejoined the POW community without penalty and even resumed command. His "leadership," however, confirmed Dramesi's belief that men fond of office politics and bureaucracy made the worst officers and POWs. When Schweitzer gossiped about rank and money, the other POWs eagerly listened, since their "uppermost" concern "was not resistance but when they would receive their next promotion and how much was the last pay raise." What truly outraged Dramesi, however, were Schweitzer's tips on dealing "with an interrogation by our own people after being released": "In essence, what we were being told was 'You don't have to tell the US debriefers anything,' and secondly, 'If you do have to talk to them, make sure you have a good lawyer.' And most important of all, 'Don't sign a thing.'" By claiming the Code "was meaningless and that it was not necessary to follow it," and by training POWs "to resist our own debriefers upon our release," Schweitzer thus turned Dramesi's world upside down.[18]

Code of Honor is most devastating, however, about a senior officer Dramesi calls "Paul Brudino." The man made a good first impression. During his first talk with Dramesi in early 1971, Brudino all but declared him his heir: " 'I've heard what you went through and I think that they killed Ed Atterberry. A lot of guys have talked about escaping but you did it. I want you to know that I really love you, I love you like a son and if there is anything that I can ever do for you—' He paused and said, 'I can do it.' " This fatherly tone, complete with shoulder hugs, reduced Dramesi to tears. He went to bed thinking that Brudino would be a friend, a leader, and perhaps a parent: "One could make great sacrifices for people like Paul." Such hopes collapsed almost immediately. Even during this first talk, Brudino resembled "a two-bit performer acting coy and trying, I imagine, in one way or another, to be modest." The way he "puckered his large lips, wrinkled his brow," and "cocked his head" was also unsettling. Then, as SRO of Room 7, he proved to be a passive resister. When an unpopular POW was yanked away, Brudino did nothing. This was bad enough—"Unity before Self," Dramesi thought, "hogwash"—but when Brudino announced, "There is nothing worth going to Heartbreak," the interrogation area, Dramesi was outraged. Brudino however went even further, compounding his hard-line sacrilege by ridiculing the great leader-heroes. "What's this unity before self shit?" he asked, and then answered his own question: "It's just another one of those goddamned stupid phrases made up by Stockdale and Denton" that had "gone out a long time ago." This speech, which so angered Howard Dunn that he and Brudino almost came to blows, left Dramesi "stunned, amazed," and confused. Was Brudino just envious, or had he just denied the POWs' duty to each other, and thus his own duty to lead?[19]

In a chapter called "The Real Hell of Hanoi," Dramesi finds him guilty on both counts. His Vichy style of leadership crushed resistance far more effectively than the Camp Authority ever had. Brudino regulated bathing hours, insisted on formal greetings for all guards, and during one "emotional tirade," he even declared, "There's not going to be an escape from this room as long as I am the SRO." Brudino justified his actions as methods for showing the Camp Authority he was in control, and thus should be recognized as SRO.

All Dramesi believed that he was showing was his unsuitability for command. Nor did Dramesi find Brudino's gestures fatherly any more. During one session, Brudino "moved very close to me, slapped me on the thigh, and said, 'John, listen, I like you; I want to be your friend.' " As he asked Dramesi to stop trying to escape, he "squeezed my leg" and "grinned"; moments later, "He leaned a little closer and squeezed my thigh again." But Dramesi remained a diehard, and soon Brudino was finding him guilty of such crimes as whistling, or laughing at jokes while waiting to bathe. When Dramesi without permission ripped down some propaganda that caricatured Richard Nixon as a criminal, Brudino sentenced Dramesi to two weeks' confinement, and though he accepted his punishment as "the quickest way to terminate the crazy scene," a perplexed Dramesi wondered, "How could I combat this insane fantasy?" In other situations, Brudino did not respond so quickly. In early 1972, "the cries and moans" of someone being beaten did not rouse him because he didn't know if the sufferer was American, or why he was being beaten. When the other POWs passively supported this decision, Dramesi confronted his worst nightmare: "Most people seemed relieved when the screams finally stopped. They could play bridge in peace now, and not be bothered with the annoying cries for help. I thought at times that I had reached rock bottom, but this by far was the Hell, the real Hell, of Hanoi." Moments like these doomed Brudino's attempts to patch things up with Dramesi as release approached. Brudino claimed that he had tried "to escape the agony" during one torture session by running "a piece of broken glass over his arm to cut his wrist. 'It was a miracle,' he explained. 'As hard as I tried, I could not cut myself.' " For Brudino, God had intervened to prevent him from becoming too hard-line. For Dramesi, since suicide was a sign of weakness, the "miracle" only proved that Brudino had lacked the guts to take the coward's way out. Dramesi sums up his fundamental disagreement with Brudino in a single exchange. "No one has told us that we can change the Code of Conduct," Dramesi told Brudino, "The guidelines stand as they exist. Our only obligation is to try to live up to those standards." Brudino then prophetically told Dramesi: "You'll see—you'll see that I'm right when the time comes."[20]

Dramesi's memoir ends a few days before *his* release. Going home with everyone else was after all something of a personal failure for this diehard escaper, and as a later release he already knew that the first POWs out had been welcomed as heroes. When he learned for certain that Ed Atterberry had died in 1969, Dramesi had wanted to grab the Vietnamese official "about the neck, and shake him like a rag doll." But instead he walked away, mumbling "'I'm sorry, Ed—I'm sorry, Ed.' Were we right? Did we do the right thing? Have we been right all these years?" *Code of Honor* is a highly crafted argument for why the answer to Dramesi's questions must be "yes." While still in Hanoi, Richard Stratton called Dramesi a gadfly—"someone that irritates others"—and that he shouldn't expect thanks for trying "to keep this group honest with itself."[21] The "group" of course saw things differently, defending what Dramesi blasted as apathy and cowardice as self-discipline or simple common sense. It is the diehard's nature, however, to be disgusted, because the extraordinary is his minimum standard. Or as Dramesi's author's note puts it:

> The object of this book is not to disgrace anyone or to dwell on the past but to present the clear and convincing truth so that we may prepare our young men and women for the future. If there is anyone who thinks that the image of the American fighting man is marred by the events and personalities presented herein, I suggest that he read this book carefully, for there is ample evidence to prove the courage, honor, discipline, and determination of our military.[22]

The Unofficial Story

When Mike Wallace asked recently returned POW Walter E. Wilber about the other prisoners' statements, he said he would "not disbelieve or repudiate them in any way." This alleged collaborator did however suggest "that the whole story had yet to be heard," and that "each person has to tell his own story." For a variety of reasons, though, many POWs have not. Late captures have deferred to the old-timers. "It was the guys who had been there longer who really suffered," explained 1972 shootdown William Angus, "I didn't want to detract from their story." For Wilber and the handful of POWs accused as traitors, silence could be considered an act of discretion. When POWs like Sergeant Ronald Ridgeway were saying they wanted to see these men "burn," or "hang as high as they can get them," attempts to justify suspect behavior would according to one general officer only "blow the wraps off it."[23] Peer pressure and public opinion also intimidated those POWs who hinted that the prisoners weren't really of one mind. These POWs did talk to reporters at first. Hubert Flesher described two distinct groups in captivity—"the superpatriots who felt we should be in there killing them by the thousands, as opposed to another faction that felt, generally speaking, that the bombing and that sort of thing was not doing any good." Flesher himself then denounced American involvement in Vietnam, called Nixon's "peace with honor" a failure, and suggested that "America may have lost the war." Other POWs set themselves apart by inadvertently contradicting orthodox Hanoi beliefs. Jungle prisoner Daniel F. Maslowski for instance was grateful to the protesters: "From the broadcasts it seemed like the antiwar movement was getting stronger, and I was really happy the American people were trying to put an end to the war. It didn't hurt my morale at all." Still other POWs stood by their tapes: "You know as well as I do we allow free speech in this country," POW Lynn E. Guenther told reporters, "At no time did any of these statements degrade the United States in any way or the way of life in our country." Such voices, however, soon faded. Since the "superpatriots" were usually high-ranking Hanoi veterans, they were the first POWs home. As a result, the dissenting POWs returned to find that the official story was already well publicized at home. The nation's desire for POWs had also complemented the senior POWs' wish to downplay most dissent. Faced with this atmosphere, those of "another faction" soon became diplomatically silent.[24]

Some jungle POWs, however, refused to let their experience be condemned, trivialized, or ignored. The degree of suffering was part of the dispute. Though it "angered pilots who were held much longer in North Vietnam," a POW's statement that "Hanoi, compared to our jungle camp, was like a Holiday Inn" was according to Kushner POW Frank Anton "in a physical sense" quite true: "Nobody starved, nobody had to work themselves to death." Shortly after the Hanoi POWs' revelations of torture, Floyd Kushner made the same point himself:

> "We've heard a lot about North Vietnam in the last few days on television," Kushner said with evident bitterness. "I've heard about solitary confinement and I've heard about being put in cells and I've heard about poor food.
> "I want to tell you I was damned glad to get to North Vietnam. I thought it was splendid . . . it was so easy being in jail and getting a couple of meals of bread and soup a day . . . I could have survived there for 50 years but in South Vietnam I couldn't."[25]

These were fighting words. Officers who felt they had passed through hell in Hanoi did not appreciate having their heroic struggles with the Camp Authority turned into quibbling over room service. Furthermore, Kushner's words attacked the Hanoi POWs' belief that as well-educated, well-trained, and virtually all-white career aviators, they *must* have performed better than the young, usually enlisted, and often black or Hispanic jungle POWs. When these jungle POWs claimed that the Hanoi Hilton did seem like *Hogan's Heroes* to them, the Hanoi POWs responded by ignoring these POWs or, if pushed, by suggesting that their death rate was high in the jungle because the prisoners were incompetent, undisciplined, and leaderless. Chapter 4 described how the official story integrated the stories of enlisted men, jungle POWs, civilians, and other marginal prisoners into the Hanoi epic. The rest of this chapter deals with how these figures told their own stories.

Some of My Best Friends Are Enlisted Men: Douglas Hegdahl

At first the Hanoi POWs dealt with enlisted men by promoting them. When three helicopter crewmen arrived in 1965, the officers set up a "sub rosa, informal 'officer's candidate school,' " as "several Air Force Academy graduates drilled Black and two other enlisted men daily on military science and tactics." SRO John Flynn promoted them to lieutenant in 1968, and though the Air Force later declared, "There is no legal basis for the senior officer of a POW camp to confer commissions during internment," Flynn's actions were confirmed in April 1973.[26] When Hanoi's most celebrated enlisted man arrived in April 1967, however, his rank remained the most important thing about him. According to *P.O.W.*, "Seaman Apprentice Douglas Hegdahl" was "one of the most remarkable characters in American military annals," but since it also called him "one of the most peculiarly effective American combatants," apparently "remarkable" meant "strange" as well as "outstanding." What did *P.O.W.* find "peculiar"? Certainly not his background. Hegdahl was the 19-year-old product of South Dakota values "that attached preeminence to God, Country, Family, and Honor." His capture was admittedly unusual. While on the *U.S.S. Canberra,* he sneaked up on deck to watch a night bombardment. A gun battery discharged as he walked under it, and "the next thing he knew, he was in the Gulf of Tonkin, regaining his senses, watching the *Canberra* recede into the darkness." Some fishermen scooped him up, and handed him over to North Vietnamese officials.[27]

At this point *P.O.W.* starts allowing Hegdahl a latitude no officer was granted. Having to bow, for instance, "did not strike the youngster as a loathsome obeisance, as it did the Americans in the Hanoi prison system." Terrified of Oriental torture—"of his genitals being squeezed and of rusty nails poked through his eyeballs"—and hazy about the Code, Hegdahl decided to behave like the village idiot—a role his captors identified as the stupid peasant, and the Hanoi POWs would have considered the dumb grunt. Forced to draw a picture of the *Canberra*, Hegdahl produced something that "looked like a small child's drawing of a tugboat." When asked about the *Canberra*'s guns, he replied, "Gee, you know anything I say will be always a guess, cuz I don't know. They don't let apprentice seamen around guns." Early success encouraged Hegdahl "to make the most of it. He would innundate them with 'sincerity'; he would be all farm-boy honesty, all open-faced, helpful innocence." *P.O.W.* gleefully supplies examples. If he had to write, Hegdahl would ask for the spelling of almost every word, and suck on his pen until he had "ink all over his tongue and face." If told he must cooperate, he answered, "Oh, I'll be happy to sweep and clean up. . . . Gee, I want to do my part. Just show me what work needs to be done." Soon the Camp Authority believed that Hegdahl "was indeed of the American peasantry and thus possessed of an intelligence and education that probably were the rough equivalent of those of his own country's peasant class." From that point on, the North Vietnamese spoke to this "ignoramus" as though "talking to a small child."[28]

Richard Stratton's early *P.O.W.* encounters with Hegdahl catch the officers' admiring yet patronizing attitude toward the apprentice seaman. Though he already had "a high opinion" of Hegdahl, Stratton was bowled over when he saw him throw dirt into a gas tank: "*This kid gets the job done*, Stratton thought. *This place is full of hot-shot pilots, but I haven't heard of anyone else sabotaging a truck!*" Hegdahl in turn, having "never been so close to so much rank," was "pleased, and awestruck" when he became Stratton's roommate. In *P.O.W.*, Stratton and Hegdahl seem like a knight and his squire, or a master and his servant. Stratton graciously told Hegdahl he needn't call him "sir." The sailor's own "thoughtful manners" made him turn away when the airman used the toilet pail, but stick his own head "in the bucket while brushing his teeth" because "Stratton couldn't stand the smell of toothpaste." This "amazing kid" with the "dumb-like-a-fox behavior toward the Vietnamese" also taught Stratton how to produce "nonsense for the enemy":

> "My airplane just blowed up . . ." Stratton wrote.
> "That's fine," said Hegdahl. "Now, why don't you say, 'I landed in a tree and decided to hang around for a while. . . .' "
> Stratton laughed. "The guys will get a kick out of that. And I'll say I landed in *the* tree, next to *the* rice paddy, like there's only one of each in North Vietnam."
> "Good. Good!" Hegdahl nodded sagely.[29]

All of Hegdahl's triumphs stemmed in fact from his talents as a fool. Forced to meet an antiwar delegation in 1968, he behaved grossly to "impress upon the American visitors that the POWs were being starved":

> He did not look at the women as they were introduced to him. Instead, he moved ravenously into the goodies on the table, seizing an orangelike fruit and biting into it, hugely, sloppily, chewing it peel and all, letting the juice squirt about and dribble down his chin. Continuing to chew the fruit, he grabbed pieces of candy, stuffed them into his mouth without bothering to remove the rice paper wrappings, chewed at them, occasionally spitting out a scrap of paper. He went on chewing and slurping at the fruit and adding more candy and peanuts as quickly as there was room in his mouth.[30]

Such antics delighted the officer POWs, even though they would never imitate them. Hegdahl's age and rank granted him a license which was also a sign of lower status—a factor that led to Stratton's decision that Hegdahl should accept parole to get a POW roster and word about torture back to America.

Accepting parole was not an option for officer POWs, as the term "fink release program" indicates; in fact, *P.O.W.* declares that of the twelve POWs who accepted early release, "Only the enlisted man, Doug Hegdahl, was not in violation of Stockdale's order—Hegdahl's release really amounted to a reluctant escape." And he was reluctant. When Stratton gave the order, "Hegdahl was shocked, silent. Then he said, 'No, Beak! I want to go home with everyone else.' " Stratton knew the order was insulting: "The youngster had been a first-rate POW. It was unfair to tell him to accept early release when he wanted to carry on. There was also the risk of grave and undeserved injury to his reputation; other POWs, who could not know the details of his departure, were likely to think harshly of the lad." Why then did Stratton, with other POWs' backing, issue the order? That "Hegdahl was quick, smart, and had committed to memory the names of scores of POWs" was not enough. Alcatraz POW Jim Mulligan had the same talents, but the idea of parole would have infuriated him. The main reason surfaced as Stratton explained his order to Hegdahl: "Look, Doug, you've made fools of the Vietnamese. You've done a damn good job as a POW. Now here's your chance to do something really important."

"Important" here was obviously relative. Officer POWs clearly felt that following the Code, supporting their fellow POWs, and resisting the "fink release program" were "really important." Hegdahl, however, was an enlisted man. Parole couldn't hurt his career as badly, and Stratton promised "to repair any damages to Hegdahl's reputation." Hegdahl felt "contempt for the role he was playing; he wanted to go home, but not early—not ahead of all the others." This reluctance caused him to botch his parole twice, "failures" which made him feel guilty, since he had disobeyed Stratton, and kept his precious information in Hanoi: "What of the 260-odd names he had memorized? Many wives and families had no idea whether these men were alive or dead, and he had been ordered to bring word of them. Had he allowed his own pride to ruin an operation? How would he explain himself to Stratton?" Hegdahl at last returned home in 1969 with the real story of the Hanoi Hilton, and apart from a stray reference, *P.O.W.* does not mention him again.[31]

Though nothing is incorrect about this version of Douglas Hegdahl's captivity, it certainly privileges the Hanoi officers' perspective. The Hegdahl who emerges from Richard Stratton's biography was far more savvy. Take Hegdahl's background. Though familiar no doubt with "God, Country, Family, and Honor," if "schoolboy confessions are taken at face value, he was a town badass. Prodded (and blushing) he admits to being a 'gang' leader of twenty or so other badasses who harassed teachers out of town and locked class weenies out on school fire escapes in twenty-below weather." Long before becoming a POW, then, Hegdahl had also learned that feigned stupidity could be a trouble-maker's perfect weapon and alibi. Nor was he overawed by the military. Enlisting because it was something to do, he found his Naval base a "prison." Headed for "postal clerks' school," his entry was delayed for six months, and he ended up off the Vietnamese coast on the *Canberra*, "manhandling heavy shells for the ship's cannon." This history supports *P.O.W.*'s claim that Hegdahl had little experience with high-ranking officers, and he did enjoy rooming with Stratton: "That was the happiest, happiest time of my captivity, the time spent with old Beak." Missing, however, are those shivers of awe which he supposedly felt in the presence of rank. Though he found Stratton "very much of an officer and a commander," Hegdahl concluded they had been put together to exploit Stratton's *very rare* sense of duty: "it was one thing to go it alone and be responsible for what's going to happen to you. It's quite another to have a troop under you (and unlike almost every other officer in the military, Navy or Air Force, that I knew, he had a real sense of command)." Hegdahl apparently never saw that marvel of hierarchy and discipline celebrated in the official story. As a good officer, Richard Stratton was an exception.[32]

Stratton's biography also notes that "an age gap and military propriety" set down "lines" which neither man crossed. The result, however, was not exactly paternal fondness and hero-worship. Hegdahl respected Stratton because he "did not treat him as either a batman or a sibling"—a quality so rare in officers that the Camp Authority actually used rank during Hegdahl's interrogations: "Don't tell him *anything* . . . Stratton's an officer and you're an enlisted man, and if you were back on board ship or back in the United States, Stratton wouldn't even talk to you." According to Stratton, this attack hit so close to home that when Hegdahl returned, "He looked kind of plaintive and looked at me and said, 'You'd talk to me, wouldn't you, if we were back home?' It was really touching in a way." Stratton's version of his parole order also reflects the heatedness of the debate, the baldness of his appeal to authority, and the firmness of his belief that Hegdahl should not be held to the same standards. *P.O.W.*'s Stratton sounds like a father or coach, assuring Hegdahl that "Gosh, Doug, you've done swell." In his biography, Stratton pulls rank—and *hard*:

"All right! You are a *seaman* and I am a lieutenant commander. I am giving you a direct order. You *will* go home and you *will* take this information out of here if you get the opportunity to go home with honor. And if anyone on the outside gives you any guff about why you've come out, you tell them, and I will stand by it when I come out. If I am wrong in ordering you out of here, then I will accept the responsibility for what I have done and they can have my butt, not yours.

"Do you understand?"[33]

Though he did admire Hegdahl's memory, Stratton was far more motivated by "a basic principle in the Navy that you always take care of the enlisted men first. If anyone should go home from Vietnam, it would first be the sick and wounded and second the enlisted men. And Doug was about as enlisted as you could get." Hegdahl recognized this belief. Stratton "always felt, since I was not a professional soldier . . . that I hadn't really known what I had gotten into; he had been trained, went through [survival] schools, was an officer, and was trained to take these chances."[34]

Stratton's compassionate sense of command was especially notable because the enlisted POWs felt ignored, exploited, and victimized by weak, stupid, or bullying officers like the ones that Stratton's order ironically enough plunged Hegdahl into the midst of. Though as intense as John Dramesi's, Hegdahl's contempt for parolees was even more cutting because of his rank. Years later he declared, "Nothing bugs me more than to hear . . . somebody say the officers behaved themselves so good [in captivity] because they *were* officers, and gentlemen." Those "princes of the realm" he encountered just before release were hardly role models. One cellmate "was an [Air Force] Academy graduate, for crying out loud . . . and he would complain, 'I'm just cannon fodder,' and he would cry and carry on and moan." Though this "totally self-centered guy" stood out as "a real baby," all the early release candidates were remarkably careless about their duties. When Hegdahl was removed from the first group to leave, he "prevailed upon his two fellow prisoners to memorize as many names as possible." The academy man claimed "he was no good at memory work"; the other man agreed only reluctantly. When Hegdahl met Lieutenant Robert Frishman and Captain Wesley Rumble, though he didn't "get preachy," he did feel "compelled to remind his two comrades of POW policy: officers were not supposed to accept release." Admittedly both men were injured, but the fact remains that "they did not respond to it at all."[35]

Nor did Hegdahl's welcome home increase his respect for the career military. *P.O.W.*'s silence about his reception saves its readers from learning that Hegdahl was basically shoved to one side. Intelligence experts decided that Captain Rumble's POW list was more accurate, and drew on Hegdahl's "phenomenal memory" only as a cross-check. Even worse, at the September 1969 press conference which exposed Hanoi's atrocities, Hegdahl sat there "tight-lipped" as the "senior man" Frishman declared himself "Stratton's chance to blow the whistle and get the facts out," even though he "had never spoken to Richard Stratton." Frishman would dominate the interviews, articles, and public appearances over the next few months. As for Hegdahl, though promoted to third-class petty officer, he soon accepted an early honorable discharge. His few public appearances made him feel like "some sort of weirdo": "After a while you feel used. I don't know how many times a Senator put his arm around me and smiled into the camera, so he could say how much he was doing for the POWs." Eventually, Hegdahl drifted back to the Navy, where as a civilian survival instructor he gave others the training he had never received. With this, "his war was done."[36] As told in Stratton's biography, then, Douglas Hegdahl's story is about how he was not *allowed* to follow the Code, or to display the sterling qualities only officers could hope to attain. After his "unwilling escape," Hegdahl confronted a military who preferred dealing with an officer who had failed as a POW and stolen Hegdahl's reason for accepting release. From at least one angle, then, the captivity of the most popular enlisted POW suggests that the aura which *P.O.W.* saw glowing around the Hanoi officers was often seen only by themselves.

The Anti-POW: George Smith and the Great American Satan

If Douglas Hegdahl was the ideal enlisted POW, Army Sergeant George Smith would have been the Hanoi POWs' worst nightmare. Captured by the Vietcong in late 1963 and released two years later, Smith was home before the Hanoi POW population had reached one hundred. What's so striking about his 1971 memoir is its inversion of the values driving so many Vietnam POW narratives. As formally conventional as the official story, Smith's memoir tells the story of how a POW comes to recognize the justice of his *captors'* cause. He had help in this task. Ramparts Press published his book; a writer for *Ramparts*, Donald Duncan, was his "editor"; and the *Ramparts* staff compiled the notes and other aids which help readers see Smith's "story in the context of the escalating war in Vietnam and the growing anti-war movement within America." In the introduction, Duncan sounds like a pro-Indian Cotton Mather. Since Vietnam was a racist war, American propaganda dehumanized all Vietnamese, and the "Vietcong" in particular. Captivity freed George Smith from these lies; the American government then persecuted him for telling the truth. Or as Duncan explains in the epilogue, "The military could not turn him loose with such a story. He had had the bad grace to come away from Vietcong captivity in reasonably good health, with no tales of torture or beatings and no rancor toward his former captors." The 1969 Frishman-Hegdahl press conference was Duncan's target here, and he goes on to show that antiwar activists could be as paranoid and polemical as any diehard POW: "Hysterical charges of torture and cruelty are still being voiced to excuse the latest decision to prolong the war, to stall the Paris talks another week, month, or year; and the grief of separated families is still being exploited to renew the old stereotype of the inhuman enemy." Smith's story is thus self-consciously revisionist. America is not a world power defending freedom, but a terrorist waging so shameful a war that in 1971, "The morale of the U.S. Army in Vietnam has never been lower." The Vietcong are not leaderless savages, but the National Liberation Front, a disciplined, courageous army which remained humane even while warding off a brutal U.S. invader.[37]

Smith is most engaging when describing his fortunes as an enlisted man. He entered the Army in 1955, on his seventeenth birthday—it got him out of the house, and his mother signed his early enlistment papers. Three years in Airborne, however, left Smith "thoroughly pissed off at the Army. 'Fuck the Army,' I said. 'I'll never come back.' " But a lack of education or marketable skills made Smith realize that "I could continue to work as a dollar-an-hour wage slave, or I could go back into the Army." Patriotism thus had nothing to do with his 1960 reenlistment. He liked hanging out with some Army people, and he'd have food and medical care even if he blew his paycheck. The boredom of movie projector repair work in New Jersey, however, soon pushed him into Special Forces. Fort Bragg served up a blend of macho Norman Vincent Peale and political fairytale—and Smith "believed everything the Army said." His instructors' version of the war was sheer fantasy: "'We've been invited to Vietnam,' they told us. We would be supporting the government of the people, they explained, or at least training an army to defend the democratic government of South Vietnam against Chinese Communists." The fiction that there were no internal enemies even appeared on the Vietnam service patch—"a picture of the Great Wall of China with a break in it and red streaming down: the Red Hordes of China streaming down into South Vietnam." All other information came on a need-to-know basis: "Ngo Dinh Diem, the 'George Washington of South Vietnam'—I didn't know who he was. I didn't know where Saigon was. Hell, I didn't know where *Vietnam* was." Smith's training was chaotic, inadequate, and demeaning. The group commander demanded a botanical garden, so Smith "spent several days spreading fertilizer, with my green beret on, as if it were my sole purpose in life." Their other leaders were just as impressive. Some men had "an alcoholic team sergeant complete with nervous tic," and Smith's "was a real redneck, loud and vulgar, ignorant," who called Claude McClure, eventually Smith's fellow POW, a "cotton-patch coon."[38] Strangers to each other and unprepared, these troops found themselves bound for Vietnam in July 1963.

Once there, "things didn't quite fit anymore." While waiting for a flight to his posting, Smith was injured in a mortar attack, and spent his first three weeks in a military hospital. When he eventually made it to Hiep Hoa, the war's full absurdity hit home. His team's "mission" was to serve as glorified security guards for a sugar mill and fields reputedly owned by Madame Nhu, but if Smith "had to summarize what we were doing in Hiep Hoa, 'nothing' would pretty much suffice." They played cards, suggested "improvements which we could never do anything about," and took medic runs into the villages. Desperate for action, their gung ho lieutenant "would sometimes climb the observation tower with his M-1—with a maximum accuracy of maybe five hundred yards—and take pot shots at farmers a couple of miles away." He also chased farmers around a field with mortars, and shelled a village by accident. Training the South Vietnamese to fight Communists— America's ostensible reason for being in Vietnam in 1963—was even more of a joke. "Well, I'll go to work for the Americans, and when it comes to a fight, I'll just run away" was the code most of these draftees, prisoners, and Cambodians lived by.[39] These motley soldiers would also change sides. Smith, Isaac Camacho, Claude McClure, and Kenneth Roraback all became POWs during an attack that began when a demo charge, probably set by one of their "trainees," went off right in their camp.

Smith had few hopes for captivity. He had watched South Vietnamese forces stick suspected VCs in barbed-wire cages or beat them to a pulp, and he also remembered what he had learned at Fort Bragg: "Guerrillas don't take prisoners." Smith was therefore stunned with his initial treatment: "We weren't being dragged behind an ox cart with only garbage and foul water to drink. We ate what the guards ate, they weren't holding any trials, and the people weren't spitting on us or beating us with sticks." Acts of compassion multiplied. McClure and Camacho both received medical attention for their wounds, and everyone got a week to "rearrange ourselves psychologically." These new POWs didn't have it easy. Though "in all fairness, the food was pretty good," Smith quickly added, "At least it was the best they had." (He also suggested that the longer a man had eaten Army food, the more he liked his jungle meals.) But the men were alive, thanks to the VC. His captors' discipline and competence also unsettled Smith. His Fort Bragg instructors had showed him a picture of "a dead, evil-looking old man in black pajamas, a 'Vietcong.' The word itself seemed to have a special meaning—that this was something like an animal." What Smith actually encountered were efficient military men who outperformed the "bunch of lazy asses" fighting for South Vietnam, and Smith's own Special Forces team as well: "A well-trained American unit wouldn't have been able to sustain the pace they did with that much equipment, and they're a hell of a lot smaller than Americans."[40]

What accounted for the difference? At this point politics start shaping the narrative.

Even before capture, Smith found America's stated reasons for being in Vietnam ridiculous. The Saigon government was collapsing, his superiors were filing fraudulent reports, and blind duty was Smith's only motivation: "After all, I *am* a professional soldier. This is the reason I am here. Even though this isn't the war of my choosing, or a war that is necessarily to the benefit of my country, I am a professional soldier and this is my job—to go fight wars." Captivity soon convinced him his captors were the only combatants with good reasons for fighting. Their energy and efficiency made him start thinking that "maybe they really do believe in what they're doing—they couldn't be *forced* to act like this." The Communist conspiracy soon faded from Smith's mind. Though Russia or China could perhaps scare people into fighting, they "couldn't force them to do it gleefully, as these guys were doing." When compared to American or South Vietnamese morale, this spirit forced Smith to conclude that "if they were out to liberate their country from whatever force was there, then that's what they were going to do." Smith also listened when the VC gave him their version of the war. The Hanoi POWs would largely ignore the Camp Authority's pamphlets and broadcasts because they were one-sided. Smith decided that knowing one side's history was better than knowing nothing. Furthermore, when he tried to present America's side to his captors, Smith sounded brainwashed and ridiculous even to himself. In time, he decided his training had made him both: "They should have told us these things in area studies at Bragg, but they didn't. Of course, if they *had* told us what he told us, we might not have wanted to go. The area studies had turned out to be a hate program that taught you to hate the Vietcong."[41]

Smith soon decided that money, not freedom, had brought him to Vietnam:

> I was a professional soldier. I was working for a man who paid me to fight wars. I'd get promoted if I did a good job, gain a little power. The fact that we were members of the U.S. Army didn't detract from the fact that we were mercenaries . . . and that was the reason I didn't give a shit about whose politics it was or what country it was. This was what I did for a living. "Go to Vietnam? Sure! Who's in Vietnam? What does it do?" It was just part of a job—who could really give a damn about the people?[42]

And yet, Smith still refused at this stage to write or tape anti-American statements. "Count me out" summed up his position: he "sympathized" with the VC, but "didn't want to fight on either side. I wanted to go home." Smith did however realize that captivity was transforming him: "I changed from my arrogance and nastiness to liking people, from my superiority to feeling that the Vietnamese were pretty good people. Some of the honest culture of an oppressed people must have worn off on me." Though it may be "difficult to imagine a worse position from which to develop a sympathetic picture of the Vietcong," this is what Smith did.[43] But something unsympathetic begins developing as well—an inverted ideological casuistry that makes Smith's memoir as harsh as many Hanoi memoirs. The crucial moment was in October 1964. All four POWs were preparing for release when Saigon suddenly executed Nguyen Van Troi, an NLF cadre who had plotted to assassinate Robert McNamara. Smith was furious: "God damn! I read that and it really pissed me off. They were going to release us! I'm sure they were going to release us. And then those guys did *this* shit!" Though he clearly just wanted out, Smith's anger was also politically motivated: "If nothing else ever caused me to lose faith in the United States government, that execution very definitely did. I certainly didn't owe any allegiance to anyone who would be that inconsiderate of our welfare, who would jeopardize us by executing some guy for *attempting* to blow up McNamara." Smith also felt his antagonism toward his captors was fading. He couldn't be "mad at the Vietnamese for not releasing us. They weren't going to have a man executed and then go ahead and release Americans." For this reason, "As far as I was concerned the United States and the Saigon government became directly responsible for our captivity from that point on."[44]

This shift came at a crucial point, because around this time these POWs began performing such dubious tasks as digging air raid shelters for themselves and milling rice. Of course survival is always a legitimate reason for labor, and the camp commander had announced " 'You must work to eat'—no work, no food."[45] Smith however presents these actions as a slippery slope into the episode when VC ordered the POWs to sharpen punji sticks for the camp's perimeter. Smith and Camacho told the commander that "we understood his position, and we didn't want to aid the war—from either side—but we could not in good conscience make weapons that might injure American soldiers." Their treatment soon decayed, the mail stopped for everyone but McClure, who had sharpened sticks immediately, and Smith, Camacho, and Roraback gave in: "How much harm would the stakes do, anyway? Unless somebody stepped on them, they couldn't do anything. . . . We looked to Camacho, the ranking man, and he said, 'Sharpen stakes.' So we all sharpened stakes. The next day we got our letters." Though calling this clash "probably the most unfortunate and unpleasant episode of the whole captivity," may seem to be a overreaction, Smith is in fact being extremely calculating.[46] Take for instance Isaac Camacho's order, and his own stick sharpening. With Smith's help, shortly afterwards Camacho escaped. For this feat, he received the Silver and Bronze Stars; once home though, he also denounced the antiwar movement. Since his welcome and statements were the opposite of Smith's and McClure's, the "sharpen sticks" episode thus tarnishes Camacho's stars and glory by showing him doing exactly the same things in captivity that the two scapegoats did. Far more seriously, though, highlighting the stakes episode also seems to be part of Smith's attempt to downplay what must have really been his "most unfortunate and unpleasant episode" in captivity, the execution of Kenneth Roraback.

Smith's memoir turns somersaults to justify his sympathy for the NLF even after they shot a fellow POW. The *Ramparts*-prepared footnote argues that Roraback and Captain Humbert Versace were killed only after the NLF had repeatedly warned Saigon not to execute three fishermen who had protested certain government restrictions. By calling the POW deaths "acts of wanton murder," but accusing the executed fishermen of "fomenting public violence," America shared South Vietnam's guilt. Most chilling, however, is the *Ramparts* note's appeal to results: "In fact, the execution of Roraback and Versace seems to have accomplished its purpose. There have been no further public executions of NLF cadres by the Saigon government. The NLF, in turn, has announced no further executions of American POWs." In the jungle, however, a huge gap lay between debating the political issues and watching Roraback get led off to his death. Smith half-heartedly argues that because the NLF often lied, no one had known for certain that Roraback was dead. The camp commander had summoned him; later, the guards removed his belongings. Although Smith "told Cook [a new POW] I thought they had shot Roraback," a "couple of shots" the next morning "could have been anything—a hunting party, somebody shooting at a monkey swinging through the camp," and the NLF "kept the radio from us for a couple of days, as if something had happened that they didn't want us to hear about." In any case, the guards never mentioned Roraback again, and Smith "didn't know what to think. All of a sudden Roraback was gone."[47]

Such uncertainties could not save Smith from charges that supporting the NLF after Roraback's disappearance was either immoral or proof of mental collapse. Smith thus shores up his defense by claiming that Kenneth Roraback's stubborn and stupid American chauvinism made his death virtually a suicide. Roraback's first appearance sets the tone. During the attack that led to their capture, Camacho "kicked at something under the little table the interpreters used for translating. It was Roraback. 'What the hell you doing under there!' " He also proved to be an incredibly annoying captive. "I was just miserable," Smith recalled, "complaining all the way, but it was nothing like Roraback's yelling and whining—'Ah, ha, oo, ee, ah!'—every time he stepped on anything that was a little bit more painful than the flat ground." Since the VC "figured, quite rightly, that he wasn't suffering any more than the rest of us," this "yowling" only made his captors "disgusted with him": "You could read the expressions on their faces, 'Oh Jesus, why did we have to catch *this* guy!'" His fellow POWs were almost as disgusted, and Camacho was prophetic: " 'They're going to shoot you, you son of a bitch,' and Roraback got scared, thinking they were." What Smith soon learned about Roraback didn't bode well either. He "just seemed to fuck up on purpose," and his motives for joining Special Forces were if anything even less respectable than Smith's: "You came in here to get *rank*, goddamn it!" he yelled at Roraback, "You couldn't make it in that damned infantry unit you were in so you came in here to make stripes!" These same stripes also encouraged Roraback to commit the unforgivable jungle camp crime of pulling rank—"NCOs don't have to do this kind of work—how about getting down in there and digging it for me." After a few episodes like this one, soon only separate cells kept Roraback from "getting thoroughly stomped." Together, these early examples suggest that both his captors and his fellow captives agreed with the guard who remarked "*Bac! Bac! Con duc!*"—"You're no good, Roraback. You're a rotten bastard. You don't work. You eat too much. You smoke too much."[48]

Roraback was at his most self-destructive during interrogations. Smith, Camacho, and McClure listened politely and agreed they didn't know why they were in Vietnam. Roraback began "trying to do the impossible—trying to indoctrinate Man with Glasses with the same silly reasoning we'd been given at Bragg." From the first, camp officials hinted that such stupidity was dangerous. "What is wrong with Ror'back?" Man with Glasses asked Smith, "Does he not understand his situation? That we have no time to play games? That there are many lives at stake? Perhaps his own?" Roraback however kept at it, and the VC passed judgment: "Roraback is a reactionary," Man With Glasses told Smith, "He cannot see." Such behavior could never of course justify Roraback's execution. What Smith suggests is that *continuing* such behavior when the threats of execution arose verged upon suicide. Shortly after Camacho's escape, the camp commander explained the "situation": "We must change our policies. We do not want to do this, but we are obliged to do so. Two more prisoners have been executed in Saigon. The Central Committee has decided that two American prisoners will be shot." Smith couldn't imagine a clearer hint to "watch your step." Though formal retaliation was the motive, the POWs who died would almost certainly be those who caused the most trouble; in fact, a newly arrived POW named Cook had told them that one POW had apparently qualified for execution by staging a hunger strike which had forced his guards to carry him. Clearly, this was no time to be what Smith had called Roraback earlier—"a fuckoff"—but Roraback stayed the course. The camp was tense—U.S. planes were napalming nearby—and the POWs had been ordered not to talk to the new prisoner. Roraback "openly and deliberately" ignored the command: "He was trying to show Cook that he wasn't being influenced. He was a dedicated soldier, even if the rest of us weren't, and never compromised with the enemy on any score." Defiance thus put him in harm's way; ridicule signed his death warrant. "You have been told many times not to talk to Cook and yet you continue to do so," the camp commander solemnly announced, "Because of this your life can no longer be guaranteed." Roraback replied by "laughing in the camp commander's face." The radio had just announced that more POWs would be executed. A frightened Smith "told Roraback he'd better play it cool," but Roraback laughed at him as well. That night Roraback disappeared.[49]

Roraback's death was therefore a case of murder, suicide, accident, and self-defense. By supporting South Vietnam's atrocities, America had forced the NLF to protect itself. By provoking his captors, Roraback cast himself as the scapegoat. The squeaky wheel got the bullet. Smith's verdict is however disturbing, largely because his reasoning resembles so closely the Humane and Lenient Treatment program that virtually every POW encountered. Roraback's faith in American ideology, his valuing of rank, and his contempt for his captors made him a diehard, and thus someone who would not go home. On the other hand, by coming "to understand the situation" and making the appropriate gestures, Smith and McClure behaved like POWs whose parole could be a propaganda coup. Smith's change of heart was undeniably sincere. He believed it when he told another POW that "the party least interested in his release was the U.S. government," and he believed that the antiwar leaders were his best chance for release: "If anything gave us hope, it was that. This was a new outlet. Since the United States government wasn't going to recognize the Vietnamese people, the peace movement was going to recognize them."[50] At his press conference in Phnom Penh after his 1965 parole, Smith even used his captors' rhetoric for describing the war. When "a woman reporter with a French accent" asked him, "What do you plan to do when you get back to the United States?" he replied that "I want to tell people the truth about Vietnam":

> "How will you do that?"
> "I will join the peace movement."
> I wasn't too sure about the last answer—I still didn't have any idea what the peace movement really was. But they had somehow influenced my release, so they sure as hell weren't the bad guys.[51]

By equating the peace movement with "the truth," Smith provoked what he saw as "a threat to other GIs not to join the peace movement." The military greeted him with a reading of "Article 31—the military version of the rights against self-incrimination under the Fifth Amendment," and then a six-month involuntary stay in Okinawa, thus confirming the VCs' prediction that "a government that will send you to Vietnam will certainly put you in jail after you get back for saying the things against U.S. policy you have." Smith and McClure were charged at first with "aiding the enemy," a crime carrying the death penalty. When fear of bad publicity led the military to drop all charges, both men were nevertheless threatened with further prosecution if they told anyone their stories. Three years passed before the trial of another POW with unwelcome opinions—Commander Bucher of the *Pueblo*—spurred Smith into writing.[52]

P.O.W.: Two Years with the Vietcong foreshadowed many later enlisted jungle POWs' experience. Like Smith, most had little interest in what the military might think about their behavior. And also like Smith, most unavoidably came to know their guards better than the Hanoi POWs ever did. Though few jungle prisoners followed George Smith's unsettling political example, the unofficial stories they told often bore a family resemblance to Smith's early and vehement antiwar allegory.

Survivors and the Long Haul: The Kushner Camp

Though a few returning jungle prisoners attacked the Hanoi POWs' God and Country rhetoric, the most dramatic dissenter was Richard H. Springman, who arrived in the

Philippines "wearing beads and a peace symbol," and told his parents "he gave himself up to the Viet Cong because he was 'tired of killing, sickened by it.' " In this case, damage control began instantly. When "Springman walked toward a crowd of greeters" at Travis Air Force Base, he found himself "intercepted by military officers, who led him back to the terminal as he raised a clenched left fist," and soon afterward, a public relations officer announced Springman was "suffering from 'periods of disorientation, mood changes, and withdrawal.' "[53] The sister-in-law of the newly arrived Private Ferdinand Rodriquez gave one major reason for the jungle POWs' subdued or rebellious returns: "No, he didn't salute or carry any flags. That was the majors and captains doing that. He was held by the Vietcong in the south, in the worst camp."[54] Though some might argue about which camp was the worst, it was undeniably a jungle camp, a form of captivity which despite *P.O.W.*'s sketchy treatment has been reasonably well documented. Besides George Smith's and Nick Rowe's memoirs, Ernest C. Brace's *A Code to Keep*, Dieter Dengler's *Escape from Laos*, and Neil Sheehan's account of Douglas Ramsey all describe jungle imprisonment. *Captive on the Ho Chi Minh Trail* deals with two missionaries captured in Laos but released from Hanoi; *No Time for Tombstones* describes two missionary POWs' martyrdom and civilian Michael Benge's survival. *Marc Cayer: Prisonnier au Vietnam* is a French Canadian civilian's memoir.

The most extensively described compound, however, was what I've been calling the Kushner camp. In addition to the *P.O.W.* account, Zalen Grant's *Survivors* is an impressive group history drawn from interviews with nine POWs. *A Hero's Welcome: The Conscience of Sergeant James Daly versus the United States Army* tells one Kushner POW's story, and Monika Schwinn and Bernhard Diehl, two German nurses held there for a time, wrote *We Came to Help*. The most controversial Vietnam POW of all cooperated in the writing of *Conversations with the Enemy: The Story of PFC Robert Garwood*, which also contains extensive quotations from the other Kushner POWs' testimony at Garwood's court-martial. Several factors account for all this attention. The camp's mortality rate—almost 50 percent—seemed to demand an explanation. Since two of its inmates later joined the Peace Committee, and since Kushner himself had strong antiwar sentiments, this camp also became the official story's example of what happens without military discipline. The Kushner POWs forcefully revised or rejected this version of their suffering. At its most basic, the dispute was over leadership. The Hanoi POWs struggled to draw precise and absolute lines of authority. What Naval rank was higher than what Air Force rank? Should rank at capture plus prison seniority outweigh a new shootdown's higher rank? The jungle POWs' questions—Should the senior officer take command? Should the other POWs obey him?—were simpler, but they often had more complicated answers. To begin with, jungle POWs often held their commanding officers responsible for their captivity. Ike McMillan declared that the officer in charge of his last mission "had no business leading a few men across the river in the first place. That's what got him killed. He was too goddamn gung ho." Jim Strictland agreed this officer "wasn't worth a damn," and even suggested that he had been shot by his own men.[55]

Nor were jungle POWs usually prepared for captivity. "None of us could actually believe we were prisoners of war," David Harker recalled, "we had subconsciously anticipated being wounded or killed—but never captured. It wasn't a war in which people were captured in the south. That was for pilots flying over the north." The VC confused matters further by denying that the POWs had officers. "Who elected you the 'Senior American POW'?" an official asked Nick Rowe, "You are not a Senior American POW, you are another prisoner just like the others because there is no rank among prisoners." Frank

Anton encountered the same policy in the Kushner camp. Their captors took pains "to show distaste for Kushner, Williams, and me because they figured we were the authority bloc and believed if anyone gave them trouble it would be us." As Anton himself admits, though, this "bloc" was very shaky; "Kushner was a captain but a doctor and therefore a noncombatant. I was a warrant officer, a pilot with no command responsibility. Williams was a first sergeant but wounded." When coupled with life-threatening conditions, this instability made it very unlikely that the enlisted POWs would blindly obey anyone they didn't respect, or suspected of pulling rank. James Daly catches this resistance perfectly when he admits "the leadership responsibility should have been Captain Kushner's," but claims he disqualified himself by being elitist and lazy: "The first time we argued was when I told him it was his turn to sweep the hootch floor. He refused. He said he hadn't gone to college for so many years to sweep floors."[56]

A profoundly coercive environment only heightened these tensions. Except for Fidel's guinea pigs, very few Hanoi POWs actually went through serious indoctrination sessions. Torture produced tapes and letters far more quickly than ideological conversion. George Smith, Nick Rowe, and the Kushner POWs all however describe serious attempts at indoctrination in the jungle. Rowe was hearing the criminal-not-POW argument as early as 1964, and this same rhetoric also governed that ludicrous and infuriating moment years later, when the "teacher" solemnly announced that after days of classes the Kushner POWs "had been given a promotion—from Criminals of War to Prisoners of War." Bernhard Diehl pointed to "the 'reeducation,' or brainwashing, of prisoners" as his captors' "avowed purpose," and the day of his capture, David Harker found himself in a one-room bamboo school house, staring at a banner that read "Welcome to Lenient and Humane Policy Towards Criminals of War."[57] While the Hanoi Camp Authority was brutally extorting propaganda material from its POWs, under far worse physical conditions jungle officials were engaged in preparing acceptable candidates for early release or exchange.

The lesson plans, discussion sessions, and "requirements" for jungle POW "students" were virtually the same for years. As early as 1963, Nick Rowe was hearing what most jungle POWs would come to know by heart:

> The National Liberation Front has dispatched us to present to you the truth of the situation in Vietnam. In the coming days you will learn of the just cause of the revolution, and the certainty of final victory. You will learn of the lenient and humane policy of the Front toward captured alien soldiers and of your duty toward the Front. Your release, sooner or later, will depend upon your good attitude and repentance of your past misdeeds, so I encourage you to have a good attitude, be well disposed toward your instruction.[58]

Classes started right after capture. Even before reaching the Kushner camp, an instructor gave Willie Watkins and James Daly "what he called a brief history of the Vietnamese people's struggle." Once there, they sat with the other POWs through classes clearly designed elsewhere: "The VC read from prepared lesson plans. They sometimes made us read the material and 'analyze' it." Veteran interrogators didn't need the paper. One official was so consistent that four years later Bernhard Diehl could still remember the lesson "word for word." Mr. Ho's two-week courses were red-letter days in the Kushner camp. From 7:00 to 11:00 a.m., then from 2:00 to 4:30 p.m., the POWs heard lectures on topics posted on the classroom's bamboo walls: "'Vietnam is one. The Vietnamese are one.' 'The Vietnamese will surely win, the U.S. will surely lose.' 'Freedom of speech is necessary in debate.' " In keeping with Ho Chi Minh's nationalist emphasis, the classes were largely historical, describing how the Vietnamese fought off Chinese, Japanese, and French aggressors in turn. The international accords signed after World War II received special attention; as for political theory, though Frank Anton recalled "a little Marxism in the indoctrination," communism was so downplayed that Nick Rowe was startled when an official started discussing Marx, Lenin, and Mao Tse-Tung. Nor was the Marxism particularly complex: "A man works in Detroit. He makes cars for General Motors. But when it comes time to buy a car he must pay for it. He is not given the car. Why? What is your opinion?"[59]

Though supposedly "*Vietnam la mot*—Vietnam is one country," the real first lesson in these classes was far simpler: academic "progress" was a POW's only hope for going home. In 1965, Smith and McClure bought their release with taped and written attacks on U.S. policy. By late 1967, the classes were so streamlined that the last lesson dealt with "the Duty of US P.O.W. at Home after Being Released by the Front." The "Struggle Form" Nick Rowe reproduces lists a number of strategies for fighting the war back in America:

> "Use the radio, television, books and papers to tell the truth.
> "Demonstrations—slogans—meetings—leaflets for struggle.
> "Refusing to eat—holding strikes.
> "Truthly participating in all struggle organization of the American people.
>   "Revolting and reaction . . . ."[60]

Regardless of what strategy the POW eventually chose, though, change was the key—and change was mandatory. Mr. Ho may claim "we have given you the right of rebirth," but he "added that we could very easily find ourselves dead if we didn't cooperate."[61]

This constant danger forced POWs to develop some markedly different strategies for surviving without selling out. Nick Rowe's captors for instance "held the key which would open the door to freedom," but the key's price—publicly supporting the NLF—"was more than I could pay." Since he "didn't want to die," Rowe "began searching for some way over, around or under that wall; there had to be a solution!" Like George Smith, he first abandoned Fort Bragg: "the theory of holding out no matter what was done to you suddenly became the scenes from the training film and not the reality facing me." Unlike Smith, though, Rowe concocted a false autobiography which he gave out only slowly and reluctantly. This is Hanoi's fallback strategy, and like his fellow officers, Lieutenant Rowe stuck to "the old 'KISS' formula, 'Keep it simple, stupid.' "[62] Even though duty or patriotism had little to do with it, the enlisted Kushner POWs often resisted indoctrination just as successfully. Willie Watkins was "happy" to get leaflets which "told about the corrupt Saigon government, said the Vietnamese didn't want Americans in Viet Nam": "We used them as rolling paper to smoke our cigarette butts." (Watkins later became a parolee, suggesting that indoctrination could have little effect even on the POWs who cooperated.) The most common strategy for dealing with the interrogators was simply to conceal a fierce anger behind surface obedience. When for example the VC boasted, "We have water buffalo and you have jets. You are bigger than we are physically. Yet we fight you and win," POWs like Tom Davis were silently saying, "And if I had a chance I would wring your fucking neck." Kushner POW Frank Anton, however, sums up best why almost all jungle POWs remained distant from their captors: "Maybe the VC were right, they had caught a rotten deal—but, still, they were sonsofbitches. It was an attitude made up partly of our racism (we're all racists, I mean, to a certain extent), our contempt for their lack of material development, and the fact that they were our captors and almost starving us to death."[63]

The reference to starvation here introduces another distinctive aspect of jungle captivity. As Floyd Kushner's April 1973 press conference made very clear, Zalin Grant was right in calling his group history of the Kushner camp *Survivors*. Between November 1967 and February 1971, approximately thirty U.S. servicemen, four German civilians, and a large number of South Vietnamese POWs were held together in the jungle. Five of the Americans were paroled, and Robert Garwood apparently joined the VC. Twelve Americans and two Germans eventually reached Hanoi: the rest of the Americans and Germans died. With the possible exception of Garwood, all of these prisoners suffered profoundly. The "typical POW," Kushner explained, "lost 40 to 50 per cent of his normal weight, shook and burned with malaria much of the time, defecated 30 to 100 times a day because of acute and chronic dysentery, bled at the gums from scurvy and suffered intense pain from a swollen liver, spleen and scrotum associated with acute malnutrition." The diet—"about three cupfuls of 'red, rotten, moldy rice' per day, the rice peppered with sand, rocks, vermin and rat feces from being long hidden in the jungle"—led to malnutrition, making the POWs susceptible to illness. Boils were a major problem, and so was a skin disease that produced "a pustular eruption . . . all over the body," and "a tremendous itching": "I recall very, very vividly 10 or 11 POWs lying on a crowded bamboo bed in the jungles of Quangnom screaming and asking God or someone to take their life so the itching would stop." At night, these POWs slept "10 and 12 to a bed while the sick and dying vomited and defecated among them." By day, they lived "barefoot and virtually without clothes in a compound littered with excrement from men too tortured by disease and starvation to clean it up."[64] Add to this sketch the fact that some POWs had battle wounds, and that Kushner was banned from serving as a doctor, and the result was a nightmare.

German nurse Bernhard Diehl has described the despair. As they spiraled down, the POWs "lost interest in everything but what concerned the most primitive human needs." At this point, "Only a few things seemed important enough to talk about. 'Eat something.' 'Don't you want to wash up?' 'Don't you want to go outside?' 'Oh, what I would give for a piece of meat!' 'What I would give for a warm blanket!'" Such suffering turned the camp into the world: "Nothing else existed. God did not exist. The Bible was just a book. Almost nothing was real to us any more." Hunger could also erase all fellow feeling—a lesson Kushner taught Diehl by sharing a dream. A U.S. helicopter gets shot down. On impact, hundreds of packages spill out—canned goods, chocolate bars, cigarettes—and Kushner frantically gathers them up and hides them, even though the pilot may still be alive. "It's sad," Kushner concluded, "but one day you'll think only about yourself. No one else, only yourself. While a helicopter pilot is bleeding to death, you will run to pick up a chocolate bar. That's what captivity is all about. In the end, the only thing that matters is staying alive." Kushner later told the press the same thing: " 'I am convinced,' he said, that those who survived 'were simply obeying the Darwinian dictum of natural selection.' " Weak men broke. Kushner "told of the mental regression of prisoners reduced to huddling in the fetal position 'sucking their thumbs and calling for mama,' and of another prisoner who 'sat on his bed with a blanket over his head for two years' in an effort to block out a world of deprivation and death." The weakest men died. Two told Kushner, "Doc, I can't hack it any more. It's just too hard to live."[65]

In this world, patriotism or duty seemed hollow or absurd. POWs "wrote or signed" the various "antiwar appeals" according to David Harker, because they "could no longer see any purpose in resisting." Their shaky physical condition could turn any punishment involving the stocks or loss of food into a death sentence; as a result, Kushner's "three rules for staying alive" stressed food, hygiene, and exercise rather than ideology or duty:

The first rule was to eat all the chow you can get your hands on . . . all your rice . . . all your manyok (a fibrous root like a potato) all the rats and the snakes and the frogs and the things we'd kill.

The second rule was to keep clean . . . take a bath every day—even when shaking from malaria and dysentery—in the cold mountain stream that flowed through the camp.

The third rule was to keep physically and mentally active.[66]

Camp conditions made even these elementary rules difficult to follow, and as everyone steadily declined, the differences between "wounded," "sick," and "lazy" began blurring for some men. Since the Kushner POWs had to do almost everything for themselves— cooking, going on manioc runs, even constructing their own compounds—not working could provoke other POWs' anger. Only death could convince some POWs that a man wasn't faking the severity of his injury or illness to avoid doing his share; and when camp officials managed to link the work issue to race, the POWs really began to buckle. By Vietnam standards, the Kushner camp had a large number of minority prisoners. Of the less than twenty black POWs who returned during Operation Homecoming, James Daly, Ike McMillan, Tom Davis, and Robert Lewis were from this camp, and early release Willie Watkins was black as well. Camp officials tried to exploit American racial tensions by asking the black POWs about their encounters with discrimination, and by encouraging them to form a separate community. That some of these men didn't get as sick as the white POWs made matters worse. Furthermore, since the ability to work is a subsistence society's greatest asset, "Willie Watkins slowly took over as camp leader. He was the strongest."[67]

And yet, most of the Kushner POWs felt that work created far more tensions than race. Watkins himself simply declared that "anybody who tells me what to do has to work at least as hard I do," and Frank Anton also noted that "Strictland got along with the blacks okay because he could work. Harker did too but he didn't like Willie. Actually it came down to who could work and who couldn't." When camp officials broke the eighteen American POWs loosely into a strong and a weak group the collapse was complete. As everyone's energy waned, the "strong" POWs increasingly resented having to work for the "weak" ones. "Petty irritations became hard resentments and then anger"; finally, the "strong" group decided that each squad "must henceforth gather its own firewood and manioc and do its own cooking." "Weak" POW David Harker was outraged: "You're crazy. Somebody will die." The "strongs" however insisted that "this is the way it's going to be." Soon Kushner's "Darwinian dictum of natural selection" was hard at work—or as Ike McMillan put it, "people started dying like hell."[68] Alarmed camp officials responded by splitting the two groups into three, and though the five black POWs were now in one group, permanent cooks for all three groups solved the no work, no food problem. But the tensions continued. Many "weak" POWs remained cool to Watkins and the "strong" POWs for their callousness, even though anger and annoyance could also erupt, as this group reaction to a dying POW suggests:

He began to make a lot of noise at night, crying over and over, "Mama, oh, Mama . . . I want my Mama."

Once in the middle of the night someone, I don't remember who, yelled, "Die, motherfucker, die!"

No one was shocked. Several people laughed. It was that kind of situation, so pathetic, but the realism of the moment because nobody could get any sleep. Later people talked about it and said what a rotten thing to do.[69]

Because these same POWs cared for the man until he died, something more than cruelty or gallows humor was at work here. Nor was the verbal abuse simply a necessary release for stressed individuals who were nursing and comforting their victim. A scene from *Survivors* reveals how broad a range of individual and group needs the Kushner POWs met while dealing with frequent death.

According to Ike McMillan, "strong" POW Dennis Hammond, or "Denny," was "one of the evilest guys in camp." When he first became ill in 1970, McMillan and other POWs started "saying things to make him angry with us, to make him want to hang on and live." These "things" were not fictions: "When a man was about to die," James Daly explained, "all the other POWs told him what they thought of him. We did this believing it might help them, might make them angry, make them want to live if for no other reason than to seek revenge." These group criticism sessions were harsh medicine—harsh and caustic, since separating what might help the dying man out from the POWs' real anger or resentment was virtually impossible. Since Denny had wanted to abandon the "weak" squad, his own compassion was notoriously slight, and his medicine was thus especially bitter, as in these sessions with Ike McMillan:

> I said, "Do you think what you did in 1968 was right, Denny? Now you're sick and can't work, can't eat or nothing, but I'm gonna do all I can to help you."
> Many days I took him to the water line and gave him a bath and washed his clothes. Each time I reminded him, I said, "I ain't gonna turn my back on you like you did us."

A formal criticism session which James Daly claims Denny himself had requested made the same point. Though they generally told him "what a rotten bastard we thought he was," their list of offenses was so detailed that the POWs seemed almost like a tragic chorus. Denny apparently *had* to recall every cruel act: "You know, you weren't very nice to Williams when he was down. Remember how you used to call him an old goat? Remember how you used to complain about sick guys with dysentery? Now look at you. The day extra peppers were thrown to us over the fence by the Vietnamese POWs you picked them up and didn't offer to share with anybody. Remember?"[70]

Though James Daly later felt bad "about the things we said against the dying"—"We thought we were trying to help. But, really, it just made things worse"—something purgative and redemptive was happening as well. The Kushner POWs were committed to having a dying man acknowledge his failings before the end, and Denny did in fact respond. When Ike McMillan brought up Denny's own behavior to the dying, he "admitted he was wrong and apologized." He also repented, however guardedly, for his past: "Yeah, I guess I was a little rotten. When I go be sure to tell my parents." Nothing theological shaped these confessions; they were simply required in return for that charity extended to *all* the dying. McMillan carried Denny to the water, where Ike bathed him and washed his clothes. Davis carried Denny to the latrine, even when some POWs still thought he should walk. As death neared, even the POWs who hated Denny most nursed him: "We knew he had crapped on himself before he ever said a word. So we got up and stripped off his clothes and somebody wiped him like a baby while the rest of us held him up. Another POW took his pants to the water line to wash them." The Kushner POWs thus responded to death in formal and contradictory ways. The past had to be confronted, and the victim must sense the others' anger. In Denny's case these encounters seemed emotionally overwrought: "The man is dying and his mind has decayed. You find yourself going crazy with him. We should have confronted him with our gripes when he has well. But we didn't. At the end it was something that just happened, something we got off our chests. You don't want the man to die. Who wants anyone to die? We were just telling him the truth."[71] The man was however cared for, and he died with a rough dignity that military protocol does not account for.

In *Survivors* and James Daly's memoir, Dennis Hammond's death on St. Patrick's Day 1970 brings the Kushner camp story to a close. Over the next ten months two important things apparently happened: conditions improved somewhat, so nobody died; and American bombing increased. In February of 1971, these POWs started walking to Hanoi, entering the system, and thus the official story, in April. Though two would join the Peace Committee, the jungle had not turned the twelve surviving Kushner POWs into Communist ideologues. Neither however had it forged them into a military unit. The Kushner POWs seldom talk about bonding through shared adversity. Except perhaps for the White House gala, their first "reunion" took place when a fair number testified at Robert Garwood's 1980 court-martial. And though a few men turned to God when the bombing escalated, religion did not bring this community together either. These "lacks" do not however prove either that survival as a POW requires military discipline at its most hierarchical, or that enlisted men generally lack the guts to fight for their lives and win. Any claims made for the jungle POWs must be tentative—they generally make very few for themselves. Some telling differences between Hanoi and jungle captivity can however be noted. First, though the Hanoi POWs might complain about food and shelter, they had no control over them. In the jungle, POWs wracked with dysentery or malaria struggled through their gathering, cooking, and building. Second, the jungle POWs faced death more directly than the Hanoi men did. "They wouldn't let us die" was a common Hanoi refrain; in the jungle, diet and disease at times meant that the POWs couldn't *stop* dying. And third, since the jungle POWs seldom had as much invested in their military careers, they were more likely to improvise, to take chances under extreme duress, to learn from the fatal mistakes other POWs made. And why not? Anything the U.S. military might do paled in comparison to what threatened the POWs right then.

How would the Alcatraz POWs have fared in the Kushner camp? The official story implicitly argues that they would have survived with their honor and military bearing intact, but we cannot know. Similarly, we can only wonder how many of the Kushner POW casualties, or of the unknown number of jungle POWs who died elsewhere, would have survived if they had gone right to Hanoi. It is I believe fair to conclude, however, that any purely ideological assessment is inadequate to the jungle POWs' experience. The Hanoi POWs and the jungle POWs had markedly different captivities, and the official story is at its worst when it harshly evaluates one group by standards carefully developed to justify and glorify the other.

The Peace Committee and Some Noncombatants

Those narratives dealing with the most controversial group of all—the Peace Committee— show how fiercely Hanoi and enlisted POWs could clash. The idea of such a group had a history—those POWs who denounced America from Korea were called the "Peace Fighters"—and like their forebears, the PCs were "bitter critics of the Vietnam War" who "refused all orders given by senior officers of the highly organized prison camps." The PCs' actions were extreme. In taped broadcasts, John Young denounced Richard Nixon and killing of all kinds, and Michael Branch advised U.S. troops to "refuse combat and just botch up all your operations." And yet, even though the case against these POWs seemed airtight, Pentagon sources told Seymour Hersh that race and rank also figured into the equation. The PCs undeniably kept speaking out, even when "advised to knock it off." But when a senior officer "attempted to pull rank on the enlisted men—they didn't take to it," and one Hersh source suggested that since "none of them are officers and some of them are black," the Hanoi POW "club is going after them."[72] PC John Young agreed, claiming that the Plantation was "sharply divided between officers and enlisted men, with many of the enlisted men opposing the war and many of the officers opposing the enlisted men—but having no access to them to impose their will." Sincerity was the real issue. Like Eugene Wilber, the PCs claimed they had freely chosen to become dissenters. "The antiwar statements are my own antiwar statements," John Young declared. The senior POWs however believed the PCs had sold out for "candy, beer, cigarettes and milk," open cell doors, and tours of Hanoi. This belief suggests that for the Hanoi POWs, the PCs' real crime was rejecting the POW command hierarchy. While John Young "denied that there was any attempt to establish a POW command structure that included enlisted men," Plantation SRO Ted Guy's "concern was not necessarily for the eight men of the Peace Committee," but with "their questioning the authority of a camp commander under prisoner-of-war conditions."[73]

Because many senior POWs believed that enlisted men collaborated almost instinctively, such insubordination outraged, but didn't surprise them. When for instance Colonel Guy realized in late 1970 that the Plantation was primarily "a prison for Americans captured in Laos and South Viet Nam, many of them enlisted soldiers and marines," he knew he had "a problem in the camp." And yet, though these men were a "typical GI cross section—guys who were AWOL when they were captured, a couple of deserters, some who had openly collaborated with the enemy," Guy proudly insisted that he restored military discipline among all of these troops—except for those in the Peace Committee.[74] These eight POWs functioned like an upside-down Alcatraz Gang. Some PCs studied Communist ideology—John Young called himself a Marxist after leaving Vietnam—and some PCs volunteered to help repair the damage caused by American bombing. PC James Daly even claims that at one ill-advised moment, the group offered to join the North Vietnamese Army. These actions sparked such bitter clashes between the PCs and the larger Hanoi community that both sides seemed to agree that only one group should return home. Warding off the PCs' questions about asylum in some neutral country, the Camp Authority had to talk them into going home. On the other side, Ted Guy claims "about a hundred men" would have happily killed the PCs: "I'm not being overly dramatic. The PCs were kept alive because I wouldn't let the others kill them, and I'll tell you that." The Hanoi POWs therefore considered the PCs the real thing—traitors who had betrayed America, joined the enemy, and now deserved to be executed.[75]

Lying between these extremes, however, were other POWs who disagreed with the Hanoi POWs *without* becoming PCs. Floyd Kushner for instance "worried about what the war was doing to the U.S., how it was hurting our country," without in PC John Young's opinion having any sympathy with his captors: "It was a strictly patriotic point of view. We felt we were patriots too, but at the same time we felt sorry for the Vietnamese because they had suffered. We felt guilty about what had happened to them. I think Kushner lacked this kind of feeling."[76] Just as importantly, though, Kushner and other POWs also lacked the feeling that the Hanoi POW command chain had any right to override the hard lessons learned in the jungle. Take the subject of parole. After years in compounds which often made early release look like the only hope for survival, the Kushner POWs firmly believed that parole offers should be accepted at once. When Ted Guy ordered them to refuse early release, then, though the colonel "might have been dedicated," Ike McMillan said to himself, "Man, you're crazy. If these people call me and tell me I can go home—I'm going home." Kushner and Anton found Guy's order equally absurd, and told him "through commo that we respected his opinion but not his judgment and if offered unconditional release we would take it." Their jungle camp's wretched conditions partially accounted for the Kushner POWs' suspicions of by-the-book commanders. Though David Harker was generally happy about reentering the command structure—"I wasn't exactly a military lover, but it made me feel sort of gung ho to know that someone was passing out orders, that we had an organization and were joined together"—even he admitted that "we had been isolated from military discipline so long that news of Colonel Guy being our camp commander was very startling." As for Kushner and Anton, after a few years of making their own decisions, both "sort of rebelled against someone telling us what to do through commo which was passed on and distorted by fifteen different people."[77]

For the Hanoi POWs, this skepticism was insubordination, even though it paradoxically kept some jungle POWs at a distance from the PCs. When an interrogator told Ike McMillan and Jose Anzaldua that the PCs "get beer and candy," the cagey McMillan replied, "Naw, man, we don't want no part of this Peace Committee. The Peace Committee is gonna get burnt." Ike's hardheaded compassion for another's suffering also turned him against the PCs. Just as he had cussed out Denny while bathing him, in Hanoi Ike found himself pitying Colonel Guy, the officer who had ordered him not to accept parole. The Camp Authority "beat that man so bad it was a shame. He was covered with bruises. He lost so much weight he looked like he'd aged fifteen years. And it was all because of the Peace Committee. The PCs told the NVA that commo came down from the most ranking officer in the camp. Boom!" The jungle POW's suspicion of all ideologues was at work here. Outside the system, POWs worried first about food, then disease, and then the boredom. National pride, military discipline, theology, and politics were luxuries, and those obsessed with such matters were either fanatics or willfully obtuse. Deflating such people was an Ike McMillan specialty. When one PC for instance solemnly said that "if my kid was a Communist I'd respect his opinion," Ike McMillan and Jose Anzaldua ended the discussion by replying, "Not us. We're imperialists."[78]

Jungle camp skepticism even divided the PCs. Though Kushner POW James Daly—a black Jehovah's Witness, an unrecognized conscientious objector, and one of the most eccentric of all Vietnam POWs—claimed he became a PC because he was morally opposed to the war, he "came to realize more and more that as a POW, as much as you're aware of the world outside and the war, and as deeply involved as you can get in talk of politics, or religion, or anything—still your real world is right there in those few rooms." Though Daly often seemed naive, confused, and even self-destructive, he still valued his own good-natured stumbling over the focused efficiency of those ideologues and bureaucrats who sent him to Vietnam despite his sincere attempts to declare himself a conscientious objector, and over the fanaticism which drove some PCs as well. Daly for instance "disliked John Young from the first minute I joined the Peace Committee" because he "seemed to force himself to believe things." Ready "to give his life for the Communist cause" without knowing "what it was all about," Young in Daly's eyes resembled those "professional military officers who were ready to die for South Viet Nam without understanding anything about the country beyond a few weak cliches."[79] As pairings like this one suggest, the ground war, the camp officials, and the other POWs could look very different to someone not tied to a party line. Since responding quickly to new threats had been the key to many jungle POWs' survival, they still tended to rely on adaptability and luck in the less dangerous but equally coercive Hanoi system. For all their reeducation sessions, the jungle POWs seldom felt they were fighting a "battle of ideas." Outside the system there was simply war, and these POWs had been unlucky enough to be captured and treated badly. Fellow prisoners were fellow sufferers; rank meant less because jungle POWs seldom bothered to draw arbitrary distinctions. Nor did shared suffering necessarily end in a sense of collective triumph. Jungle POWs were generally awed by their own survival, and they seldom moralized or drew noble conclusions because fate and luck—forces the official story generally downplayed—seemed to have played so large a part in their captivity.

In January 1973, when he knew he would make it back to America, Kushner POW David Harker mused on his captivity:

> I thought about the jungle, the men who wouldn't be going home, the twelve of us who had survived. So many things had happened, so much we wanted to forget. We knew each other better than our wives would ever know us. We were beyond the simple emotions of love and hate, forever joined by the most intimate exposures of our deepest selves, made brothers by that drive to survive when all seems lost.

Though Harker uses the sports and fraternity rhetoric which the Hanoi POWs were so fond of, he hardly claims the conventional POW victory. In the official story, dead men were saints or washouts, martyrs or suicides. The jungle POWs stayed jagged. Things happened, but in no discernible pattern; men died, changed, and survived without American military values exerting any certain influence. Neither duty or affection but the fact of surviving made the Kushner POWs "brothers"—the point a fellow POW made as he punctured Harker's reverie: "As I stood thinking about how very few men have ever known each other this way, Ike McMillan slipped up behind me and whispered, 'Harker, you can have my one twelfth of the sunshine now.' "[80]

The Enemy Within—Robert Garwood

> . . . Hammond caught sight of Garwood in the door. "Holy shit!" he said to Zawtocki, "A white gook!"
>
> *Conversations with the Enemy*[81]

> Bob was an American. He was a deserter. Perhaps his fellow countrymen will find harsher names to call him, but I cannot condemn him.
>
> BERNHARD DIEHL[82]

The witchcraft hysteria of the 1690s "made only one relationship between white and Indian conceivable—that of captive to captor, helpless good to active evil." As Richard Slotkin explains, though eating the same food, sleeping in the same places, and braving the same dangers of ongoing warfare inevitably blurred the boundaries between Indian and colonist, for these very reasons the New Englanders remained adamant: "Even the metamorphosis of a white man into an animal later became an acceptable part of the Puritan myth, but not the loss of one's identity as English and Christian."[83] As the jungle POWs arrived in Hanoi almost three centuries later, they too faced a fiercely Puritanical scrutiny. Since words could be extorted and terrified individuals could sincerely become antiwar, the senior Hanoi POWs weren't especially concerned about propaganda statements. The real worry was whether a POW had *essentially* changed—become "a white gook." Posture, gestures, and language were the warning signs here. As Elaine Scarry notes, since human beings learn "to stand upright, to walk, to wave and signal, to listen, to speak" within "particular 'civil' realms, a particular hemisphere, a particular nation, a particular state, a particular region," whether "residing in one fragile gesture or in a thousand," the individual's "loyalty to these political realms" will be more "deeply and permanently" engraved in these actions than in "those disembodied forms of patriotism that exist in verbal habits or in thoughts about one's national identity."[84] A way of squatting or eating from a bowl could in short be more damning than an antiwar statement—a fact that led the Hanoi POWs to ban the learning of Vietnamese, "thus maintaining our separate status, making no concessions that would even hint of collaboration with the enemy, and forcing our captors to address us in English."[85]

The total traitor would therefore be someone whose speech and gestures confirmed a physical defection, and Marine Private Robert Garwood bore the full force of POW hatred directed at such monsters. Captured on September 28, 1965, he left Vietnam in 1979—six years *after* Operation Homecoming. He was notorious long before his return. *P.O.W.*, *Survivors*, James Daly's *A Hero's Welcome*, Schwinn's and Diehl's *We Came to Help*, and debriefing testimony "from hard-core officers" and "from foot soldiers, a warrant officer, a doctor—from blacks, whites, from Hispanic soldiers" all insisted that "Garwood had chosen to give his allegiance to the enemy, and in this he was alone, separate from the other prisoners." As his biographers Winston Groom and Duncan Spencer note, however, Robert Garwood was more than "separate." His survival skills, apparent good health, and fluent Vietnamese led other POWs to link Garwood to "one of the barracks-room myths of the Vietnam War, the man called 'Super Charlie,' or the 'White Cong.' " Someone "either crazed by battle, brainwashed, or simply perverse," this monster "joined the Viet Cong and combined technology with jungle cunning," thus abandoning "not only his country and his ideology, but also his hemisphere and his race." This "depth of evil bordering on insanity" was the same depravity Cotton Mather saw in colonists seduced by the satanic forest.[86] What the New Englanders and the Vietnam POWs never expected, however, was that this mutant might come back from the jungle. How could someone change his fundamental nature *twice*?

Robert Garwood's 1979 return from Vietnam set off a storm for other reasons as well. Though hardly pleased that Garwood was one of theirs, the Marine Corps saw him as a chance to right past wrongs. After Operation Homecoming, the Marines had been prepared "to prosecute every individual who was guilty of breaking the code or behaving in such a way that unfavorable notice was taken by a fellow prisoner." But the other service branches issued a blanket amnesty, then dismissed the charges POWs Jim Stockdale, Ted Guy, and Ed Leonard filed as private citizens. The decision in 1979 to charge Garwood with desertion therefore "must have reflected the venom that the officers who made up the Marine mentality felt about the whole shabby 'Operation Homecoming' business." Garwood was also a convenient whipping boy for the Vietnam War itself. By 1979, the military blamed treachery at home and in the field rather than defeat by a dedicated military force for America's failure in Vietnam. The "turncoat" Garwood thus "took on an almost religious significance as a scapegoat whereby all the losses and effort wasted, the cries and hopeless blood could be made right and fair." The prosecutors went after this Garwood at his court-martial. His defense counsel countered by presenting Garwood "as an example of the peculiar wastage of Vietnam—a man who because of inhuman conditions became a creature of the enemy's own creation, a zombie, a brainwash." As the White Gook vied with the Manchurian Candidate in court, Garwood therefore became a "symbol of the whole tragedy of America in Vietnam—part war, part collapse, part a disturbing mental sickness that leaves everyone uncertain, including any thinking jury."[87]

Robert Garwood ends this chapter on alternative narratives because his story responds so directly to other memoirs and histories. As Groom and Spencer explain, the first hint that Garwood had assumed "a large, if one dimensional, image without facts to deflate it" came when the bewildered officials who first met him in 1979 found that "the Garwood they had in hand, the skinny man with the smudged eyes who kept asking for ice cream and Winstons, was nothing like the Garwood they had heard of." His court-martial further obligated him to supply alternative versions for the most damning accounts of his behavior as a POW—accounts which were in some cases already in print. And in 1983, *Conversations with the Enemy*, a biography written with Garwood's cooperation, claimed to tell his story once and for all—even though Garwood has been publicly revising it ever since. Near the end of this biography, Groom and Spencer pose some difficult questions: "And so what was Garwood? A traitor? A patriot? A hero? Or simply an unfortunate, trying to make the best of a horrible and impossible situation?" Though his biographers say "the only thing for certain is that Bobby Garwood is a survivor," their book takes the form of an *apologia* or defense, time-honored genres which address the charges and half-truths always swirling around a prominent figure.[88]

What made Robert Garwood's case striking is that his defense rests almost entirely upon events that no one else could confirm or deny. The relatively short but intensely controversial time Garwood spent with the Kushner POWs was sandwiched between long periods of isolation. The handful of American POWs he knew between September 1965 and September 1967 all died in captivity. Even during the two key years, his contacts with the Kushner POWs were irregular, since he lived in another part of camp and was often sent out into the jungle. And after his last encounter with these POWs, in October of 1969, Garwood spent the next nine and a half years alone. *Conversations with the Enemy* sets the murky ends against the traitorous middle. The story of Garwood's first two years must account for that familiarity with his captors which the Kushner POWs found so damning. The story of his later years must explain why he did not return in 1973, but did come home to face prosecution six years later. Claims very similar to *P.O.W.*'s shore up Groom's and Spencer's forensic exercise. They speak of "hundreds of hours of interviews," of "a voluminous file of tapes, notes, transcripts and other documents." Though the authors admit the possibility of bias, since "the recollections of many of the principals go back more than fifteen years, and some are obscure, bitter, or self-serving," the authors nevertheless "firmly believe that this telling is as close to the truth of the Garwood matter as it is humanly possible to get"—and since the only possible source for huge periods was Garwood himself, this belief might actually be more solidly grounded than Hubbell's.[89]

The first third of Garwood's biography describes an easily influenced yet fire-breathing victim. Born fittingly on April 1, 1946, into "a strange little family" which Garwood himself called "a little better than white trash," he endured a childhood apparently designed to produce a deeply troubled adult. Though Groom and Spencer deny the lawyers' claim that "young Bob's life was some kind of Dickensian hell," their biography leans heavily toward Faulkner or Flannery O'Connor. A roustabout father, a strict grandmother, a crippled Uncle Buddy suffering "from some sort of dimly understood palsy," and a 300 pound stepmother who seemed "to be literally drowning in excess weight" were the important people in Garwood's life. His mother had fled. As a child and as an adult, Garwood displayed an "inability to avoid the control exercised over him by others." Whether "his father, his stepmother, his grandmother, the juvenile court, the Marine Corps, the Vietnamese, or more recently his squadron of lawyers," authority figures always dragged "Garwood, the innocent, yearning to be free," into situations "from which he would not or could not escape." Once in a fix, Garwood typically remained "more or less inert" until he unexpectedly kicked out.[90] Indirectly, one such kick landed him in the Marines. After getting into trouble as a teenager, Garwood impulsively entered a juvenile detention home rather than return to his family. A recruiter visited the home, and Garwood enlisted in late 1963, but Corps life wasn't all that thrilling either. His only combat training came in boot camp, and he bounced from California to Okinawa, and then to Vietnam, in support units—"driver" comes closest to describing his duties. A listless, directionless teenager with no role models, few talents, and a habit of acting impulsively, Robert Garwood was therefore a poor prospect for jungle captivity.

Given this history, his early performance is all the more surprising. Ambushed while waiting to pick up an officer at a fishing village, Garwood supposedly shot one, and possibly two VC before being overwhelmed. After nine days of marching from village to village as a traveling show, he made his first escape attempt. Locked in a bamboo cage after being recaptured, he reacted to a series of horrifying events shortly afterwards by trying another escape. Some time later, he decided that the cost of accepting early release was just too high, and ruined his departure ceremony by publicly *refusing* parole: " 'I thank the SVNFL for their consideration,' he said quickly, shocking himself by deviating from the text he had been given, 'but I feel that I am not worthy of their consideration and decision and wish to decline in accepting the selection. I feel that I should work harder and study more about the Vietnamese culture.' "[91] Resisting capture, attempting escapes, and refusing parole thus describe Garwood's captivity up until June 1967, a few weeks before meeting Luis Ortiz-Rivera, the first POW who survived to testify against him.

When patriotism and captor relations became the issue, however, poor training, horrendous conditions, and Garwood's enlisted status get stressed. Like many enlisted men, he began his "reeducation" with no weapons for fighting back. As Mr. Ho, the official who would later run the Kushner camp programs, began the first lesson, "Garwood stared at him stupidly": "He had never been exposed to the Communist line or propaganda of any sort before, and amazingly, his Marine training had included no course of instruction in how to deal with such methods except the bare and stark statements of the code of conduct." All Garwood had ever "thought about was putting in my time and going home. I didn't know who the Vietnamese were, what we were fighting about and I really didn't care."[92] These remarks therefore begin laying the foundations for a defense against charges of collaboration. Such political ignorance not only makes any claim that Garwood deserted to become an NLF warrior seem farfetched, but also starts shifting any blame for his performance toward the military itself. As Korea's General Dean remarked, you can't judge troops harshly when you haven't given them a good reason to fight.

Garwood's lessons were almost identical to what other jungle POWs heard. When he asked about the Geneva convention, Mr. Ho answered that America's undeclared aggression meant that "*you* are not considered a prisoner of war, and cannot enjoy the international policy as a prisoner of war, but fall under the policy of a criminal of war." When Garwood refused to sign a "Fellow Soldiers Appeal" because "it's against the code of conduct," Mr. Ho's reaction was equally formulaic: " 'Code of conduct!' Ho spat. 'I know all about your code of conduct. But you see, your code of conduct does not and cannot apply here. Let me remind you once again, you are not considered to be a prisoner of war. . . . ' " The ten regulations Mr. Ho read out echoed those posted in Hanoi and other jungle camps. Two aimed at the Code—do not try to escape or make contact with other POWs— and four more dealt with health and diet—eat everything, wash yourself, don't hide food, and "use WC for all body waste." Another two concerned the guards—stand at attention for them, and ask their permission to leave your quarters—and one rule—"no singing of U.S. imperialist songs"—seems to have been written for Garwood. One rule, however, "You must try hard to learn Vietnamese customs and language," doesn't appear in other

POWs' accounts.[93] As I've already noted, camp officials didn't seem very interested in teaching Vietnamese, and many POWs felt it was their duty to resist such learning. In Garwood's case, though, this rule accounts in part for his ability to serve as a translator in the Kushner camp.

Garwood's methods for resisting interrogation also resembled those of other POWs. Although Garwood knew "where the intelligence command for the whole First Corps was located, and the names of most of the top officers," Mr. Ho didn't ask "any real questions of military value," and as his political lessons proceeded, Garwood became annoyed: "This guy is going to teach me about America? This guy is going to teach me American history? This guy is ignorant as shit. I'm not going to let him tell me about my own country." Like the stereotyped rednecked Marine, then, Garwood resisted angrily and instinctively at first. In time, though, he decided to avoid "the dysentery, the malaria, the unconscious wavering near total darkness" by adopting the same fallback strategy so many Hanoi POWs followed. He picked some worthless topics he could talk about forever—his vehicle, the motor pool—and he also told some lies about his past, always remembering "what he had told Ho, what he hadn't told him." Significantly, this strategy duplicates Richard Stratton's, the Hanoi POW who seemed to be under enemy control but was actually resisting. Garwood continued this parallel by mistakenly assuming, like Stratton, that other POWs and officials back home would see through any propaganda statements. "No piece of propaganda has ever affected our troops, it's too damn ridiculous," Garwood rationalized when signing a "Fellow Soldiers Appeal," "Anyone who picked it up would know I did it under pressure."[94] Though a poorly trained enlisted man, then, as a POW Garwood was a soft-liner with hard-line tendencies who only fell back when left with nowhere to hide.

The degree of Garwood's early suffering made his fortitude all the more remarkable. The physical horrors fully bore out Mr. Ho's remark that "it is so easy to die here in the jungle," and Garwood's forced presence at staged executions added a whole new dimension of terror. Sitting on bleachers with some ARVN POWs, Garwood watched in horror as two blindfolded Vietnamese whom Ho called "cruel agents" were forced to play Russian roulette. When this preview of *The Deerhunter* reached its inevitable conclusion, Garwood was left in "a state of barely controlled hysteria" which serves to undercut further any claim that he crossed over to the enemy. How could a terrified Indiana boy have possibly united with sadists capable of such horrors? Garwood remembers resolving to "wait. Simply wait, surviving in any way he could. Survival, he thought, could become the whole and complete object of his everyday existence. He would live through every day simply to get to the next in the faith that some day the war would end, and there would be no more reason to keep him."[95]

To this point, Garwood's biography makes him look more like the POW most memoirs present as a good resister than like a deserter, but the arrival of a thin, bearded, and ragged figure draped in a plastic sheet changed Garwood's life forever. This specter was Army Captain William F. Eisenbraun, a seventeen-year veteran whose extensive training made him arguably the best-prepared American captured in Vietnam. He spoke "what appeared to Garwood to be perfect Vietnamese," and he didn't stand on ceremony: " 'Cut out the Captain shit,' Eisenbraun said. 'You're the first American I've seen in six months, and we might as well go by a first-name basis.' " This informality did not mean that "Ike" refused to command. His belief that "There is a good chance that we can survive, but we gotta stick together"—was basically "Unity before Self." Another recommendation, however, had weighty consequences. When Ike announced that "the first thing you'll have to do is to start learning the Vietnamese language," Garwood "was surprised and thought, Shit, as long as he knows it, that's one of us, why isn't that good enough?":

> "It's a benefit," Ike said. "It's a better chance for us. If I get sick. If we get separated. You've got to understand what these people are saying, and if you know the lingo there are damn few surprises on their side, at least as far as I've known. You help your chances of survival, you don't hurt them."[96]

No sympathetic attachment to Asians lay behind Ike's own language skills. He claimed Korea was "colder'n shit. Girls don't fuck worth a damn. Booze was flat," and in Vietnam, "gooks and slopeheads" were his English names for the captors, "slant-eyed bastards." Language was therefore not a concession but a weapon. Since "most Vietnamese had no more than a first- or second-grade education," fluency would make it easier for Ike and Bobby, "with superior education and advanced culture" to outsmart their captors.[97]

Language was only one of the many skills Eisenbraun passed on to his troop. Garwood later claimed that "he taught me everything I learned about the jungle," as recognizing special foods, herbal medicines, and vitamin C sources so quickly became second nature, that even his guards thought "the Americans were becoming 'real Vietnamese.' " Eisenbraun set policies for escape and resistance as well. Since he estimated the chances for a successful escape at "one in ten thousand," Ike advised waiting for American intelligence operations to find them. He also advised doing "whatever the VC tells us to do. Don't piss them off. Every one of those guards out there has had a family member killed by one side or the other, and they're itching for any kind of excuse to blow your ass away." Supplying propaganda materials fell under this order. Garwood was amazed "that Eisenbraun, the hard professional soldier who had been through torture, would simply sit down and write the facts about himself for the commander," and while Ike was "ashamed" himself "about some of the things I've said and done," he would "probably keep on doing them as long as my survival depends on it. Ashamed and alive." A relieved Garwood then confessed to signing a "Fellow Soldiers Appeal," and Ike decided "it did more good than it did harm." Since the VC probably dropped copies near U.S. bases, American military officials now "know you are alive, and that you have been captured, and this will give you hope that maybe some kind of rescue operation may get underway."[98] The same logic governed Ike's advice about parole. When the VC began preparing Garwood for early release, he asked Ike what to do. Ike told him exactly what Richard Stratton would tell Douglas Hegdahl in Hanoi: "They'll use you. Any way they can, they'll use you. This is gonna be propaganda, Bob. You've got to promise me you'll draw the line to where it may harm another American. Other than that, do anything you have to do to get out of here and let somebody know we're alive." In this instance, and in so many others, this "gaunt, bearded man of thirty-four" seemed "all things" to Garwood: "comrade in arms, friend, leader, officer in charge, almost a father, almost the father he never had."[99] Perhaps most importantly, however, Ike is also Garwood's alibi. In one of the more mind-boggling arguments found in any Vietnam POW narrative, what his fellow POWs considered the strongest signs of Garwood's collaboration—his jungle skills, his fluent Vietnamese, his obedience to camp officials—are actually proof that he had followed his commanding officer's orders to the letter. Garwood had not gone native, he had gone Eisenbraun.

Garwood's complete and naive trust left him frighteningly vulnerable when Ike betrayed him. The catalyst for this disaster was Corporal Russell Grissett, whose arrival was Garwood's greatest misfortune as a POW. Grissett was "a good grunt"—fairly strong, not too bright, and no leader—but malaria sapped his strength, and he lacked Garwood's or Eisenbraun's survival instincts. Since Grissett wouldn't learn Vietnamese, he also never knew what his fellow POWs were saying to camp officials. What turned Grissett into Garwood's nemesis was a failed escape that had terrible consequences for all three POWs. Though Eisenbraun had discouraged such attempts, before Grissett arrived Ike had made a pact with Garwood not to warn each other if they did decide to try. That way, "if the one or the other is recaptured, he'll know nothing to tell." Nevertheless, when Garwood discovered that Ike and Grissett had made a break without telling him, he found himself "fighting a wave of panic that was almost nausea. He felt hurt and betrayed. He hadn't been included, though he was the strongest of the three. He thought ridiculously of being jilted by Eisenbraun. He felt a sting of hate toward Grissett." When the two escapers were recaptured, Ike then wounded Garwood to the quick:

> "Bob, you've probably gonna hate me for telling you this, but if me and Russ had got clean away, they'd have probably killed you. They would have never believed that you don't know nothin' about this."
> Garwood looked at him blankly. "You knew that when you escaped?"
> "Yeah, I knew it. It was a possibility."[100]

This betrayal was however far less disastrous for Garwood than the failed escape's effect on Grissett. The guards had told him that Garwood had informed on the escapers, and while in this biography at least Garwood's shock and Eisenbraun's confession prove the charge was false, Grissett wasn't too bright, and his punishment in the stocks left him a "changed man"—obedient and eager to write statements. When the VC then forced these POWs to witness the execution of an ARVN POW, Grissett was even further reduced to a "cringing terrified prisoner," and therefore the perfect choice for "leader of the Americans."[101] The Vietnamese accordingly moved him in with three newly arrived POWs— Luis Ortiz-Rivera and Agusto-Santos, the Puerto Ricans who were later paroled, and Robert Sherman, who died in captivity.

Mentally unstable and certain that he had been betrayed, Grissett proceeded to destroy Garwood's reputation. Meanwhile, some distance away Ike started his slide toward death which would rob Garwood of his certainties. Eisenbraun realized his early advice had gone sour. Now certain that Garwood would have "to go it alone," in his last days Ike tried to prepare his troop "for the long haul." He first told Garwood that the growing POW population had turned their language fluency into a liability: "We know too much about 'em. If they release anybody, they'll release someone who doesn't know Vietnamese. Hell, we know names, dates, places, we know too much." Ike also warned Garwood about Grissett: "Russ still believes, from the day of our escape attempt, that you told the bastards one thing or another that got us recaptured"—fatherly advice that has added significance for Garwood's biography, since by branding Grissett a vindictive and unreliable source, Ike calls into question from the grave all secondhand stories about Garwood's captivity before he met the Kushner POWs. Most important of all, Ike instructed Garwood to behave in precisely the way that the Kushner POWs found so suspicious. "You gotta try to find ways to help the others, Bob," Ike advised, "but don't tell them":

> I don't want them to be in the role that they have to depend on you. If they start making demands, it'll never end. If you steal one cup of rice, they'll want two. Because you speak Vietnamese, they're gonna think you're not taking chances. Because you know the guards, they're gonna say you've got it easy. Don't let this happen.[102]

Happen however it did, as events managed to blacken Garwood's reputation further. When Ike Eisenbraun died in September 1967, Garwood was not only devastated, but left in a nasty situation. To the new POWs, a Vietnamese-speaking American could only look like a crossover. To his captors, Garwood's skills now made him a potential "provocateur who could stir up resistance among the other prisoners—even if it were as little as learning to live off the land and eke out their rations with what they could find in the forest."[103] Perhaps for this reason, shortly after Ike's death the VC moved Garwood to another camp for two months—an interval that allowed Grissett to brief new POWs on Garwood without fear of contradiction, and provided a convenient period for Garwood's supposed ideological conversion. As the narrative arrives at the most controversial years of Garwood's captivity, then, he was isolated from the other POWs, his worst enemy had control over his reputation, and the one person who could back up Garwood's version of his captivity was dead.

Of *Conversations with the Enemy*'s over 400 pages, 170 cover the time before the Kushner camp events, 65 deal with that period itself, and 40 more with his court martial, when "ten ex-POWs told the jury members Garwood appeared to them to be one of the enemy, living apart from the POWs, serving as guard and interpreter."[104] Presumably on his lawyers' advice, Garwood himself remained silent. As the record of what he could have said, however, his biography is almost too complete. "The Vietnamese forced me to," he seems to say, "and Eisenbraun, my senior officer, ordered me to. But actually I didn't do anything at all, many POWs did the same or worse, and anyway, I was only trying to help!" Such overkill results from the book's calculated efforts to present Garwood as a walking refutation of the Kushner POWs' charges. Since he disappeared for long periods, for instance, the other POWs concluded he was getting better treatment or even serving in the NLF. In the biography, though, the dying Eisenbraun predicted that since the new camp policy "was to keep the prisoners in a state of total dependency," Garwood would be quarantined as someone who had refused parole, and who therefore might urge other POWs to think twice about being cooperative. The accusations of preferential treatment get dealt with in the same way. When the Kushner POWs started dying, they saw Garwood's relatively good health as proof of treason: "Sure Garwood, you're eating at the guard's kitchen, and you don't see none of the guards starvin' to death, who are you tryin' to shit? We got eyes." Actually, though, Ike's survival teaching was Garwood's salvation. He ate "insects and wild herbs and roots"; he "could catch a rat with his hand and kill it and eat it, he could make marginal soap out of a banana leaf, and he could make tea from leaves and he knew the magic of the betel." His "collaboration" was thus jungle sense—the one thing that Russ Grissett had perversely refused to develop. If only the Kushner POWs had "known what he knew, they might have survived," Garwood thought sadly. But his efforts were doomed, simply because he "could not seem to teach the new Americans to eat insects and rats."[105]

The VCs' own wish to destroy Garwood's reputation added to his troubles. When first removed from isolation to serve as a translator, he knew he was in serious trouble. Translating, carrying the radio to the Kushner POWs' compound for Radio Hanoi broadcasts, and serving as a group leader during reeducation sessions would make Garwood look like a VC functionary to POWs "who had only Grissett to tell them he wasn't collaborating but only surviving." When however Garwood asked to be relieved of these duties, the camp commander called the POWs together and announced that from now on, "Bob will be known as Mr. Dau to you." According to his biography, "Dau" meant "freedom fighter"; camp officials also told the other POWs that Garwood used a bullhorn at the front lines to urge American troops to join the NLF.[106] Garwood himself admitted his behavior and frequent absences must have seemed suspicious. But he also knew that

only a well-organized and perceptive group could have avoided drawing false conclusions—and these qualities were hardly the Kushner POWs' strongest traits. According to
Garwood, at one point the doomed First Sergeant Williams even told him that the officers'
dereliction of duty was more serious than anything Garwood had done. Williams felt "scorn
and horror" for what he thought Garwood had done—"I can't believe an American can
act in the way you did"—but he granted that youth and inexperience were partially to
blame. The POWs Williams "could not excuse were Anton and Kushner, men of higher
education who had failed."[107] Garwood's strongest support from the grave, however,
comes from his nemesis. After he moved in with the new POWs, Russ Grissett fluctuated
between sidling up to Garwood and pandering to the other men. After thoroughly poisoning
Garwood's reputation, however, Grissett took ill, and like Ike Eisenbraun, his dying words
to Garwood warned him about the other POWs:

> . . . "Stay away from 'em, Bob. Stay away."
> "Stay away from who?" Garwood said.
> "Other Americans," Grissett whispered. Garwood explained that his advice was
> going to be hard to follow.
> "I'm tellin' you if you ever come down here, don't ever come down alone."[108]

This exchange perfectly illustrates a fundamental principle of Garwood's defense: the less
someone knew about him, the more he was hated. Ike knew him best, and liked him;
Grissett had stayed at a distance and mistrusted him. The Kushner POWs knew nothing
about his early captivity and hated him; officials back in America were most vindictive of
all. Thus Grissett's death was a disaster: "Once it was Eisenbraun, Grissett, and Garwood.
Now the links had been broken and no one would know who he was, what he was, what
he had gone through. There would only be the accusation and the hatred, the 'facts' that
were close enough to a kind of truth, but still very far from it."[109]

The most damning accusation, however, was that Garwood had become the creature
of American military nightmares, the White Cong: "You been here so long you've turned
into a gook," Dennis Hammond told Garwood, "You don't sit, you squat, you chew that
red shit, you dress, eat, walk, carry things like one of them. The only thing left is when
your skin starts turning yellow." Garwood realized that "his stained pajamas, his filthy
hands, his feet that looked like the feet of some scaly animal" made him look like "some
kind of Oriental experiment that was failing to jell," but this Frankenstein monster had
many creators besides itself. The VC had abused him from the start. His commanding
officer had taught him the language and jungle skills which later alienated him from the
other captives. By rejecting Garwood's help, Russ Grissett and the Kushner POWs pushed
him further into the jungle as well. And finally, the military and America itself should take
some credit for that motley figure the jungle POWs encountered: "There he was, a white
Caucasian, AK strapped to his pack, black pajamas, sandals, beard—and behind him three
men in U.S. fatigues. He thought wearily he looked the worst of a hippy, a grunt, and a
gook, all rolled up in one."[110]

The chapters dealing with the ten years following Garwood's late 1969 separation
from the Kushner POWs are less detailed. Placed in isolation as a "special category" POW,
he was badly hurt during a bombing raid in 1970. After a long recovery, like most jungle
POWs he made the long trek north, where a hospital stay had him "nearly back to normal"
by Christmas. He entered Son Tay Prison Camp in February 1971—three months *after* the
rescue attempt—and began "a sort of hibernation."[111] Segregated from the Vietnamese
POWs held there, over the next few years Garwood built a fish pond and tended a vegetable

garden while the other American POWs went home and Saigon fell. Two events from this period do however get special attention. The first episode ties into what has made Robert Garwood so interesting to some people today. Though he himself was isolated, the camp commander told Garwood the prison population was "composed of both American and Vietnamese prisoners." Warning lights go off here—no American POWs released in 1973 were held at Son Tay after the raid. Guards also "inadvertently" mentioned that "members of the French Legion force, made up of Spaniards, Moroccans, Algerians, expatriate Germans and others" were running a dairy nearby. Though "most of them" were supposedly "crazy," they spoke Vietnamese well, and the guard claimed there were also a lot of them: "At one time, there were over two hundred," he said. "I don't know how many are there now." The reasons given for this state of affairs understandably depressed Garwood. "Vietnam is not so stupid as to release all prisoners," one guard explained, "What would prevent the U.S. from coming back and bombing Hanoi again?"[112] Though these reports of live Caucasian captives have greatly interested those in the MIA/POW movement, they also form part of Garwood's defense. Military officials treated Garwood in 1979 like the POWs who chose to stay in Korea, but dribbled home later. Live POWs in Vietnam would allow Garwood to claim that *like other prisoners still there*, he had been held back as insurance.

Garwood's second key experience was a heavily symbolic representation of his fate as a POW. A camp official named Ky often told Garwood about his wife Hoa, who did "the most dangerous type of intelligence" in the South. In the summer of 1974, she arrived at Son Tay. Tall for a Vietnamese, "without the short-legged look," she wore high heels and gold jewelry—a ring, bracelet, watch, necklace, and earrings. Her hair had a wave, and she lit her cigarettes with a gold Zippo lighter. She was also assertive, playful, and self-assured—"unlike any other Vietnamese woman" Garwood had ever seen. Hoa paid special attention to Garwood, asking for his opinions about female beauty and American women, and for details about his sexual experiences with Vietnamese women. Soon the inevitable happened, making Robert Garwood the only American POW to claim he had sexual relations with a Vietnamese woman while in captivity. The writing is at its most conventional here. Darting tongues, "svelte slippery" bodies, and Garwood's "manhood" all played their parts, leading up to his "uncontrollable wave" of passion and guilt. The biggest cliche, however, is Hoa herself. "This is what you Americans like," she giggled while acting out the American GI fantasy of being serviced by an Asian sex toy: "She sat, legs crossed, combing her hair, a slight smile playing about her lips. 'How do you feel?' she said, still with the friendly tone, like a girl you would meet in school. 'I have never seen anybody come so fast,' she said flippantly. 'Ky takes forever.' She smiled the whore's smile." These drugstore novel passages do not however erase an important affinity between Hoa and Garwood. She had done her "duty to the revolution" by posing as a South Vietnamese whore and getting military information "any way I could" from the easily seduced American officers. Now that the Americans were leaving, however, she faced a terrible fate. Though "It's not the same as being unfaithful," sleeping with the enemy for whatever reason had turned her into a pariah: "She could not even tell another Vietnamese because of the social code. Even her closest friend would discard her as a whore." Hoa thus turned to Garwood, who "as a nonperson, a prisoner and an American, was the one safe person she could speak to," and Garwood in turn "felt an instant kinship with the woman, tormented by a guilt she couldn't discharge."[113] Like Hoa, he had lived for long periods among his enemies, and survived by adapting. But their success was also their undoing, since such contact always seems to contaminate. Hoa and Garwood therefore shared the common fate of being victims in danger of punishment for doing the right thing.

The rest of Garwood's captivity whips by. Put in charge of the motor pool for a huge reeducation camp, through some clever moves he got to Hanoi and passed his name to a foreign visitor, thus forcing the North Vietnamese to release him. Garwood's defense at his court-martial seems grossly inadequate, largely because he never got to tell the story we've been reading. Garwood was found guilty of interpreting during indoctrination sessions, of informing on other POWs, of questioning POWs about military and escape matters, of trying to indoctrinate POWs, of suggesting they defect, of guarding other POWs, and of assaulting POW David Harker. The charges that could have led to lengthy imprisonment, or even the death penalty, were dropped, and his sentence was relatively light: "The jury ordered Garwood reduced to the lowest rank, a dishonorable discharge, forfeiture of pay and allowances."[114] Apart from his huge legal bills and other debts, then, he was basically free—free, but maimed for life. As the preeminent Vietnam POW scapegoat, Robert Garwood remained a victim of his upbringing, his captors, and his fellow POWs; of the U.S. military, the legal process, and America's troubled relationship to its own past; and ultimately, of fate. Robert Garwood has however proved consistent in his inconsistency. *Conversations with the Enemy* appeared in 1983. In late 1984, though, Garwood undercut his own authorized biography by claiming in a front-page *Wall Street Journal* interview that he had personally seen "at least 70 Americans held prisoner in Vietnam as of the late 1970s"—roughly twenty men in mid-1973, thirty to forty at a railway crossing in 1977, and as many as sixty in 1978. He also offered a possible explanation for the Americans' continued captivity: the Vietnamese could be using them for terrorist training, "to show that Americans are only human, that we do suffer duress and stress." Although this article admits that "Mr. Garwood isn't the most credible of witnesses," interviewer Bill Paul presents Garwood as a sincere penitent ready to talk: "The U.S. government had sought to interview Mr. Garwood about his Vietnam experiences when he returned to the U.S., but he refused to cooperate. He didn't take the stand at his court-martial. And he didn't tell of POWs still living in Vietnam in his 1983 biography, 'Conversations With The Enemy.' He has come forward now, he says, because he wants to clear his conscience."[115]

Over the years, other writers have suggested further reasons for Garwood's initial silence. In 1987, Robert Colvin believed that litigation, the court-martial, and Vietnamese threats to harm American POWs had sealed Garwood's lips. Scott Barnes, an earnest player on the MIA movement's fringes, wrote in the same year that Garwood had told him in early 1986 about "personally" helping to bury some POWs "who had died long after the war had ended." Even more stunningly, Barnes also claims that Garwood "admitted that he had collaborated. 'I am not trying to make excuses for what I did,' he told me, 'but I was only a nineteen-year-old kid, tortured and starved, wanting to come home.' " Most recently of all, in her 1990 book *Kiss the Boys Goodbye*, Monika Jensen-Stevenson presents Garwood as the victim of a wide-ranging 1980s conspiracy to suppress his firsthand knowledge of live American POWs in Vietnam. And so it goes, as Garwood's story shifts in its emphasis, details, and revelations. Regardless of what may be discovered, though, I suspect Robert Garwood will have the last word.[116]

Everyone recalls that moment from *The Wizard of Oz* when the Wicked Witch of the West sinks into the floor, shrieking "I'm melting, I'm melting!" Evil getting its full reward is as memorable as it is rare. The more important scene, however, occurs shortly afterward, when Toto pulls back a curtain to reveal that Oz, the Great and Powerful, is a special effects show staged by an insignificant someone who shrieks, "Pay no attention to the man behind the curtain!" The Vietnam POW scapegoat memoirs also fluctuate between great projected stories, with all their conflicts, political statements, and allegories, and the captives themselves as they suffer through the boredom and pettiness of captivity. Just as unmistakably, though, through the force of contrast these narratives often expose the tiny individuals operating the mighty official story as well. By documenting how the mainstream POWs reacted to them, renegade or scapegoat POWs suggest that from the outside, unity before self could look like false group bravado fueled by guilt, or like the huddling instincts of sheep, or even like a misery which not only loved but demanded company. Outsiders' memoirs also remind us that no group can see farther than the shared experience of its membership. Since POWs who lived closely with their guards or did a great deal of manual labor had a different captivity than the Hanoi POWs did, the official story's limitations result as much from ignorance as from malice. And finally, the jungle narratives especially argue by implication that the Hanoi POWs' strongest convictions could seem self-indulgent or even suicidal when the goal was simply survival.

Since the Vietnamese guards and officials are hardly likely to write memoirs, these narratives from the official story's other sides therefore provide the only perspective on the many versions of the official story other POWs have told. And establishing that perspective is particularly important before dealing with the most deliberate and evaluative POW writings of all—those of the SRO of Alcatraz.

· 8 ·

Keeping the Faith— James Bond Stockdale

> If you have an earnest desire toward philosophy, prepare yourself from the very first to have the multitude laugh and sneer, and say, "He is returned to us a philosopher all at once;" and "Whence this supercilious look?" Now, for your part, do not have a supercilious look, but keep steadily to those things which appear best to you, as one appointed by God to this particular station.
>
> EPICTETUS[1]

Commander James B. Stockdale was the quintessential senior POW. From the moment he was captured in September 1965 until the day he left Hanoi, he was the highest-ranking Navy POW, and though crippled by his shootdown, Stockdale proved so troublesome that he eventually landed in Alcatraz, and then in total isolation when he proved too disruptive even among the diehards. Despite these hard-line credentials, Stockdale was respected by a remarkably wide range of POWs. Though John Dramesi was often disgusted by his commanders, he admired Stockdale: "Peg was willing to lead, to live by the code of conduct as much as he was physically able. To me, he had been and continued to be the leader of resistance in Hanoi." But soft-liner Richard Stratton also praised Stockdale as an intelligent "hard-liner" who "gradually accepted Stratton's method of resistance and was himself, in turn, assailed for weakness by some of his fellow officers in the prison system."[2] Stockdale's own history was remarkably varied. As an Annapolis graduate and a carrier air group commander, Stockdale was one of the Navy's elite. But he had also done graduate work at Stanford, and his fondness for the humanities led this "amateur student of philosophy" to close his returning remarks with a quotation—"Nothing is so sweet as to return from the sea and listen to the raindrops on the roofs of home"—which the *New York Times* credited to "an unknown Greek poet," but which Stockdale himself identifed as Sophocles.[3] As a Hanoi SRO, his actions often reflected his training in law, history, and ethics. Whether composing those pragmatic guidelines known as BACK US, or developing resistance strategies for the entire community, Stockdale self-consciously functioned as a Platonic philosopher and warrior king. And though rank may have granted him his authority, he struggled to prove worthy of the POWs' trust.

Jim Stockdale's meditations on captivity have extended far beyond his own experience in Hanoi. He has published two books. At well over 450 pages, *In Love and War: The Story of a Family's Ordeal and Sacrifice During the Vietnam Years* is one of the longest POW memoirs, and one of the most distinctive, since Sybil Stockdale's chapters on her own battles as a founder of the League of Families comprise as complete a memoir as

Jim's. His second book, *A Vietnam Experience: Ten Years of Reflection* is a selection of essays and addresses which catch "the essence" of his thoughts.[4] Significantly, both books appeared in 1984. Though busy with teaching, lecturing, and administrative duties—he was the president of the Naval War College, and then briefly the president of the Citadel, before becoming a Hoover Institute research fellow and a philosophy lecturer at Stanford—Stockdale was not someone who would have rushed into print anyway. An aphoristic writer who found "tempering" the best metaphor for moral progress under stress, he was no friend of blind obedience or knee-jerk political and religious orthodoxy. As a POW and writer, however, he accepted the challenge of reconciling appeals to God, Country, and Duty with the facts of Hanoi captivity.

Some have found this task a dishonest one. A letter responding to a *New York Times* op-ed piece about how valuable Stockdale had found his training in philosophy declared "there must be something wrong with a philosophy, no matter how beautifully described, which enables a man to come to terms with raining bombs on innocent civilians—and to emerge with his 'self-respect' intact."[5] But Stockdale himself knew very well the difficulties involved in looking for meaning or value in the experience of those Americans held captive during the national disaster that was the Vietnam War: the search has in fact been his principal reason for writing. What other POWs took on faith or accepted as their duty, he struggled to place on some rational or ethical ground. As a student of history, he knew how narratives, laws, orders, and pacts have always helped challenged individuals to endure. And finally, his tenacity at ferreting out the universal principles for his actions and beliefs has made him the most articulate and informative POW on what the official story could supposedly teach Americans who would never enter an enemy's cell.

The Making of a Philosopher Warrior

Sybil Stockdale's "favorite fantasy" as a child "was that I was really a royal princess, and that a handsome prince had already been chosen as my future husband." Her dream came true, for Jim Stockdale was one of the Navy's "princes of the realm, the blood royal."[6] This distinctively American oxymoron of republican royalty rests on an ideal of simultaneous equality and excellence. Stockdale found this "dynamic tension" in his parents: "I don't mean friction; I mean a permanence through stabilized stress, almost like the old Greek concept of unity through opposing forces." For this reason, listing his parents' differences "in temperament, in background, in likes and dislikes, in education," begins Stockdale's self-portrait.[7] Vernon Stockdale left school at sixteen to care for his parents and sister. At twenty he became the timekeeper for a bathroom fixtures company in Abingdon, Illinois, where except for two years in the Navy, he worked until he retired. The Navy had been important to Vernon—it "was freedom, it was his first look at the big wide world, it was his 'college' "—and it became the future he wanted for Jim: "From the time of my first memories, there had been no question about it: I would be going to Annapolis to make a career in the navy dad loved so much." On the night before Jim entered the academy, when Vernon proudly told his son that "I want you to try your best to be the best man in that hall," an American success story spanning two generations was thus complete.[8]

His mother's equally heartfelt remark—"You must not humiliate us"—reveals the nature of Jim's other formative influence. Vernon was a working man, at home with the crew. Mabel Stockdale measured success by how far one rose above the common or vulgar. She came by her attitudes honestly. Though Vernon became her "hometown beau" when she was twenty-one, she did not feel free to marry until her father, who "didn't consider Stock good enough for his well-educated daughter," died nine years later.[9] Well educated she was. The family had moved to Abingdon so the children could attend Hedding College, where Mabel received her B.A. in English and history. After a year's graduate work in Chicago, she taught in New Mexico and Montana before returning to Abingdon. Though extremely happy in her marriage, this English, drama, and public speaking teacher with a love for Shakespeare and Latin and German poetry still impressed upon her son the value of higher education and culture.

These greater goods came at a cost. "My childhood was never carefree or even particularly happy," Stockdale recalled, "because from my earliest memories I was always behind, always had debts to pay." Jim grew up knowing he must excel—"excel across the board in studies, music, oration, drama, athletics. From the time I entered the first grade, an inner voice periodically said to me: 'To dope off, to just smell the flowers, is a waste, is lazy, is inconsiderate of your parents, and must be paid for with conscience-stricken remorse.' " Although Vernon's obsessively hard work during the Depression fueled Jim's "awful drive, that tough-minded determination never to be put down," his mother's values tended to dominate. Even school meals showed her pride—"when the blizzards came and everybody took a lunch box, I had to take one fully equipped with napkins and silverware"—and winning a major music competition and performing superbly in a play were the only two accomplishments which Jim felt "really scored" with Mabel Stockdale. Not surprisingly, then, Jim's own "awful drive" was to succeed in the eyes of both parents. Though he excelled academically and artistically, he worried about being seen as that "chubby little mama's boy who was always at the top of the honor roll but unable to fight his way out of a paper bag." To prove he "was as tough inside as the next kid," on school competition days "the spoiled little rich boy" would play his piano or violin selection, then dash off to the track meet. Though short and slight, Jim also insisted on playing football— another of Vernon's loves—and in a direct challenge to Mabel, he worked one summer as a "beast of burden" at his father's plant.[10] From an early age, then, Stockdale set out to embody that "dynamic tension" which enriched his parents' marriage. While he loved learning and high culture, and met his mother's demands for excellence, his father's work ethic and common touch kept Jim from drifting into intellectual elitism.

History helped keep these forces in balance. His parents had lived through World War I, and Jim spent most of World War II at the Naval Academy. Both conflicts enjoyed widespread popular support, and Mabel Stockdale went along with Annapolis for Jim because it represented the highest level of military excellence at a time when all men served. Military success, however, never "scored" with Mabel, and after the war she started applying pressure. "Jim's mother was upset" in 1949, Sybil Stockdale recalled, "because he'd applied for flight training at Pensacola. She talked him into applying for a Rhodes scholarship where he'd be safer. She wasn't too happy with me for not opposing the flight-training idea; she wanted me to help her influence him to become a lawyer."[11] Mabel's reasoning here seems fairly transparent—except during a national emergency, Jim should not waste his talents in the limited sphere of military service—and in his writings Stockdale responds to this disapproval by insisting that his love for humanistic learning had been crucial to his success as a POW leader.

Jim Stockdale's military career showed clear signs of his mother's challenge. One set of postings mapped out the rise of an elite aviator. After learning to fly at Naval Air Training Command, he passed through aircraft carrier training, and mastered jets at the Test Pilot School at Patuxent River. Time as a flight instructor and a stint at Survival School led to a tour in a fighter squadron. Then, after a "sabbatical" at Stanford, he served in Vietnam as a fighter squadron commander on the aircraft carrier *Ticonderoga,* where he figured prominently in August 1964's Tonkin Gulf incident. In 1965, he reached "the apex of every naval aviator's flying career" by becoming the carrier air group commander (CAG) on the *U.S.S. Oriskany,* "sometimes referred to as the 'Big Risk.'"[12] As an aviator and officer, then, Stockdale's career ticket had all the right punches. During this steady rise, however, he kept track of his intellectual needs. His Stanford "sabbatical" was crucial, as in mid-career, he entered a two-year M.A. program approved as training for a future posting "in strategy, plans, and policy in the Navy Department." Courses in economics and comparative Marxist thought and a thesis on Southeast Asia gave Stockdale a knowledge of Vietnam and Communist ideology that few POWs, or even few camp officials, could match: "I felt ten feet tall, even when forced to kneel before that irate political cadre. I could look him in the eye and quietly tell him: 'Lenin didn't say that. You're a deviationist.' "[13] He also studied "brainwashing" in the Korean War POW camps, which gave him a valuable perspective on the Code, and he fell deeply in love with philosophy. So much did Stockdale enjoy Stanford that he asked the Navy for permission to complete a doctorate. The answer forced him to make the most important decision of his life: "I could go up the operational aviation command chain or go for a Ph.D. and become a specialist, but not both."[14] The choice threatened to rip him in half. Though excellence would always be the goal, he now had to bear in either his mother's or his father's direction.

World events, this time in Southeast Asia, left him with one choice. The Vietnam War was starting, and Stockdale "could never have lived with myself knowing that I had dodged the ultimate challenges of what I had spent my life preparing for: I had to take command of that air group." He returned to active duty, however, determined that his humanities training would direct his extremely technical and practical life. Plato and Dostoyevsky would go with him on air assaults, and still later Marxist ideology and Arthur Koestler would help him compose POW rules in Hanoi. This ambition was hardly a new one—philosopher warriors and kings ruled in Plato's *Republic*—and on shipboard, Stockdale happily developed a reputation as a commander with balls *and* brains. Since his first two names actually were James Bond, he used "Double-O-Seven" as his voice call, and the sailors "painted '007' on 'my' plane in every squadron, and on all of their tow tractors, starting jeeps, forklifts, and crash cranes." At the same time, though, he "posed as a sort of absent-minded professor and made a joke about my not being able to keep up with all the changes that were being installed out there on the ship by the week."[15]

This blend of secret agent and quirky academic impressed POWs like Robinson Risner, who described Stockdale in a way he would have liked: "He had a shock of iron-gray hair falling down over one eye, which gave him a remarkable likeness to the writer Carl Sandburg. He loved philosophy and intrigue and was an outstanding leader—one of my dearest friends." Jim Mulligan also noted the same curious union of strengths:

> He had a brilliant mind, and was liberally educated. He was the antithesis of the military mind stereotype I had grown accustomed to serving with. Stockdale was a striver. I was convinced that he had the abilities needed and would push himself to the utmost to reach the top. I was also convinced that Jim Stockdale was a fighter who would always find a way to come out a winner, even in Hanoi. He was a first class intellectual superior to any one else I knew in military service.[16]

Stockdale himself credited the entire range of his education for his success. The Naval Academy had continued that "familiarization with pain" which began with high school football—"you have to practice hurting. There's no question about it"—and had taught him in plebe year how "to take a bunch of junk and accept it with a sense of humor." Stanford, however, had not only been "a major force in molding my own personality as a leader," but had also prepared him better "for being a prisoner of war than did the traditional survival and evasion training." At times the least admirable skill proved the most valuable. When tortured into writing something, Stockdale found that "graduate school was the best of all preparations for this life of 'fire and fall back,' 'cross and double-cross.' I went after that paper as if it were a bluebook in an international-law exam and started cranking out the bullshit."[17] Humanities training also left him wary of chapter-and-verse approaches to military operations. He enjoyed most assignments that demanded ingenuity and creativity—night landings on an aircraft carrier, for instance:

> What a joy to be alive and to perform so effortlessly the arabesques of maneuver I'd worked so long and hard to perfect. It was no longer a matter of memorized procedures and geometric designs; it was free-form art, intuition over reason, with only the utilitarian aim of getting to that carrier's ramp, lined up, on speed, ready to go into the arresting wires with as much fuel remaining as I could keep in the tanks.

Off the Vietnam coast in 1964, Stockdale enjoyed a "life of change and flexibility," and he thanked "Providence for the totally unexpected joy of having command during a period of such instability that I could do damned near anything I wanted to—provided the squadron delivered under pressure."[18]

An irony pervades these words, however, since Stockdale at that time played a key role in the event which dragged pilots back under "the 'by-the-numbers' rules of the navy." With the Tonkin Gulf incident, "civilian override of recommendations of on-scene military commanders," in Stockdale's opinion the Vietnam War's fatal flaw, "came into full sway" even though "its pitfalls were most dramatically demonstrated on August 4, 1964." When the destroyers *Maddox* and *Turner Joy* reported themselves under attack that night, he flew out to provide air support. Two days before, when the *Maddox* had skirmished with some boats, Stockdale had led the air attack. On August 4th, he spent a confusing and dangerous night firing at invisible targets radioed up from the *Maddox*. When he read through a transcript of the destroyer's communications after returning to his ship, Stockdale concluded that "spooked operators and spooked equipment" had been the enemy. The only consolation therefore to be taken from this "Chinese fire drill" was that "at least there's a commodore up there in the Gulf who has the guts to blow the whistle on a screw-up, and take the heat to set the record straight." Within hours, though, an astonished Stockdale was leading a reprisal bombing raid for this imaginary attack. The White House had ignored the whistle—and by announcing that America would hit North Vietnamese targets *before* Stockdale took off, President Johnson also endangered his own troops. Magazine stories about the night of August 4th raised Stockdale's suspicions about the American media as well. *Time* reported that two of six Russian-built vessels sank; *Life* put the American boats under continuous torpedo fire. Though *Newsweek* admitted it didn't know how many enemy boats there were, it claimed that one definitely went down, and torpedoes missed the U.S. destroyers by only 100 feet. A shipboard visit from two Defense Department officials on August 11, four days after Congress had passed the Tonkin Gulf Resolution, worried Stockdale most of all. After some hemming and hawing, one man confessed, "We were sent out here just to find out one thing: Were there any fuckin' boats out there the other night or not?" For Stockdale, "That said it all." He knew "what was to come: Washington's second thoughts, the guilt, the remorse, the tentativeness, the changes of heart, the backout"—and with this backout, "a generation of young Americans would get left holding the bag."[19]

Books like Neil Sheehan's *A Bright Shining Lie* and David Hackworth's *About Face* tell the stories of military men whose combat abilities were matched only by their contempt for those responsible for the Vietnam disaster. Stockdale also separates the acts of true warriors from the bureaucratic fumblings in Washington. Before the Tonkin Gulf incident, "I'd seen myself as a shield of protection between my pilots and the North Vietnamese; now I saw myself as a shield of protection between my pilots and McNamara's Pentagon whiz kids." His leadership strategy changed. Group unity and technical execution became the only virtues. Stockdale didn't hold patriotic pep rallies—partly because "things like that just aren't done in elite fighting groups," but also because he refused to deliver "a very odd speech that would extol an obstructionist bureaucracy, and that's what *government* was beginning to mean to me." Stockdale himself was pessimistic. Though his Southeast Asian studies had led him to conclude that the "tinderbox situation" in Vietnam would have meant "war in due course anyway," his philosophy training made him believe in the notion of the just war, and as "one of the few men in the world who really understood the enormity" of the retaliatory attacks, he was horrified that "we were about to launch a war under false pretenses, in the face of the on-scene military commander's advice to the contrary." Stockdale decided not to tell his pilots about "the Tonkin mess," since "it would never do to disillusion those wonderful young men of mine with the real truth of that story."[20] His own respect for truth however led him to share his version of August 4, 1964, with some friends before returning to Vietnam in 1965. What he knew made him very apprehensive about capture: "If my captors had read my name in most any American newspaper of a year ago after the Tonkin Gulf episodes, the simple confession they might be able to torture out of me would be the biggest Communist propaganda scoop of the decade: 'American Congress Commits to War in Vietnam on the Basis of an Event that Did Not Happen.' " It was hardly surprising, then, that during his first days of captivity, Jim Stockdale dreamed of telling a friend that "we're doing it all wrong over here in this war and we're going to get into a lot of trouble."[21]

Rage and Calculation—The Processing of James Stockdale

Since the Camp Authority replaced the bureaucrats as his immediate concern, in some ways captivity was simpler for Stockdale—simpler, but not simplistic, for he seldom made the racial or ideological jabs other POWs were fond of. Like John Dramesi, Stockdale felt that assuming superiority over his captors would endanger POW resistance. Respect kept you wary and sharp, as his fantasy of standing at Ho Chi Minh's deathbed suggests: "What would I say? 'You old son of a bitch'? No, I'd probably say something like 'Goodbye, you old bastard. You know how this game is played. You didn't snivel—*and neither will I!*' " The Camp Authority's bureaucratic attitudes were however no more attractive than they were in American officials. Submission was his interrogators' goal. They boasted to other POWs they would make a "domestic animal" out of Stockdale, and the furious interrogator who yanked him from Alcatraz in January 1969 wanted "to know only one thing. Will you be my slave or not?" Stockdale's processing and his reactions followed the common pattern. When torture forced Stockdale to produce the required letters, tapes, and confessions, he "felt guilty at my failure to do better in the ropes, and fear of swift and severe retribution." He also looked forward to "a life of continuous shame without friends or self-respect," and an eventual "return to America that would disgrace my family, my hometown, and my service." That the information was extorted simply for bureaucratic purposes only made matters worse. Everyone involved knew that "My Secret Report on the Defenses of My Ship," "My Secret Report on Aircraft Tactics over the Target," and "My Secret Report on All the Targets I've Struck" were all worthless, but obedience, not information, was the Camp Authority's goal. After looking up the word, one official even agreed that he was assembling a "blackmail" package, complete with undated letters and tapes describing Stockdale's physical condition as poor, in case the Camp Authority ever decided "to give me the ax."[22]

Stockdale launched two attacks on this fill-in-the-blanks mentality. The first involved throwing wrenches into the procedures; offering "helpful" hints, for instance, about the American command chain, which led his interrogators into accepting and misdirecting some patently ridiculous letters. His second strategy, deliberately erratic behavior, was designed to make him look like a bad propaganda risk. His moment of revelation came in May 1966. When told to get ready for a press conference, Stockdale blew up. Ranting and raving, he shook his fists and threw papers around: "I didn't care. What had I to lose? Better to go down in flames *here* than drag my country through the muck in front of the whole world." The Camp Authority's response to this outburst changed his understanding of captivity forever: "Cat's face showed real panic; my mental snapshot of his distorted face became the most valuable icon I was to acquire that first year. That guy was actually in trouble! He was really worried. The hierarchy had stuck him with a pop-up requirement, he had gotten a late start, and I had turned into a wild-eyed erratic lunatic." Stockdale now knew that processing, not conversion, was his captors' goal. Like the U.S. paper-pushers behind the Tonkin Gulf incident, these camp officials "are not ideologues so much as they are just ambitious bureaucrats," and therefore turned on "the axle of chain-of-command bureaucracy, the axle of careerism." Since a POW with "a subtly unstable personality" would be such a career functionary's last choice for public display, this discovery left Stockdale awestruck: "Wow, are there lessons in all this! What's that old crap I used to hear about how military officers should maintain their bearing, remain calm and courteous, and project personal dignity, no matter what? By holding to that ethic, you automatically volunteer to have a ring put in your nose and be led downtown to be slaughtered at a Communist press conference." At this moment, Stockdale realized that the "indispensible attributes" for a POW were "not only tough-mindedness and physical courage, but skill in the dramatic arts as well"—the skill his mother had earnestly cultivated—and this lesson learned, he began charting out an elliptical path through captivity.[23] His strategy was both successful and satisfying. "Now I want you to know I'm through with you," Rabbit told him, "I hate you. All we have been doing is just furnishing you a stage on which to perform. You are the world's greatest actor. And you love it!" Stockdale agreed: "I had become a good actor. That was the only way to stay even with these bastards, and I *was* loving it."[24]

This faith in unpredictability also left Stockdale with little sympathy for raging, bigoted ideologues, or cunning careerists on his own side. Neither Alcatraz, nor solitary, nor the ropes depressed him as much as the time he spent in a cell with "Lieutenant Colonel John Doe." Though no collaborator, Doe felt the Camp Authority was "omniscient" and "omnipotent." Because he believed "the only way to keep these Communist bastards away from you is to live like a totally silent mouse," he told Stockdale that "if you communicate, I guarantee you I'll screw you in the end." Stockdale concluded this apparent cowardice actually masked a rage aimed at anyone, friend or foe, whom Doe found threatening. "There was no doubt that he hated the North Vietnamese," but what really drove Doe was a right-wing, vitriolic, and racist anger at being an American under an Asian Marxist's control: "He pressed his obsession with destroying communism to the point that I got the idea he thought 'having it way down here' for ultra-right causes could somehow make up for his revulsion to being slapped around when one-on-one with a tough commissar." Clearly, the cellmates "were at opposite philosophical poles," but even though Doe's "thought processes disgusted" Stockdale, he still tried to reach him through an analogy: "You're a big Las Vegas gambler—when you go up to that crap table, do you set about to *hate* the croupier? No, you've got to mousetrap him, and keep your mind clear, free of hate, if you're going to win. Same thing here with Communists. Think of ways to skin those sons of bitches alive, but don't hobble yourself emotionally by going around all choked up in a seething ideological rage all the time." Doe however was unreachable, and when Stockdale managed to contact other POWs briefly, he said he was "locked up with a psycho"—"there was no other quick, clear, truthful way to say it." Even so, this entire experience was "a quagmire of moral dilemmas" that Stockdale "never felt comfortable with": "Maybe I had been too nice to Doe. Should I have just forced myself to ignore him and joined the covert communication system the first week? In hindsight, we would have been split up immediately, and both been better off. But what about Unity over Self?"[25]

Since the second enemy to POW unity, the amoral careerist, was flawed before captivity, and since his actions were unswervingly self-interested, he posed an even greater danger to POWs like Stockdale who believed that a society resting upon personal advancement rather than ethical absolutes was a fool's and cynic's playground. The debates over escape and the actions of one particular POW were Stockdale's cautionary examples of what self-serving attitudes led to. Like John Dramesi, Stockdale felt that a POW's early feelings about escape often foreshadowed his later levels of resistance. In a 1980 essay, he described the escape debate as a clash between value systems. The pro-escape POWs were the "romantics or idealists," who asked "people to accept risks and to pay costs in support of an *idea*." The anti-escape POWs were "the profit-and-loss guys, the bottom-line guys, the efficiency worshipers—the systems analysts, if you will," who always asked, "What's in it for me?" As self-proclaimed "leader of the romantics," Stockdale blamed the small number of escape attempts on "a faint-hearted colonel" whose profit/loss methods for dealing with matters of honor "pushed two years' work down the drain."[26] In another place, Stockdale even uses Dramesi's favorite image to make a related point: "Winning consisted of establishing a credibility of defiance that precluded the enemy's leading the captive around like a placid bull with a ring in his nose."[27] Stockdale explores the personal consequences of careerism through his portrait of a "handsome, smart, articulate, and smooth" POW who was also "almost sincere," "obsessed with success," and "a classical opportunist." This man's tragic flaw was his inability to stand firm: "When the going got tough, he decided expediency was preferable to principle." For this reason, this POW willingly made radio tapes and accepted privileges during the bad times, but returned to the POW fold when conditions improved and release seemed certain. This reunion was hardly a successful one: "You can sit and think anything you want," Stockdale declared, "but when you insensitively cut down those who want to love and help you, you cross a line. He seemed to sense that he could never truly be one of us." A pitiful, contemptible figure, "the tragedy of his life was obvious to us all," and when this man died "in an accident that strongly resembled suicide," shortly after Operation Homecoming, Stockdale reports that "tears were shed by some of his old prison mates" at the waste.[28]

This moralistic tone appears whenever Stockdale's subject is careerism. He blamed American "corporate life, board life, hierarchical life" for infecting some POWs with "that slide to accommodation we are told is necessary to get something accomplished, and that invitation to moral weakness." The Camp Authority deftly attacked this Achilles' heel: "Step one is getting the American prisoner to make a deal, a reasonable deal; *any* deal will do for a start. From my own experience I can state that a Prisoner Interrogator's Handbook would list among suggested openers, 'Let us reason together,' 'You Americans are a sensible, pragmatic people; meet us halfway.' " When a POW resisted, he was therefore pitting ethics against business, values against technology, justice against litigation, and leadership against management. Stockdale saw his own captivity as a gleaning of ethical wheat from careerist chaff—"The values were there, but they were all mixed up with technology, bureaucracy, and expediency, and had to be brought up into the open." As a result, he became a bitter enemy of all managerial approaches to leadership. "It's obvious by now that I'm tired of being told that national policy decisions must be restricted to a bottom-line process, and that honor and idealism have to be checked at the door," he wrote in 1980, "I think that's wrong from a moral standpoint, and it's particularly wrong now if we are to keep the public ethos and public policy out of conflict." The same "idealistic" arguments fueled his 1981 attack on an enticement system for encouraging national service. The "marketplace business ethic" which tried to bribe new recruits with money, educational training, or choice of duty station dangerously downplayed those ethical imperatives of "duty, honor, and country" which were "the true meaning of service."[29]

The same fear that a "Madison Avenue mentality is aiming us toward that bifurcated society of fighting fools and thinking cowards" also drove Stockdale's 1982 essay, "Military Ethic Is Not at Home with Business Values," which argued that "successful management, company and personal profit, and rational self-interest" can never replace the military values of "loyalty, obedience and courage." This management model had doomed America's Southeast Asia operation as early as 1961, "when Defense Secretary Robert Strange McNamara and his Whiz Kids took over the Department of Defense" and tried "to manipulate rather than fight the Vietnam War" almost "as if it were the Ford Motor Company with a knock in the engine and an unfavorable balance sheet." By asking, "How can we do it?" rather than "Should we do it, and will we persevere?" these functionaries ensured disaster. Though applying "rational management principles to planning and waging a war" was obviously necessary, because "war is an irrational undertaking and there are no tenets of rationality to which all men subscribe," the "strategists, the analysts, and the tacticians" proceeded "on incomplete if not erroneous assumptions about the nature of man and the nature of war." He delivered the same message to a meeting of the Armed Forces Communications and Electronics Association. Though the POWs "were in a position where we knew more about how to run a prison organization than anybody else in the world," too much faith in "systems" or "lines of authority" had paralyzed officers who were "ill at ease" because they couldn't "touch base with headquarters." Since in Hanoi the American handyman had often outwitted the Vietnamese engineer, Stockdale concluded that "we complicate matters by always looking for a perfect system. A perfect system serves an idiot—it is bound to be too complex. I think there is a lot of wisdom in old Admiral Gorshkov's maxim that 'the best is the enemy of the good enough.' "[30]

At his most expansive, Stockdale denounced these tendencies as signs of an ethical malaise which threatened America itself. He welcomed Aleksandr Solzhenitsyn's Harvard commencement address, with its harsh attacks on "the insidiousness of creeping legalism" and the resulting "mutation of ethics." Stockdale agreed with his fellow longtime prisoner of a totalitarian regime that "legality" and "regulations" bore no necessary relation to good and evil. He also feared a slide toward "laws, courts, regulations" and "conformity to specified rules of conduct," since it could only weaken our "moral obligation to ourselves, to our service, to our country." Stockdale was especially revolted, however, with how this slide had spawned military officers who lived by "fads and buzzwords," traded "checkoff lists for common sense," and worshipped "error avoidance and careerism." Laboring "far from the canons of ethics and decency," by groveling before the "administrative bodies" controlling salary and advancement, such officers were "amoral gnomes lost in narrow orbits" and "relativists without any defined moral orientation."[31] Captivity therefore profoundly convinced Jim Stockdale that a person's ethical orientation placed him on one side or another of an unbridgeable gap between integrity and duplicity, honor and shame.

Going through Channels—The Processing of Sybil Stockdale

One further reason for Stockdale's disgust with functionaries was perhaps his intimate knowledge of how the U.S. government had handled the POW issue. This came from his wife, Sybil, whose own battles with government bureaucrats, the military hierarchy, and the American media as she tried to protect Jim's interests were almost as horrifying as his own. Though she eagerly read a marriage manual called *The Navy Wife* as a newlywed, like her husband, Sybil Stockdale was something of an anomaly. Her childhood had also featured strong contrasts. Her father's dairy made farm work second nature to her, but Sybil lived for her tap dancing and ballet lessons: "If I'd had long legs and a liberated mother, I think I might have become a Rockette." When Sybil was accepted into Mount Holyoke College, her "mother was more thrilled than I. She had always wanted to go there but because of the expense had to settle for Normal School, the local teachers' college." Sybil also went to Stanford before Jim, receiving her M.A. in education in 1959, and she taught both before and after his shootdown. Since "Navy tradition dictated that, as the wife of the commanding officer of a fighter squadron, I should guide and help the younger wives," Jim's promotions brought Sybil more duties as well. She welcomed the responsibility: "I'd been a Navy Relief volunteer for years and an officer in numerous wives' organizations. I liked being president best because it seemed easier to me just to be in charge of everything while others did the hard jobs."[32] In hindsight, then, it seems perfectly natural that Sybil Stockdale would organize the wives under her husband's Hanoi command.

Given the POW wives' initial experience with the military and government, such leadership was essential. Four months before Jim's shootdown, Sybil attended an "unusual event": a meeting for wives which "gave guidelines about how to conduct yourself if your husband was shot down and taken prisoner in Vietnam."[33] These rules were basically a Wives' Code of Conduct: don't talk to strangers, don't tell anyone but relatives your husband is a captive, don't comment on any information the North Vietnamese might release, don't use endearments when writing, and above all, don't intercede in any way on his behalf. Right after Jim's capture, Sybil was the obedient Navy wife, but as she encountered the same kind of bureaucracy that had botched the Tonkin Gulf incident, her trust wavered. The Navy's "by-the-book" answers to her finance questions meant that she could not learn right away whether she would continue to receive Jim's pay. Though "completely disappointed by the incompetence of the system," she tried to remain patient, but as the mortgage payment neared, she lost her temper and "screeched" at some functionary. Her answer came in two hours. Equally appalling foul-ups soon followed. In 1966, Sybil learned that she couldn't join a savings plan for military currently in a combat zone because the bill's drafters had forgotten about the POWs. Even worse, in late 1967 a letter arrived from the Navy Bureau of Personnel, informing Jim, now in his third year of captivity, that he had been selected for deep draft command. Sybil's reaction set her agenda for the future: "How could they possibly be so incredibly screwed up? Wasn't there any system of coordination? What could I do to impress upon them that Jim was in prison in Vietnam, being tortured?"[34]

In-service rivalries and condescension to dependents also disgusted Sybil. A full calendar was the official excuse when Sybil's request as head of the League of Wives for a meeting with the newly elected Richard Nixon was turned down. A friend however set her straight: "The military aide to the president is an air-force general and he's not about to have a navy wife see the president unless an air-force wife is there too."[35] Thanks to a grimly humorous 1967 luncheon with Admiral Moorer, the new chief of naval operations, Sybil was already familiar with such jockeying. Mrs. Moorer and Admiral Semmes, the officer Sybil held responsible for the Navy's "rotten job" on POW matters, were also present as she read out a list of indignities which POW dependents had suffered. One wife "was told she was lucky to be getting her husband's pay, because he wasn't doing what he'd been sent to do"; on a more personal note, Sybil described how "sloppy bungling" had endangered Jim's covert communications. She ended by asking "if there was any one officer who was in charge of prisoner affairs to the extent that his career would be damaged if he made life-threatening mistakes." The meal that followed only sharpened her point. Though happy with a "lovely-looking cold plate," Sybil couldn't help but notice that everyone else was served "hot sirloin tips and gravy, mashed potatoes, and creamed peas." (She also noticed how disgusted the Admiral's wife was—"I guessed Admiral Moorer would hear more about this luncheon.") The "smooth-talking" Admiral Semmes was less perceptive. When he blithely tried to buy Sybil off with a job as civilian liaison to Navy wives, she was so "genuinely enraged that he still didn't understand the depth of my disillusionment and dismay" that for the first time she said "exactly what I believed, without any reservation" to a high-ranking official: "Bluntly, I told him that if I told others like myself about his performance, they'd be more inclined to jump out the window than leave feeling better."[36]

This was an important moment. Though she never renounced the military or government, Sybil Stockdale declared here that she would not obediently defer to authority. Over the years, she skirmished with a number of pompous top brass. In January 1972, for instance, when an "air force general at the western White House who thinks he's God Almighty" blasted her over the phone for accusing the president's staffers of watering down a Nixon statement on the POWs, Sybil told her mother she was "surprised" she hadn't lost her own temper with this "incredibly rude" official. Sometime later, when this same official tried to bribe her with a ride to Washington on a White House plane, she told his secretary "that Mrs. Stockdale does not care to ride anywhere with General Hughes." In May 1970, Sybil had also fended off some retired military men's sexist and profit-oriented attempts to take over the league: "They would set themselves up as its paid officers in downtown Washington offices. We wives would be allowed to come in and lick envelopes or open mail." Things fell into confusion as she strung out the agenda at the league's annual meeting. Only when the apparent scatterbrain suddenly announced that time was up did "the pitchman for the take-over plan" realize that "he'd been had."[37]

These military troubles were nothing, however, when compared to Sybil's problems with civilians. Politicians ignored, avoided, or patronized her for years. Everett Dirksen, the Republican senator from Jim's home state, solemnly told her that the military had free rein to conduct the war, but he later signed a letter to Mabel Stockdale which claimed

Sybil had asked about Jim's release. Sybil was insulted: "Senator Dirksen's letter made me sound cheap and shallow. Why hadn't he written Jim's mom about what we really discussed?" Democrats, however, were generally worse. In 1970, Allard Lowenstein, a onetime Stanford faculty member and antiwar congressman, agreed to meet Sybil in the Los Angeles airport. During a fifteen-minute runaround, Sybil barely got in a word as Lowenstein babbled on about bipartisan congressional committees. After he dismissed her—"His office would be in touch with me. Sorry he had to run. 'Duty calls' "—Sybil could only be "glad Jim didn't know how his great friend had just behaved." What truly infuriated her, however, was the Johnson State Department's benign neglect. In May 1966, Sybil was still in awe of government officials, and she felt her heart pounding during her meeting with an assistant of Averell Harriman, "ambassador-at-large" for POW issues. In July, she barely restrained her anger when Harriman himself admitted he didn't know what the Pentagon was doing about the POWs and their families, thus making a mockery of his assistant's claims "that everything possible was being done to ensure that our men were well-treated, but unfortunately these things couldn't be talked about." One year later, Sybil's awe of Washington had faded, but when she "sharpened the tone of my questions," Harriman "didn't appear to pay any attention. It was almost as if he were giving a monologue. I left feeling frustrated and depressed."[38]

Sybil was especially upset because she knew Harriman had firsthand reports about POW torture. Jim himself had smuggled this information out in his letters to Sybil. This awareness accounted for her bitter response to a 1967 State Department "white paper" on POW treatment: " 'We reluctantly come to the conclusion that some of the US airmen were being subjected to emotional and physical duress, which is a flagrant violation of the Geneva Convention.' I supposed it would be too ungentlemanly to use the words *torture*, or *leg irons*, or *handcuffs*. Besides, we wouldn't want to upset the American people." Years of study had also made her "cynical and sarcastic" at times. Within days of Jim's shoot-down she was reading "every item about Vietnam in the newspapers and magazines," and memorizing "the provisions of the Geneva Convention Relative to the Treatment of Prisoners of War." The summer of 1968 was her POW university. She "pored over *The Prisoners of Korea, The Road to Calumny, In Every War But One, In the Presence of Mine Enemies,* and many more books and articles of a similar nature." As a result the pompous telegram she received from Harriman when she went public with her cause only confirmed her decision: "No, Ambassador Harriman, I thought when I finished reading this message, I'm not sure I do realize the welfare of the men is uppermost in your mind; nor do I think you, of all people in this world, should be advocating early releases, which are a violation of the Code of Conduct."[39] The more congenial Nixon team also learned how strong she could be. In January 1971, Henry Kissinger skipped a meeting with a league delegation, sending his assistant, Alexander Haig, instead. After hearing the "long, familiar line about how concerned everyone was about our situation," in a voice that "shook with rage," Sybil declared that "we don't want to wait two months to see Dr. Kissinger, General Haig. We want to see him in two days. We'll still be here on Monday, and if he cares about our men, he'll somehow make the time to see us. We're tired of being put off. Do you understand what we're saying? Are we communicating with you?" Kissinger showed up—and a good thing, for "if he had put us off, it would have meant a declaration of war between us and the White House."[40]

Encounters like this one explain why Sybil stayed true to "my Jim's navy"; in fact, her contacts with civilian officials were often at the Navy's request. The Pentagon had requested her to meet with Harriman, and Naval intelligence officer Bob Boroughs "then asked if I'd go over to the State Department and ask them what they were doing about our men being held in Hanoi." His request left Sybil "a little puzzled," and when Harriman asked, "How are they treating you over at the Pentagon?" she became thoroughly bewildered: "Weren't these people all members of the same government?" But Sybil's own loyalty was clear, as she became one of the military's most reliable sources about the State Department. The degree of her dedication was remarkable. When for instance a State Department official agreed to talk to POW families only if reporters and military officers were barred, though she "had no idea whether this was legal or proper," Sybil agreed when Bob Boroughs asked her "to wear a hidden tape recorder to the meeting and return the tape to him."[41] As early as 1966, she was also helping Naval intelligence turn her letters into perhaps the best code link between Washington and Hanoi. Jim's first two letters were much longer than the six- or seven-line messages POWs were soon confined to, and he seemed to be hinting about camp conditions and other POWs. Sybil helped Navy intelligence officers identify and decode odd statements. Strange references to family friends proved to be information on downed POWs; phrases like "detailed and numerous conversations" suggested "lengthy interrogations" to Sybil; and allusions to Dostoyevsky and Arthur Koestler's *Darkness at Noon* pointed toward solitary and inhumane treatment. Since Jim was obviously trying to establish official contact, Sybil began encoding Navy messages into her own letters. A faked photograph of Jim's mother carried the code, and Sybil's letters were written on an invisible carbon paper which Jim then used to smuggle his own messages out. A single January 1967 letter carried out over forty POWs' names and confirmed "torture, irons, solo."[42] Jim turned another letter into an epic:

> On goes the list of prisoners, starting with the names I've acquired since January 2. Then I write on, explaining that the solar plexus of this war machine is the Hanoi propaganda radio station, the pump-up motivator of the whole country. That *must* be destroyed. I give them my best estimate of where the prison camps are, and I tell them that the main railroad tracks running north and south along the coast are about a mile and a half due east of this place, the Zoo, and that we can hear the trains roll out of Hanoi heading south every night just after dark. I tell them what questions are being asked and what new weapons the Vietnamese are curious about in recent military interrogations of new shootdowns, and so on.[43]

This subterfuge profoundly altered Sybil's sense of contact with Jim. Although she did the actual encoding, the military's "need-to-know" security often meant that "Bob Boroughs wouldn't give me a clue" about what the contents were. This was stressful enough: Sybil encoded her "letters to Jim early in the morning to be as sure as possible I wouldn't make an error that could cause his execution." This covert activity also erected a barrier between husband and wife. Intimate details were masks for messages; sentences were twisted sideways to carry their secret freight. The rush to get Navy information out led Jim to write slapdash "cover" letters: "Blah blah blah blah blah. For God's sake, just keep saying noncontroversial things, platitudes, whatever . . . Poor sweet Syb, what a sketchy, messy letter I had to rush off to you."[44]

Back in America, reading some messages in late 1971 made Sybil realize "once more" just "how little Jim's and my letters had to do with our own communication. They were primarily the product of covert communication with Naval Intelligence. This fact gave them an impersonal aspect that seemed almost unworthy of our love." And yet, although the Stockdales' "personal lives" seemed to be "on hold"—she would not write an uncoded letter until September 1972—Sybil insisted "it was this very covert communication that sustained our morale."[45] This sense of self-sacrifice guided her public actions as well. The left's condemnation of all military activity, including the "illegal" air war most POWs had been waging when captured, hardly made these liberals attractive allies. Nevertheless, her "mission to maintain pressure on the governments in both Washington and Hanoi" made Sybil seek out an interview with Dick Cavett in July 1972 because his audience "was a segment of the population I really wanted to reach": "the young, stay-up-late, idealistic voters most easily taken in by McGovern's impossible-to-fulfill promises." The show's producers were barely interested. Sybil had to pay her own way to New York, and one of Cavett's assistants "warned me the show was not political and I was not to make any political statements" even though "as the show unfolded, it became clear that Dick Cavett would make the political statements and I was to be Mrs. Dumb Dumb Navy Wife who could only sit and wring her hands." Sybil held her own: "When his remarks seemed to me critical of the present administration, I reminded him that Johnson, Rusk, and McNamara had gotten us into this war. . . . I was glad to have told his audience where they could order POW bracelets and not too sorry later to hear that the program had been canceled."[46] Experiences like this one explain why Sybil occasionally served as President Nixon's liaison to the American people on certain Vietnam issues. Both sides benefited from the relationship. Sybil needed information, aid, and political action; Nixon's staff, as a friend told her, knew she could "influence other families." The payoffs could be blatant. The president's first meeting with POW families in December 1969 was immediately followed by a press conference which Sybil rather than the president led. Although very nervous— "I've heard that the Washington press corps is a brutal, mean, and ruthless crowd"—she did so well that the Committee to Re-elect the President had her accept on Nixon's behalf a petition from the Vietnam Veterans Against the War at the 1972 Republican National Convention.[47]

Sybil was of two minds about such actions. Admiral Semmes's attempted bribe had disgusted her, and her familiarity with government incompetence hardly made supporting Richard Nixon a knee-jerk response. But backing the president and the government if at all possible certainly fit best with Jim's values and her own. Sybil and many other Vietnam POW dependents had for instance refused to sit with the wife of the *Pueblo*'s Commander Bucher at a POW wives' meeting because her public attacks had demeaned "her service and her country in the eyes of the world." Her infuriating encounters with North Vietnamese officials also left Sybil more comfortable with the casually racist attitudes of some American officials than Jim might have been. When some Navy men dropped by with the news that Jim had been promoted, but secretly, because "we don't want to give the slant-eyes any reason to watch him any more closely than they already do," Sybil recalled, "How good it was to hear male voices in this house and have the fun of making drinks and exchanging nonsense remarks." For much the same reason, elected officials who drubbed the North Vietnamese made her profoundly grateful. When Congressman Mendel Rivers "made no bones about the fact that the North Vietnamese were barbarians; that our men were living in hell itself; and that if he had his way about it, he'd bomb North Vietnam into the Stone Age," he sounded like Colonel Doe, Jim's "psycho" roommate. After two years of official silence, however, Sybil "was shocked as well as refreshed to hear him shout all these things at the top of his lungs. Almost everyone else patted us on the head, told us to pray and try not to worry, but here was one Washington official who was not afraid to tell the truth about his perceptions." In a 1968 letter to her friends, Sybil's own tough opinions caused her to blast Dr. Benjamin Spock and Eugene McCarthy, and announce her own intention to vote for Nixon. With customary Stockdale candor, Sybil mentioned that her oldest son "felt my ideas were saturated with emotionalism and lacking intellectual reinforcement," and she later realized that "if I was absolutely honest with myself, I probably felt Nixon would bomb the enemy into submission and end the hostilities in a few weeks."[48] In any case, though, Sybil Stockdale was no praying, shrinking victim who just wanted her husband home. She did her duty, chose sides, and fought.

As the numbers of Americans who jumped on the POW bandwagon turned Sybil's last years before Operation Homecoming into as much of an administrative nightmare as her husband's, she marked progress by noting when influential figures joined the cause. A call in late 1968 from Governor Ronald Reagan was "the first time any public official had made an extra effort to help me or gone out of his way to be kind," even though Reagan's call was itself an answer to "an irate telegram" Sybil sent when refused an appointment with the governor. Secretary of Defense Melvin Laird's May 1969 denunciation of the North Vietnamese really turned the tide. "A high official in the Nixon administration was going on the record," and Sybil was ecstatic—"My heart sang during the drive to school, and I smiled that evening as I watched the news." The White House seal of approval soon brought the league some important allies. *Reader's Digest* and other companies provided financial help, "a real sign that we were making progress," and when Senator Robert Dole organized a tribute in Constitution Hall, the guest list contained "Vice-President Spiro Agnew; Senator Barry Goldwater; assorted congressmen; an astronaut; a mayor; movie actor Bob Cummings; the DAR's president general; entrepreneur Ross Perot; assorted POW and MIA wives; et cetera."[49] And yet, like Jim, Sybil struggled to maintain that "dynamic tension" between excellence and equality. Though more highly educated than almost everyone she dealt with, she hated officiousness and condescension, regardless of the source. Her own abilities, like her husband's, made careerism a constant temptation, but she held fast to those values which she felt guided their family life, the military, and America itself, even if many Americans seemed headed in another direction. At their most fervent, then, both Stockdales declared their independence from the cynic, the amoralist, the elitist, and the bureaucrat, standing instead with their family, their fellow sufferers, and their country.

The Philosophy of Imprisonment

Because years of enforced isolation allowed him to piece together a credo of captivity and duty, saying what the Stockdales' experience should mean to other Americans fell largely to Jim. So strong were his leanings toward philosophy that they turned an interrogation into one of his most enjoyable Hanoi experiences. In the spring of 1966, Stockdale sparred with Nguyen Khac Vien, "a name with which I had become familiar through my research in graduate school." A medical doctor and "master Communist propagandist," in the 1950s Vien had organized protests in France against its Vietnam policies. Though "an intellectual of sorts," Vien was above all an ardent cultural nationalist, as his book *Vietnam: A Long History* and his essay on "Historical Background" for the anthology *Vietnamese Literature* both testify to. Stockdale instantly knew he was about "to have my brain picked. He was probably going to write propaganda booklets and had asked to talk to an 'American intellectual' from the dungeons." Stockdale also knew that this battle-scarred revolutionary "was too sophisticated in the ways of Vietnamese prisons to be alarmed" by a filthy and crippled POW. Vien's comments about North Vietnam's "programmed saturation propaganda-bombing of the West" filled Stockdale with "a new feeling of horror": "Our country has not the capability to defeat you on the battlefield. But war is not decided by weapons so much as by

national will. Once the American people understand this war, they will have no interest
in pursuing it. They will be made to understand this. We will win this war on the streets
of New York." Given these comments, why then did Stockdale find his time with Vien
"sheer entertainment"? Stanford provided the answer. Though Vien tried to keep "his
intellectual roots obscure," Stockdale recognized that force which cut through nationality,
race, and ideology—the force of an educated, rational mind. Vien's questions "tracked
right out of a textbook of old-fashioned Western Philosophy I," and "after so long a
drought" Stockdale thrilled "to again talk to somebody who actually knew who Plato
was, someone who could openly smile when I deflected his discussion of the definition
of *justice* to the arguments of the all-night debate about that same subject on Cephalus's
porch in Piraeus 2,400 years before." Method was the common ground: "Vien and I held
opposite views on almost every point raised, but what a charge it was to talk to a man
urbane enough to take a hit when I ridiculed the idea of any sane person comparing
LBJ to Hitler, and then tacitly grant me the point without going into a theatrical rage."
Stockdale in short delighted in this "hour-long verbal Ping Pong game" because similar
debates with camp officials and other POWs were so rare. Nor was this the two opponents'
only affinity. As the POW who worked hardest to set the POWs' captivity within that cluster
of values making up humanistic learning, like Vien, Stockdale was his community's principal
philosopher, ideologist, and propagandist. The Vien-Stockdale encounter was a meeting
between two philosopher-kings—the brains of their bodies politic.[50]

This self-image shapes Stockdale's narrative. Though his knee could jerk as quickly
as anyone's, for instance, he almost always looked for the ethical stimulus behind the
jerk. Take the POWs' political conservatism. In 1979 Stockdale declared that eight years
in Hanoi had produced "the biggest bunch of hawks in the world"; in 1982, he remarked
that "I thought, during the war, after it, and still today, that Barry Goldwater had the
only sensible outlook: either move quickly against Hanoi with repeated high impact
non-nuke hammer blows from the air or forget it." Many POWs of course made similar
remarks, but Stockdale struggled to place this militance within Western philosophy's
long debate over the nature of war. Stockdale believed that America's fundamental error
was its refusal to accept what war actually was. Neither "a crusade, a mistake, a crime
or a conspiracy," the Vietnam War was a "tragedy" which resulted from "a misguided
experiment of the Harvard Business School crowd—the 'whiz kids'—in achieving foreign policy objectives by so-called rational game theory, while ignoring the reality and
obstinacy of human nature."[51] The student of war's history knew better, as Stockdale
demonstrates through references to Will Durant, Baron von Clausewitz, and Alfred
Thayer Mahan, an early president of the Naval War College. Durant once told Stockdale
that human beings were "all mixed up" because "we seem to be working on the assumption that if we're nice to other people they'll be nice to us. I can tell you that in the
last 4000 years there's practically no evidence to support that view." Ethics must therefore
take refuge in the exercise of "power," which Mahan called the force that permits "moral
ideas to take root." Clausewitz was Stockdale's favorite authority on the force that war
unleashes, and the actions which leaders must therefore be ready to carry out. When
Stockdale attacked bureaucrats for not realizing that "while war as political theory may
be perfectly rational, warfare in practice is most decidedly not," he drew his support
from the Baron's remark that "war is a trinity with its rational element being outweighed
two to one by the combined elements of chance ('within which the creative spirit is free
to roam') and blind natural force ('primordial violence, hatred and enmity')." Citations
like this one set Stockdale apart from the other POWs. During the 1972 Christmas

bombings, he stood "with scores of American POWs and cheered while unmistakable commitment was registered as B-52 bombs thundered into military targets all night, night after night in late 1972, and felt the collapse of an enemy's will."[52] Because he was certain that the strength of national will ultimately determined the victor, Stockdale had been horrified by Vien's claim that "we will win this war on the streets of New York." The key to the struggle lay where North Vietnam planned to attack, for as Stockdale later wrote, Napoleon, Pericles, and "forty years in uniform, and particularly that decade of war and life behind enemy lines, have taught me that more than any other factor, military success or failure depends on the moral sentiment, the ethos, the spirit of the man in the street." While other prisoners saw these bombings as a glorious revenge, or even as intimations of the apocalypse, Stockdale thrilled to the Christmas bombings as evidence of that "unmistakable commitment," if only Richard Nixon's, that had been missing from America's actions in Vietnam.[53]

He also welcomed the bombings because they fit within his vision of the Vietnam POW story as an allegory for how rationality, tradition, and civilization will prevail even within the crucible of war. This belief was all the more remarkable for being almost exclusively secular. Though his parents had "both honored the Protestant beliefs of their pioneer mothers," they "almost never attended services" and found "churchiness" amusing and small-minded. When he joined a church as a teenager—largely to meet girls—"that fact was of absolutely no concern at home," and although Sybil describes how her own "strong personal relationship with God" grew during her early married years, Jim and his fellow pilots had faith primarily "in themselves and their aircraft." Because Sybil believed that "there came a time when you could proceed only by having total faith in God's existence and love," she looked carefully at Jim's Hanoi letters for signs of such faith. Nor did Jim disappoint her. "Be assured that above all, I have securely found God," he wrote, and he ended another letter with a confession that "this experience has taught me to love Him completely, and hopefully to better serve Him (and to better serve you all), when I get home." Jim's claims that "God was his roommate," however, seemed designed to comfort Sybil as much as to proclaim a spiritual awakening.[54] Even when he experienced it, Jim's skepticism about the miraculous was very strong. When guards burst into his cell while he was encoding a letter home, for instance, Jim prayed "like I've never prayed before." Suddenly "the face of Christ in the big stained-glass window behind the altar of the Naval Academy chapel" appeared before him, provoking a response that was pure Stockdale: "What is this, a religious experience? I just don't have those. What does it mean? That I'm going down the tubes? That he is 'welcoming me aboard' in heaven?" The answer was neither of the above. Either Divine intervention or sheer luck kept the guards from finding the incriminating evidence lying in front of them. It's significant as well that Jim's Christ was an Annapolis Jesus, given another vision Stockdale had in solitary. When a head seemed to emerge from the cell's brickwork, "To me in that hour of hopelessness, it looked like the back of the bronze head of Tecumseh, the old Indian chief, as seen looking up the sidewalk toward the front steps of Bancroft Hall at the Naval Academy." If anything, this vision inspired Stockdale more, since it reminded him of "how it was to accumulate obligations, all that precious emotional baggage, that self-doubt, that conscience, all those debts to pay"—that duty to family, in short, which he had felt since childhood.[55]

Instead of *Pilgrim's Progress*, then, Stockdale's memoir resembles most those enquiries into truth he found in Plato or Descartes. He thought of his captivity as a grim form of schooling in human nature—what he later described as a "big laboratory experiment":

It is a very expensive experiment, so expensive that even here in America we couldn't afford it. The reason is that the subjects are humans and it takes about 50 of them full time, 24 hours a day, for four years. Now these subjects will be very healthy, college-educated men in their 20s, 30s (some of us even our 40s). Each will be sealed individually in a box ten feet long and four feet wide. They will be prevented from seeing each other throughout the four-year period. They will have no pencil, no paper, no books. They must live in absolute silence. They will be traumatized, or crystallized with an outside threat, and I, as an insider, will take mental notes of what makes them tick. During this four years I will select out five or six general traits, traits that are rather different than you might expect. Now after this experiment, if what I report isn't "information about human nature," what is it?[56]

Stockdale saw "human nature" as most fundamentally an issue of selfhood. Sir Thomas More was "the hero of selfhood," for instance, because More proclaimed "his human right to conscience and dignity" even though it led to his death. Lying "beneath issue-oriented fallouts, and I hope even beneath attitudes," Stockdale found five essential traits in his fellow POWs. These men were "*ritualistic, poetic, fascinated* by *astronomy, numbers*, and *music* (the seven liberal arts were not pulled out of a hat, after all), *highminded, private.*"[57] As noted in chapter 5, many POWs recited poetry and meditated on astronomy, numbers, and music, and though "ritualistic" may suggest religion, Stockdale was actually referring to the POWs' talent for following routines. These three traits were however outgrowths of the last two, since he felt all important human activities must be grounded in the self (privacy), and consistent with how people should function in groups (high-mindedness).

Privacy was so valuable that Stockdale condemned even well-intentioned trespassing on another's "sacred turf":

> . . . we all had the experience of a fit of exuberance at suddenly "putting the universe together" in our individual hearts and minds, and of trying to relay these wonderful religious or at least generally inspirational keys to the kingdom next door. A very polite and tentative wall touch in reply usually told us "thanks a lot but no thanks." A supressed irritation was there and it was clear that what was meant was "I know that you're performing an act of love, but you're getting into my private territory." "That solar plexus of my soul is mine alone."[58]

With roots in Aristotelian and stoic notions of personal sovereignty, in Christian doctrines of personal responsibility for salvation, and in English Common Law's ideas of property, this "irritation" has as distinguished a history as religion. In captivity, though, Stockdale found the self's mistrust of collectivist values—Christian, Marxist, or American—especially valuable. Leaders must be extremely sensitive to this mistrust; in fact, half of the ten leadership principles Stockdale lists in a 1981 essay are actually about personal sovereignty. Principle 8, for instance, "*Living in harmonious ant heaps is contrary to man's nature*," arose out of "The Grand Inquisitor" section from *The Brothers Karamazov*. According to Stockdale, the Grand Inquisitor "believed that mankind is best served, not so much by seeking the bread of heaven, as by being furnished the bread of earth—social services, and so on—of being protected from want and the ravages of war." In such a clergyman's eyes, Christ had doomed the human community by arousing personal conscience, and thus unleashing the self's energy. Dostoyevsky's Jesus did not of course reply, but after quoting the Inquisitor's maxim that "it is to mankind's advantage to live all in one unanimous, harmonious antheap of universal unity," Stockdale denounces all such collectivist visions as not just "contrary to man's nature," but dangerous enemies as well.[59] As Principle 7, "*People do not like to be programmed*," implies, ego-driven freedom always rebels against bureaucratic notions of equality which suppress the will's impulses. Stockdale blamed this "leveling of America" on a spineless and relativistic government which has "convinced too many people they are good simply because they *are*." What saved him from adopting some *Ubermensch* theory, however, was his belief in "dynamic tension"—or as Principle 6 put it, *"Freedom and absolute equality are a trade-off,"* since "if you push individual freedom to the limit, you lose equality; if you subordinate every social value to equality, you lose freedom."[60]

In Hanoi, Stockdale became convinced that freedom was identical with self-consciousness. He shared Viktor Frankl's belief that "he could continue resistance as long as he remembered that he, alone, was in possession of the fundamental *freedom* of shaping his own attitude about what was going on." Also present in the old saw that "Stone walls do not a prison make, / Nor iron bars a cage," this belief informs Principle 4, *"Compulsion and free will can coexist,"* and Principle 5, *"Every man can be more than he is."*[61] These tributes to the self did not however turn Stockdale into Ayn Rand. While he believed freedom could help individuals resist compulsion, he also agreed with the Grand Inquisitor that many human beings were their own greatest foes. This grim truth anchored Stockdale's understanding of torture. If nothing can match the soul's potential for punishing itself, then torture's real objective is civil war, for as Elaine Scarry explains, by trying to make "the person in great pain" see "his own body as the agent of his agony," by trying to instill "not only the feeling 'my body hurts,' but the feeling 'my body hurts me,' " the torturer aims for a sense of "self-betrayal in pain" which leads to "self-hatred," "self-alienation," and ultimately to the will's disintegration.[62] Stockdale knew very well how pain could rudely introduce soul to body—so well that he staged painful experiments to learn whether the mind and body were truly distinct entities. When fasting left him almost "ready to spill my guts just looking for a friend," Stockdale had his answer: "I tapped to the guy next door and I said, 'Gosh, how I wish Descartes could have been right, but he's wrong.' He was a little slow to reply; I reviewed Descartes's deduction with him and explained how I had discovered that body and mind are inseparable." This apparent bad news was however actually a source of comfort and strength. Since their minds "had the weakness of being an integral part of our bodies," pain could force the POWs to do things. Submitting during torture was thus not self-betrayal. A POW failed only when he avoided pain by doing what the enemy wanted, or when he accepted his torturer's claims, lost faith in himself, and despaired: "That's what really tears you apart, there's where the real problem occurs, when you allow yourself to be scared and guilt-ridden."[63] It's not surprising, then, that Stockdale found "lots of meaning" in the last stanza of Henley's "Invictus":

> It matters not how strait the gate,
> How charged with punishments the scroll,
> I am the master of my fate;
> I am the captain of my soul.[64]

Stockdale proudly aligned himself with those philosophers who believed that self mastery was the foundation for all successful human communities. During a 1979 West Point address, he began his remarks by claiming that ethics and the self were first married in Athens. Drawing on Plato's and Aristotle's notion of *arete*—"virtue or moral excellence"—he argued that the good individual did "what was *expected* of him depending on his particular station in the world," but also displayed "those virtues of character proper to a human as a human." The first expectation governs military discipline and duty, but for Stockdale the second expectation precedes it, since communities only act ethically when their citizens seek to embody the "human" virtues. Fear of punishment for instance should not prevent people from lying, but "because not to keep your word is dishonest, below the dignity of man, the opposite to virtue (arete)." Stockdale's portrait of Immanuel Kant, which could also serve as a self-portrait, makes the same point. Though he "happened to be a religious man," Kant never relied "on religion as a justification for any of his ideas; he relied only on what he called pure reason." After observing that a "law we set for ourselves is *free* in contrast with the eternal law which is *compelling*," Kant tried to explain how this free law, whether as "the voice of conscience" or as "the obligation to do our duty," soon becomes as compelling as the laws of God or State. This is the "categorical imperative," Kant's "name for this inbred, self-imposed restraint, for the command of conscience within that tells us that the only true moral act is done from a pure sense of duty. So you can't ask what benefits will accrue from performing your duty. You must do your duty because it *is* your duty. Period."[65]

The world's lack of interest in this compulsion was for Stockdale a strong sign of its importance. Though captivity had placed him in surroundings that opposed his desires, such restraint wasn't unique to imprisonment. Military history teaches that ethical individuals always stand in hell's furnaces. After quoting General Sherman—"War is cruelty and you can't refine it"—Stockdale told the West Point cadets that a knowledge of "perfidy, of violence, of terror," in Joseph Conrad's words, was one of their duties. Leadership Principle 2, "*Life is not fair*," thus leads naturally into Principle 9: "*The self-discipline of stoicism has everyday applications*." Leaders must deal with "the lack of a moral economy in this universe," for as Stockdale says elsewhere, "To handle tragedy may indeed be the mark of an educated man, for one of the principal goals of education is to prepare us for failure."[66] This belief set Stockdale slightly apart from the other POWs. Because "many people have a great deal of difficulty with the fact that virtue is not always rewarded nor is evil always punished," in Hanoi "most guys" believed "it was really better for everybody to be an optimist." Partially because he "knew too much about the politics of Asia," and partially because "some people believe what professional optimists are passing out and come unglued when their predictions don't work out," Stockdale was a pessimist. This perspective did not however necessarily lead to despair. "Over time, we started getting a boost out of our bad luck," Stockdale recalled, "I can remember Howie Rutledge saying 'Talk about World War II, I've been in solitary confinement longer than World War II lasted.' So we made destitution a prestige item." For this reason, Stockdale was drawn to Pascal's wager—the practice of mentally betting on the worst outcome so that "losing" is a relief.[67] It was stoicism, however, that gave the greatest comfort. When a Stanford professor gave him Epictetus's *Enchiridion* as a parting gift, Stockdale had been puzzled: "I was an organizer of men and a fighter pilot, concerned with the technology of the age. How could the foundations of the Aurelian stoical school apply to my daily life?" The answer came in Hanoi, where a badly wounded Stockdale was forced to separate "what is in my power from that which is not" and to remember that "lameness is an impediment to the leg, but not to the will." By insisting that "life isn't fair," Epictetus also ruled out "any thoughts of being punished for past actions," thus rendering the question "Why me?" ridiculous. Since the "number one problem" in captivity was that people could not "accommodate" themselves to an amoral world, Stockdale "learned to be selective" about whom he shared his dark stoic comfort with: "It's a strong message which upsets people." Nevertheless Stockdale believed that stoicism was the key to the Hanoi POWs' generally admirable performance. Since chance rather than merit so often places people in their social roles, ethical integrity largely depends on playing this role well: "Remember that you are an actor in a drama of such sort as the Author chooses," Epictetus remarks, "if short, then in a short one; if long, then in a long one. If it be his pleasure that you should enact a poor man, or a cripple, or a ruler, or a private citizen, see that you act it well. For this is your business—to act well the given part, but to choose it belongs to another." In this dramatic metaphor, Stockdale also found an ethical guide for leading. Though very few men shared Stockdale's pessimism, "ninety-eight percent" left Hanoi with their "sense of dignity and self-respect intact" because they played to the hilt the roles that a few senior men assigned them.[68] For this reason, a leader's principal virtue was "high-mindedness"— a term with philosophical and historical significance. If chance and uncertainty, what Stockdale calls "the ultimate destabilizers," threaten everyone, it seems only reasonable that individuals would help each other endure the ensuing pain and bewilderment. Confessing to others after torture, for example, helped men "realize fear and guilt are your enemies, and not pain." In this way, "friendship and support" helped men transform their personal suffering, the "fire that was meant to destroy us," into "a saving fire, as a cauterizing agent, as a temperer of what became our steel."[69]

Three of Stockdale's leadership principles—"*You are your brother's keeper*," "*Duty comes before defiance*," and "*Moral responsibility cannot be escaped*"—insist on this obligation to others. This duty was not simply the lesson of Hanoi, but of America's heritage, and even of Western civilization. Though Stockdale admitted that "pure patriotism and loyalty to our Commander in Chief" could spur most Vietnam POWs' resistance, he also insisted on placing this resistance within the "traditional Anglo-Saxon legal viewpoint," found in Blackstone and the American Bill of Rights, that a free society could still set "certain limits to the civil rights of soldiers." At his most expansive—this time at a commencement—Stockdale declared that Americans are "products of the culture of Greece, inherited by the Romans and transferred by the Fathers of the Church with the religious teaching of Christianity and progressively enlarged by a countless number of artists, writers, scientists and philosophers from the beginning of the Middle Ages until now." In Hanoi, Stockdale decided that this heritage was suffering from a "self-inflicted wound" with "no biological roots"—that romance with mediocrity he called the "leveling of America." The cure was "excellence," a standard "born of the human will" which always realizes that "civilization is but a thin veneer on society, and we are but one generation removed from barbarism."[70]

For Jim Stockdale, leaders are those individuals who embody their society's values, but also filter them through a sense of history and of life's tragic dimensions. This historical sense guards against America's frequent drifts toward an "egalitarianism of ideas" that Stockdale blames on the social sciences and "trendy psychological chitchat." Since "busy people, particularly busy opportunists" in these fields lack "the yardstick of four thousand years of recorded history," they tend "to view their dilemmas as unique and so unprecedented that they deserve to make exceptions to law, custom, or morality in their favor to solve their problems."[71] The military leader must avoid this perspective like the plague. As Alfred Thayer Mahan once declared, "The great warrior must study history," and the four traits Stockdale finds in those leaders "assured a place in history" make the same point. Trait one, a predisposition "to continual self-improvement," and trait two, personal integrity, stress once again the individual will. Trait three, "having the emotional stability to handle failure," saves the leader from despair, even though he knows that no "natural moral economy prevails by which evil is punished and virtue is rewarded." Stockdale found this stability by becoming "familiar with examples of men who have successfully coped with failure in the classical and religious past"—examples like Job, or the Greek tragic heroes, or above all the writer of Ecclesiastes, whose words rang so true to Stockdale in Hanoi: "I returned and saw that the race is not always to the swift nor the battle to the strong, neither yet bread to the wise nor riches to men of understanding, but time and chance happeneth to them all." The fourth leadership trait, leadership ability, invokes a "broader version of leadership; a quality which can properly be called *teachership*."[72] After looking for "a good seagoing job" after his return, Stockdale soon knew that "high command of a peacetime military force was not for me." When offered the presidency of the Naval War College, however, he jumped. Stockdale "wanted to teach people about war," and he also agreed wholeheartedly with the sentiment that a teacher "is a witness to guide a pupil into the promised land; but he must have been there himself." For this reason, Stockdale soon began drawing on his Hanoi experience when enhancing the curriculum at the college. The booklist for his leadership course could have come from the standard Great Books course found at most liberal arts colleges: "Plato's *Dialogues*, Aristotle's *Nichomachean Ethics*, Immanuel Kant's *Fundamental Principles of the Metaphysics of Morals*, Arthur Koestler's *Darkness at Noon*, Herman Melville's *Billy Budd*, Albert Camus' *The Plague*, Joseph Conrad's *Typhoon*, and Stephen Crane's "The Open Boat."[73]

All the training in the world will not however guarantee performance in times of profound stress, as Stockdale's account of an early 1967 interrogation demonstrates. When he asked an official what the criteria for membership in the Communist Party were, "Rabbit had replied quickly, assuredly, and emotionally: 'There are only four. First, you have to be smart enough to understand the theory. Second, you have to be seventeen years old. Third, you have to be selfless and willing to work without the aim of personal gain. And fourth and most important, you must have the *innate* ability to influence others.' " The first three requirements were predictable; it was the truth of the last requirement that impressed Stockdale because he recognized it in his own community. When tortured into writing down the names of his "central committee," Stockdale listed all the POWs in rank order. "This is our organization," he explained, "It is a lineal responsibility list. It is like a snake you can't kill—the head will always grow back: Take me out and Denton will take over; take Denton out and Jenkins will fill in." Stockdale knew very well, however, that some POWs lacked the ability to influence others, and furthermore, that his captors already knew who the real "central committee" was. "What were leaders to one side were troublemakers to the other," and the cadres "were used to looking for them" because "it is the leader/troublemakers who make communism work."[74] Hence the glory of being chosen for Alcatraz, that "dark place" reserved for those "darkest criminals, who persist in inciting the other criminals to oppose the Camp Authority." Neither rank nor resistance in themselves qualified a POW. As Stockdale put it, "You had to be a threat to the North Vietnamese prison system to get to Alcatraz."[75] This same threatening ability also distinguished true warriors from military bureaucrats. Shortly after leaving Hanoi, Stockdale was happy to learn that a friend had been promoted, even though he was "nothing like those flashy Washington-oriented bastards who always seemed to be looking over the head of mere fighter pilots, trying to see something way up ahead of us all." Stockdale was furious to learn, however, that the government had not charged those "few POWs who had illegally accepted parole," nor planned to prosecute those men accused of collaboration by their fellow POWs.[76]

As all these examples suggest, Stockdale believed that all the most important battles are waged between bureaucrats, technocrats, and "business-oriented systems analysts" on the one side, and individuals driven by hard-won ethical principles on the other. In these battles, morality confronts engineering, contemplation confronts action, philosophy confronts social management—the humanities, in short, confront the social, administrative, and applied sciences. Though fully aware of his chosen profession's managerial bent, Stockdale insisted the values which define the humanistic tradition must also govern the military leader. As a moralist, he must study ethics; as a jurist, he must advocate justice; and as a teacher and philosopher, he must believe in preserving these values. For this reason, the best training for captivity was neither Survival School, nor a rabid commitment to American ideology, but "a broad, liberal education that gives a man at least enough historical perspective to realize that those who excelled in life before him were, in the last essence, committed to playing a role." Stockdale's electives program, designed to complement the War College's core curriculum of "strategy, economics, and operations," shows how committed he was to this position. (He personally taught "Foundations of Moral Responsibility.")[77]

The same principles also informed the official story, the events leading up to it, and its eventual significance for all Americans. As soldiers imprisoned during a failed war, the POWs could have seen their lives as suspended or wasted. Instead, they turned their captivity into a triumph by reenacting those events which make up Western ethical history. As always, this process began with the individual. After some time in solitary, a condition imposed "in an attempt to sever our ties with one another and with our cultural heritage," the POW realized that "unless he gets some structure, some ritual, some poetry into his life, he is going to become an animal." This need drove the POW into covert communication, and as "lives and dreams" were shared, "common practice in united resistance" became possible. Leadership emerged when "codified law commences to emanate from the senior prisoner's cell," and in time, "a body politic of common customs, common loyalties, common values takes shape." Of course, this narrative appears in scores of POW memoirs and histories. Stockdale stands out because he explicitly argues that the official story echoes the course of Western history. Mark Van Doren once remarked that "before proclaiming a man educated, one would ask this question about him: Could he refound his civilization?" Stockdale's own history of the POWs repeatedly reveals "how desperately we needed to refound our own civilization in those prisons of North Vietnam."[78] Nor did release complete the task. Captivity made the POWs very sensitive to those domestic forces which they blamed for America's failure in Vietnam, for the chaos at home during the late 1960s, and even for the misfortunes of their commander in chief, Richard Nixon. Stockdale's writings were thus only the most elaborate and allusive version of a POW article of faith governing the official story and its conforming memoirs and histories. Refounding their own country's civilization would be one of the POWs' most pressing duties after their welcome had faded a bit, and they picked up their pens to write.

When Richard Nixon announced the Vietnam accords, Sybil Stockdale reacted stoically: "No shouts of joy. No tears of elation on my part. I warned myself again to be careful, not to get my hopes too high." A number of briefings also made her cautious: "We wives had been told the men would probably be sexually impotent and might be hostile toward those they loved." Jim felt doubtful and uncertain as well. "What will they think of me down there, Syb and the boys?" he wondered as his plane prepared to land in San Diego. "My hair is totally white now. I can't see to read (too many months in the dark, too many weeks in the blindfold) . . . I'm forty-nine years old and crippled and can't raise my left arm."[79] None of these concerns however could shake the Stockdales' faith that endurance was an essential quality for individuals, families, and nations. When addressing the crowds at Travis Air Force Base, Jim Stockdale fittingly said that it was good to be home. But he also placed this sentiment within that longer perspective he always searched for: "As that Athenian warrior and poet Sophocles wrote over 2400 years ago, 'Nothing is so sweet as to return from sea and listen to the raindrops on the rooftops of home.' " This brought Sybil comfort: "He's still referring to his beloved Greek philosophers, so I know he's in fairly good shape."[80] The days ahead brought recognition and frustration. Though Jim received the Medal of Honor, and Sybil the Navy Distinguished Public Service Award, the first edition of *In Love and War* closes with the upheavals brought about by Jim's earnest but failed efforts to prosecute those men considered collaborators. The revised edition describes his tumultuous years in education and public service, and still later, the 1992 presidential campaign saw Stockdale as the running mate of the quixotic H. Ross Perot. Stockdale's saturnine nature, however, seems to have let him take these events and upheavals in stride.

Whether *In Love and War* glows with the aura of truth its writers so earnestly intended for it, or whether it stands as only the most ambitious and skillful of many Vietnam POW attempts to grant their experience a significance it never possessed, is up to the reader to decide. As I've tried to suggest throughout this book, however, the entire project represented by orthodox and heretical POW histories alike has implications stretching far beyond simple matters of acceptance or contempt. This fight for meaning, and the nation's tradition of waging it, continues.

Notes

Introduction: America's Vietnam POWs

1. NY:2:14:16.
2. United States. II 932-1106. For other comprehensive lists see Wyatt n.p., *4th Allied P.O.W. Wing* 4-6, Hubbell, 606-18, and Schlitz, 29.
3. *4th Allied P.O.W Wing* 4-5; Groom 313-14.
4. *4th Allied P.O.W Wing* 17.
5. *4th Allied P.O.W. Wing* 4-7.
6. Schemmer 282; Hunter 190.
7. Hunter 190.
8. WP:4:5:20.
9. Rowan 13.
10. Hunter 199.
11. Hubbell 382-93.
12. Alvarez I 20-24.
13. Karnow 682.
14. Hunter 190.
15. Stockdale II 190.
16. Rowan 28; Wyatt n.p.—cites VIVA as its source—and Schlitz 29 confirms 16 AF dead; Schemmer 282.
17. The POWs were Atterberry, Schmidt; Cameron, Connell, Cobeil; Frederick, Storz, Sijan. The information is everywhere; LA 4:3:18. lists the "neglect" victims.
18. Grant *passim*.
19. Colvin 161, 155.
20. Colvin 164-71, WSJ 12:4:1, 22.
21. Jensen 51.
22. Schemmer 12.
23. Gaither 119; Dunn 20; Stockdale I 108; Hubbell 210.
24. Rutledge 94.
25. Hunter 197.
26. Mulligan 37; Rowan 86; Hubbell 211.
27. Rutledge 94.
28. Heslop 271.

29. Hunter 198; NY:1:9:12; NY:1:26:11.
30. Denton 178–79.
31. NY:2:18:1; NY:4:30:38.
32. NY:2:27:4.
33. NY: 2:20:4; NY:2:24:28.
34. WP:2:24:1, 11; NY:4:1:IV:15.
35. CT:4:7:2.
36. LA:4:9:8.
37. NY:2:18:IV:2; Naughton 2.
38. Hunter 198; Naughton 2; Mallicoat 23.
39. WP:4:3:IV:7.
40. NY:2:7:39.
41. CT:4:3:14.
42. LA:4:12:2.
43. NY:3:28:47; NY:3:3:16.
44. WP:2:13:8.
45. LA:2:1:22.
46. WP:3:20:B1.
47. NY:5:25:1, 16.
48. WP:12:5:31.
49. LA:5:25:2; NY:11:4:23; WP:4:8:6.
50. WP:10:13:16.
51. LA:5:11:3.
52. LA:6:12:26; Hunter 203; K. Johnson 41.
53. NY:6:2:21.
54. NY:6:4:7; NY:6:5:6.
55. NY:6:28:7; NY:6:29:9; NY:7:4:22; NY:7:4:1.
56. K. Johnson 41.
57. Schemmer 282.
58. Hunter 199; Chesley preface.
59. NY:5:25:16.
60. Amnesty 161; NY:3:30:1, 18; LA:4:9:8.
61. McGrath viii.
62. CT:3:17:12.
63. NY:3:6:12.

I The Code, the Rules, and the Body

1. Walzer 147.

1. The Fighting Man's Code

1. Dunn 23.
2. Grant 341.
3. Rowe 331.
4. Kinkead 15, 17.
5. Kinkead 156.
6. Kinkead 128.
7. Kinkead 39, 166.
8. Kinkead 164, 159.
9. Kinkead 105.
10. Kinkead 175.

11. Biderman 168, 271, 167, 238.
12. Barker 201-3; Holt 33-34; Hitchens 48.
13. Dunn 18; Naughton 3; Kinkead 190.
14. Plumb 281; Day 89; LA:2:17:26.
15. NY:2:18:1; LA:2:17:26.
16. Hitchens *passim*; NY:3:21:45.
17. Gallery 148.
18. Gaither 46; Denton 36.
19. Walzer 148, 151, 166.
20. Walzer 166.
21. Holt 64.
22. Powers 295.
23. Grant 107; Mallicoat 29.
24. Stockdale II 446.
25. Jensen 48.
26. Gallery 149; Schemmer 9.
27. Walzer 166.
28. Hitchens 52.
29. Grant 126, 128.
30. Rutledge 85; Rowan 89.
31. Plumb 223.
32. Rutledge 85.
33. Gallery 149; Richardson 61.
34. Dunn 25.
35. Grant 293.
36. Kinkead 172, 185.
37. Biderman 171.
38. Walzer 156.
39. Gallery 150.
40. Hunter 193; Rowan 17-18; E. McDaniel 87; Stockdale I 8-9; CT:9:11:2.
41. Coker 43, 46.
42. Heslop 181.
43. Dunn 21; Denton 28.
44. Plumb 168.
45. Coker 43-44; Stockdale II 356.
46. Mulligan 217.
47. NY:7:15:38.
48. Hitchens 67; NY:7:15:38.
49. Hitchens 48.
50. Stockdale I 18-19.
51. Kinkead 130.
52. Biderman 216.
53. Gallery 138.
54. NY:3:21:45.
55. Grant 60-61.
56. Dunn 26; Plumb 167.
57. Gaither 33.
58. K. Johnson 43; Gaither 35.
59. Blakey 100; Stockdale II 168-69.
60. Denton 37.
61. Levie 650.
62. Kinkead 51, 60, 52, 66.

63. Walzer 149.
64. Smith 282, 287, 290.
65. Heslop 276; Hitchens 62.
66. Stockdale I 19; Dunn 23; Stockdale I 10–11.
67. Chesley 158.
68. Smith 296; Grant 275; Rowan 165.
69. Dunn 21–22.
70. Jensen 77.
71. Plumb 167; LA:7:1:VII:3.
72. Stockdale I 10; II 247, 250–251, 247.
73. Denton 37.
74. Stockdale II 250–2; S. Johnson, 127.
75. Naughton 10–11; see Alvarez I 235 for the "irrelevant" name.
76. Plumb 170–71.
77. Rowan 165.
78. Jensen 78.
79. Dean 90.
80. Stockdale I 36.
81. Dunn 27.
82. Hitchens 51.
83. Grant 56; Blakey 164; Mallicoat 26.
84. Hubbell 395.
85. Grant 282, 339.
86. NY:6:3:IV:3.
87. Dunn 23; Jensen 15.
88. Hitchens 51–52; Holt 31; Stockdale II 149.
89. Hubbell 62; Risner 70; Stockdale II 179.
90. Hitchens 55, 66–67.
91. Wehrun 147; NY:10:8:33.
92. Ball 57.
93. Stockdale II 218.
94. Ball 76–77.
95. Stockdale II 296; I 101.
96. Armbrister *passim* (quotation on 386–87); Bucher 321.
97. Dunn 20.
98. Hitchens 61; Mulligan 259, 256.
99. Heslop 235–36.
100. Rowan 225.
101. Jensen 154; Plumb 259.
102. Mulligan 276, 243; LA:2:9:20.
103. NY:2:1:17; NY:2:6:1.
104. Blakey 317; Jensen 169; Rowan 155.
105. Hubbell 601–3.
106. NY:7:28:4; Dunn 22, 26; Hitchens 64.

2. Camp Authority and the Rules of the Game

1. Schwinn 78.
2. Levie 506.
3. Levie 533.
4. Dean 112.
5. Kinkead 160–61.

6. Alvarez I 34; Risner 23; Groom 43; Rutledge 24.
7. Jensen 26.
8. Stockdale II 167, 158; I vii.
9. Stockdale II 312.
10. Holt 31.
11. Biderman 127.
12. Levie 654–55.
13. Smith 129; Rowe 366.
14. Hitchens 54–55; Levie 649.
15. Holt 54–55.
16. Jensen 74; Heslop 254.
17. Plumb 62–75.
18. Jensen 74; Rowan 229.
19. Hubbell 113. Among the sources are Stockdale II 151–52, NY:6:3:13, Heslop 254–56, Jensen 74–76, Plumb 75, and Hubbell 113; my quotations come from McGrath 112–13, which provides complete versions of the first and second sets of rules.
20. Jensen 74; Stockdale I 7; Hubbell 113.
21. McGrath 113–14.
22. Hubbell 114.
23. Holt 40.
24. Foucault 125, 122.
25. Levie 652.
26. Biderman 251–55; Barker 79; Biderman 54n, 60n.
27. Denton 76.
28. Stockdale I vii, 32, 138, 32.
29. Stockdale I 138; Heslop 275–76; Stockdale II 149.
30. Foucault 235–36, 6–7.
31. Heslop 258; E. McDaniel 56–57.
32. Foucault 237.
33. Stockdale II 114.
34. Dean 86.
35. Gaither 74; Dramesi 154–55; Schwinn 37.
36. Schwinn 53, 59.
37. Mulligan 53; Rowan 104.
38. E. McDaniel 38; Stockdale II 183.
39. Stockdale II 165, 285.
40. Foucault 253–54.
41. Gaither 52; Denton 78.
42. Mulligan 73.
43. Stockdale II 253–55.
44. Stockdale II 272, 255, 343.
45. Rutledge 47; Stockdale II 175.
46. Rowan 109.
47. Chesley 50–51; Naughton 8.
48. Kinkead 116, 52.
49. NY:1:28:1; Holt 35; Amnesty 163.

3. Torture and War's Body

1. Horne 196.
2. Scarry 3.
3. NY:4:7:11; LA:4:19:25.

4. LA:6:9:II:4.
5. Chafee 17; Amnesty 160; Fall 23.
6. Jensen 92.
7. Smith 58.
8. Stockdale II 158.
9. Stockdale II 185.
10. Naughton 5.
11. Jackson 115; Risner 177-79; Rutledge 70; Stockdale I vii.
12. Chesley 67.
13. Amnesty 166.
14. Peters 2, 153, 3, 7.
15. Ruthven 94; Peters 68.
16. Amnesty 162.
17. Ruthven 239.
18. Scarry 47.
19. WP:4:11:22; NY:4:30:38.
20. Smith 253-54, 301n; Rowe 209-12.
21. Scarry 28.
22. McConnell 194; Rowan 44.
23. Holt 51; Smith 119-24.
24. Risner 140-44.
25. Richardson 48.
26. Peters 5, 77-78, 6-7.
27. Rowan 43, 237, 44.
28. Foucault 25; Peters 88; Foucault 16, 9.
29. Peters 40, 54; Foucault 37-38; Peters 57, 66.
30. Chesley 57; Hubbell 373.
31. Risner 31; Stockdale II 155; Risner 161; Stockdale I vii.
32. Scarry 49.
33. Chesley 57.
34. E. McDaniel 39; Rutledge 25; Plumb 65.
35. Richardson 47.
36. Peters 186, 77-78.
37. Ruthven 217.
38. Peters 138.
39. Ho Chi Minh, *passim*.
40. Scarry 12; Quoted in Peters 180-81.
41. Peters 5.
42. Alleg 13.
43. Blakey 36, 91, 96.
44. Blakey 97.
45. Hunter 192.
46. Gaither 50; NY:2:15:16; Rowan 76.
47. Quoted in Hitchens 49.
48. Stockdale II 156, 176, 172.
49. Scarry 35, 27.
50. Stockdale I 124-25.
51. Foucault 262.
52. Rutledge 51; Holt 64; Stockdale II 188-89.
53. NY:4:10:22; Naughton 13.
54. Rutledge 30; Rowan 145, 143.
55. Heslop 113; Rowan 42.

56. Rutledge 28; Risner 132; Denton 56.
57. Chesley 66.
58. Jensen 43; Stockdale I 89–90.
59. Coker 45.
60. K. Johnson 41; Rowan 26.
61. Rowan 41–42.
62. Naughton 7.
63. Stockdale I 8; Rowan 87.
64. Stockdale I 102–3.
65. Denton 55–56.
66. Blakey 122.
67. Rowan 215.
68. Plumb 217.
69. "Playboy Interview" 82.
70. Blakey 207, 210–12.
71. Ruthven 295.
72. Scarry 21, 27.
73. Blakey 395; Stockdale I 17, 21.
74. NY:4:30:38; NY:3:31:4.
75. Scarry 144.
76. WP:3:30:13; LA:3:30:1; LA:4:3:18.
77. LA:4:11:14.
78. NY:4:30:38; NY:3:4:28; NY:3:30:18; NY:3:30:1.
79. NY:4:30:38.

II The Official Story and the Big Picture

1. Hubbell vi.

4. The Official Story

(Unless otherwise indicated, all page references are to Hubbell.)

1. 309–12.
2. Plutarch 406–7.
3. Colvin 161.
4. Schemmer 11; Risner 19; Stockdale I 33; Hubbell 304; Stockdale I 33–34.
5. Schemmer 280.
6. Chesley 107; Rowan 247.
7. Plumb 281.
8. Naughton 3; Stockdale I 7.
9. Plumb 287.
10. Rowan 83; Coker 42.
11. Naughton 4, 6–7.
12. Naughton 10.
13. Hackworth 9.
14. Coffee 265; Heslop 218; Denton 142–43.
15. Mulligan 237.
16. Denton 168; Heslop 218.
17. Naughton 2; Schlitz 27.
18. Schlitz 26, 25, 27–28.
19. v–viii.
20. Chesley ix.

21. iv.
22. vi.
23. xi–xiii.
24. 6.
25. 10.
26. 18.
27. 7–8.
28. 28.
29. 32.
30. Alvarez I 79.
31. 30.
32. 5–6.
33. 28.
34. 33.
35. 35–37.
36. 41–44.
37. 44–46.
38. 44.
39. 48, 54, 52.
40. 58.
41. Denton 28; Hubbell 59.
42. 61, 63–64.
43. 75.
44. 78–79.
45. 83–85.
46. 86–87.
47. 87.
48. 80.
49. 89.
50. 92, 90, 93–94.
51. 95.
52. 101, 104–5.
53. 108, 117–18.
54. 121.
55. 112–13.
56. 114.
57. 129, 131–32.
58. 135–36.
59. 138, 135, 138–39.
60. 150.
61. 153.
62. 153–54.
63. 158.
64. 177.
65. 163, 181–82.
66. 184–87.
67. 187.
68. 190–91, 187, 191–93.
69. 193.
70. 197.
71. 223, 211.
72. 210, 209.

73. 223-24.
74. 235.
75. 264.
76. 236, 283, 285.
77. 261-62.
78. 273-74.
79. 239-40, 248.
80. 288.
81. 297, 281, 304-5, 324, 325-26.
82. 346-47.
83. 361.
84. 383.
85. 393.
86. 417.
87. 395-96.
88. 399-400.
89. 416.
90. 418-19.
91. 417.
92. 419-20.
93. 422-24.
94. 467, 468-69.
95. 484-85.
96. 516, 543.
97. 572-73.
98. 517.
99. 402-3, 414-15, 535.
100. 411.
101. 413.
102. 512, 530-31, 533.
103. 426.
104. 429.
105. 432-34.
106. 440, 444.
107. 457, 462.
108. 475-77.
109. 355-60.
110. 491, 493.
111. 493-94.
112. 494-95, 496, 543.
113. 497; for Day's own account, see Day 151-68.
114. 496.
115. 498-500.
116. Amnesty 160.
117. 513-16, 519-20.
118. Denton 177.
119. 518; Denton 151.
120. Denton 151-52; Hubbell 549.
121. 540, 541.
122. Stockdale II 400.
123. 549.
124. 542; Risner 214.

125. 548-49; Risner 214.
126. 544-46; Risner 220.
127. 548.
128. 529, 566-67.
129. 568.
130. 571.
131. 572-74.
132. 582.
133. 595-96.
134. 479.
135. 525, 481.
136. 480, 482.
137. 525, 524, 526.
138. 554.
139. 563.
140. 558, 559.
141. 560-61.
142. 577, 548.
143. 577.
144. 581.
145. 583-84.
146. 601-3.
147. 590-92.
148. 599-600.

5. The Big Picture

1. Stockdale II 165.
2. George Day for instance structures his memoir on *The Inferno*.
3. Slotkin 94, 96.
4. Slotkin 102, 95.
5. Biderman 104-13.
6. Dean 85.
7. Slotkin 101, 104-5.
8. Risner 53.
9. Denton 5; McConnell 49-50; Naughton 3.
10. Smith 100; Grant 62; Stockdale II 153; Smith 107-8; N. McDaniel 20.
11. Rowan 231.
12. Rutledge 84.
13. Jensen 40; Blakey 17; Stockdale II 190; Rowan 38; Blakey 17.
14. McGrath 1; Dengler 209; Heslop 35.
15. Gaither 7; Rowan 184; N. McDaniel 8; Grant 219.
16. McGrath 2; Blakey 17.
17. Plumb 56; E. McDaniel 35; Jensen 40; Rowan 34; Rowan 38; McConnell 163.
18. Jensen 40.
19. McGrath 4.
20. Heslop 9-10.
21. Rowan 37.
22. Norman 115.
23. Laffin 158.
24. Plumb 177; Norman 116; Plumb 177; Risner 178.
25. Heslop 119; Sidey 36.

26. Jensen 58; Schwinn 204-5.
27. Rowan 12; Mallicoat 27; Schwinn 74; Stockdale II 340; Rowe 133-34; Norman 122-25.
28. Jensen 72.
29. Dramesi 145-47; Grant 134; Stockdale II 184.
30. Scarry 10.
31. Heslop 311, 139, 148.
32. Jensen 117; Plumb 179; Jensen 103.
33. Jensen 133; Alvarez I 231.
34. Coffee 265; LA: 3:30:LA:3; Mulligan 251; Denton 124, 142; N. McDaniel 38-40.
35. Gaither v, 68, 98, 114, 120, 123, 125, 129, 145.
36. Rowan 13; E. McDaniel 139.
37. E. McDaniel 139; CT:9:12:7; E. McDaniel 98; Plumb 239; CT:9:12:7.
38. E. McDaniel 98; Heslop 59; Plumb 89-90; Norman 179; Chesley 79; Day 229.
39. E. McDaniel 141; Jensen 121-22; E. McDaniel 142; Jensen 121-22; Norman 178-9.
40. CT:9:12:7.
41. Naughton 4.
42. E. McDaniel 112; Dramesi 60; Denton 88.
43. Gallery xi.
44. Slotkin 127, 118.
45. Alleg 25.
46. Barker 30; Levie 644-45; Deane 10, 169; Dean 130-31.
47. Greene 176. See Drinnon, esp. 374-428, for further discussion.
48. Grant 51.
49. Rowan 11.
50. E. McDaniel 104; Chesley 38; E. McDaniel 33-34.
51. Plumb 117, 93, 117, 52, 94, 96.
52. Plumb 113-14, 102, 93, 117-18.
53. E. McDaniel 34; Blakey 36; Risner 21.
54. Gaither 128; Grant 43; Jensen 88.
55. Plumb 97; Gaither 128; Plumb 97.
56. V. Nasmyth 182; Day 119.
57. Sheehan 335; Gaither 128; E. McDaniel 54.
58. E. McDaniel 39, 49; Chesley 51; Gaither 26; E. McDaniel 140.
59. Risner 236; E. McDaniel 49; CT:3:3:4.
60. Quoted in Drinnon 371.
61. Plumb 57; Day 117; Rowan 40; Blakey 308, 346; Risner 32; NY:4:30:38.
62. Frishman 11; Gaither 92; Plumb 105, 192.
63. Blakey 97; E. McDaniel 49.
64. Blakey 185.
65. Grant 193.
66. Fall viii, vi.
67. Halberstam 38; Fall ix.
68. Holt 38.
69. Holt 56; Schwinn 167-68; Groom 20.
70. Rowe 260; Stockdale II 115.
71. Risner 140.
72. Grant 196.
73. Hubbell 195-97.
74. Jackson 114-18; Rowan 28; Jackson 117-18.
75. Risner 22; Stockdale II 114, 233-34.
76. LA:4:4:5.
77. Plumb 108-9, 116.

78. Chesley 55.
79. Drinnon 314n.
80. Mallicoat 27.
81. NY:3:2:1.
82. Plumb 69-70, 111.
83. N. McDaniel 21. The following survey of names is gleaned from all of the POW memoirs and histories.
84. Hubbell 363; Dramesi 123.
85. Smith 134.
86. Smith 5.
87. Grant 59; Rowe 237.
88. LA:3:26:5.
89. Deane I 76.
90. Hubbell 351-53; for Day's own account, see Day 70-77.
91. Hubbell 437; NY:3:30:18; HSB 3:6:7.
92. Plumb 103-4, 99-100; Daly 155.
93. Hubbell 509, 528.
94. Hubbell 489-90.
95. Guarino 192.
96. Barker 132; Rowan 115-16; Grant 316.
97. Barker 132; Chesley 79, 93; Coffee 181; Rowan 90.
98. Rowan 115-17; Coffee 181.
99. Plumb 101-2; Rowan 115; Plumb 101, 129.
100. Dramesi 78.
101. Dramesi 164.
102. Dramesi 185.
103. Mulligan 226-27.
104. Dramesi 143.
105. Schwinn 66-67; Alvarez I 117.
106. Denton 104, 110-11.
107. Alvarez I 197-98.
108. Plumb 100.
109. Rowan 116; V. Nasmyth 181-82; Rowan 91.
110. Daly 182, 147.
111. E. McDaniel 101; Dramesi 53.
112. Dramesi 147; Day 42; Plumb 238-39.
113. Rowan 91.
114. Plumb 89; V. Nasmyth 193, 319.
115. V. Nasmyth 250; S. Nasmyth 317, 316.
116. Plumb 262; Jensen 205; Blakey 318.
117. Gaither 68, 126, 131.
118. Blakey 13; Rowan 249.
119. Jensen 125-29.
120. Rowan 94; Denton 64.
121. NY:2:5:13; WP:3:5:3.
122. N. McDaniel 16, 77, 96.
123. Heslop 178.
124. N. McDaniel 48; NY:3:6:10; Jensen 190; Rowan 94.
125. NY:3:6:10; NY:2:5:13.
126. LA:2:18:9.
127. Jensen 148-49; LA:6:9:5; Jensen 149; LA:6:9:5.
128. Terry 297.

129. Alvarez I 238, 242, 239, 242.

130. Plumb 16, 31-33, 153-56, 163.

131. Plumb 268-69, 275, 272, 276, 275.

132. Plumb 276-77, 278-79.

133. Mulligan 102.

134. WP:4:5:13; Stockdale I 9; Plumb 49.

135. Kinkead 210.

136. Plumb 49; Jensen 25; E. McDaniel 16; Chesley 96; Rowan 63.

137. Plumb 236-37; Mallicoat 27.

138. Denton 53; Stockdale I 11.

139. Slotkin 119-20, 138.

140. FitzGerald 367-68; Drinnon 443-47; see also Melling.

141. Quoted in Drinnon 456.

142. Drinnon 375; McConnell 37.

143. Plumb 56; Chesley 56; Day 103; McConnell 54.

144. Coker 46; Jensen 177.

145. Plumb 234; Rowe 287; Denton 8; Jensen 203; NY:2:15:16.

146. Risner 182; Denton 8; Risner 185.

147. Rutledge 84.

148. Chesley 107; E. McDaniel 15-16.

149. Scarry 81.

150. E. McDaniel 113, 15; Hubbell 524; Naughton 13.

151. Hubbell 152.

152. Scarry 105; Heslop 135; N. McDaniel vii; Rowan 251-52.

153. Schwinn xi; Coker 42; E. McDaniel 51.

154. Smith 127; Rowe 211, 245, 164.

155. Rowe 164; Rowan 81; Rowan 195-96.

156. Daly 235; NY:2:16:14.

157. Smith 304; Jackson 114.

158. Holt 29, 55.

159. Slotkin 99, 130, 99-100, 130, 95.

160. Denton 17; E. McDaniel 131, 88; Blakey 334, 358.

161. NY:3:11:50; Hubbell 440, 515; Gaither 143.

162. NY:3:11:50; Slotkin 108; E. McDaniel 87-88; Hubbell 354-55.

163. NY:2:1:18; Heslop 21-22; Stockdale II 204.

164. NY:1:30:15; NY:2:8:16; NY:2:18:3. For more information about antiwar POW/MIA families, see Keenan.

165. Stockdale II 261, 175.

166. Rowe 404-6.

167. Slotkin 120-21.

168. Slotkin 141.

169. Denton 127-28; Hubbell 182.

170. Stockdale I 99-101.

171. Slotkin 99, 129.

172. Jensen xi.

173. Stockdale II 252.

174. Grant 82; Daly 236-37; Grant 327.

175. Plumb 136-37; Naughton 9-10, 12.

176. NY:1:31:17; CT:2:20:2:1; NY:2:14:16.

177. N. McDaniel 68; Plumb 271; Stockdale II 435.

178. NY:2:1:17; Heslop 316-17; Heslop 320; WP:5:25:B3; Heslop 318.

179. Jensen 23, 25.

180. Jensen 171, 182, 188, 183, 187.
181. Jensen 202-3.
182. Plumb 18, 16-17, 14, 17.
183. Heslop 311-12.

III One Man's View

1. Laffin 24.

6. A Prophet Returns to His People

1. "The Love Song of J. Alfred Prufrock," ll. 94-95.
2. Gaither 144.
3. Rowan 27; Heslop 173.
4. Mulligan 166.
5. Chesley 4, 27.
6. Slotkin 112.
7. Chesley 140, 138.
8. Slotkin 110-11; Barker 192-93, 141-42.
9. N. McDaniel 99-100; Risner v-vi.
10. Biderman 41; Levie 664.
11. NY:4:1:62; Mulligan 17; Holt 35.
12. Mulligan 82, 127, 94, 53.
13. Mulligan 7-11, 27-28.
14. Mulligan 102, 27.
15. Mulligan 7, 18-20, 22, 104.
16. Mulligan 10, 16, 12, 10, 43.
17. Mulligan 122, 51-52, 41, 51.
18. Mulligan 260-61, 17.
19. Mulligan 123, 48, 87, 207, 123-24.
20. Mulligan 206, 262.
21. Mulligan 73, 69-70.
22. Mulligan 212, 211, 259.
23. Mulligan 19, 94, 142.
24. Mulligan 214, 19, 154.
25. Mulligan 260, 262, 265, 120.
26. Mulligan 175, 205.
27. Mulligan 66, 107-8,144-46, 234.
28. Mulligan 144.
29. Mulligan 298.
30. Denton 70, cover.
31. Denton 12, 1, 83.
32. Denton 140; Stockdale II 292; Hubbell 487.
33. Denton 143-44; Hubbell 487; Denton 148-49.
34. Denton 125-26, 152-53, 156, 165.
35. Denton 170-71.
36. Blakey 211-12; Rowan 183.
37. Denton 181.
38. NY:2:13:14.
39. Slotkin 94-95.
40. White 338; Harris 160.
41. Slotkin 96.

42. Gaither v; N. McDaniel vii–viii.
43. Slotkin 108, 113–14.
44. Heslop 139; Mulligan 93–94; Day 156–80; Jensen 71; E. McDaniel 171.
45. NY:1:31:1.
46. Rutledge 90; NY:2:20:4; N. McDaniel 51; Heslop 106.
47. Mulligan 292; Jensen 160.
48. Chesley 82, 86; Jensen 37; Plumb 49; Chesley 4; Heslop iv, 93–94, 4–5.
49. Rutledge 14, 17–18, 20.
50. Chesley 7, 9, 11.
51. Hubbell 50; Mulligan 183.
52. Chesley 20; Denton 8; Hubbell 120, 125.
53. Heslop 135; E. McDaniel 61; Chesley 111, 114.
54. Rowe 231.
55. Rutledge 46, 98.
56. Slotkin 101n.
57. Rutledge 56; Gaither 35–37, 40.
58. Denton 93.
59. E. McDaniel 107, 111–14, 118–19.
60. E. McDaniel 119, 121, 176.
61. NY:2:14:16.
62. Slotkin 103.
63. Risner 62, 3–4.
64. Risner 34.
65. Risner 36–44.
66. Risner 53, 62.
67. Risner 32.
68. Slotkin 109.
69. Risner 110, 185.
70. Risner 228, 256, 264.
71. McConnell 15.
72. McConnell 250.
73. McConnell 118, 179, 120–21.
74. McConnell 179, 148, 178.
75. McConnell 127, 129, 126–28.
76. McConnell 129, 180, 164, 175–76.
77. McConnell 176, 175, 183, 188, 200.
78. McConnell 182–83.
79. McConnell 208.
80. McConnell 209.
81. McConnell 208, 210.
82. McConnell 249.
83. McConnell 217–18.
84. McConnell 224–25.
85. McConnell 233, 226, 228, 237.
86. McConnell 243, 245.
87. Jensen 60; Rutledge 35–37.
88. E. McDaniel 42; Chesley 158.
89. Heslop 145.
90. Rutledge 64; E. McDaniel 132.
91. Chesley 52.
92. Jensen 140–41.
93. Chesley 76, 20, 33, 131.

94. E. McDaniel 135.
95. Rutledge 53, 77.
96. Hubbell 544–45.
97. N. McDaniel 61.
98. Plumb 85.
99. Heslop 147.
100. LA:3:18:17; N. McDaniel 114.
101. Jensen xi, 207.
102. Jensen 209.
103. Jensen xi, 204.
104. Slotkin 111, 129–30.

7. The Story's Other Sides

1. Kinkead 194.
2. Biderman 180, 1n; Barker 147.
3. Denton 97.
4. Coker 45; E. McDaniel 106, 159–60.
5. Dramesi 62, 69.
6. Dramesi 35, 20, 29, 31.
7. Denton 157; Dramesi 185, 182–83.
8. Dramesi 181, 172, 176.
9. Coker 45.
10. Dramesi 27.
11. Dramesi 144.
12. Coker 46; Dramesi 79–80.
13. Dramesi 197–98, 163, 98.
14. Dramesi 76, 109, 97, 99, 97.
15. Dramesi 247.
16. Barker 86; Dramesi 203, 195.
17. Dramesi 262, 219–20, 252, 258.
18. Dramesi 219, 239, 237–38, 239–40.
19. Dramesi 207, 206–7, 219, 221–22.
20. Dramesi 225, 230–31, 235–36, 249, 268.
21. Dramesi 271, 248.
22. Dramesi 11.
23. NY:4:2:3; CT:9:12:7; CT:9:10:5; NY:4:2:3.
24. LA:3:8:21; CT:2:26:1; NY:2:28:9.
25. Grant 297; WP:4:4:5.
26. WP:5:6:16; NY:4:7:9; LA:2:16:10.
27. Hubbell 252–53.
28. Hubbell 255–56, 258–60.
29. Hubbell 284–87.
30. Hubbell 336.
31. Hubbell 274, 313–14, 375–76.
32. Blakey 162–63, 178, 182.
33. Blakey 185–87.
34. Blakey 188–89.
35. Blakey 197–98, 229, 239.
36. Blakey 241, 251, 267, 270.
37. Smith 9, 290, 15, 11.
38. Smith 31–32, 35–38.
39. Smith 45–47.

40. Smith 58, 73, 78, 88, 138, 92, 104.
41. Smith 62, 105, 122.
42. Smith 125–26.
43. Smith 176, 271, 13.
44. Smith 184–85.
45. Smith 190, 195.
46. Smith 217, 219.
47. Smith 301, 253–54.
48. Smith 20, 94, 95, 103, 95, 213, 95, 212–13, 117, 213.
49. Smith 127–28, 178, 241, 228, 149, 252–53.
50. Smith 272, 263.
51. Smith 281.
52. Smith 290, 282, 286, 293.
53. CT:2:20:2:1.
54. NY:2:16:14.
55. Grant 22, 20.
56. Grant 92; Rowe 200; Grant 133, 155, 157.
57. Rowe 119; Grant 142; Schwinn 76; Grant 83.
58. Rowe 115.
59. Grant 107; Schwinn 79; Grant 131, 133; Rowe 402; Grant 133.
60. Rowe 289.
61. Grant 140.
62. Rowe 116, 122.
63. Grant 31, 134, 143.
64. WP:4:4:5.
65. Schwinn 101, 114; WP:4:4:5; WP:4:4:1.
66. Grant 192; WP:4:5:12.
67. Grant 155.
68. Grant 156, 161–62, 171.
69. Grant 175.
70. Grant 228–29.
71. Grant 229–30.
72. Levie 646; NY:3:16:1, 2.
73. WP:6:8:1, 4; Grant 343.
74. Grant 268, 286–87.
75. Daly 208; Grant 326.
76. Grant 283.
77. Grant 292–93.
78. Grant 289, 306, 288.
79. Daly 217; Grant 310.
80. Grant 322.
81. Groom 170.
82. Schwinn 83.
83. Slotkin 144–45, 112.
84. Scarry 109.
85. Chesley 55.
86. Groom 320, 317.
87. Groom 319, 336, 318, 388, 354.
88. Groom 394.
89. Groom 11.
90. Groom 62–63, 40, 65–67, 40.
91. Groom 16, 26–27, 57, 140.

92. Groom 42, 133.
93. Groom 43, 52, 46.
94. Groom 53, 43, 59.
95. Groom 44, 55–56, 61.
96. Groom 78–79.
97. Groom 82, 87, 85.
98. Groom 87, 82–84.
99. Groom 137, 87.
100. Groom 101, 84, 102–3, 106.
101. Groom 113, 152–53.
102. Groom 153–54.
103. Groom 162.
104. Groom 387.
105. Groom 162, 188–89, 172, 187–88.
106. Groom 180, 220, 231.
107. Groom 208–9.
108. Groom 216.
109. Groom 217.
110. Groom 178, 171, 178.
111. Groom 239, 246, 249.
112. Groom 247, 258.
113. Groom 261, 264, 270–71, 269.
114. Groom 391–92.
115. WSJ: 12:4:1, 22.
116. Colvin 165; Barnes 211; Jensen-Stevenson *passim*.

8. Keeping the Faith–James Bond Stockdale

(I = *A Vietnam Experience*; II = *In Love and War*)

1. Epictetus 338.
2. Dramesi 183; Blakey 211.
3. NY:2:16:14; II 437.
4. I ix.
5. NY:4:1:IV:15; NY:4:12:44.
6. II 37; Blakey 205.
7. II 76.
8. II 64–65, 69.
9. II 69, 63.
10. II 287, 290–91, 287, 68.
11. II 48.
12. II 77.
13. II 60, 94.
14. II 60.
15. II 60, 91, 98.
16. Risner 100; Mulligan 247.
17. II 8; I 141; II 175.
18. II 21, 10.
19. II 27, 24, 29, 34, 36.
20. II 88, 90, 25, 90.
21. II 94, 117.
22. II 354, 265, 294, 176, 329–31, 338.
23. II 182–84.

24. II 338.
25. II 393-94, 397, 394, 396-97.
26. I 97-98.
27. McGrath vi.
28. I 29-31.
29. I 92, 28, 98-99, 106.
30. I 110-11, 20, 83-84.
31. I 50-51.
32. II 39-40, 53.
33. II 78.
34. II 121, 144, 227.
35. II 304.
36. II 220-22.
37. II 408, 374-76.
38. II 223, 372, 136, 216.
39. II 456, 224, 121, 216, 298, 300.
40. II 384-85.
41. II 142, 136, 142, 231.
42. II 131-32.
43. II 201.
44. II 210-11, 308, 373, 198.
45. II 390-91.
46. II 414, 418-19.
47. II 366, 421.
48. II 228, 212, 228, 298.
49. II 303, 308, 318, 373.
50. II 179-81.
51. I 75, 109.
52. I 24, 21-22.
53. I 95.
54. II 287, 81, 126, 129, 230.
55. II 202, 353.
56. I 129.
57. I 135, 130.
58. I 134.
59. I 120, 42-43.
60. I 119-20.
61. I 41, 119.
62. Scarry 47.
63. I 32-33, 74-75.
64. II 350.
65. I 67-68, 70-71.
66. I 71, 118-20, 73.
67. I 75, 71.
68. I 4, 34-35, 68, vii.
69. II 276; I 75.
70. I viii, 118-20; McGrath vi-vii; I 48, 66.
71. I 116.
72. I 15, 46-49, 47.
73. I 6, 13, 15, 118.
74. II 273-75.
75. II 278, 403.

76. II 434, 444–45.
77. I 13, 73, 8, 39.
78. I 93–94.
79. II 427, 439, 438.
80. II 437, 441.

Bibliography

Books and Articles

Alleg, Henri. *The Question*. Trans. John Calder. Jean-Paul Sartre. Preface. London: John Calder, 1958.

Alvarez, Everett, with Anthony S. Pitch. *Chained Eagle*. New York: Donald I. Fine, 1989. (I)

Alvarez, Everett, with Samuel Schreiner, Jr. *Code of Conduct*. New York: Donald I. Fine, 1991. (II)

Amnesty International. *Report on Torture*. American Edition. New York: Farrar, Straus and Giroux, 1975.

Armbrister, Trevor. *A Matter of Accountability: The True Story of the Pueblo Affair*. New York: Coward-McCann, 1970.

Ball, Harry P. "Prisoner of War Negotiations: The Korean Experience and Lesson." *Naval War College Review* 21 (Sept. 1968): 54-87.

Barker, A. J. *Prisoners of War*. New York: Universe Books, 1975. In England, *Behind Barbed Wire*, 1974.

Barnes, Scott, with Melva Libb. *Bohica*. Canton, Ohio: Bohica Corporation, 1987.

Biderman, Albert D. *March to Calumny: The Story of American POW's in the Korean War*. New York: Macmillan, 1963.

Blakey, Scott. *Prisoner at War: The Survival of Commander Richard A. Stratton*. Garden City, New York: Anchor Press, Doubleday, 1978.

Brace, Ernest C. *A Code to Keep*. New York: St. Martin's 1988.

Brown, Wallace L. *The Endless Hours: My Two and a Half Years as a Prisoner of the Chinese Communists*. New York: Norton, 1961.

Brownlie, Ian, ed. *Basic Documents on Human Rights*. Oxford: Clarendon, 1971.

Bucher, Lloyd M., with Mark Rascovich. *Bucher: My Story*. Garden City, New York: Doubleday, 1970.

Cawthorne, Nigel. *The Bamboo Cage: The Full Story of the American Servicemen Still Held Hostage in South-East Asia*. London: Leo Cooper, 1991.

Cayer, Marc. *Marc Cayer: Prisonnier au Vietnam*. Tel que raconte au journaliste Yves Leclerc. Montreal: Ferron Editeur Inc., 1973.

Chafee, John H. "P.O.W. Treatment: Principles versus Propaganda." *United States Naval Institute Proceedings* 97 (July 1971): 14-17.

Chesley, Captain Larry. *Seven Years in Hanoi: A POW Tells His Story*. Salt Lake City, Utah: Bookcraft Inc., 1973.

Clark, Marjorie A. *Captive on the Ho Chi Minh Trail.* Chicago: Moody Press, 1974.

Clarke, Captain Douglas L. *The Missing Man: Politics and the MIA.* Washington, D.C.: National Defense University Press, Research Directorate, 1979.

Clinton, Susan Maloney. *Everett Alvarez, Jr.: A Hero for Our Times.* Chicago: Childrens Press, 1990.

Coffee, Gerald L. *Beyond Survival: Building on Hard Times—A POW's Inspiring Story.* New York: G. P. Putnam's Sons, 1990.

Coker, George T. "P.W." *United States Naval Institute Proceedings* 100/9/859 (October 1974): 41–46.

Colvin, Rod. *First Heroes: The POWs Left Behind in Vietnam.* New York: Irvington Publishers, 1987.

Daly, James A., and Lee Bergman. *A Hero's Welcome: The Conscience of Sergeant James Daly versus the United States Army.* Indianapolis: Bobbs-Merrill, 1975.

Day, George E. *Return with Honor.* Mesa, Arizona: Champlin Museum Press, 1989.

Dean, William F. *General Dean's Story.* As told to William L. Worden. London: Weidenfeld and Nicolson, 1954.

Deane, Philip [Svoronos-Gigantes, Gerassimas]. *Captive in Korea.* London: Hamish Hamilton, 1953. (I)

_____. *I Should Have Died.* New York: Atheneum, 1977. (II)

Dengler, Dieter. *Escape from Laos.* San Rafael, California: Presidio Press, 1979.

Denton, Jeremiah A. *When Hell Was in Session.* New York: Reader's Digest Press, 1976; reprint Mobile, Alabama: Traditional Press, 1982.

Dramesi, John A. *Code of Honor.* New York: Norton, 1975.

Drinnon, Richard. *Facing West: The Metaphysics of Indian-Hating and Empire-Building.* New York: Meridian, 1980.

Duncan, Donald. "The Prisoner." *Ramparts* 8 (Sept. 1969): 51–56.

Dunn, Howard J., and W. Hays Parks. "If I Became a Prisoner of War . . . " *United States Naval Institute Proceedings* 102/8/882 (August 1976): 18–27.

Eliot, T. S. "The Love Song of J. Alfred Prufrock." *Selected Poems.* London: Faber and Faber, 1961.

Epictetus. *Discourses and Enchiridion.* Based on Trans. by Thomas Wentworth Higginson. Roslyn, New York: Walter J. Black, Inc., 1944.

Falk, Richard A., Gabriel Kolko and Robert Jay Lifton, eds. *Crimes of War: A Legal, Political-Documentary, and Psychological Inquiry into the Responsibility of Leaders, Citizens, and Soldiers for Criminal Acts in Wars.* New York: Random House, 1971.

Fall, Bernard B. " 'Unrepentant, Unyielding': An Interview with Viet Cong Prisoners." *The New Republic* February 4, 1967: 19–24.

FitzGerald, Frances. *Fire in the Lake: The Vietnamese and the Americans in Vietnam.* Boston: Little, Brown, 1972.

4th Allied P.O.W. Wing. Phoenix: NAM POWs, Inc., 1977.

Foucault, Michel. *Discipline and Punish: The Birth of the Prison.* Trans. Alan Sheridan. New York: Vintage, 1979.

Franklin, H. Bruce. *M.I.A. or Mythmaking in America.* New York: Lawrence Hill, 1992.

Frishman, Robert F. "I Was a Prisoner in Hanoi." *Reader's Digest* 95 (Dec. 1969): 111–15.

Gaither, Ralph. *With God in a P.O.W. Camp.* As told to Steve Henry. Nashville: Broadman Press, 1973.

Gallery, Daniel. *The Pueblo Incident.* Garden City, New York: Doubleday, 1970.

_____. "We Can Baffle the Brainwashers!" *The Saturday Evening Post,* January 22, 1955: 20ff. In Gallery above, 133-146.

Garrett, Richard. *P.O.W.* London: David and Charles, 1981.

Grant, Zalin. *Survivors.* New York: Norton, 1975.

Greene, Graham. *The Quiet American.* New York: Viking, 1956.

Groom, Winston, and Duncan Spencer. *Conversations with the Enemy: The Story of PFC Robert Garwood.* New York: G. P. Putnam's Sons, 1983.

Guarino, Larry. *A P.O.W.'s Story: 2801 Days in Hanoi.* New York: Ivy, 1990.

Hackworth, David H., and Julie Sherman. *About Face.* New York: Simon and Schuster, 1989.

Halberstam, David. *Ho.* New York: Random House, 1971.

Hansen, Kenneth K. *Heroes Behind Barbed Wire.* Princeton, New Jersey: Van Nostrand, 1957.

Harris, Stephen R., with James C. Hefley. *My Anchor Held.* Old Tappan, N.J.: Fleming H. Revell, 1970.

Hefley, James and Marti. *No Time for Tombstones: Life and Death in the Vietnamese Jungle.* Wheaton, Illinois: Tyndale House, 1974.

Heslop, J. M., and Dell R. Van Orden. *From The Shadow of Death: Stories of POWs.* Salt Lake City: Deseret, 1973.

Hitchens, Harold L. "Factors Involved in a Review of the Code of Conduct for the Armed Forces." *Naval War College Review* 30 (Winter 1978): 47-71.

Ho Chi Minh. *Ho Chi Minh on Revolution: Selected Writings, 1920-1966.* Ed. Bernard B. Fall. New York: New American Library, 1967.

Holt, Philip R. "Prisoners of War: Prescriptive Conduct and Compliance in Captive Situations." *Naval War College Review* 21:4 (Dec. 1968): 29-79.

Horne, Alistair. *A Savage War of Peace: Algeria 1954-1962.* New York: Viking, 1977.

Hubbell, John G. *P.O.W.: A Definitive History of the American Prisoner-of-War Experience in Vietnam, 1964-1973.* New York: Reader's Digest Press, 1976.

Hunter, Edna. "The Vietnam POW Veteran: Immediate and Long-Term Effects of Captivity." *Stress Disorders Among Vietnam Veterans: Theory, Research and Treatment.* Charles R. Figley, ed. New York: Brunner/Mazel, 1978: 188-206.

Jackson, James E. "Eighteen Months as a Prisoner of the Viet Cong." *Ebony* 23 (August 1968): 114-119.

Jensen, Lieutenant Colonel Jay R. *Six Years in Hell: A Returned POW Views Captivity, Country, and the Nation's Future.* Bountiful, Utah: Horizon Publishers, 1974.

Jensen-Stevenson, Monika, and William Stevenson. *Kiss the Boys Goodbye: How the United States Betrayed Its Own POWs in Vietnam.* With material from Captain Eugene "Red" McDaniel. Toronto: McClelland and Stewart, 1990.

Johnson, Kathryn. "A Return Visit with POW's—10 Years Later." *U.S. News and World Report* March 28, 1973: 40-43.

Johnson, Sam, and Jan Winebrenner. *Captive Warriors: A Vietnam POW's Story.* College Station, Texas A & M University Press, 1992.

Karnow, Stanley. *Vietnam: A History.* Harmondsworth: Penguin, 1984.

Keenan, Barbara Mullen. *Every Effort: A True Story.* New York: St. Martin's, 1986.

Kinkead, Eugene. *In Every War But One.* New York: Norton, 1959.

Knightley, Phillip. *The First Casualty: From the Crimea to Vietnam: The War Correspondent as Hero, Propagandist, and Myth Maker.* New York: Harcourt Brace Jovanovich, 1975.

Laffin, John. *The Anatomy of Captivity.* London: Abelard-Schuman, 1968.

Langbein, John H. *Torture and the Law of Proof: Europe and England in the Ancien Regime.* Chicago: University of Chicago Press, 1976.

"Let's Go Home." *Soldiers* 28:4 (April 1973), np.

Levie, Howard S. ed. *Documents on Prisoners of War.* Volume 60 of *Naval War College International Law Studies.* Newport: Naval War College Press, 1979.

"Life as a War Prisoner—First-Hand Accounts." *U.S. News and World Report* October 16, 1972: 66-67.

Mallicoat, D. "A PW Returns." *Soldiers* 28:9 (Sept. 1973): 23-29.

McConnell, Malcolm. *Into the Mouth of the Cat:The Story of Lance Sijan, Hero of Vietnam.* New York: Norton, 1985.

McDaniel, Dorothy Howard. *After the Hero's Welcome: A POW Wife's Story of the Battle Against a New Enemy.* Chicago: Bonus Books, 1991.

McDaniel, Eugene, and James L. Johnson. *Before Honor.* Philadelphia: A. J. Holman, 1975. Published in paperback as *Scars and Stripes.* Eugene, Oregon: Harvest House, 1980.

McDaniel, Norman A. *Yet Another Voice.* New York: Hawthorn Books; W. Clement Stone, Pub., 1975.

McGee, Patrick. "Theory in Pain." *Genre* 20 (1987): 67-84.

McGrath, John M. *Prisoner of War: Six Years in Hanoi.* Annapolis, Maryland: Naval Institute Press, 1975.

Melling, Philip H. *Vietnam in American Literature.* Twayne's Literature and Society Series. Boston: Twayne, 1990.

Mulligan, James. *The Hanoi Commitment.* Virginia Beach, Virginia: RIF Marketing, 1981.

Myers, Thomas. *Walking Point: American Narratives of Vietnam.* New York: Oxford University Press, 1988.

Naughton, Robert J. "Motivational Factors of American Prisoners of War Held by the Democratic Republic of Vietnam." *Naval War College Review* 27:4 (Jan. 1975): 2-14.

Nasmyth, Spike. *2355 Days: A POW's Story.* New York: Orion, 1991.

Nasmyth, Virginia, and Spike Nasmyth. *Hanoi Release John Nasmyth: A Family Love Story.* Santa Paula, California: V. Parr, 1984.

Norman, Geoffrey. *Bouncing Back: How a Heroic Band of POWs Survived Vietnam.* Boston: Houghton Mifflin, 1990.

O'Daniel, Larry J. *Missing in Action: Trail of Deceit.* New York: Arlington House, 1979.

Peters, Edward. *Torture.* Oxford: Basil Blackwell, 1985.

"Playboy Interview: Jane Fonda and Tom Hayden." *Playboy* 21:4 (April 1974), 67-90, 180-84.

Plumb, Charlie. *I'm No Hero: A POW Story as Told to Glen DeWerff.* Independence, Missouri.: Independence Press, 1973.

Plutarch. "Sayings of the Spartans." *Plutarch's Moralia* Volume 3. The Loeb Classical Library. London: Henemann, 1927.

Powers, Francis Gary, with Curt Gentry. *Operation Overflight: The U-2 Spy Pilot Tells His Story for the First Time.* New York: Holt, Rinehart and Winston, 1970.

Presley, Virginia. *22 Stayed.* London: W. H. Allen, 1955.

Purcell, Ben and Anne. *Love and Duty.* New York: St. Martin's, 1992.

Randle, Robert F. *Geneva 1954: The Settlement of the Indochinese War.* Princeton: Princeton University Press, 1969.

Reid, Pat, and Maurice Michael. *Prisoner of War.* New York: Beaufort, 1984.

Richardson, Walton K. "Prisoners of War as Instruments of Foreign Policy." *Naval War College Review* 23:1 (Sept. 1970): 47-64.

Risner, Robinson. *The Passing of the Night: My Seven Years as a Prisoner of the North Vietnamese.* New York: Random House, 1973.

Roberts, James C. *Missing in Action.* Washington, D.C.: The Fund for Objective News Reporting, 1980.

Rowan, Stephen A. *They Wouldn't Let Us Die: The Prisoners of War Tell Their Story.* Middle Village, New York: Jonathan David Publishers, 1973.

Rowe, James N. *Five Years to Freedom.* Boston: Little, Brown, 1971.

Ruthven, Malise. *Torture: The Grand Conspiracy.* London: Weidenfeld and Nicolson, 1978.

Rutledge, Howard, and Phyllis Rutledge. *In the Presence of Mine Enemies.* Old Tappan, New Jersey: Fleming H. Revell, 1973.

Scarry, Elaine. *The Body in Pain: The Making and Unmaking of the World.* New York: Oxford University Press, 1985.

Schemmer, Benjamin F. *The Raid.* New York: Harper & Row, 1976.

Schlitz, William P. "The POWs Return." *Air Force Magazine* 56 (April 1973): 25-29.

Schwinn, Monika, and Bernhard Diehl. *We Came To Help.* Trans. Jan van Heurck. New York: Harcourt Brace Jovanovich, 1976.

Sheehan, Neil. *A Bright Shining Lie: John Paul Vann and America in Vietnam.* New York: Random House, 1988.

Sidey, Hugh and Margery Byers. "Memories of Divided Families." *Life* 69 (Dec. 4, 1970): 36-43.

Slotkin, Richard. *Regeneration Through Violence: The Mythology of the American Frontier, 1600–1800.* Middletown, Connecticut: Wesleyan University Press, 1973.

Smith, George E. *P.O.W.: Two Years with the Vietcong*. Berkeley: Ramparts Press, 1971.

Stockdale, James. *A Vietnam Experience: Ten Years of Reflection*. Stanford: Hoover Press Publication, 1984.

Stockdale, James and Sybil. *In Love and War: The Story of a Family's Ordeal and Sacrifice During the Vietnam Years*. New York: Harper & Row, 1984. Revised and updated edition, Annapolis, Maryland: Naval Institute Press, 1990.

Terry, Wallace. *Bloods: An Oral History of the Vietnam War by Black Veterans*. New York: Random House, 1984.

United States. Cong. Senate. Select Committee on POW/MIA Affairs. *Hearings on the U.S. Government's Efforts to Learn the Fate of America's Missing Servicemen*. 102 Cong., 1st sess. 2 pts. Washington: GPO, 1992.

Wagaman, Winnie, and Norman J. Brookens. *Civilian POW: Terror and Torture in South Vietnam*. Hagerstown, Maryland: Warm Welcomes Designs and Publications, 1989.

Walzer, Michael. *Obligations: Essays on Disobedience, War, and Citizenship*. Cambridge, Massachusetts: Harvard University Press, 1970.

Wehrum, John E., Jr. "The Status of United States Prisoners of War Under the Code of Conduct for the Armed Forces." *Catholic University Law Review* 1 (1971): 133–151.

White, William Lindsay. *The Captives of Korea: An Unofficial White Paper on the Treatment of War Prisoners*. New York: Scribner's, 1957.

Wolfkill, Grant F. *Reported to Be Alive*. New York: Simon and Schuster, 1965.

Wyatt, Captain and Mrs. Frederic A. *We Came Home*. Toluca Lake, California: P.O.W. Publications, 1977.

Newspaper Articles

(Listed by paper, in chronological order)

Chicago Tribune

1973

Mullen, William. "18 POWs Head Home after Peek at Miniskirts," 2:20:2:1.

Mount, Charles. "POWs Deluged with Propaganda," 2:26:1, 4.

Houston, Jack. "Peaceniks Delayed Release: POWs," 3:3:4.

Chamberlain, John. "POW Patriotism Is Understandable," 3:17:12.

Rekasis, Joe. "Who Remembers Disabled GIs?" 4:3:14.

Farrar, Fred. "Top POW Recounts Red Torture," 4:7:2.

Sneed, Michael. "Two Former POWs Find Readjustment Takes Time," 9:10:1, 5.

Sneed, Michael. "I Became a Better Person, Ex-POW Says," 9:11:2.

Sneed, Michael. "Tedium Was the Enemy for POWs," 9:12:7.

Honolulu Star-Bulletin

1992

"Vietnam War POW Says Gay Guards Raped Him," 3:6:7.

Los Angeles Times

1973

"Text of Nixon's Press Conference," 2:1:22-24.

"POWs Won't Face Penalty for Remarks," 2:9:20.

"Promotion of POWs Studied," 2:16:10.

Meagher, Ed. "Vietnam POWs Not Beaten Down; Lessons from Korea Credited," 2:17:26.

Hager, Philip. "Alvarez Home to a New World: Fashions, Cars and Women's Lib," 2:18:1, 9.

"U.S. Failed to Win Viet Goals, Ex-POW Avers," 3:8:21.

Wheeler, John T. "Ex-POWs: What It's Like to Put Pieces of Life Back Together," 3:18:1, 16-17.

"POW Camp Bristled With Hate," 3:26:5.

Abramson, Rudy. "Free to Talk At Last, Ex-POWs Tell of Torture," 3:30:1.

"POW Poets Wrote of Love, Home and Mice," 3:30:LA:3.

"Militia May Have Killed 100 Downed U.S. Pilots," 4:3:18.

Loh, Jules. "U.S. POWs Whistled Up Morale," 4:4:5.

"POWs Say Rehearsed Talks Helped Outlook," 4:9:8.

"Antiwar Leaders Reply to Criticism of Actions," 4:11:14.

"News in Brief: The World," 4:12:2.

Chapman, Robin. "Prove It, Jane Fonda Says of POW Torture," 4:19:25.

"Told to Blur POW Report, Doctor Says," 5:11:3, 27.

"News in Brief: The Nation," 5:25:2.

"Former POWs Lay a Comrade to Rest," 6:9:5.

Fonda, Jane. "Jane Fonda Amplifies on Her POW Stand," 6:9:II:4.

"Divorce Ends Marriages of 39 POW's," 6:12:26.

Butler, Ray E. "Military is Tied to a Code . . . That No Longer Serves," 7:1:VII:3, 7.

New York Times

1973

"Egress Recap is Given New Title: Homecoming," 1:9:12.

Finney, John W. "100-Man P.O.W. Airlifts Expected to Start Feb. 10," 1:26:1, 11.

Gwertzman, Bernard. "Hanoi Lists of P.O.W.'s Are Made Public by U.S.," 1:28:1, 26.

Kaufman, Michael T. "P.O.W. Kin in Tristate Area Rejoice," 1:30:15.

Finney, John W. "A Marine Returns from the Officially Dead," 1:31:1, 17.

Turner, Wallace. "Base on Coast Prepares for Arrival P.O.W.'s," 1:31:17.

Sterba, James P. "P.O.W.'s Greeters Told to De-emphasize the Military," 2:1:17.

"All Freed P.O.W.'s to Get Lifetime Baseball Pass," 2:1:17.

"Room Prepared For Son's Return," 2:1:18.

Roberts, Steven V. "Wives Waiting for P.O.W.'s With Hope and Anxiety," 2:5:1, 13.

Sterba, James P. "P.O.W. Conduct Barred as Topic," 2:6:1.

Reston, James. "A Debt of Honor," 2:7:39.

Roberts, Steven V. "Sister of P.O.W. Thinks He Will Face a 'Shock'," 2:8:16.

Van Gelder, Lawrence. "Happy Hubbub Envelops Homes as Families Await Their P.O.W.'s," 2:13:1, 14.

"Flag at Full Staff Today for Captives," 2:14:16.

"First 2 P.O.W.'s Land in U.S., 'Grateful, Overwhelmed, Proud'," 2:14:16.

Roberts, Steven V. "20 Former P.O.W.'s Land At Air Base in California," 2:15:1, 16.

Sterba, James P. "P.O.W. Says All Upheld War Aims," 2:16:14.

Roberts, Steven V. "The P.O.W.'s Show Pride and Gratitude," 2:18:1, 3.

Roberts, Steven V. "Thoughts on Reentering 'The World'," 2:18:IV:2.

Sterba, James P. "Managing the P.O.W.'s: Military Public Relations Men Filter Prisoner Story in a Careful Program," 2:20:4.

"Muzzled P.O.W.'s . . . ," 2:24:28.

"Brainwashing Laid to U.S.," 2:27:4.

"A P.O.W. Concedes He Assailed War," 2:28:9.

Hersh, Seymour M. "Vietcong Captive Tells of 7-Year Ordeal," 3:2:1, 3.

Roberts, Steven V. "The P.O.W.'s: Focus of Division," 3:3:16.

Roberts, Steven V. "Unshakable Will to Survive Sustained P.O.W.'s Over the Years." 3:4:28.

Roberts, Steven V. "P.O.W. Wives Who Chose New Life Face Dilemma," 3:6:10.
Hersh, Seymour M. "P.O.W.'s Planned Business Venture," 3:6:12.
Roberts, Steven V. "Two Ex-P.O.W.'s: Their Clashing Views Reflect Generation Gap," 3:11:50.
Hersh, Seymour. "Eight May Face Courts-Martial For Antiwar Roles as P.O.W.'s," 3:16:1, 2.
Marshall, S. L. A. "Behavior of P.O.W.'s . . . ," 3:21:45.
Lifton, Robert Jay. "Heroes and Victims," 3:28:47.
Roberts, Steven V. "Former P.O.W.'s Charge Torture by North Vietnam," 3:30:1, 18.
Roberts, Steven V. "Captain Says Resistance by P.O.W.'s Forced Captors to Be Brutal," 3:31:4.
Hersh, Seymour. "Pilot Recalls 'Bad Attitude' Made Him Suffer in Hanoi," 4:1:1, 62.
Stockdale, James B. "Back from Hanoi," 4:1:IV:15.
"P.O.W. Who Made Antiwar Statements in Hanoi Recalls 'Pressure of Conscience'," 4:2:3.
"Promotions of 3 P.O.W.'s To Lieutenants Confirmed," 4:7:9.
"Jane Fonda Grants Some P.O.W. Torture," 4:7:11.
"Ex-P.O.W. Says Enemy Used 'Pro' Torturers," 4:10:22.
Gross, Milton S. "Letter to the Editor," 4:12:44.
Roberts, Steven V. "P.O.W.'s Felt Their Mission Was to Resist," 4:30:1, 38.
Herbers, John. "Ex-P.O.W.'s Cheer: President Says It Is Time to Stop Making Heroes of Thieves," 5:25:1, 16.
"Ex-P.O.W.'s to Get Health Counseling For 5-Year Period," 6:2:21.
"P.O.W.'s Had List of Prohibitions," 6:3:13.
Ayres, B. Drummond Jr. "Falling Out Among the Heroes," 6:3:IV:3.
Saxon, Wolfgang. "Despondent P.O.W. Apparent Suicide," 6:4:7.
"Air Force Making 'Deep' Study of Suicide by Indochina P.O.W.," 6:5:6.
"Marine P.O.W., 24, Charged With Collaboration, Kills Himself," 6:28:7.
Sterba, James P. "P.O.W.'s Wife Says U.S. Killed Him," 6:29:9.
Finney, John W. "7 Former P.O.W.'s Freed of Charges of Aiding Enemy," 7:4:1, 22.
Roberts, Steven V. "Antiwar P.O.W.'s: A Different Mold Scarred by Their Combat Experiences," 7:15:1, 38.
"Army Secretary Defends P.O.W.'s: Says Air Force Officer Had No Authority Over G.I.s," 7:28:4.
Binder, L. James. "Codes of Conduct . . . ," 10:8:33.
"Ex-P.O.W. to Run in Dakota," 11:4:23.

Wall Street Journal

1984
Paul, Bill. "*Veteran's Tale*: Robert Garwood Says Vietnam Didn't Return Some American POWs," 12:4:1, 22.

Washington Post

1973
Cannon, Lou. "With a Phone Call, Life Begins Again: Nixon Hears Returnees' Thanks," 2:13:1, 8.
"POWs Deny U.S. Coaching: Their Patriotic Words 'Came From the Heart'," 2:24:1, 11.
Aarons, Leroy F. "Free Navy POW Sure U.S. Did Right in Asia," 3:5:3.
Buchwald, Art. "The Outlook for a POWerless Nixon Administration," 3:20:B1.
Chapman, William. "POWs' Nightmarish Ordeal: Tales of Torture, Beatings, Months in Solitary," 3:30:1, 13.
Jacobs, Jody. "A Night to 'Let It Loose' for Ex-POWs," 4:3:IV:1, 7.
Ringle, Ken. "POWs Pleaded for Death: Captive of Vietcong Describes 5-Year Ordeal," 4:4:1, 5.
Ringle, Ken. "The Horror of POW Life: Death by Starvation," 4:5:1, 12.
Barker, Karlyn. "The Horror of POW Life: 'Cried Like a Baby'," 4:5:1, 13.
"Caucus Hits Black Ratio Among POWs," 4:5:20.

"Ex-POWs Plan Political Work," 4:8:6.

Goldman, Ivan G. "Recently Captured POWs Not Harmed," 4:11:22.

Claiborne, William. "POWs Get Better Reception," 5:6:1, 16.

"Their Cheers, their Tears, their Day," 5:25:B1, 3.

Claiborne, William. "Ex-POW Recalls His Antiwar Role," 6:8:1, 4.

"Honor Canceled Due to Race, POW Claims," 10:13:16.

Swindle, Orson G. "Letters to the Editor," 12:5:31.

Index

DATE DUE

DEC 0 5 2002	
NOV 1 8 2003	
AUG 0 3 2004	

BRODART, CO.   Cat. No. 23-221-003

#27069201